The Popular Music Studies

The Popular Music Studies Reader brings together classic texts and essential new writings on popular music. The *Reader* places popular music in its cultural context, looks at the significance of popular music in our everyday lives and examines the global nature of the music industry.

The *Reader* maps the changing nature of popular music over the last decade and considers how popular music studies has expanded and developed to deal with these changes. Articles discuss the increasing participation of women in the industry and the changing role of gender and sexuality in popular music, the role of new technologies, especially in production and distribution, and the changing nature of the relationship between music production and consumption. The *Reader* is divided into parts, each with an introduction by the editors. The parts are:

- Music as Sound, Music as Text
- Making Music
- Subcultures, Scenes and Tribes
- Popular Music and Everyday Life
- Musical Diasporas
- Music Industry
- Popular Music and Technology
- Popular Music Media
- Popular Music, Gender and Sexuality.

Contributors: Rick Altman; Philip Auslander; Mavis Bayton; Andy Bennett; David Brackett; Michael Bull; Tia DeNora; Alice Echols; Kodwo Eshun; Susan Fast; Simon Frith; Paul Gilroy; Andrew Goodwin; Joanne Gottlieb; Dai Griffiths; Jocelyne Guilbault; Daniel Hallencreutz; Bob Hanke; David Hesmondhalgh; Rupa Huq; Keith Kahn-Harris; Marjorie D. Kibby; James P. Kraft; Dave Laing; Tony Langlois; Joseph Lanza; Susan McClary; Tom McCourt; Richard Middleton; Maria Pini; Dominic Power; Simon Reynolds; Tricia Rose; Eric W. Rothenbuhler; Barry Shank; Helena Simonett; Jeff Smith; Richard Smith; Philip Tagg; Paul Théberge; Sarah Thornton; David Toop; Jason Toynbee; William Tsitsos; Steve Waksman; Gayle Wald.

Andy Bennett is Professor in the Department of Communications, Popular Culture and Film at Brock University in Canada. He is the author of *Cultures of Popular Music* (2001) and *Popular Music and Youth Culture: Music, Identity and Place* (2000). **Barry Shank** is Professor of Comparative Studies at Ohio State University. He is the author of *Dissonant Identities: The Rock 'n' Roll Scene in Austin, Texas* (1994). **Jason Toynbee** is Lecturer in Media Studies at The Open University. He is the author of *Making Popular Music: Musicians, Creativity and Institutions* (2000).

The

Popular

Music

Studies

Reader

Edited by

Andy Bennett, Barry Shank and Jason Toynbee

Routledge
Taylor & Francis Group

LONDON AND NEW YORK

First published 2006
by Routledge
2 Park Square, Milton Park, Abingdon, Oxon OX14 4RN

Simultaneously published in the USA and Canada
by Routledge
270 Madison Ave, New York, NY 10016

Routledge is an imprint of the Taylor & Francis Group

Editorial matter, introductions and selections
© 2006 Andy Bennett, Barry Shank and Jason Toynbee
Contributions
© 2006 the contributors

Typeset in Perpetua by
Florence Production Ltd, Stoodleigh, Devon.

Printed and bound in Great Britain by
TJ International Ltd, Padstow, Cornwall

British Library Cataloging in Publication Data
A catalogue record for this book is available from the British Library

Library of Congress Cataloging in Publication Data
The popular music studies reader/edited by Andy Bennett, Barry Shank
and Jason Toynbee. – 1st ed.
    p. cm
Includes bibliographical references and index.
1. Popular music – History and criticism.   I. Bennett, Andy, 1963–
II. Shank, Barry.   III. Toynbee, Jason.
ML3470.P688 2005
781'.64–dc22   2005005252

ISBN10: 0–415–30709–0 (hbk)
ISBN10: 0–415–30710–4 (pbk)

ISBN13: 9780415 307093 (hbk)
ISBN13: 9780415 307109 (pbk)

Contents

Notes on editors

Andy Bennett is Professor in the Department of Communications, Popular Culture and Film at Brock University in Canada. Prior to studying for his Ph.D. at Durham University, he spent two years in Germany working as a music teacher with the Frankfurt Rockmobil project. He has published articles on aspects of youth culture, popular music and local identity in a number of journals including *British Journal of Sociology, Sociology, Sociological Review, Media Culture and Society* and *Popular Music*. He is author of *Popular Music and Youth Culture: Music, Identity and Place* (2000, Macmillan) and *Cultures of Popular Music* (2001, Open University Press), editor of *Remembering Woodstock* (2004, Ashgate) and co-editor of *Guitar Cultures* (2001, Berg), *After Subculture* (Palgrave, 2004) and *Music Scenes* (Vanderbilt University Press, 2004). Andy is a former Chair of the UK and Ireland branch of the International Association for the Study of Popular Music (IASPM) and co-founder of the British Sociological Association Youth Study Group. He is a Faculty Associate of the Center for Cultural Sociology at Yale University, an Associate of PopuLUs, the Centre for the Study of the World's Popular Musics, at Leeds University and a member of the Editorial Boards for the journals *Sociology* and *Leisure Studies.*

Barry Shank is Professor of Comparative Studies at Ohio State University. He is the author of *Dissonant Identities: The Rock 'n' Roll Scene in Austin, Texas* (Wesleyan, 1994) and *A Token of My Affection: Greeting Cards and American Business Culture* (Columbia University Press, 2004) as well as numerous articles on popular music, race and popular culture, and theories and methods of American studies. He is an Associate Editor of *American Quarterly*, and has served on the editorial boards of *American Music* and *Popular Music*. His current project is a study of abstraction and embodiment in musical performances that are resistant to fascism. The Long Ryders continue to perform without him.

Jason Toynbee is Lecturer in Media Studies at The Open University. Before becoming an academic in the early 1990s, he was a builder and sometimes a singer too. Jason completed a Ph.D. at Coventry University which he later turned into a book called *Making Popular Music: Musicians, Creativity and Institutions* (2000, Arnold). He has written several other pieces on creativity and music, and is now researching links between copyright, authorship and symbolic form across a number of genres. He is also co-editor of *Analysing Media Texts* (Open University Press, 2006), and a member of the Editorial Group of the journal *Popular Music*.

Notes on contributors

Rick Altman is Professor of Cinema and Comparative Literature at the University of Iowa. He is author of *The American Film Musical* (Indiana University Press, 1999), *Film/Genre* (BFI, 1999), and *Silent Film Sound* (Columbia University Press, 2004). His articles on film sound and Hollywood genres have been translated into over a dozen languages.

Philip Auslander is a Professor in the School of Literature, Communication, and Culture of the Georgia Institute of Technology (US). He is the author most recently of *Liveness: Performance in a Mediatized Culture* (Routledge, 1999) and the forthcoming *Performing Glam Rock: Gender and Theatricality in Popular Music* (University of Michigan Press).

Mavis Bayton was a member of Oxford's first all-women rock band in the late 1970s punk period. This experience led her into researching women's popular music-making which culminated in her Ph.D. and then the pioneering book *Frock Rock* (Oxford University Press, 1999). She is currently a tutor at Ruskin College, Oxford, and also a singer–songwriter and one-woman blues performer.

David Brackett is Associate Professor in the Faculty of Music at McGill University, Montreal. His publications include *Interpreting Popular Music* (Cambridge University Press, 1995; reprint University of California Press, 2000) and *The Pop, Rock, and Soul Reader: Histories and Debates* (Oxford University Press, 2005). His current work focuses on the relationship between genre and identity in twentieth-century popular music.

Michael Bull is a Senior Lecturer in Media and Film at the University of Sussex and has written widely on sound, music and technology. He is co-editor of *The Auditory Culture Reader* (Berg, 2003) and is presently writing a monograph entitled *Sound Moves: iPod Culture – an Urban Experience* for Routledge, to be published in 2005. He is Chief Editor of *The Senses and Society* journal.

Tia DeNora teaches sociology at Exeter University. She is author of *Beethoven and the Construction of Genius* (University of California Press, 1995), *Music in Everyday Life* (Cambridge University Press, 2000) and *After Adorno: Rethinking Music Sociology* (Cambridge University Press, 2003). She is currently doing research on music and science in Beethoven's Vienna and on music, spirituality and transcendence.

Alice Echols is the author of *Daring to Be Bad: Radical Feminism in America, Scars of Sweet Paradise: The Life and Times of Janis Joplin* (University of Minnesota Press, 1990) and *Shaky Ground: The Sixties and Its Aftershocks* (Columbia University Press, 2002. She is an Associate Professor of English at USC and is currently working on *Upside Down: Disco and the Remaking of American Culture*.

Kodwo Eshun writes about the interface between art, music, technology and science fiction. He is author of *More Brilliant Than the Sun: Adventures in Sonic Fiction* (Quartet, 1999), and is a contributor to, among other publications, *The Wire, i-D, Spin* and *The Guardian*.

Susan Fast is Associate Professor of Music at McMaster University, Ontario. Her recent work is focused on constructions/representations of identity in popular music performance. She is author of the book *In the Houses of the Holy: Led Zeppelin and the Power of Rock Music* (Oxford University Press, 2001).

Simon Frith has been Professor of Film and Media Studies at Stirling University, Scotland, since 1999. Recent publications include *Music and Copyright*, edited (with Lee Marshall) for Edinburgh University Press (2004) and 'What is bad music?' in Christopher J. Washburne and Maiken Derno's *Bad Music* (Routledge, 2004). He chairs the judges of the Mercury Music Prize.

Paul Gilroy is currently Chair of the Department of African American Studies at Yale University. His teaching on questions of race and social theory operates at the junction points between sociological concerns and the humanities. He is researching automotivity and its relationship to consumer culture, and continuing work on the institution of racial orders, especially in colonial territory. Current writing projects involve a consideration of Britain's post-colonial melancholia, given as the 2002 Wellek Library lectures and a survey of New World black musics in the twentieth century.

Andrew Goodwin is Professor and Chair of the Department of Media Studies at the University of San Francisco. He is the author of *Dancing in the Distraction Factory: Music, Television and Popular Culture* (Routledge, 1993) and is currently completing a novel, *Enjoy the Silence*.

Joanne Gottlieb is currently a social worker who works with adolescents in New York City.

Dai Griffiths is Head of Music at Oxford Brookes University. He has recently published a monograph on Radiohead's *OK Computer*, as well as various chapters, including studies of words in pop songs, cover versions and the history of pop music since punk. His mother knew John Cale's mother, both of them hailing from Garnant in South Wales.

Jocelyne Guilbault is Professor of Ethnomusicology at the Music Department of the University of California, Berkeley. She is the author of *Zouk: World Music in the West Indies* (University of Chicago Press, 1993) and of several articles on theory and methodology in popular music studies. Her current research focuses on the politics and aesthetics of the calypso music scene in the Caribbean and its diaspora.

Daniel Hallencreutz is founder and Managing Director of a research consultancy company called Intersecta AB and is affiliated to the Centre for Research on Innovation and Industrial Dynamics at Uppsala University. He has a D.Phil. in economic geography from the Department of Social and Economic Geography, University of Uppsala, and has research interests in regional development, industrial competitiveness, growth policies and the cultural industries.

Bob Hanke is a sessional Assistant Professor in Communication Studies, and the Joint Graduate Programme in Communication and Culture, at York University, Toronto. He has co-edited a special issue of *Topia: Canadian Journal of Cultural Studies* on technology and culture. Recent solo works include 'For a Political Economy of Indymedia Practice' in the *Canadian Journal of Communication* and 'McLuhan, Virilio and Speed in the Age of Digital Reproduction' in *Marshall McLuhan: Critical Evaluations in Cultural Theory* (Routledge, 1998).

David Hesmondhalgh is Senior Lecturer in Media Studies, Faculty of Social Sciences, The Open University. He is the author of *The Cultural Industries* (Sage, 2nd edn, 2006), and editor of *Western Music and its Others* (with Georgina Born, University of California Press, 2000), *Popular Music Studies* (with Keith Negus, Arnold 2002), *Understanding Media: Inside Celebrity* (with Jessica Evans, Open University Press, 2005) and *Media Production* (Open University Press, 2006).

Rupa Huq is Senior Lecturer in sociology at Kingston University, London. Previously she taught at the University of Manchester. Her book, *Beyond Subculture: Youth and Pop in a Multi-ethnic World,* will be published by Routledge in 2005. Her research interests are combined with being a practitioner of DJing, motherhood and politics.

Keith Kahn-Harris is an Associate Lecturer at the Open University and a freelance research consultant. He has been a visiting fellow at universities and educational institutions in Sweden, Finland, Israel and Australia. He has published a number of articles on Extreme Metal culture and was co-editor (with Andy Bennett) of *After Subculture* (Palgrave, 2004). A full list of his publications can be found at www.kahn-harris.org.

Marjorie D. Kibby is a Senior Lecturer in Communication and Culture at the University of Newcastle, Australia. Her research publications focus on issues of identity and community online, and in particular on the personal and cultural effects of the use of the Internet in everyday life.

James P. Kraft is Associate Professor of History, University of Hawaii at Manoa, Honolulu. He is author of *Stage to Studio: Musicians and the Sound Revolution, 1890–1950* (Johns Hopkins University Press, 1996) and has written extensively in the field of the social and economic history of music.

Dave Laing is a writer and researcher based in London. His books include *The Sound of our Time* (Quadrangle Books, 1969) and *One Chord Wonders* (Open University Press, 1985). He is an editor of the *Continuum Encyclopedia of Popular Music of the World* and a member of the editorial board of *Popular Music History*.

Tony Langlois lectures in the School of Media and Performing Arts at the University of Ulster, Northern Ireland. His published articles are concerned with the cultural politics of music in North Africa and Europe.

Joseph Lanza, the author of *Elevator Music* (St Martin's Press, 1994), was the Executive Producer for the two-disc collection entitled 'Music for TV Dinners'. He also contributes frequently to *Time Life Music*. He has written several other books, the most recent being *Vanilla Pop: Sweet Sounds from Frankie Avalon to ABBA* (Chicago Review Press, 2005).

Susan McClary (Ph.D., Harvard, 1976) specialises in the cultural criticism of music, both the European canon and contemporary popular genres. McClary is author of *Feminine Endings: Music, Gender, and Sexuality* (University of Minnesota Press, 1991), *Georges Bizet: Carmen* (Cambridge University Press, 1992), *Conventional Wisdom: The Content of Musical Form* (University of California Press, 2000), is co-editor with Richard Leppert of *Music and Society: The Politics of Composition, Performance and Reception* (Cambridge University Press, 1987). She was awarded a John D. and Catherine T. MacArthur Foundation Fellowship in 1995.

Tom McCourt is an Assistant Professor of media studies at Fordham University, New York, and the author of *Conflicting Communication Interests in America: The Case of National Public Radio* (Praeger, 1999).

Richard Middleton is Professor of Music at the University of Newcastle upon Tyne, England. He is the author of *Pop Music and the Blues* (Gollancz, 1972) and *Studying Popular Music* (Open University Press, 1990), editor of *Reading Pop* (Oxford University Press, 2000) and co-editor of *The Cultural Study of Music: A Critical Introduction* (Routledge, 2004). A new book, *Voicing the Popular*, will be published by Routledge shortly.

Maria Pini completed her Ph.D. on Woman and Contemporary Social Dance Cultures at Goldsmiths College, London. After this, she took up a Postdoctoral Fellowship at the University of Western Sydney where she wrote *Club Cultures and Female Subjectivity: The Move from Home to House* (Palgrave, 2001). Until August 2004, Maria was a Lecturer in the Media and Communications Department at

Goldsmiths College. She has spent the past seven months working on a forthcoming book written with Valerie Walkerdine, on video diaries and auto-ethnography.

Dominic Power is an Associate Professor at the Department of Social and Economic Geography, Uppsala University, Sweden. His research is concerned with regional and industrial competitiveness, and the workings of the cultural industries, in particular the design, fashion and music industries. His most recent book is *Cultural Industries and the Production of Culture* (co-edited with Allen J. Scott, Routledge, 2004).

Simon Reynolds writes about pop culture for magazines including *The New York Times*, *Village Voice* and *The Wire*, and posts regularly at Blissblog, http://bliss out.blogspot.com. His latest book *Rip It Up and Start Again: Postpunk 1978–84* is set for 2005 publication by Faber & Faber (UK/Europe) and by Viking Penguin (North America), with a postpunk website at www.simonreynolds.net.

Tricia Rose is Professor of American Studies at UC Santa Cruz. In addition to *Black Noise* (Wesleyan Press, 1994), she is also co-editor with Andrew Ross of *Microphone Fiends: Youth Music and Youth Culture* (Routledge, 1994) and is also the author of *Longing to Tell: Black Women Talk About Sexuality and Intimacy* (Farrar, Straus and Giroux, 2003). More information on the author can be found at www.triciarose.com.

Eric W. Rothenbuhler is Professor of Communication at Texas A&M University, co-editor of *Media Anthropology* (in print), author of *Ritual Communication: From Everyday Conversation to Mediated Ceremony* (1998), co-editor of *Communication and Community* (2001), and author or co-author of more than fifty articles, chapters, essays, and reviews on media, ritual, community, media industries, popular music, and communication theory.

Helena Simonett received her Ph.D. in ethnomusicology at the University of California, Los Angeles, and is currently teaching at Vanderbilt University, Nashville. She conducted extensive research on Mexican popular music and its transnational diffusion. Her publications include *Banda: Mexican Musical Life across Borders* (Wesleyan University Press, 2001) and *En Sinaloa nací: Historia de la música de banda* (Association de Gestores del Patromino Historico y Cultural de Mazatlan, 2004).

Jeff Smith is an Associate Professor and the Director of the Film and Media Studies Program at Washington University in St Louis. He is the author of *The Sounds of Commerce: Marketing Popular Film Music* (Columbia University Press, 1998), and is currently at work on an essay on Richard Linklater's film 'School of Rock'.

Richard Smith is Senior Associate Editor of *Gay Times*. He is the author of *Seduced and Abandoned: Essays on Gay Men and Popular Music* (Cassell, 1995), and edited a collection of Kris Kirk's music journalism, *A Boy Called Mary* (Millivres-Prowler, 1999). He has contributed to the books *Drag: A History Of Female Impersonation in the Performing Arts* (ed. Roger Baker, Continuum, 1995) and *Intoxication: An Anthology of Stimulant-based Writing* (ed. Jeff Noon, Serpent's Tail, 1998).

Philip Tagg studied music at Cambridge and education at Manchester in the 1960s, and at the same time was also active as a songwriter, arranger and musician in both the 'classical' and 'popular' fields. From 1971 to 1991 he taught music history, analysis, film music and keyboard harmony at the University of Göteborg (Sweden). In 1991 he initiated work on EPMOW (*Encyclopedia of Popular Music of the World*). From 1993 to 2002 he taught at the University of Liverpool's Institute of Popular Music. He was appointed Senior Professor of Musicology at the Université de Montréal in November 2002.

Paul Théberge is Canada Research Chair in Technological Mediations of Culture, at the Institute for Comparative Studies in Literature, Art and Culture, Carleton University, Ottawa, where he teaches courses in music, sound in film, technology and culture. He is presently conducting research on music, the Internet, and processes of globalization.

Sarah Thornton (1965–) published her Ph.D. as a book called *Club Cultures: Music, Media and Subcultural Capital* (Polity, 1995) and is co-editor of *The Subcultures Reader* (Routledge, 1997). She writes a monthly pop sociological column for *Art Review* and is working on an ethnography of the contemporary art world.

David Toop is a composer and author. He has published four books: *Rap Attack* (Serpent's Tail, 1999), *Ocean of Sound* (Serpent's Tail, 2001), *Exotica* and *Haunted Weather* (Serpent's Tail, 2004). In 2000, he curated 'Sonic Boom: the Art of Sound' for London's Hayward Gallery. His first album was released on Brian Eno's Obscure label in 1975; since 1995 he has released seven solo CDs. He is currently an AHRB Research Fellow in the Creative and Performing Arts, based at the University of the Arts, London.

William Tsitsos teaches Sociology at the University of Arizona.

Steve Waksman is Assistant Professor of Music and American Studies at Smith College, Wolverhampton, MA. His research and teaching interests are in the history of US popular culture – especially music, but also film, television and literature – during the nineteenth and twentieth centuries, and in the intersection of race, gender and sexuality. In 1998, his dissertation, 'Instruments of desire: the electric guitar and the shaping of musical experience', won the Ralph Henry Gabriel Prize awarded by the American Studies Association; the project is now a book published by Harvard University Press in 1999. Currently, he is writing an interpretive history of heavy metal and punk rock, tentatively titled 'The noise of youth: rethinking rock through the metal/punk continuum'.

Gayle Wald teaches English at The George Washington University. In addition to riot grrrl, she has published on boy bands, 'girl' performers and blue-eyed soul. Her current book project, forthcoming from Beacon, is *Music in the Air*, about the gospel singer-guitarist Sister Rosetta Tharpe.

Acknowledgements

The following extracts were reproduced with kind permission. While every effort has been made to trace copyright holders and obtain permission, this has not always been possible in all cases. Any omissions brought to our attention will be remedied in future editions.

Altman, R. (1992) 'The material heterogeneity of recorded sound', in Altman, R. (ed.) *Sound Theory, Sound Practice*. New York: Routledge/American Film Institute. Reproduced by permission of Routledge/Taylor & Francis, Inc.

Auslander, P. (1996) 'Liveness as performance', *Performance and Cultural Politics*, Elin Diamond (ed.), Routledge. Reproduced by permission of the author and publisher.

Bayton, M. (1998) 'Constraints', in *Frock Rock: Women Performing Popular Music*. Oxford: Oxford University Press. Reproduced by permission of the publisher.

Bennett, A. (1999) 'Subcultures or neo-tribes?: Rethinking the relationship between youth, style and musical taste', *Sociology*, 33 (3), pp. 599–617, © BSA Publications Ltd. 1999, by permission of Sage Publications Ltd.

Brackett, D. (1995) 'Family values in music? Billie Holiday's and Bing Crosby's "I'll Be Seeing You"' from Brackett, D. (1995) *Interpreting Popular Music* © Cambridge University Press, reprinted with permission of the author and the publisher.

Bull, M. (2000) 'Filmic cities and aesthetic experience' from *Sounding Out the City: Personal Stereos and the Management of Everyday Life*. Oxford: Berg, pp. 85–96.

DeNora, T., 'Music and Self-identity', from *Music in Everyday Life*. Cambridge: Cambridge University Press, pp. 75–108), 2000, © University of Cambridge Press, reprinted with permission of the author and the publisher.

Echols, A. (2000) 'Little girl blue'. Excerpts from *Scars of Sweet Paradise: The Life and Times of Janis Joplin* by Alice Echols © 1999 by Alice Echols. Reprinted by permission of Henry Holt and Company, LLC and Time Warner Book Group UK.

Eshun, K. (1998) 'Futurhythmachine', *Crash Media*, 8. Reproduced by permission of Mute/Metamute/Mutella/Openmute www.metamute.org.

Fast, S. (1999) 'Rethinking issues of gender and sexuality in Led Zepplin: a woman's view of pleasure and power in hard rock', from *American Music*, 17:3, copyright 1999 by the Board of Trustees of the University of Illinois. Used with permission of the University of Illinois Press.

Frith, S. (1988) 'The industrialization of music', from *Music for Pleasure: Essays in the Sociology of Pop*, Polity. Reproduced by permission of the publisher.

Gilroy, P. (1993) '"Jewels brought from bondage': black music and the politics of authenticity", from *The Black Atlantic: Modernity and Double Consciousness*, Verso. Reproduced by permission of the publisher.

Goodwin, A. (1992) 'Rationalization and democratization in the new technologies of popular music', in Lull, J. (ed.) *Popular Music and Communication*. Newbury Park, CA: Sage. Reproduced by permission of the publisher.

Gottlieb, J. and Wald, G. (1994) 'Smells like teen spirit: riot grrrls, revolution and women in independent rock'. Excerpts from Gottlieb, J. and Wald, G., 'Smells like teen spirit'. Copyright (1994) from *Microphone Fiends* by Andrew Rose and Tricia Rose (eds). Reproduced by permission of Routledge/Taylor & Francis Books, Inc.

Griffiths, D. (1999) '"Home is living like a man on the run": John Cale's Welsh Atlantic', *Welsh Music History*, 5. Reproduced by kind permission of the author and The University of Wales Press.

Guilbault, J. (1993) 'Zouk and the isles of the Caribees'. Excerpts from Jocelyne Guilbault, 'Zouk and the isles of the Caribees', from *Zouk: World Music in the West Indies*, 1993, The University of Chicago Press. Reproduced by permission of the publisher and author.

Hanke, R. (1998) '"Yo Quiero Mi MTV!": making music television for Latin America', in Swiss, T., Sloop, J. and Herman, A. (eds) *Mapping the Beat: Popular Music and Contemporary Theory*, Oxford: Blackwell, pp. 219–45. Reproduced by permission of Blackwell Publishers.

Hesmondhalgh, D. (1998) 'The British dance music industry: a case study of independent cultural production', *British Journal of Sociology*, 49(2). Reproduced by permission of Blackwell Publishers.

Huq, R. (1996) 'Asian kool? Bhangra and beyond', in Sharma S., Hutnyk J. and Sharma A. (eds) *Dis-Orienting Rhythms: The Politics of the New Asian Dance Music*. Reproduced by permission of Zed Books.

Kahn-Harris, K., '"Roots"? The relationship between the global and the local within the Extreme Metal scene', *Popular Music*, 19 (1): pp. 13–30, 2000, © University of Cambridge Press, reprinted with permission of the author and the publisher. (Previously published under the name of Keith Harris.)

Kibby, M.D., 'Home on the page: a virtual place of music community', *Popular Music*, 19 (1), 2000, © University of Cambridge Press, reprinted with permission of the author and the publisher.

Kraft, J., 'Musicians in Hollywood: work and technological change in entertainment industries, 1926–1940', *Technology and Culture*, 35 (2) (1994). © Society for the History of Technology. Reprinted with permission of The Johns Hopkins University Press.

Langlois, T., 'The local and global in North African popular music', *Popular Music*, 15 (3), 1996, © University of Cambridge Press. Reprinted with permission of the author and the publisher.

Lanza, J. (2004) '"Beautiful Music": The rise of easy-listening FM', from *Elevator Music: a Surreal History of Muzak, Easy-Listening and other Moodsong*. The University of Michigan Press. Reproduced by permission of the publisher.

McClary, S. (1991) 'This is not a story my people tell: musical time and space according to Laurie Anderson', from *Feminine Endings: Music, Gender and Sexuality*, University of Minnesota Press. Reproduced by permission of the author and the publisher.

Middleton, R. (1986) 'In the groove, or blowing your mind? The pleasures of musical repetition', from Bennett, T., Mercer, C. and Woollacot, J. (eds) *Popular Culture and Social Relations*. Milton Keynes: Open University Press). Reproduced by kind permission of Tony Bennett.

Pini, Maria (1997) 'Women and the early British rave scene', in McRobbie, A. (ed.) *Back to Reality? Social Experience and Cultural Studies*. Manchester: Manchester University Press. Reproduced by kind permission of Maria Pini.

Power, D. and Hallencreutz, D. (2002) 'Profiting from creativity? The music industry in Stockholm, Sweden and Kingston, Jamaica', first published in *Environment and Planning A*, 34, pp. 1833–54. Reproduced by permission of Pion Ltd, London.

Reynolds, S. (1998) 'War in the jungle', from *Energy Flash: a Journey Through Rave Music and Dance Culture*, Macmillan, London. Reproduced by permission of the publisher.

Rose, T. (1994) 'Voices from the margins: rap music and contemporary black cultural production' from *Black Noise: Rap Music and Black Culture in Contemporary America* by Tricia Rose, Wesleyan University Press, 1994. © 1994 by Tricia Rose. Reprinted by permission of Wesleyan University Press.

Rothenbuhler, E.W. and McCourt, T (1992) 'Commercial radio and popular music: processes of selection and factors of influence', in Lull, J. (ed.) *Popular Music and Communication*. Newbury Park, CA: Sage. Reproduced by permission of the publisher.

Shank, Barry, *Dissonant Identities: The Rock 'n' Roll Scene in Austin, Texas*, Wesleyan University Press, 1994. © 1994 by Barry Shank. Reprinted with permission of Wesleyan University Press.

Simonett, H., 'Technobanda and the politics of identity', from *Banda: Mexican Musical Life Across Borders* by Helena Simonett, Wesleyan University Press, 2001. © 2001 by Helena Simonett. Reprinted by permission of Wesleyan University Press.

Smith, J., 'Popular songs and comic allusion in contemporary cinema', in Robertson, Wojcik, P., and Knight, A. (eds) *Soundtrack Available: Essays on Film and Popular Music*, copyright, 2001, Duke University Press. All rights reserved. Used by permission of the publisher.

Smith, R. (1995) 'Housewives choice: female fans and unmanly men', from *Seduced and Abandoned: Essays on Gay Men and Popular Music*, London: Cassell. Reprinted by permission of The Continuum International Publishing Group.

Tagg, P. (1994) 'Subjectivity and soundscape, motorbikes and music' from: Järviluoma, H. (ed.) *Soundscapes. Essays on Vroom and Moo*, Tampere. Reproduced by kind permission of Phil Tagg.

Théberge, P. 'Music/technology/practice: music technology in action' from *Any Sound You Can Imagine: Making Music/Consuming Technology* by Paul Théberge, Wesleyan University Press, 1997. © 1997 by Paul Théberge. Reprinted by permission of Wesleyan University Press.

Thornton, S. (1995) 'Subcultural capital and club cultures', from *Club Cultures: Media and Subcultural Capital*, Polity, pp. 98–105. Reproduced by permission of the publisher. (Material drawn from two separate sections of *Club Cultures* (see pp. 11–14 and 98–105). New title added at author's request.)

Toop, D. (1995) 'Scanning: aether talk', from *Ocean of Sound: Aether Talk, Ambient Sound and Imaginary Worlds*, Serpent's Tail, pp. 33–65. Reproduced by permission of the publisher.

Toynbee, J. (2000) 'Making up and showing off: what musicians do,' from *Making Popular Music: Musicians, Creativity, and Institutions*, London and New York: Arnold Press and Oxford University Press. Reproduced by permission of Edward Arnold.

Tsitsos, William, 'Rules of rebellion: slam dancing, moshing and the American alternative scene', *Popular Music*, 18 (3): pp. 397–407, 1999, © University of Cambridge Press. Reprinted with permission of the author and the publisher.

Waksman, S. (1999) 'Black sound, black body: Jimi Hendrix, the electric guitar and the meaning of blackness'. Reprinted by permission of the publisher from 'Black Sound, Black Body: Jimi Hendrix, the Electric Guitar, and the Meanings of Blackness' in *Instruments of Desire: The Electric Guitar and the Shaping of Musical Experience* by Steve Waksman, pp. 167–206, Cambridge, MA: Harvard University Press, © 1999 by the President and Fellows, Harvard College.

Andy Bennett, Barry Shank
and Jason Toynbee

POPULAR MUSIC ISN'T WHAT IT USED TO BE. People have been saying this for years, of course, especially people of a certain age such as the editors of this book. Yet there is a sense in which music at the start of the twenty-first century is changing in important ways. Popular music as we now know it emerged at the beginning of the last century, taking shape through what were then revolutionary new media, particularly sound recording and broadcasting. As Simon Frith points out in Chapter 26, its subsequent history has been marked by a surprising degree of continuity. Millions were buying and listening to records during the 1920s, and the same conditions apply now, except that the audience can be measured in billions. Music radio was born in the 1920s, and today we are listening to at least as much as we ever did. Bands that recorded and played live became the dominant type of performing unit in that second decade, and bands with a similar combination of skills are still hard at work as you read.

Connected to this technological continuity is a stylistic one. From before the 1920s to as late as the early 1960s, a particular type of popular song, the 'standard', held sway. It featured sentimental lyrics, a 32-bar verse and middle 8 structure, and was sold to a mass audience primarily in the US, although increasingly to the rest of the industrialised world too. Overlapping with this style for a few years, a new popular mainstream then emerged during the 1960s. Despite rock's very different sound and mood, it actually had a lot in common with popular music of the preceding era. Both styles brought together a mass audience. Both incorporated an African-American influence while at the same time excluding African-American performers. And both were sold by a music industry that sought to nurture long-term stars and promote them to a single, well-defined market. Perhaps the main difference between the two was that there was a distinct British version of rock as well as a North American style. Apart from this factor, however, it is a story of continuity – until some time in the mid-1980s, that is, when things begin to change.

We need to be careful here. The division of the past into historical periods is fraught with problems. We may easily impose a spurious unity on a span of years, perhaps by focusing on one or two features at the expense of others that do not fit so easily together into a chronological block. This is especially true of 'the present', by which is meant the recent past. Often we are tempted to read the present as a brave new world: the future arrived early. Popular music's ideology of the new makes this temptation stronger, while recent theories in cultural studies and related fields further reinforce it, reflected in the spread of concepts such as post-modernism, the network society or globalisation. All of these propose a radical break with the past.

Nevertheless, and with this cautionary note in mind, we want to suggest that contemporary popular music is undergoing change in three broad areas. It is such change, together with its impact on research, that provides the rationale for the *Popular Music Studies Reader*. The time is right to collect together work written in a period when the sounds, institutions and social formations of popular music are shifting – a period of transition, in other words.

What changes are we talking about? First, there has been the fragmentation of markets, styles and constituencies. The formation that Will Straw (1990) calls 'heartland rock' – that is the culture and aesthetic practices centred on post-1960s guitar-based music – has been eclipsed. It is not that rock is over, as has been announced on numerous occasions, but rather that rock is no longer at the centre of youth culture or of the music industry's attention. Instead, it takes its place as one among many styles and markets. Arguably, as Andy Bennett describes in Part Three, rock represents just one of the various 'neo-tribes' (Maffesoli, 1996) that make up contemporary youth culture: hip-hop, house music, bhangra, (pre-) teen pop, and so on. And, of course, there are older tribes too, each with distinctive tastes, each pandered to by the musical media and products. True, an ideology lingers on, sometimes in the music industry itself, according to which rock still has a special political-cultural mission. But in practice, these days rock is a niche market and style.

It has been suggested that rock's aesthetic of 'authenticity' – its association with both personal expression and values of community – was actually no more than a means of accruing cultural capital. By exercising rock taste, one set oneself above others who had a lower form of engagement with music, one based merely on its use as entertainment. One might infer, then, that the eclipse of rock has meant the advent of a more democratic music scene where strategies of distinction are much less significant. In fact, what seems to have changed is that cultural capital is no longer *exclusively* associated with rock. Instead, it is likely that the person of taste is becoming an 'omnivore' (Peterson and Kern, 1996), someone who is able to move between styles and in this way produce a personalised menu of the 'cool'.

Interestingly, the fragmentation of music is associated with what on the face of it seems to be a counter-tendency towards homogenisation. Classical music was until recently considered the binary opposite of popular. It thus provided a useful benchmark against which popular music might be defined. However, classical music is itself becoming increasingly popular, literally in the sense that many people buy it, but also because it is used in popular contexts, such as film, television and advertising soundtracks. In 2005, the US trade magazine *Billboard* published four classical album charts, including 'Top Classical Crossover' and 'Top Classical Budget'. Again, we should not push this line too far. Live opera, for example, remains the preserve of the privileged few, defiantly unpopular in both economic and cultural terms. But the emergence of popular music as an all-encompassing form, one that can incorporate an apparently uncongenial sound and style such as 'classical', is surely now an irreversible process.

The second factor affecting change is globalisation – the growing interconnectedness of cultures and economies around the world. This is undoubtedly having an effect on the production, reception and form of popular music. As we hinted above, some accounts of globalisation make very strong claims about the scale of the changes wrought by it (see, for example, Lash and Urry, 1994). Our assessment of globalisation is more temperate. For one thing, to argue that globalisation has been both sudden and intense is to ignore its long history. In the mid-nineteenth century, Marx and Engels pointed out that '[t]he need of a constantly expanding market for its products chases the bourgeoisie over the whole surface of the globe. It must nestle everywhere, settle everywhere, establish connections everywhere' (1967, p. 83). Significantly, popular music was an early global commodity, with record companies establishing branches around the world for both marketing and the recruitment of talent at the beginning of the twentieth century (Gronow and Saunio, 1998). This might seem to render the Anglo-American centred history of popular music (recounted in the first two paragraphs of this chapter) rather problematic. What about French *chanson,* Greek *rembetika* and Cuban *son*?

Yet the Anglo-American history can be defended, on the grounds that it was indeed music from the US and Britain that flooded world markets in the twentieth century, establishing first the Tin Pan Alley song and then the sound of rock as hegemonic global styles. In other words, globalisation in its first phase was very much a matter of one-way flow. Certainly, there were national and regional popular forms, but by and large these were limited to their own locales.

Is this still the case, though? It appears that the recent history of popular music has been one of increasing hybridisation. Anglo-American music (particularly from the Black Atlantic tradition – see Chapter 20 by Gilroy in Part Five) is not only being appropriated and mixed with local styles in music scenes around the world, but the indigenised forms are returning to the 'core' music-producing countries for further hybridisation. Take, for example, Indian popular music and in particular the soundtracks to Hindi (or 'Bollywood') musicals. For many years musicians in Mumbai produced music based on the *ghazal* and other traditional forms which had an enormous, yet tightly delimited market. The audience for both films and soundtrack recordings was confined to the subcontinent and to diasporic communities of Indians around the world, most importantly in Britain. However, as this music has become increasingly influenced by Anglo-American dance music – electronic production techniques, house and break beats etc. – so too it has started to resonate, quite literally, in studios in the West. In 2005, rap and R & B artists are using Bollywood sounds, and in a further twist, there is renewed interest in the Jamaican dance-hall genre, a style that has already incorporated Indian modalities. (Listen, for example, to the 'Indian Riddim' used by Elephant Man, Capleton and others on Various Artists, 2002.) Other examples and case studies in hybridity are found throughout the *Reader*, especially in Part Five.

It could be argued, then, that in its multiple flows of sound and style, globalising pop represents something epochal – namely, the beginnings of a shift towards the reciprocal exchange of music across the world. Still, we should emphasise that this is only just starting to happen. Moreover, any such process is vulnerable, not least because it is occurring in a world system built on economic *in*equality: the contradictions between musical exchange and mutuality on the one hand, and a widening gap between rich and poor on the other are severe indeed.

The third major factor contributing to change in popular music is economic through and through. The advent of digital technology in production, but perhaps even more significantly, in distribution, threatens to destabilise the music business. As we write, academic work on this subject is only just beginning to be published. Yet it is already clear that the recording industry is having to make major adjustments to its 'business model' in order to cope with up- and down-loading of music on the Internet. The basic issue here is that the spread of Internet access has enabled the distribution of music at a marginal cost to a great swathe of consumers, at least in rich industrialised countries. No longer restricted to lending hard copies of records to their friends or making tapes, music fans can now 'file share' with millions of others. The recording industry rightly sees this as a threat to its well-established profit-making strategies. These have depended on being able to maintain 'turnstiles' at every point music is used, such that no person or organisation can access music without paying. The turnstiles have included shops, as well as the licensing deals between record companies and radio stations or other 'secondary users'. What has kept everyone going through the turnstiles is copyright law.

Now, however, the promiscuous interconnectivity of the Internet makes the turnstile model very difficult to enforce. It is impossible to check every file exchange between millions of different PCs across the world. Nevertheless, it is likely that new kinds of digital surveillance and encryption such as 'watermarking', combined with the rigorous application of more punitive copyright laws, will ultimately make file sharing marginal. Or, in a slightly different perspective, by taking up Internet distribution itself, the recording industry will effectively commodify the Internet, leaving the genuinely mutual exchange of music on the sidelines. That said, the music industry is clearly going through a difficult period. Technological developments – those forces of production that drive capitalism – also present problems for it, and such problems will surely persist and even intensify over the shelf-life of this *Reader*.

We have been keen in this Introduction to underline the change and turbulence that popular music is going through in the contemporary period, while also pointing to the dangers associated with taking such an approach. We might note that the desire to explain, articulate and even amplify the new is powerful among academics, partly because status in the profession so often depends on innovation. One of the most efficient ways of demonstrating academic innovation is through revealing what is new in the world. It is, then, particularly laudable that, by and large, practitioners of popular music studies have avoided this lure, while at the same time enormously expanding their knowledge in an under-researched area of human experience.

For years, popular music studies was doubly marginalised. Not only was its subject a form of *popular* culture, and therefore despised by many in the academy for whom culture was synonymous with elite art, it was also *music,* and as a result it was treated with distrust by positivists in the social sciences and humanities. Music, this objection went, referred to nothing, it had no meaning. Neither of these criticisms has disappeared (for rebuttal, see virtually any of the contributions in the *Reader*), yet popular music studies has now emerged as a globally established and multi-disciplinary field. The international community of popular music scholars continues to grow, as does the range of specialisms that they bring to their work. At the time of writing, the academic backgrounds of popular music researchers span a variety of disciplines, including musicology and ethnomusicology, anthropology, sociology, media and cultural studies, politics, linguistics, history and English. Many of these scholars are members of the International Association for the Study of Popular Music (IASPM), which has expanded enormously since its inception in 1981. And there are now a number of smaller, local IASPM branches throughout the world that hold annual and biennial conferences and seminars. Popular music studies, we might say, has been globalised.

Over the same period, the number of courses in popular music has grown. Students can now take a popular music module or course on a wide range of programmes from music (strangely, this still means *classical* music) to media studies. There are even a few dedicated degrees in the subject now. Ultimately, it is the growth in student numbers that explains the expansion of research and publishing in the field. This *Reader*, for example, has been published on the assumption that there is a large and developing market for a volume that wraps up recent texts inside a single jacket. It constitutes a compilation album – but perhaps this is too easy an analogy. The expansion of popular music studies has also been characterised by an increasing diversity in the range of topics researched. In addition to ongoing work in established areas of popular music scholarship – notably the music industry, textual analysis and audience studies, the 1990s saw the emergence of new areas of interest such as music scenes, local music-making practices and the impact of new technologies – for example, digital recording, MP3 and the Internet, on patterns of popular music production and consumption. We have discussed the broad historical context of some of these topics already.

Another developing focus of research has been on the relationship between popular music and diaspora, really a subset of the field of globalisation studies. With the increasing flow of people around the world, music has proved to be a key resource providing a cultural bridge between displaced peoples across the globe, their homelands and a yet-to-be-realised cosmopolitan world culture. The emphasis on global flows presents a new approach to popular music that reshapes the field across its various sub-areas. This approach focuses not so much on the origins of musical styles, but takes as its object what happens to musical culture when it moves across space and time. The studies in this area build on the transformative work by Paul Gilroy (1993 and in Chapter 20), and insist that popular music styles can no longer be contained within a single national tradition. Indeed, as work on music and diaspora has demonstrated, the effect of globally established musics such as reggae and rap has been the forging of trans-local diasporic communities. Thus, musical globalisation is not only about the movement of musics, but also about the movement of peoples. Part Five is devoted to this topic.

Since the mid-1990s, an increasing concern among popular music scholars has been the more mundane applications of popular music in everyday life. There is a growing understanding of popular music's significance as a personal resource for individuals, with a range of individual characteristics such as identity, biography and personal memories being articulated with reference to particular songs or pieces of music. Furthermore, popular music is now an acknowledged part of the every-day soundscape, being heard in a diverse range of public spaces, including shops, cafés, bars, gyms and on public transport. The introduction of the Sony Walkman in the early 1980s, and the subsequent development of more sophisticated personal stereo formats over the last twenty years, has added a significant new dimension to this everyday quality of musical experience by enabling the user to choose his/her own individual soundscape. Pieces on popular music and everyday life may be found in Part Four.

However, contemporary popular music research is not exclusively concerned with the here and now. The most recent literature indicates that the field of popular music studies is quickly coming to recognise its necessary historical component. So, although the field has typically focused on post-Second World War musics, that very era has become historical. Similarly, discussions of the contemporary impact of population flows, technological developments, as well as generic or stylistic trans-formations have encouraged engagement with these processes before the war. For example, the impact of the electrical microphone enabled the softer more intimate singing associated with both Bing Crosby and Billie Holiday. Such a singing style became absolutely central to pop singing styles after the Second World War. David Brackett investigates the complex implications of this in Chapter 4. Similarly, the encounter across racial lines that has typically been associated with rock and roll was clearly prefigured in the swing era and in the rise of early country music. Increasingly, popular music studies are engaging the historical contexts of these demographic, stylistic and technical developments. Chapters with a historical focus can be found throughout the *Reader*.

To repeat, then, it is the rapid expansion in the range of topics now researched and taught under the rubric of popular music studies that provides the rational for this volume. Given that the current leading popular music reader, Frith and Goodwin's (eds) (1990) *On Record: Rock, Pop and the Written Word*, was published over ten years ago and has not been subsequently updated, there is a need for a new edited reader in popular music studies whose content takes into account devel-opments in popular music scholarship and research during the last fifteen years.

Due to the volume of work published during this period, it is clearly impossible to present a collection of studies that is entirely representative. Nevertheless, in choosing the selections presented here, we have endeavoured to include material that is as comprehensive and diverse as possible in terms of its coverage of popular music studies over the last fifteen years. The topics covered in the nine sections of the *Reader* represent the key areas of research and debate that characterise popular music studies at the beginning of the twenty-first century.

In compiling the studies contained in the *Reader*, we have also attempted to reflect as much as possible the different disciplinary orientations of popular music researchers. Where appropriate, the sections in the *Reader* comprise material published by scholars spanning a range of disciplinary backgrounds. Additionally, the book reflects the increasingly global flavour of popular music studies. Alongside North American, UK and central European studies, the work of researchers from Japan, Oceania, Scandinavia and South America is also featured.

Finally, we have tried to acknowledge the contribution of authors who, although working outside the conventions of academic research and writing, have nevertheless produced work that has been highly influential on the direction and approach of popular music studies during the last fifteen years. The work of writers such as David Toop, Joseph Lanza, Kodwo Eshun and Alice Echols has added a new depth of understanding of the historical and technological developments that have shaped popular music production, performance and reception since the mid-1950s. These authors also bring a fluency and allusiveness to the writing, which is not just a matter of style: such writing illuminates its topic – namely, fluent, allusive popular music.

PART ONE

Music as sound, music as text

Introduction to Part One

■   Barry Shank

IN THE PAST DECADE, popular music studies has begun to develop its own strategies of formal analysis. Where traditional musicologists have often had little to say about the harmonic structure, pitch patterns or interwoven themes of popular music, a new generation of scholars is now articulating categories of formal analysis and careful listening procedures that isolate key patterns of affective signification. Most of the efforts to create a popular musicology eschew the traditional jargon while continuing to uncover musical meaning. Focusing on aspects such as the function of repetition, the effects of particular timbral qualities, and the ways in which vocal styles and musical strategies encode place, race, class, and gender, the articles we present here link musical sounds with socially inscribed and embodied meaning.

Part One begins with Richard Middleton's classic analysis of repetition. Middleton reminds us that one of the classic critiques of popular music is that it all sounds the same or that it is repetitious. He points out that all music contains repetition. In fact, repetition is one of the key sources of musical pleasure. A more accurate way to state the critique would be to say that popular music has its own patterns of repetition. Theodor Adorno linked the repetitions found in popular music to its industrial conditions of production. Middleton finds the pleasure produced in and through repetition to be located at the intersection of several sets of determinations, conditions of production, the psychological construction of listening and performing subjects, the larger political economy, and the effects of musical traditions. He identifies a spectrum of repetition patterns that range from repeating very small units (i.e. riffs) to the repetition of larger units at the level of the phrase or even longer. The shorter patterns he calls 'musematic,' the longer ones, 'discursive.' Where musematic repetition appears, there tends to be a corresponding surface complexity. Where discursive repetition dominates, the surface sounds are often more straightforward. While the pleasure taken in repetition might indeed signal a repetitious working environment, it can also evoke a hypnotic condition of 'being sent,' a feeling of transcending the limitations of one's immediate context.

Susan McClary articulates an important use of musical repetition in her analysis of the musical style of Laurie Anderson. As McClary points out, traditional musicology is not very helpful in trying to identify why Anderson's songs work. Once traditional theory names the two chords that repeat in 'O Superman,' for instance, there is not much more for it to say. But McClary sees that insistent repetition as precisely the source of productive meaning in the song. McClary identifies a pedal on middle C that reorients the traditional relationship between the Ab major chord and its relative minor, C minor. Where in traditional musicology, the major chord is heard as the more stable tonal center (i.e. 'masculine') and the relative minor is heard as a momentary movement away from that center (less stable and, therefore, 'feminine'), the C pedal encourages us to hear the C minor chord as at least the equal of the Ab. McClary's analysis of gender in Anderson's music is not limited to harmonic structure. Anderson's performance style enters as well. In McClary's analysis, Anderson's strategies of electronically mediating and distancing the sounds produced by her violin focuses the audience's attention on the embodied nature of musical performance while escaping the objectification of female bodies common to traditional performance styles. Anderson's evocation of the necessary embodiment of musical performance works in parallel with her leveling of the harmonic field to reorient the gendered hierarchy of traditional music and traditional musicology. McClary's analysis enables us to hear and see the embodied meaning in Anderson's music.

Where Middleton and McClary call our attention to aspects of musical structure and performance, Dai Griffiths focuses on John Cale's voice to show us how particular vocal timbres and elements of singing styles can evoke place, home, and a specific ethnic subjectivity (in this case, Welsh). Griffiths listens across Cale's recorded output, identifying moments of intensifying the vocal line such that the *sound* of the voice becomes the key signifying element, working with but also over-coding the melody and the lyrics. Griffiths links this use of vocal intensity to Welsh history and to the effects of the rapid industrialization that have produced, among other things, a particular dark humor, a near complete loss of the Welsh language, and a distinctive rasp to Welsh voices. Griffiths teaches us to hear these qualities in Cale's screams, in the ways in which he rushes the vocal line near the ends of songs, in his use of sardonic laughter and in the ways in which his vocals sometimes sound squeezed, as though emerging above ground after a long day in the coal mines. As Griffiths puts it, 'The Cale voice is most immediately recognizable as that of the psycho-drama.'

David Brackett provides us with an alternative approach to the voice. Brackett shows us how two recordings of the same song by two different singers, Bing Crosby and Billie Holiday, can evoke two very different sets of musical meanings. Just as Griffiths used Cale's voice to link musical sounds to a particular context, Brackett insists that 'the voice never means only by itself, but as a means of evoking the signifying associations with that voice'. In 'I'll be Seeing You', Brackett has located a key text for identifying the specific associations that contribute to the social construction of musical meaning. A common associational linkage suggested by the voice sends us towards the person and the biography of the singer. This is the direction that Griffiths took us in. Brackett, however, encourages us to consider additional contexts that shape our understanding of the identities of the singers. It would not do simply to link Holliday's version with the facts of her biography and contrast that with Crosby's. Their recordings do not merely reflect the commonly known facts of their lives. For example, the critical discourse at the time the songs were recorded gave much greater credence and significance to Crosby's recording. Audiences were assumed to be familiar with Crosby's real name, his image and style, as well as the physical condition of his bandleader. No similar knowledge about Holliday was assumed. While the review of Holliday's recording had to justify its space in the pages of *Downbeat*, Crosby's recording was discussed in a matter of fact way that indicated its immediate acceptance by jazz critics. Today, however, Holliday is categorized more as an artful singer while Crosby's style evokes a more casual popular style. Crosby's persona was developed in and through his work in films as well as his work in music, and Brackett shows how this persona helped reinforce the timeliness of Crosby's version of the song. Intriguingly, however, that timeliness has worked to limit the aesthetic reception of Crosby's version today. Brackett's point is that questions of aesthetic value, even the value that is produced in and through the voice, cannot be answered solely by reference to the person singing. The meaning and the value of the vocal contribution has to be understood in a complex array of contexts that include shifts in prestige of the various codes (musical and social) articulated in the text.

Philip Tagg begins his analysis of subjectivity and soundscape with the image of a baby screaming. The sheer survival of the dependent young human is dependent upon that person's ability to cut through all surrounding noise with the intensity of his or her wail. Tagg takes off on this commonly known fact to remind us that different cultures have different patterns and norms whereby the subject emerges out of the sonic background. Careful listening to the relative volume and timbre of popular musical sounds can then tell us something about the relationship between the individual subject and the social structure out of which that subject emerges. Tagg uses the example of heavy metal music, which he argues is 'essential to the survival of underprivileged young people living in harsh urban environments,' to make his case. He argues that the sounds of a successful environment – the quiet purr of a nice auto, the soft hum of the shopkeeper's lights – can sound oppressive to those who feel no ownership of or access to that success. Indeed the musical layers of heavy metal display a homological relationship with the class structures of industrialized societies. Against a background of heavily compressed and densely packed sound, the lead vocals and solo instruments much display intensity, high pitch, sharp timbres and even louder volume in order to be heard. Tagg argues that the pleasure of heavy metal derives at least in part from the ability of its musicians and fans to take symbolic control over an oppressive social structure by rising above its noise musically.

Each of these pieces encourages us to listen carefully to popular music and to develop ways of analyzing and decoding musical meaning that respond to the same qualities that the fans and musicians find meaningful and pleasurable. As popular music studies continues to grow and develop, new analytical strategies will emerge. Their usefulness will ultimately be dependent upon how well they link musical meaning, musical pleasures to the social, economic and cultural conditions within which those meanings and pleasures are experienced.

Chapter 1

Richard Middleton

IN THE GROOVE OR BLOWING YOUR MIND?
The pleasures of musical repetition

I N RECENT YEARS THE QUESTION of the pleasure of popular music has been placed firmly on the agenda for discussion. Partly, this has been the result of a spillover from work on the pleasures of literary and film texts; partly, it was the result of a realization that existing sociological, subcultural and musicological studies of popular music had neglected this vital area – the area, after all, that would appear to do most to legitimate the existence of the music from the listener's point of view. While early studies devote most of their attention to the performer, what is largely lacking so far is any sustained examination of the pleasures produced by musical syntaxes themselves.

The most widely applicable aspect of popular musical syntaxes is that of repetition, and this in turn bears closely, in all its manifestations, on questions of like and dislike, boredom and excitement, tension and relaxation – in short, the dialectics of musical pleasure. Almost all popular songs, to a greater or lesser extent, fall under the power of repetition. Why is this and what are the effects?

'It's monotonous'; 'it's all the same'; it's predictable': such 'popular commonsense' reactions to popular music have probably filtered down from the discussions of mass-culture theorists. From this point of view, repetition (within a song) can be assimilated to the same category as standardization (as between songs). Of course, the significance of the role played by such techniques in the operations of the music industry can hardly be denied; it is, however, equally difficult to reduce the function of repetition simply to an analysis of the 'political economy' of popular music production and its ideological effects.

Common-sense criticisms of the prevalence of repetition in popular music usually derive from a specific analytical error: a particular conventionalized proportion of repetition to non-repetition is naturalized; most popular music is then said to transgress this norm. As already suggested, this view mostly trickles down from mass-culture theories that see repetition in popular music as a function of a specific

mode of production and its associated social relation. But all music contains repetition – though of an enormous variety of types. I would like to see the extent and
nature of repetition in a given music as produced by and located at the point where
several sets of determinations intersect: the 'political economy' of production; the
'psychic economy' of individuals; the musico-technological media of production and
reproduction; and the effects of musical–historical traditions. The syntactic conventions of musical traditions have a certain inertia and a certain relative autonomy,
overdetermining the socially and historically specific configurations resulting from
the operations of the previous factors. The importance of repetition in African-
American musics hardly needs establishing. But before we can understand the
significance of this fact and of the kind of repetition involved, we need to locate
repetition itself as a syntactic variable, within an overall theory of musical syntax.

Analytically, we can posit two (ideal) structural types: the *monad* and the *infinite
set*. One might argue – still on a strictly theoretical level – that whereas natural
language, because of its denotative function, 'tends towards' an extreme of total
differentiation, music, because of its self-reflexive character, 'tends towards' an
extreme of total sameness. Such an argument would base itself on the observation
that, considered as sets of coded conventions, musical syntaxes are marked by
an unusual degree of predictability; indeed, music's basic materials, rhythm and
pitch, are actually 'cut out' from the natural spectra by the workings of periodic
repetition. At the (theoretical) ultimate, then, music reduces to infinite repetition.
In reality, however, one would have to fix these two extremes not to particular
signifying systems but to tendencies or dispositions within signifying practice as a
whole. Thus, in practice, different musics and different language-systems are
located at different points on the line between the extremes.

Within musical practice we can envisage a scale stretching between the monad
and infinite set on which actual syntaxes are positioned at a variety of points. Since
music is a multiple parameter system (pitch, duration, timbre, etc.) and, almost
always, a multiple later system (melody, bass, accompaniment, riffs, rhythm section,
backing vocals, call and response, etc.) particular syntaxes do not sit neatly at one
particular point on the spectrum. Rather, different syntactic processes are mixed
up together; moreover, in the mixing, they do not remain wholly themselves; they
are articulated together, each mediating the other (thus, a binary switch chord-
oscillation – say a tonic-subdominant riff – can be worked into a melody digitally
organized as to pitch relationships), and the whole being given a gradual crescendo.
Moreover, since music is a temporal system, different syntactic processes can
operate simultaneously on different structural levels.

Within a particular music or individual song, the existence, role and nature of
repetition is a major distinguishing tool for analysis, helping to indicate synchroni-
cally existing differences in relation to other musics and songs, and also helping to
mark out historical changes in musical styles. But to do the distinguishing is no easy
matter. The significance of repetition is closely bound up with its role in the total
syntactic structure – i.e., with the nature of what is repeated and with the relationship of the repetition to the other processes that are present. The variety of
ways in which repetition can be used is potentially infinite. Again, however, we can
distinguish certain basic models. First, I would like to differentiate between what I
shall call *musematic* repetition and *discursive* repetition. Musematic repetition is the

repetition of short units; the most immediately familiar examples – riffs – are found in African-American musics and in rock. Discursive repetition is the repetition of longer units, at the level of the phrase. The effects of the two types are usually very different, largely because the units differ widely in the amount of information and the amount of self-contained 'sense' they contain, and in their degree of involvement with other syntactic processes. Moreover, musematic repetition is far more likely to be prolonged and unvaried and discursive repetition to be mixed in with contrasting units of varying types. The former therefore tends towards a one-levelled structural effect, the latter to a hierarchically ordered discourse. They may be tentatively characterized as 'epic-recursive' and 'narrative-lyric', respectively. Repetitive recursive frameworks are often combined with a surface displaying complex, minutely inflected, often improvised variation, while the narrative-lyric model tends towards the developmental type, most strikingly developed in the European art tradition.

The basic models outlined here are often correlated with oral and literate modes of composition respectively. However, it would be better to see these modes of production not as crudely technologically determined, but as actively summoned into development and strongly mediated by the needs of distinct socio-economic configurations. The principles of musematic repetition and recursive structures are certainly suited to the methods of oral composition; similarly, discursive repetition and hierarchically organized structures can be more easily worked out on paper. But there are plenty of examples of discursive repetition in orally created music and of musematic repetition in written pieces.

Complete coverage of repetition practice in popular music is well beyond the cope of a short essay. Here, I will illustrate a few basic types, some interactions between them and an overall historical change. I shall draw my examples from three sources: nineteenth-century British popular music; Tin Pan Alley song (c. 1900–39); rhythm and blues, and rock music.

In nineteenth-century music hall song, repetition is usually discursive – at the level of the phrase. Quite often the repeated phrase is slightly altered for harmonic reasons. As a rule, indeed, varied repetition, when it occurs, does not play off a relationship between recursive framework and variative detail so much as it approaches the technique of sequence or the technique of phrase-structure repetition. In the latter, the surface details change but there is a kind of parallelism or analogical repetition between phrases on the level of harmonic-rhythmic structure and basic melodic shape. Perhaps the most typical repetition technique in music hall song is that of sequence – typical because it is at the same time repetitive and non-repetitive: the unit of repetition is worked into a larger unit of narrative flow or lyrical symmetry. Even when shorter units – approaching musemes – are repeated in music hall song, they are almost always drawn out into a longer line through sequence. Sequence is a way of holding on to at least some of the power of repetition while, as it were, cutting it down to size and stitching it into other structural processes. Sequence composes time; it makes us aware of rise and fall, a discursive hierarchy, and thus refers us to irreversible experiences.

The prevalence of sequence in this kind of song confirms a general tendency there to absorb repetition into more complex structures. It is a tendency that can be traced back easily to the bourgeois song styles of the eighteenth and nineteenth centuries. There, too, one notices that repetition is confined to the melodic level: at the extreme, it strikes one as the icing on the cake, the cake itself being mixed from narrative-harmonic ingredients. The influence of African-American music can already be heard in a few nineteenth-century popular songs, particularly in America, and with this influence came musematic repetition. When ragtime hit Tin Pan Alley, this influence became a flood. Musically, however, there was no clean break: the techniques of phrase-repetition, phrase-structure repetition and sequence remained important, and indeed Tin Pan Alley song, from 1900 to 1939, can be seen as involved in a constant struggle between the two traditions.

Classic early examples of Tin Pan Alley incorporation of musematic repetition are Irving Berlin's 'Alexander's Ragtime Band' of 1911 and Lewis Muir's 'Waiting for the Robert E. Lee,' written the following year. By the jazz age, the technique was endemic. However, musematic repetition was still generally worked in with older-established techniques – phrase-building and sequence. Often, musemes are treated sequentially in a traditional way. Sometimes they are coupled with longer units that are sequentially repeated. The further we move from Tin Pan Alley towards theatre song, and from the 1920s into the 1930s (there are two relation-ships here, historically intertwined), the more musematic repetition tends to be worked into complex analogue-based structures. In the hands of the Broadway masters – George Gershwin, for example – quite complex fusions can result. At the same time as incorporating some musematic repetition, Tin Pan Alley songs retained the use of discursive techniques; indeed, the classic ballad form of the period (a 32-bar AABA) relies on them for its overall structure. Moreover, repetition is still almost totally confined to melody – although the occasional song hints at the use of short harmonic cells.

Musematic techniques, as a primary structuring device, first broke through in a big way, in mass-audience popular music, in the work of the 1930s swing bands (in the form of riffs). Where exactly in music history this technique originated is difficult to say, but in the end it is less important to identify particular sources than to locate the technique in general everyday (oral) practice in black culture; this, of course, is what recordings, out of marketing and other considerations, have always under-represented. Thus, black bands in the 1930s often made up 'head' arrange-ments based on simple riffs for dancing; only afterwards, if successful, were they sometimes given lyrics and worked out properly. However, musematic techniques, while undoubtedly suited to the oral composition methods common in rhythm and blues and rock, should not simply be correlated with folk spontaneity. Elaborate studio-created pieces based on riffs are not uncommon (the Beach Boys would be a classic case here – for example, 'God Only Knows' and 'Good Vibrations'); and, after all, it is the new electro-mechanical media that have made possible the fade out (the ultimate form of repetition, since it actually does fulfil itself in monadic silence).

Lionel Hampton's celebrated 'Flyin' Home' can serve as a classic example of riff technique, on its way from swing to rhythm and blues. For examples of the techniques' assimilation by jump and rhythm and blues bands in the 1940s, almost any of Louis Jordan's recordings are excellent sources. In all these cases, the rela-tionship between riff framework and variative detail (improvised solos, inflected instrumental playing) is important. From this point, riff techniques spread through almost all black popular music. Riffs can comprise more or less the whole piece; alternatively, they can be a framework underneath vocal and/or instrumental variative elaboration. They can be continuous or worked into an antiphonal call-and-response pattern. They can be unchanging in pitch level or be pitch-layered against an (often 12-bar blues) chord progression. They can be melodically memorable or chiefly rhythmic in impact. Always their effect, to a greater or lesser extent, is to level out the temporal flow, challenge any narrative functionality attaching to chord patterns and verse sequences, and open up the syntactic field for rhythmic elements to dominate. The shorter and more insistently repeated the riffs, the more powerful these effects.

From rhythm and blues, these techniques permeated rock 'n' roll and from there spread widely within rock. Again, the variety of usage is considerable. For instance, combinations of riffs can be worked into chord patterns, as often happens in, say Rolling Stones songs. Or the riffs can be virtually the whole framework, with perhaps an important role for surface variative detail; a classic example is Led Zeppelin's 'Whole Lotta Love'. Of more general importance to a study of musematic repetition in African American and rock music is the fact that it encompasses not only melody but also rhythm and harmony. Developments in rhythm are too extensive and various to be covered properly here, but it is worth noting that rhythm emerges as a distinct layer in jazz and rhythm and blues, notably through the use of identifiable syntactic units by drummers: 'back beat' and eight-to-the-bar patterns, etc. Just as melodic musematic repetition stems from African-American musical practice, so the harmonic equivalent – short chord sequences, usually two or three chords, repeated – clearly has its origins in black music. This technique appears in early gospel music; from there it passes into the work of secular vocal groups and early soul singers and becomes a staple ingredient of black music from the 1960s on. This soon became a primary rock technique. Its effect is to cut back the differentiation of harmonies, the narrativity of harmonic syntax, to a minimum. The Who's 'My Generation' in which a continuous two-chord oscillation is supplemented by a melodic riff, illustrates one common type of application. Once again, some of the most interesting examples are compromises; the classic source here is the work of the Beatles, a large proportion of Lennon–McCartney songs being based on the working of harmonic riffs into a discursive structure, usually derived from AABA ballad form.

Repetition is often associated with the phenomenon of being 'sent', particularly in relation to 'hypnotic' rhythmic repetitions and audience trance: a collective loss of the self. Repetition does its work precisely on the terrain where social determination, signifying practices and the relative constants of the human condition intersect. Within the psychic economy, repetition appears to us only in complex mediated forms. Within signifying systems, too, repetition does not represent itself as natural, nor purely as instrumental or purposeful. Instead, we can say that its forms represent a cultural work – or rather that they exist and are worked out at the point where socially constructed cultural codes and the structure of the subject meet. Repetition, at its simplest, is the minimum step into the game of language and culture.

What this conception opens up for us is a apace within which specific manifestations of repetition-practice in popular music can be located as manifestations of a complex cultural game into which play a variety of social and psychic forces. Musematic repetition would seem to be more basic – more involved with desire and death – while discursive repetition involves more of the ego and the self. The game can be disrupted, the sense of self lost. For instance, the very force of repetition can, as it were, obliterate the significance of content; as continuous repetition approaches that point where we know that change is ruled out, the point of monadic unity, then the game effectively ceases. A good deal of popular music privileges this rhythmic obstinacy, reiteration to excess, and obliterates organization and variety; a hypnotic abandon to this energy is also the expression of an energy.

It should by now be clear, in general terms, how the ensemble of social determinations breaks upon the pleasure-field. 'Pleasure' is a social term; similarly, people and syntaxes repeat themselves in socially determinate ways. There is no need, however, to see this process as monolithic or unidetermined. It is open to struggle. Certainly, the various pleasures of musical effects are not like bran-tub goodies, freely or randomly available; they come ideologically sorted, shaped and wrapped. But the ensemble of forces in the field is too complex and too dynamic to be regarded as a completely homogeneous totality; how can, say, a thumping rhythm-and-blues riff be turned simply into a collective rubber stamp? The production of musical syntaxes involves active choice, conflict, redefinition; at the same time, their understanding and enjoyment take place in the theatre of self-definition, as part of the general struggle among listeners for control of meaning and pleasure.

Chapter 2

Susan McClary

THIS IS NOT A STORY MY PEOPLE TELL
Musical time and space according to Laurie Anderson

IN HER COMPOSITION 'Langue d'amour' – just after she has retold the Adam and Eve story and just before she moves into the ecstatic stasis that ends the piece – Laurie Anderson says:

> This is not a story my people tell. It's something I know myself. And when I do my job I am thinking about these things. Because when I do my job, that's what I think about.

She thus casually evokes a typical ethnographic situation in which a native informant delivers authentic folklore to an anthropologist.

But there are problems here: who are the individuals referred to as 'my people'? Who is this speaking and why are her stories different? Our narrator is not a trustworthy informant: by her own admission, she is refusing to deliver what is always understood to be the desired anthropological commodity-authentic, transparent access to 'the stories my people tell.' Even the language of naive storytelling is corrupted by the slang phrases of popular culture, such as 'happy as a clam' or 'hothead': clichés that are plenty meaningful but that disrupt our ability to hear the story as the pure voice of the 'folk.'

Anthrospeak notwithstanding, this is not a primitive myth at all, but rather a pointed retelling of our own Western narrative of origin. Moreover, the story is being told by a woman and from a woman's point of view. With the lightest of touches, Anderson sets up what seems at first glance the standard binary oppositions underpinning Western knowledge: anthropologist/primitive, human/nature, truth/fiction, authenticity/corruption, Western/non-Western, male/female. Then she tilts them slightly, so that they begin to slip. Their bedrock certainty just evaporates.

Laurie Anderson's work always involves several discourses, all operating simultaneously, all interconnected in unpredictable, sometimes contradictory ways. It is virtually impossible to separate out any one aspect of her pieces for examination without violating her own insistent violation of the genre boundaries that organize the traditional art world. Most critics of drama, film, performance art, and postmodern culture accept, and even celebrate this in their analyses of her work. But while such multimedia approaches are indispensable when one deals with Anderson, one prominent aspect of her work – the musical – almost always gets slighted in such accounts for the simple reason that nonmusicians have difficulty verbalizing about music and its effects.

Unfortunately, the academic musicians who know how to talk about music have shown little interest in Anderson's work. Most of the analytical techniques that have been developed in academic music theory slide right off her pieces. Because much of her music is triadic, the harmonic theory designed for the analysis of the standard eighteenth- and nineteenth-century repertories might seem relevant. But all harmonic theory can do is to label the pairs of alternating chords that often serve as the materials for her pieces. Musicians often dismiss Anderson's music as being nothing more than this, as though it were intended for beginners in ear-training classes: 'O Super man' gives the boneheads eight minutes to hear the difference between two chords. Next week, a three-chord structure. After a year, maybe a Mozart sonata. Finally, Schoenberg or Carter. For these are, of course, the stories – the *authorized* stories – 'my people' tell, in both concert hall and classroom.

In this chapter I focus on the musical dimension of Anderson's work. If her music resists analysis as we practice it in the academy, it is not necessarily because her pieces are faulty according to universal, objective criteria, but rather because her premises are different. As it turns out, Anderson's musical experiments – the stories she tells herself when she does her job – can tell us quite a bit both about the discursive conventions of the standard repertories and also, by extension, about music theory as it is practiced in the academy. Because they resist many of the categories of traditional music theory, her pieces demand that we develop a new set of analytical questions. Accordingly, this essay concentrates on some very basic issues: the organization of space and time in Anderson's music and musical performances.

American musicology and music theory have rarely been interested in examining the temporal and spatial dimensions of music per se. The scarcity of literature in this area is emphasized by Robert Morgan's pioneering article, 'Musical Time/ Musical Space' (1980), which develops some useful ways of considering various kinds of spatial relationships within music. However, except for a brief aside in which he mentions pieces that deliberately exploit spatial arrangements within performance sites, Morgan's comments address only the metaphorical space within compositions: qualities of high and low, of relative distance, of surface and background. Many aspects of Anderson's pieces can fruitfully be discussed in these terms and I will return to them later. But there are other spatial issues at stake in music issues that are not only neglected but actively repressed by most professional musicians and theorists, and Anderson forces us to become aware of these submerged, though crucial, issues.

The most significant of these issues concerns the physical source of sound. In many cultures, music and movement are inseparable activities, and the physical engagement of the musician in performance is desired and expected. By contrast, Western culture – with its puritanical, idealist suspicion of the body – has tried throughout much of its history to mask the fact that actual people usually produce the sounds that constitute music. As far back as Plato, music's mysterious ability to inspire bodily motion has aroused consternation, and a very strong tradition of Western musical thought has been devoted to defining music as the sound itself, to erasing the physicality involved in both the making and the reception of music. The advent of recording has been a Platonic dream come true, for with a disk one can have the pleasure of the sound without the troubling reminder of the bodies producing it. And electronic composition makes it possible to eliminate the last trace of the nonidealist element.

The genre known as performance art arose in the 1960s and was in part a reaction against this erasure of people from art. One of the principal features of performance art is the insistence on the artist as a performing body. Gone is the division of labor in which a composer constructs an object and passes it on to a performer who executes faithfully the demands of the master. In performance art, artist and performer are usually one, and the piece is that which is inscribed on and through the body. The radical separation of mind and body that underwrites most so-called serious music and music theory is here thrown into confusion.

Anderson's compositions rely upon precisely those tools of electronic mediation that most performance artists seek to displace. In order to put this aspect of her work into perspective, it is important to recall that most modes of mechanical and electronic reproduction strive to render themselves invisible and inaudible, to invite the spectator to believe that what is seen or heard is real. By contrast, in Laurie Anderson's performances, one actually gets to watch her produce the sounds we hear. But her presence is always already multiply mediated: we hear her voice only as it is filtered through Vocoders, as it passes through reiterative loops, as it is layered upon itself by means of sequencers. For some pieces, she attaches contact mikes to drum machines and produces sounds by striking various parts of her body; for others, she speaks through a pillow speaker located inside her mouth. The closer we get to the source, the more distant becomes the imagined ideal of unmediated presence and authenticity. Anderson deliberately plays with those anxieties provoked when a voice is not securely grounded in a particular body. She insists on and problematizes her mediation.

The problem this extreme mediation calls up is sometimes referred to as 'man versus Machine,' and in fact many reviewers of Anderson's work have assumed that she too is merely critiquing the alienating influence of the media on human authenticity. But to interpret her work in terms of that standard dichotomy is to ignore her obvious fascination with gadgetry. As she has remarked:

> It's true that there is a lot of alienation in songs like 'Big Science' and 'O Superman.' All of my work that deals with machines, and how they talk and think, is inherently critical. That's certainly the bias. But I think many people have missed an important fact: those songs themselves are made up of digital bits. My work is expressed through technology – a lot of it depends on 15 million watts of power.

If Anderson's work refuses the options offered by the traditional man-versus-machine dichotomy, it is in part because she is not a man. The fact that hers is a *female* body changes the dynamics of several of the oppositions she invokes in performance. For women's bodies in Western culture have almost always been viewed as objects of display. Women have rarely been permitted agency in art, but instead have been restricted to enacting – upon and through their bodies – the theatrical, musical, cinematic, and dance scenarios concocted by male artists. This raises the stakes enormously and makes much more significant Anderson's insistence on her self-representation within the performance space.

When Anderson involves herself with electronics, she confuses still other habits of thought grounded in gender difference. For it is supposed to be *man* who gives birth to and who tames the machine. But as Anderson wrestles with technology, she displaces the male subject who usually enacts that heroic feat. And by setting up an implied alliance and identification with the machine, she raises the conventional anxiety of the self-directed robot – the living dolls of science fiction or Gothic stories of the uncanny, but a living doll who is self-created, who flaunts her electronic constructedness. 'As she says in her piece "Closed Circuits," 'You're the snake charmer, baby. And you're also the snake.'

For all these reasons, musical space in Laurie Anderson's music is multiply charged. No longer merely a metaphorical concept, the space within which her music occurs is the arena for many kinds of cultural struggles. It is electronically saturated at the same time as it insists on the body – and not simply the neuter body that has been erased from consideration in music theory, but the problematic female body that traditionally has been the site of the spectacular.

But whether a woman performer denies or emphasizes her physical presence, it is always read back onto her. Anderson is sometimes criticized, for instance, for presenting gestures 'from which spontaneity and joy tread: [read: sexuality] have been banished,' or for preventing the audience from identifying with her, for withholding the kind of nurturing presence we expect women performers to deliver. She walks a very thin line, foregrounding her body while trying not to make it the entire point. As she puts it:

> I wear audio masks in my work – meaning, electronically, I can be this shoe sales man, or this demented cop, or some other character. And I do that to avoid the expectations of what it means to be a woman on a stage.

I would like to move now into the music itself. Many of the same dilemmas that Anderson faces as a woman on stage confront her again when she decides to compose. How does a woman composer negotiate with established musical discourses? What options are available and what do her choices signify?

Music is generally regarded as a neutral – a neuter-enterprise – because of the desire not to acknowledge its mediation through actual people with gendered bodies. Some women composers accept this position and write music that is indistinguishable from that of their male colleagues. Many of them chafe at the suggestion that their sexual identity might have something to do with their music, and understandably so: for centuries it has been thought that if women did write music, it would sound frail and passive – that is, it would sound the way dominant culture assumed that women were and should be. In the last few decades, many women have risen in the area of composition to command the respect of both male and female peers – respect not as women composers, but as composers, period. I want to stress here once again that I very much admire the accomplishments of these women.

However, Laurie Anderson is a performance artist whose priorities lead her not only to acknowledge but to insist upon her gender identity in her work, in the music as well as the more theatrical components. But it is not at all obvious how to make gendered differences audible in music, nor is there a single theoretical position on this matter. Some feminist artists endeavor to create images of feminine eroticism in order to celebrate their own experiences and to seize control of the representation of the female body that has been thoroughly colonized by pornography throughout Western art history. This option often produces exuberant, liberatory work, but it threatens to reinscribe the old patriarchal notion that women are simply and essentially bodies, are reducible to their sexualities. Recently, theorists such as Teresa de Lauretis and Denise Riley try to imagine new social realities – worlds in which the celebration of the erotic need not reduce women back to sex objects, in which the intellect and the body can be mutually supportive and collaborative. I want to argue that Anderson's work enacts a similar position as it continually shifts back and forth across boundaries, sometimes focusing on social critique and sometimes on developing new models of pleasure.

'O Superman,' the 1981 hit single from the extended work *United States*, is a good example of Anderson in deconstructive mode. The musical constant in 'O Superman' is a pedal on middle *c* on a single syllable: 'ha ha ha.' In performance, one watches as Anderson generates this sound and establishes its technological reiteration through a delay mechanism. It gives the impression of being expressively authentic, as though it exists outside of or prior to language, and it evokes powerful though contradictory affective responses; alternately, it may be heard as sardonic laughter or as anxious, childish whimpering. It runs for the duration of the composition, changing only when it is thrown temporarily out of kilter through phasing. Its apparent shifts in meaning are due solely to context, for the sound itself is frozen into place electronically.

Two alternating chords inflect the pedal harmonically: an A major triad in first inversion and a root-position C minor triad. It is her dependence on such minimal musical materials that makes some musicians dismiss Anderson as unworthy of serious analytical discussion. But like many other aspects of Anderson's work, the music often is carefully organized in terms of austere binary oppositions, the kinds of oppositions that structuralists such as Saussure and Lévi-Strauss revealed as lying at the foundations of Western thought and that poststructuralists have been concerned with deconstructing. The binary opposition she has chosen is not innocent and, as the piece unfolds, we learn a good deal not only about 'O Superman' but also about the premises of Western musical discourse and our own postmodern condition.

The triadicity of 'O Superman' invites listeners to read its materials in terms of the traditional codes of tonal procedure. Indeed, some critics hear Anderson's music as a simplistic return to the familiar, reassuring comforts of tonality in reaction against the intellectual rigors of serialism. Yet as easy as it may be to label the individual moments in the piece, we run into trouble as soon as we try to fix the two chords in terms of a tonal hierarchy. The pedal is first harmonized by A major, which serves as the reference point for much of the piece. The C minor harmonization appears initially as a brief inflection that is quickly altered back to A.

There are a few details, however, that make the relationship between the alternatives slightly uneasy. First, the only difference between the two chords is the choice between the pitches A flat and G. The dramatic action of the piece hangs on that flickering half-step. Second, the A chord is in first inversion and is thus somewhat flimsy, while the presumably decorative C minor chord is very solid. Third, the semiotics of tonal music associate major with affirmative affective states (hope, joy) and minor with negative states (sadness, depression). And as the piece swings between these two stark triads, one is encouraged to hear the alternation as a happy/sad dichotomy. But the fact that the major alternative is always unstable (because it is in inversion) and the minor always stable suggests that security ultimately lies with the negative option. Thus, although the major triad was established first (and therefore has some claim to the status of 'tonic'), it is increasingly heard as an inflection poised to resolve to C minor.

In other words, even although we are given only two closely related triads, it is difficult to ascertain which is structural and which ornamental. Consequently, the affective implications of the opposition become confused. Usually in tonal narratives, we are led to desire affirmative, major-key states while dreading the minor. And we are likewise accustomed to define structural stability in terms of the initial tonic and to expect that dissonances will be resolved for purposes of narrative closure. But what about a piece that mixes up these two mechanisms of desire and dread, when clinging to hope spells unstable illusion and certainty comes only with accepting dread?

Anderson's piece is in some ways like a performed-out analytical reduction of the axes upon which many such tonal pieces turn. Nothing extraneous is present – she gives us only the binaries that underlie and inform the more complex narratives of the tonal repertory. But the fact that the hierarchical relationship between her two chords is undecided means that there is not even the potential security of the tragic ending. Anderson's monologue causes us to map the alternations with certainty at first: man/machine, home/alienation, and so on. But then things become confused, as Mom becomes machine, and the clichés of American patriotism become codes of totalitarian control. Finally, we are left with the ambiguity of the initial sound and the undecidability of the binarisms. Duration and accent turn out to count enormously in this piece, for it is only through relative temporal and textural emphasis that one or the other of the chords achieves prominence, thus offering us a point of reference, at least for the moment. The most awful part of the piece begins with the words 'So hold me, Mom,' when both chords finally appear in root position, both equally oppressive. Near the end, after the singing has concluded, predictable periodic phrasing occurs for the first time. An inexorable bass ostinato enters and over it the two chords switch on and off mechanically. These fade until finally we hear only the original track: laughing or whimpering, human or electronic – all or none of the above.

At stake in the verbal text of 'O Superman' are issues such as self versus other, home versus the public sphere, autonomy versus external control. As her performance splits her into multiple identities, as the security of Mom becomes indistinguishable from national security and human becomes indistinguishable from technological, many of the constants upon which we habitually depend are thrown into turmoil. In her music, as the structural is confused with the ornamental, as the musical semiotics of desire and dread, of hope and disillusion, of illusion and reality get mapped and remapped, inscribed upon and erased from the same two chords, the tidy structures of formal analysis – those assurances of unitary control – become hopelessly tangled.

But deconstruction is only one of Anderson's interests. 'Langue d'amour' appeared in both *United States* and later, in a more elaborate version, on the 1984 album *Mister Heartbreak*. Its musical materials too are elemental. Four pitches (D, E, G, and A) cycle through the bass in a synthesized sound that evokes drumming. The pitches occur in any sequence – order and hierarchy don't matter here. Likewise, although there are strong pulses, there is no regular metric organization. The piece encourages physical motion, but it refuses to regiment that motion. Surface events in the piece are unpredictable, yet because they take place within an enclosed musical space that is securely bounded by these few pitches, nothing unexpected happens. Narrative is thus sacrificed for the sake of sustained pleasure.

Layered on top of the mix are the sounds of what are identified as electronic conches–teasing glissandos that slide upward, smearing the certainty of diatonic articulation. Even Anderson's voice is split off into several registers at once by means of the Vocoder – unitary identity is exchanged for blurred, diffused eroticism. Eventually, the decisiveness of verbal speech is abandoned for a prolonged moment of musical jouissance, in which the murmured text – 'Voici, voilà la langage de l'amour' and 'La, la, la, la' – puns continually on 'tongue': the tongue of love, the tongue that flickers in and out of the snake's mouth, the tongue inciting feminine ecstasy.

This is most emphatically not a story my people tell, if by 'my people' is meant official Western musical culture, for feminine pleasure has either been silenced in Western music or it has been simulated by male composers as the monstrous stuff requiring containment in *Carmen* or *Salome*. Indeed, Anderson's text invokes the primal story of feminine containment – the biblical account of man's seduction by woman, the hurling of mankind into history and narrative. That original story has informed our culture ever since. Retelling it from Eve's point of view quietly eliminates the pathos, the lethal mixture of desire, dread, and violence that compels narrative structure.

By suggesting that Anderson produces images of feminine pleasure in this piece, I do not mean that there is something essential about the female body and its experiences or that her artistic processes are irrational. On the contrary: what Anderson is doing is very complex, both musically and intellectually. It relies heavily on her deconstructions of the presumably neuter terms of Western music, and it requires that she manipulates the materials of music so as to produce alternative metaphors, for if many people have experienced the 'structure of feeling' conveyed by Anderson, she has had to work very hard to organize pitches and rhythms so that listeners recognize it in the music. But having isolated and analyzed the elements that have underwritten patriarchal narratives of control throughout history, she now has a space within which to assemble those elements in accordance with a different organization of time.

While women have been marginalized with respect to Western culture for most of its history, our perspectives from the margins have offered some advantages. For example, we have been privy both to the public displays and explications of official masculine culture – including the ways in which male artists construe women – as well as to experiences not accounted for within that official culture, but which Anderson and a few other women are beginning to map.

So far as we know, only one man – Tiresias, the seer in Greek mythology – has had the opportunity to experience both feminine and masculine realms: he was permitted to live in the body of a woman for several years and then was changed back into a man. When asked who had the greater erotic pleasure, he answered that women's jouissance was seven times that of a man. For divulging this information, he was struck blind. As I do not want to repeat his mistake by insisting on the superiority of Anderson's erotic imagery in 'Langue d'amour,' I will conclude with this:

Think of it.
Think of it as.
Think of it as a new way.
Think of it as a new way of structuring time.

Chapter 3

Dai Griffiths

'HOME IS LIVING LIKE A MAN ON THE RUN'
John Cale's Welsh Atlantic

> I've no business being in rock and roll. I've said it over and over again
> that I'm a classical composer, dishevelling my musical personality by
> dabbling in rock and roll.

THIS LINE OF JOHN CALE'S autobiography *What's Welsh for Zen?*, suggests the confusion and ambiguity at the heart of his now substantial output. There is, on the one hand, a profound sense of disdain for rock and roll, the art form which, after all, has sustained him for nearly forty years; but at the same time, on the other hand, there is a faith in individuality and self-expression that is either supremely confident – would you talk about your musical personality? – or, as 'over and over again' suggests, the sense that no one is listening, an indication of someone who lives, as Cale's great obsessive song has it, 'down at the end of Lonely Street'. Some of the soundbites that Cale comes up with are like the ones you would get from some of rock's loners and blabbers: Zappa, Costello, Lennon, Van Morrison; Morrison is another Celt on record reminding everyone that pop music is just his way of slumming it: 'I personally don't have anything to do with rock, in any shape or form . . . I just find it hard to be a so-called pop. It conflicts with creativity.' Cale is bothered seemingly less by commerce per se – although he and Morrison are both well clear of hits and have had to keep on producing – but by a more refined and reified idea of classical music. That Cale (or Victor Bockris, his editor) feels no need for inverted commas anywhere in the phrase 'classical composer' in a book published in 1999 says it all; it starts to point us away from the simple observation about the difference between pop music as having to do with playing in bands and classical music as writing orchestral music, and towards the complex roots for this mix-up in South Wales, and perhaps by extension, in a certain moment of the Celtic mindset. This is a Celticism that festers underneath Victorian recreations, a Wales that makes big money out of industry and is willing to lose its language accordingly; it is a scenario that finds the Celts and the Jews embarrassingly interrupting the speeches at a conference on the postcolonial; a crowd that refuses to leave a wake held for the modern, holding up the intended celebrations of the postmodern, until they are absolutely sure that the booze and drugs really have run out. Another of the guiding theses here is that John Cale presents a worn, jaded, belated version of the adjective 'Wagnerian', taking control of the whole caboodle from songwriting through singing and playing to production, with even some svengali activity on the side, the story played to a bust of Beethoven on top of the piano, and enacted with staggering levels of drug-taking and sexual adventure.

The keyword for Cale is flight: born in Garnant, near Ammanford in South Wales in 1940, he went to college in London and then took a chance and moved to New York City in 1963. After a period with LaMonte Young's Dream Syndicate, he met Lou Reed and formed the Velvet Underground, at the time part of the group gathered around Andy Warhol. Cale left the Velvet Underground in 1968 after participating in only the first two albums; although both were commercially unsuccessful, it is fair to suggest, and possible to demonstrate, that they are among the most influential of all pop albums, with legacies in glam rock, punk rock and indie or alt-rock. After one collaborative work with composer Terry Riley, he began in 1970 to record as John Cale, issuing a total of eleven solo albums mostly containing music recognizably in a rock genre relatively new at the time, as well as further collaborative albums with Brian Eno, Lou Reed (again) and Bob Neurith. Throughout this time Cale is back and forth between America and Europe, with particular success, it seems, in France. Latterly, he has begun to issue non-vocal music more recognisably in a neoclassical or contemporary genre, largely soundtracks to French feature films, as well as one orchestral setting of poems by Dylan Thomas and, most recently, ballet music in Holland.

What I intend to do in this essay is to read Cale's work against the westward movement of the Celtic diaspora. I will then mount a steady and straightforward review of his work focusing on the voice. A final section will return directly to the Welsh focus, suggesting effectively that Cale's exile has been, heroically enough to my mind, a necessary phase that has already enabled calmer but hopeful creative conditions to emerge in Wales itself.

Voice

'There's only one good use for a small town – you hate it, and you know you'll have to leave': perhaps Lou Reed's enduring contribution to the pop song, building on the lead suggested by Bob Dylan, is precisely his way of incorporating in preference to lyric's various fastidiousness the blunt prose statement, and this particular assertion describes a point where Reed, Cale and Andy Warhol all find themselves deracinated in the 1960s. 'He's completely mad,' Reed once said of Cale, 'but that's because he's Welsh'. Cale's rootlessness and what sounds like madness are most palpable in his voice.

Cale once described for a television programme a scene from his childhood: 'It would be very quiet on a Sunday. You could hear the people with pneumo walk up the street. I would be able to tell when somebody was going by the house 'cause I could hear the rasping.' From a novelist, this would be striking enough; from a musician, and a musician who sings, somehow it feels different: the awareness of a tiny code of sound to set alongside all of the other sounds and noises that go to make up recorded performances. The story about the miners struggling up the hill illustrates a moment in the history of South Wales that presumably happened again and again, as village upon village began to contain this trace, and is thus a reminder that while much of the discourse of race turns on visual appearance, social history can also be inscribed in voice, sound, and noise. Pneumoconiosis, or 'pneumo', the source of the 'rasping' wheeze that Cale would hear, is a chest condition that afflicted miners, and a symbol of how South Wales transformed from its rural to its industrial base, in a complex movement alongside and contrary to a Celtic mythology preserved as a version of pastoral. Cale's voice is that of industrial South Wales, and from this point, two musico-cultural points can be made. There is a Cale voice which is that of the lyric tenor (at its most charming on *Paris 1919*), a voice able to recite like Richard Burton: Cale's lyric voice would not of itself merit attention for plenty of equivalents are found in numerous male voice choirs. In addition, however, there is also the Cale voice whose character is suggested even in song-titles alone – 'Fear', 'Guts', 'Sudden Death', 'Taking Your Life in Your Hands' – once memorably described by Ian Penman as being 'to normative pop lyricism what a Francis Bacon Pope is to a Page Seven Fella'.

When recording his voices, Cale's production principles – 'nothing counts unless the tape is running' – tended to leave those features open like scars on the face, and which in their screams and noise and psychoses invite us to turn again to Roland Barthes. Barthes's essay on vocal grain, the lineage of which traces back through Julia Kristeva through Jacques Lacan to Sigmund Freud, his Oedipal scene and studies in hysteria, ends with the suggestion that 'the simple consideration of "grain" in music could lead to a different history of music from the one we now know', one in which less would be made of the technical idea of music without tonality. That history would also constitute a history of social sediment in the voice, of the landscape of noise: 'it *would* be very quiet on a Sunday.'

The voice's extremities in Cale will often accompany a consideration of the extremities of life. The Cale voice is most immediately recognizable as that of the psycho-drama, a scream or a strangulated whine, a cry or shout. As lineage, Cale was as likely to have been crossing genre from musical modernism: Berg's operas or Ligeti's sets of *Aventures*, for example. In pop music's terms, there was the voice of sanctifying gospel (Aretha Franklin, 'Amazing Grace'), burning soul (James Brown, 'Cold Sweat') and psychedelic fantasy (Arthur Brown, 'Fire'); it might be a precedent as simple as the scream towards the end of The Beatles' 'Hey Jude' that points further, since with Cale the thematic material spills into the sense of ending, of how the three-minute record might stop in or fade into some existential netherworld. The first example appears on Cale's first album for Island Records, *Fear*: there was preparation in 'Ghost Story' on *Vintage Violence*, but *Paris 1919* was notably and lyrically calm throughout. *Fear*'s title track announces some of the key slogans of the Cale psycho-drama: 'home is living like a man on the run', 'life and death are things that you do when you're bored', 'say: fear is a man's best friend'. The track ends at a full stop, following a careful fragmentation: cymbals and jerky bass serve as creepy accompaniment to a voice that is finally left to expressionist ranting; the phrase 'so say: fear is a man's best friend' is stretched and distorted, its rhythm elongated and compressed. Performed live in later years, Cale would take leave of the song much faster: in London 1984, the line repeats twice only before 'say' screams away over dissonance; in Paris 1992, the dissolve occurs on only the second repetition, the voice this time over piano clusters. It's as though Cale builds a sudden brick wall to contain the earlier fade, with resultant effect on song form.

The trick of 'Fear is a Man's Best Friend' was to serve Cale well: repeated over the years in examples such as 'Guts' and 'Rollaroll' on *Slow Dazzle* ('Guts' in France in 1992 receives an update very similar to 'Fear'), 'Engine' on *Helen of Troy*, 'Wilson Joilet' and 'Russian Roulette' on *Honi Soit*. By the time of 'Magazines', a track about military hardware on *Caribbean Sunset*, the Cale ending sounds like self-reference. In between the last two, however, is *Music for a New Society*, the *ne plus ultra* of Cale's binding of vocal deposit and thematic reference. *Music for a New Society* represents a genuine extremity, a point beyond which there was no point. The record contains three great moments of ending: the creepy laughter at the end of 'Thoughtless Kind', the line and manner of delivery that ends 'Sanities' ('a strong though loving world to die in'), and the all-out roar that ends 'Damn Life'.

As thematic marker, Cale's voice is something that binds together several of his 'exile' features: mothers and wives, deracination, violence and madness, death. 'Dirtyass Rock 'n' Roll' in the Cale song had made him 'feel like an undercover Sigmund Freud', and the drama of family romance is here in pulp fatness. Cale found in the Presley hit 'Heartbreak Hotel' a suitable map of this emotional landscape. On *Slow Dazzle*, his vocal performance is all horror-story hisses and screams, while the instrumental space of the band's crisp chords in Presley's original is filled with ominous, Munch-like swirls. By 1992, several versions later, performed live, 'Heartbreak Hotel' had become a remarkable song almost in the manner of text-setting, with florid piano embellishment.

Cale's voice is the marker of removal from origin, the mark of nature that emerges with Wales as accent and with a number of early obsessions: on all thematic fronts, ageing brings with it a playing-down, a compression and containment of earlier expression. There is a characteristic obsession with the figure of the mother, starting with 'Half Past France' on *Paris 1919*, and prevalent on *Fear* with 'Where to, my son?' in the title track, and on 'Gun', where a link is made between the mother and exile: 'Mother of plenty, mother of none, you got me cornered, I'm still on the run'. The theme is seemingly exorcised on *Music for a New Society*, with 'Sanities' perhaps its endpoint. 'Sanities' is the story of a woman whose mother, 'white with time', bluntly calls her a failure; 'choirs of angels' enable her to elude the charge. She enters a 'friendship' which turns into a marriage; it is, however, a marriage 'made in the grave'. In a moment of deep, one might say Germanic, expressionism, there is a 'searchlight' that finds her 'cockleshell and sure'. A remarkable list of cities – to which I shall return – follows before the ending, 'a strong though loving world to die in'. This is a strange and harrowing track – it's hard not to elide Cale himself into the female protagonist – and the tying together of motherhood and exile, rather understandably, appears to stop at that point.

An even more remarkable calming over time is found in Cale's reference to religion and the church. 'Tell Me Why', on the recent *Walking for Locusts* does something that the earlier records would hardly have dared: just before three minutes into the track, Cale goes gospel. There's a barrage of 'world beat' percussion around here, that Cale had used at inordinate length in movement 6 of the Warhol score, *Eat*; but there is also the Lafayette Inspirational Choir, gospel-derived backing vocals having been one of pop music's most insidious reference points since Madonna's 1989 single 'Like a Prayer'. The very end of 'Tell Me Why' is characteristically questioning, but hearing Cale singing 'There's a saviour looking on' can't help but feel like Garnant's last laugh. 'I'm the church and I've come to claim you with my iron drum,' Cale was told on 'Paris 1919'. The pithy 'Save Us' on *Helen of Troy* is perhaps the most subtle: 'save us from the house of God' is the running theme, with Cale adding in some churchy organ as coding. By 'The Sleeper' on *Artificial Intelligence*, Cale's agnosticism reaches an extreme point, with a weird but Welsh comparison of himself and his lover with Jesus and, yes, Satan. Cale's pact with the devil is tribute to the way that Wales's Nonconformist chapel mentality (and nonconformist rather than modernist may be the most suitable epithet to describe Cale) pervaded even someone raised in the established Church.

If thematically there are gradual changes in the voice's role, vocal drama pervades the very form of the songs themselves: a Cale trait is for vocal intensity effectively to take the space of a song's melody and divide it through anti-lyrical words into much smaller diminutions. A simple example is found in 'Mary Lou' on *Guts*, where the chorus hook (at 0.36):

X   X   X   X   (X
Ma-ry   Ma-ry   Ma-ry (Lou

is compressed (at 1.47) into

x x x
Ma-ry   Watch out me Watch out Watch out Ma-ry (Lou

This followed by a hearty scream over half of the next line. Another fine example is found in 'Leaving it Up to You' on *Helen of Troy*, where the space formerly occupied by the desolate line 'Looking for a friend, looking everywhere', is padded out to contain, first, 'And if you gave me half a chance, I'd do it now, I'd do it now, right now, you fascist', and then, 'I know we could all feel the same like Sharon Tate, and we could give it all, we could give it, give it, give it all'. The syllable count increases and the whole nature and tenor of the words shift dramatically in the short but regularly divided time: other examples are to be found on 'Cable Hogue' and on 'Wilson Joilet'. [. . .]

To end this section, however, it is worth briefly mentioning Cale as reciter: this has a subplot all its own and again sees transformation across time. The earliest solo example links the story of 'The Jeweller' on *Slow Dazzle* back to 'The Gift' on the Velvet Underground's *White Light/White Heat*, where the voice is in both cases rather pinched and foppish, as though living up to some given idea of what English short-story recitation ought to sound like. In truth, several songs were blurring the distinction of speech and song: much of *Music for a New Society* — 'Sanities' again — can stand as example. By the time of 'A Dream' on the Warhol tribute, *Songs for*

Drella, Cale's spoken voice is far more engrossing: the Welsh deposit is still there, but the voice is calm and intimate. When Cale performs other texts – Kerouac, Swedenborg, Rimbaud and Oscar Wilde– it is often as reciter: the Dylan Thomas 'settings' too are notably syllabic and flatly nonexpressive. With *Last Day on Earth*, the Neurith collaboration of 1994, an assured spoken voice is now doing something far less parochial.

Conclusion

> Libraries gave us power.
> People who don't change will find themselves like folk musicians,
> playing in museums and local as a mother-flicker.
>
> Chwi a gewch wybod y gwirionedd, a'r gwirionedd a'ch rhyddhâ chwi.
> [And ye shall know the truth, and the truth shall make ye free.]

What's Welsh for Zen? ends as it begins in Wales, and Cale struggles, especially towards the conclusion, to articulate the effect of the homeland and his deracination. Cale's descriptions of the homeland sometimes cross the line between nostalgia and senti-ment; his relation to Wales, with so much spatial and temporal distance between them, seems primarily nostalgic and devoid of irony; bitterness, when it appears, is turned inwards on the home rather than directed with any anger towards the social condition of South Wales. It is a far cry from the biggest Welsh band of the 1990s, Manic Street Preachers who, especially on *The Holy Bible*, produced precisely such a sustained diatribe; that said, the band has always remained in the UK if not in Wales itself, and, unlike Cale, its members are all monoglot English speakers. If earlier I suggested that Cale's exile left behind a certain state-sponsored version of Welsh music, then is it now possible to see him as the fulcrum, the Welsh Atlantic as a kind of necessary removal that leads to the current condition of Welsh music?

Cale appears to have spotted his heirs in Gorky's Zygotic Mynci – of all the rush of bands to have appeared from Wales, the one that most preserves a tension between the Welsh and English languages. Listening to Gorky's single releases, or an album like *Barafundle*, makes one wonder why Cale is so hung up on the idea that his work in pop music is some kind of delayed adolescence awaiting its proper elevation to the classical pantheon, even while he himself has to ascend to Parnassus through supplying music for mixed-media forms: settings of poetry, music for the dance or – for so many of its finest practitioners, the lowest of the low – film music. To turn back to a fairly basic essentialism, it's a Welsh thing: Garnant has stood its ground and is asking for more. The great irony is that Cale's carrying of the myth of modernity – genius, originality, Beethoven – has presaged a far more significant development: staying cool about the English language. With this, several things follow.

First, the culture of South Wales has a model of how to proceed, since any specifically Welsh-language emphasis always tended to downplay it. Second, the idea of being innately bilingual becomes something confidently to be asserted rather than hidden away as an uncertain split of personality. Third and finally, the markers of Wales, listening to John Cale would suggest, are musical traces that sometimes can be heard and at other times need interpretation. The flag, the anthem, the rugby shirt and dressing up as Druids once every year, all of these may be one thing, but what one is really engaging with and defending in the idea of Wales is something far more complex and contradictory, and listening critically for its musical trace is a good place to start.

Chapter 4

David Brackett

FAMILY VALUES IN MUSIC?
Billie Holiday's and Bing Crosby's 'I'll Be Seeing You'

IN 1944, BING CROSBY rested securely atop the entertainment industry. Multiple tie-ins with the movie studios, movie theaters, recording studios, and radio stations saturated the United States and much of the Western world with his image and voice. His activities as entertainer in the armed forces, his pleasant roles in movies, and his affable presence as radio host all made him welcome in the homes of middle America, as well as in the columns of critics who referred to him with the collegial monikers of 'Der Bingle' and 'The Groaner.' At this time, Billie Holiday also possessed a strong and recognizable, if not as well-known, image and sound. Known as 'Lady Day' or 'La Holiday' to jazz connoisseurs, her voice generated a radically different response from listeners, and her image presented a contrast to Crosby's All-American 'Everyman.'

Both of these singers recorded renditions of the song 'I'll Be Seeing You' in 1944. The public and the music industry treated these performers and their recordings very differently: in the quantity of copies bought; in the amount of radio play received; and in the degree and kind of press coverage allotted. In terms of their recorded performances, it is doubtful that any listener, then or now, would have mistaken one of these recordings for the other.

This chapter will focus on the reception and interpretation of these two recordings; this focus also raises several issues that impinge on the act of interpretation. First, the conjunction of these recordings permits us to explore the impact of institutional factors on the reception of a musician's work, as well as the impact of these factors on the critical status and 'popularity' of a performer. Second, the juxtaposition of these two very different performers provides an opportunity to explore the idea of voice: as we listen to a recording, respond to it, and interpret it, do we necessarily connect the sounds we hear to what we know of the historical personage singing them? If we do, how does this connection work, and what aspects of the biological author influence interpretation? The last section will consider the connection between the musical sounds of these recordings of 'I'll Be Seeing You,' the idea of the musical code, and the types and kinds of interpretations accorded Billie Holiday and Bing Crosby.

A tale of two (or three) recordings

'I'll Be Seeing You' was written in 1938 by Sammy Fain and Irving Kahal as part of the show *Right This Way,* and a version of it was recorded in the late thirties by the 'popular chanteuse' Hildegarde. Following the re-release of Hildegarde's recording late in 1943, many versions were subsequently recorded and/or released in 1944. Bing Crosby recorded his version on February 17 with the John Scott Trotter Orchestra. He had begun featuring it on January 13, 1944 in his hour-long NBC radio variety show *Kraft Music Hall*, a show that 'gave him continual exposure in millions of homes'; and he continued to include it on broadcasts until July 27, 1944. This recording first appeared on the best-selling retail record charts on April 22, 1944 and ascended to the number one position on July 1, 1944, where it remained for four weeks. Bing Crosby's recording remained a total of twenty-four weeks on the best-seller charts.

Billie Holiday recorded her version on April 1, 1944, about six weeks after Crosby recorded his. It did not appear on the pop charts although her producer, Milt Gabler, described the song as a 'a pretty big hit.' Several other recordings of the song appeared that year, including a performance sung by Frank Sinatra in his last record released with the Tommy Dorsey Orchestra (they had recorded the song in 1940). While it did not reach number one, the Sinatra/Dorsey version first appeared on the charts on May 20, 1944, rose as high as number four, and remained on the charts for a total of seventeen weeks.

Style and history

The reader may wonder *why* Billie Holiday and Bing Crosby received the kind of critical attention they did, as well as why they were represented by certain types and degrees of popularity. If we attempt to answer this question by using a discussion of critical discourse and biography, we may be led back to a set of stark oppositions: Bing Crosby, the white male, became supremely important through the efforts of publicity agents and his own efforts to provide the public with what they wanted – in other words, he was a commercially co-opted 'sell-out.' On the other hand, Billie Holiday, the African-American female, triumphed over racism and personal adversity to reach the few listeners who were prepared to receive the unvarnished presentation of her soul. Yet Holiday was more than willing to 'reinvent' herself when she thought it would bring her more publicity; and an important aspect of Crosby's image was the notion that he was simply 'acting naturally' and being paid for it. Beyond questions of the relationship between the images of these two performers and the notions of commerce and artistry, it is important to remember that at different times, both singers were lauded for revolutionizing popular singing, for changing the role of the popular singer, and for revitalizing popular music with jazz – and hence American – elements. Both singers modified the horizon of what constituted acceptable popular singing; both made their mark through the presentation of new mixtures of innovation (difference) and tradition (similarity). Yet the different contexts in which their styles became known and in which they circulated crucially affected the degree and kind of impact their music could have.

Crosby's early recordings from the late 1920s through the early 1930s are now those of his recordings most often canonized and lauded for their innovation. Critics praise these recordings of Crosby primarily for his relatively sophisticated sense of swing for a popular singer, and for his ability to combine this with a relaxed type of vocal projection that exploited improvements in microphone and recording technology. On the other hand, a diachronic analysis reveals Crosby's continuity with previous singers: his sense of swing derives from approaches based in vaudeville and the minstrel show. Biographical evidence strongly suggests that minstrel performers such as Al Jolson and Eddie Cantor were stronger influences on the young Crosby than King Oliver or Bessie Smith, although during Crosby's tenure with Paul Whiteman he was exposed to the playing of Bix Beiderbecke and Eddie Lang. The resultant 'sense of swing' therefore bears traces of emotional detachment not apparent in contemporaneous approaches of singers and instrumentalists with a different relationship to swing, such as Louis Armstrong or Jack Teagarden. To combine these observations, Crosby's 'relaxation' appears related both to the exploitation of technological innovations and to a certain distance from the 'hot' music of the time.

Not surprisingly, the fact that much of the 'jazz' influence upon Crosby arrived via the minstrel show informs much of his work: it features prominently in his role and performance in blackface as 'lazy minstrel man' Dan Emmett in the 1943 movie *Dixie*; it figures in the exchange with Johnny Mercer during 'Mr. Gallagher and Mr. Sheen' (in which Crosby sings 'swing is really much too ancient to condemn/in the jungles they would play, in that same abandoned way'); it surfaces in the dialect during 'Ac-Cent-Tchu-Ate the Positive' (recorded in 1944); it made possible his participation in a minstrel show with Al Jolson in 1947, as well as his inclusion of the numbers 'I'd Rather See A Minstrel Show,' 'Down in Jungle Town,' and 'Roll Dem Bones' during the last year of broadcasting his General Electric sponsored radio show (1954).

Throughout the 1930s and early 1940s, both jazz and minstrel influences lessened in Crosby's recordings, and he increasingly favored a wide variety of styles, including novelty numbers, 'hillbilly' tunes, sentimental ballads, medium-fast swing, Western-style numbers, and proto-rhythm and blues. This eclecticism resulted, at least in part, from the influence of the owner of Decca Records, Jack Kapp, who eschewed improvisation for a relentless canvassing of mainstream taste. Kapp also concentrated the bulk of his production and promotion energies on Crosby. Crosby displayed his versatility at the session at which he recorded 'I'll Be Seeing You,' by recording the relatively hard swinging 'On the Atcheson, Topeka, and the Santa Fe' (although even his swing-based songs retain a distinct 1920s sensibility).

An examination of Holiday's early recorded work reveals a rather different set of issues from those raised by her recording of 'I'll Be Seeing You.' One of the main differences between her period of greatest critical acclaim, 1935 to 1938, and a recording such as 'I'll Be Seeing You' (or many of the post-1939, post-'Strange Fruit' recordings) is that the earlier recordings present the vocalist more nearly as an equal partner with the instrumentalists, and that this, combined with the variety of tempi, lessens the sense of 'dramatic presentation' found in the post-'Strange Fruit' recordings. While the Harlem audiences for which she first performed recognized the originality of her approach, they also could recognize that aspects of her style were founded in practices that were circulating among other well-known jazz performers. These audience members were not necessarily jazz 'connoisseurs' such as John Hammond, who haunted uptown night spots looking for the 'latest thing,' but rather 'regulars' at places such as Basement Brownie's, Dickie Wells' Clam House, or Pod's and Jerry's Log Cabin, all on West 133rd Street in Harlem; these venues attracted customers who were used to appraising musician's improvisations in a variety of contexts that included well-rehearsed acts as well as jam sessions.

In 1939, Holiday began performing at the Cafe Society, a Greenwich Village nightclub that was the first New York nightclub to admit an integrated audience. Here was an audience, largely composed of white liberals, seeking more than mere 'entertainment'; and such a setting undoubtedly encouraged Holiday to record a song that she had initially rejected, 'Strange Fruit.' Other writers have been almost unanimous both in noting the shift in style that followed this recording and in their disparaging remarks about the changes in Holiday's style after this point, generally regarding these changes as a 'corruption' of a previously pristine sensibility. However, many other listeners, apparently not bothered by Holiday's fall from grace, have heard an almost unbearable pathos in this recording. When we consider the historical exigencies of the recording, it becomes difficult to regard it as some kind of 'sell-out.' While Holiday did initially resist recording and performing the song, she became convinced of its importance; and this coincided (and was perhaps aided) by her performing the song in a context in which the audience wanted to be moved by a song with lyrics that referred to social injustice. Holiday's response to this was to increase the emphasis in her performance on the emotional resonance of the text, an element already important in her style, but one that now assumed greater importance.

Performance, effect, and affect

During the years 1943 and 1944, songs that appeared on *Billboard*'s popularity charts could be organized into five basic categories based on style, genre, and ensemble. In this period, songs in the 'vocal with orchestra' (sometimes referred to as 'vocal w/accompaniment') and 'band with featured singer' (sometimes known as 'vocal refrain') categories are the most numerous. 'Vocal with orchestra' refers to songs in which the singer is the 'leader' on the date, backed by a more or less anonymous orchestra, with the recording dominated by the vocal. Approximately half of the songs surveyed in this category were slow in tempo, with minimal jazz or blues elements. The lyrics were invariably about love. On some of the medium tempo songs, the instrumentation of a big band was extracted for passages of the song. The songs featuring 'big band' instrumentation were also the songs that conveyed the strongest sense of 'swing,' and were most likely to include improvisational elements and pitch/rhythmic inflection. These tunes, or sections thereof, merge with the other most common type of tune during those years, the category of the 'band with featured singer.' These recordings were identified by the name of the bandleader, with the names of the singers listed after that of the leader. While the majority of these tunes feature jazz elements, instrumental improvisation, and a sense of swing at a variety of tempi, some of these tunes are slow ballads, feature string sections (as in Harry James' band), or are very 'square' rhythmically; in other words, except for the labeling and the relative paucity of non-jazz instruments, these songs closely approximate the approach of those in the first category. Two categories constituting a smaller percentage of songs in the hit parade are the 'novelty' tune and the 'band instrumental.' The remaining category, 'vocal with small group,' occupied an intermediate level of popularity. These small group recordings during the 1943–1944 period invariably featured black groups, with musical elements either prominently derived from gospel (as in the vocal groups mentioned above), or from jazz and incipient R&B (as in the King Cole Trio or Louis Jordan).

Bing Crosby's and Billie Holiday's recordings of 'I'll Be Seeing You' represent extreme examples of style categories on opposite ends of the affective spectrum. Crosby exaggerates almost all the aspects of the 'vocal with orchestra' approach noted above: the tempo is extremely slow; there is no question that this is an orchestra, not a big band; and the mix and arrangement leave no doubt that this is a singer accompanied by an orchestra, not a band which happens to feature a singer. An unusual aspect is the very prominent and almost constant use of tempo rubato (although Crosby and his arranger, John Scott Trotter, used this technique in other songs of the period, such as 'Too-Ra-Loo- Ra-Loo-Ra,' 'Where the Blue of Night,' and 'The Bells of St. Mary's'): the slow ballads by other singers in the 'vocal with orchestra' category always convey a strong pulse even at a slow tempo. Holiday exaggerates certain features of the 'vocal with small group' compared to the other examples mentioned earlier. The tempo is extremely slow throughout; the song is a *torch* song, unlike the other medium-tempo bounce tunes of King Cole and Louis Jordan; and the vocal is clearly the center of the recording, unlike the other songs of this ilk, which feature the band or group vocals.

Performance – the recordings

In his recording of 'I'll Be Seeing You,' Crosby delivers the lyrics straightforwardly in his 'crooning' vocal style. This delivery is meant to convey a feeling of intimacy and many listeners of the time felt that it did. Crosby believed that his popularity depended on the communication of 'presence,' achieved technically through the technique of close-miking. Owing at least in part to his many appearances in movies, and to the orchestral scoring – which is reminiscent of movie musical scoring – this song creates the impression of someone playing a role in a film. The diction ('mornin' sun') recalls Irish ballad singing, and this may well have reminded audiences of the role of Father O'Malley that Crosby had recently played and won an Oscar for in the 1943 movie *Going My Way* (a role he reprised in 1945 in 'The Bells of St Mary's'). The effect is as if the scene has suddenly turned serious, a situation that the audience knows is only a temporary foil for the overwhelming lightheartedness of life, which is precisely the type of context that would have surrounded a song like this in a movie such as *Going My Way*. We can imagine Bing at an 'old café,' at a 'park across the way,' in almost any small town in the US in the early 1940s.

Even though the song was not written during the war, it belongs to a type of song about generalized loss that was common and popular during World War II. This type of song differed from earlier Tin Pan Alley songs of loss and separation, in that rejection is not the cause for the separation of the characters in the song's lyrics; this allowed listeners who were separated from their families to identify with the song's sentiments. 'I'll Be Seeing You' fits comfortably into this category and, indeed, Crosby was closely associated with entertaining the troops during the war; and he included many other patriotic songs, some with overt references to the war. With his well-entrenched image of the 'American Everyman,' we can assume that many people felt consoled by his generic rendering of a soothing, uncompli-cated tale of a person stranded in a small town by a loved one.

In Billie Holiday's performance we no longer hear the qualities with which Crosby's audience identified; Holiday increases the overtone content during the repetition precisely at the point where she changes the melodic line to a higher register ('and when the night is new'), and at the beginning of the last line ('but I'll'), thereby creating a 'richer,' 'warmer,' 'brighter' sound and heightening the sense of climax in this line.

What is interesting is that, even if we examine a song that both Holiday and Crosby recorded earlier in their careers, 'Pennies from Heaven' (1936), we find many of the same differences observed in 'I'll Be Seeing You.' Again, Holiday favors a steady tempo, while Crosby chooses a rubato approach; again, Holiday takes greater liberties with the notated melody; and again, Holiday is accompanied by a small jazz group, Crosby by an orchestra. In this recording, Crosby *does* vary the melody considerably: note his insertion of the low Os on the words 'pennies from,' his adoption of the quarter note rest in the first, third, and seventh measures, a rhythmic motive that does not arise until the ninth measure of the sheet music. Other notable aspects of this include the arrangement, with its perpetual use of accelerandi and ritardandi, which creates the effect of shifting meter, and the frequent scoops up to pitches, both of which occur as a trademark in Crosby's work of this period. On the affective level, Crosby's recording also seems 'carefree' rela-tive to his version of 'I'll Be Seeing You,' which is appropriate, given the optimistic tone of the lyrics of 'Pennies from Heaven.'

Holiday's 'Pennies from Heaven' contrasts with Crosby's (as well as her recording of 'I'll Be Seeing You') in that it is performed at a medium, bouncy tempo, radiating a kind of exuberance lacking in her version of 'I'll Be Seeing You.' Holiday, as she did in 'I'll Be Seeing You,' exploits the presence of a clear pulse by creating a series of accents against that pulse (note again how few pitches land directly on beats), creating a sense of swing. She too includes a prominent 'trill'-type ornament, featuring it more prominently in this passage than does Crosby, despite it being one of his trademarks. An important difference in their use of this ornament is the placing of it in the respective recordings: Holiday's tends to occur immediately before the barline, contradicting the emphasis of the downbeat and thereby increasing the rhythmic drive and complexity. Crosby's ornament occurs here (as well as in his other recordings) as primarily a melodic decoration and, as such, does nothing to enhance the rhythmic drive (this would be difficult to do in both of the Crosby recordings discussed here since they do not contain 'rhythmic drive' in the jazz sense of the term). Holiday in some respects modifies the melody less than Crosby: in the first line ('Ev'ry time it rains, it rains/pennies from heaven') she interjects fewer new pitches into the written line. Holiday's recording emphasizes relatively dissonant pitches compared to Crosby's recording. Many of these enhanced dissonances result from her propensity to compress a melody, to simplify it by reducing the number of pitches.

The interpretation and analysis presented here of 'I'll Be Seeing You' (and to a lesser extent 'Pennies from Heaven') contains implied aesthetic values that can be understood in terms of 'undercoding' and 'overcoding.' The way in which Crosby's recording activates codes seems, at a distance of fifty years, to be relatively 'overcoded': that is, aspects of this recording – the orchestral scoring, the 'expressive' rubato – have turned into clichés through use in advertising and the mannerisms of countless lounge singers. This is due partly to the enormous popularity and influence of the music at the time. Paradoxically, the cultural cachet of Billie Holiday's music has risen, owing to some extent to its very inaccessibility at the time of its initial dissemination, and to the way in which her style has not lent itself easily to imitation on a mass scale. Therefore, it retains those qualities of 'individuality' that allow us to receive it now as 'undercoded.' Perhaps what may have seemed clear, reassuring, and unequivocal at one time, now appears to belong *too much* to its own time, and to lack resonance in ours. And, conversely, a recording that offers competing perspectives, that may seem to mock itself, to laugh at itself, to question its own discourse, may have more to offer later generations even if it mystified the listeners of its own day. Of course, here too the idea of musical 'competence' is crucial: a listener who grew up listening to Bing Crosby and who never had much interest in jazz, Billie Holiday, or post-rock 'n' roll pop music, may revel in nostalgia upon hearing Crosby's version and feel that Holiday's version is overly mannered. A person steeped in Western art music with little enthusiasm for jazz may find the orchestral arrangement, the shifting meters, and the use of rubato in Crosby's recording intriguing, while judging the tempo and arrangement of Holiday's recording static and uninteresting. A fan of contemporary popular music with little or no exposure to popular music of the 1940s may complain that both Crosby's and Holiday's recordings are too slow, have little energy, and that they sound 'old.'

What I have tried to demonstrate in the discussion of the 'musical code' and by the analysis of certain features of the recordings of 'I'll Be Seeing You' is that the musical message can never be reduced to the mere communication of the biography of the performer. If Billie Holiday's music only communicated tragedy and sadness, it would result in a one-dimensional aesthetic experience that could hardly satisfy anyone lacking an over-romantic sense of his or her own tragedy (which is not to say that her music had nothing to do with her life). And if Bing Crosby's music seems somewhat 'overcoded' now at a distance of fifty years, we need not let that blind us to the artistic questions that his work answered. Questions of aesthetic value are intimately linked not only to an individual song's reception history, but as well to historical shifts in the prestige of various codes articulated by a text; and these shifts may fluctuate inversely to the initial dissemination of a recording, as an initially popular style saturates the musical soundscape, thereby eventually creating a sense of 'overcoding.' Furthermore, for any recording artist and recording attributed to him or her, there are a host of other factors unique to that context that must be considered: media images of the performer, and the history of the emotive and axiological connotations associated with any given style and genre, to name a few. Interpretation forms in the complex space between codes that may emphasize the entanglement of the motivations that we attribute to the performers with the information conveyed by the musical codes.

Chapter 5

Philip Tagg

SUBJECTIVITY AND SOUNDSCAPE, MOTORBIKES AND MUSIC

Baby's soundscape

A T THE AGE OF MINUS FOUR MONTHS most humans start to hear. By the time we enter this world and long before we can focus our eyes on objects at different distances from ourselves, our aural faculties are well developed. Most small humans soon learn to distinguish pleasant from unpleasant sounds and most parents will witness that any tiny human in their household acts like a hyperactive radar of feelings and moods in their environment. You know it's no use telling baby in an irritated voice 'Daddy's not angry' because the little human sees straight through such emotional bullshitting and starts howling.

But baby's hearing isn't what most parents notice first about sound and their own addition to the human race. It is more likely that they register the little sonic terrorist's capacity to scream, yell, cry and generally dominate the domestic soundscape. Babies are endowed with non-verbal vocal talents totally out of proportion to other aspects of their size, weight and volume: they have inordinate lung power and vocal chords of steel, it seems, capable of producing high decibel and transient values, cutting timbres and irregular phrase lengths, all vehiculating messages such as 'change my nappies' and 'produce either breast or bottle for immediate consumption'. Maybe these tiny humans have to yell not so much because they can't speak as because they need to dispel whatever state of adult torpor we happen to be in, be it watching TV, chatting, reading or, worst of all, sleeping. Babies seem to know in advance that sharp timbres at high pitch and volume carry extremely well, cutting through whatever constant underlying hum or mumble there may be in the adult world, be it idle conversation, the TV on in the background, fridges, ventilation, etc. Also, irregular rhythms and intonation by definition avoid the sort of repetition that can gradually transform into ambient (background) sound: a baby's yell is always up front, foreground, urgent, of varying periodicity and quite clearly designed to shatter whatever else mother, father, big sister or big brother is doing. That sonic shattering is designed to provoke immediate response. Desires and needs must be fulfilled *now*, they cannot wait.

'Now' is the operative word in this context. Sonic statements formed as short repetitions of irregularly varying length are also statements of urgency, as well we know from the anaphones of news and documentary jingles – important, flash, new, the latest update. Babies seem to have no conscious past or notion of future: all is present. The baby's lack of adult temporal perspective in relation to self is, of course, related to its lack of adult senses of social space. This is in turn related to baby's egocentricity, essential for survival, and to omnipotence the poor little soul is forced to abandon in order to survive in the process of growing up and being an adult.

Sound, subjectivity and socialisation

Different cultures and subcultures establish and develop different patterns and norms for what course the process from baby via child to adult should run. The ultimate goal – being an ideal male or female adult – depends on whatever the society in question, on account of its material basis and cultural heritage, sees as desirable, useful and good. Assuming we have all been babies and if, as I suggest here, baby's power over the domestic soundscape is a biological necessity in the early development of every human and if this state of sonic domination must largely be relinquished for that individual to survive, then we ought to gain important insights into how any culture works by studying patterns of socialisation that relate directly to non-verbal sound. Assuming that one of music's main functions is to vehiculate socially relevant images of affective behaviour, states and processes in the form of non-verbal sound, this means studying music in that society. I want to suggest here that music plays an essential part in socialising us as subjects in whatever culture we belong to and that our changing relationship as subjects to the soundscape (from egocentric sound dominating individual to one of cooperative interaction) can be traced in the way that foreground and background are vehiculated in the music of different cultures. After all, we all carry a small, vulnerable but omnipotent little version of ourselves inside us until the day we die and, like it or not, each of us will have to find forms of containing, training and socialising that little idiot throughout our lives. Since non-verbal sound is so important to the construction of our emotional personality, music, perhaps more than any other symbolic system, is probably where we can best study how different cultures and subcultures at different stages of their development contain, train and systematise our subjectivity.

Psychotherapists in the urban soundscape

In 1983 I found myself having to explain the expressive qualities of heavy metal to psychotherapists at a weekend conference called 'Creativity in the Arts'. I did not succeed, partly because there was at that time considerable adult panic about the perceived aggressive qualities of the music and I was claiming that such music was essential to the survival of underprivileged young people living in harsh urban environments. Not until I met two of the conference participants on the street did I manage to get the basic point across. The noise of the traffic was such that the psychotherapists could no longer speak to each other in the wonted pacificatory and confidential tone of their trade. To make themselves understood, they had to shout *above* the din of the traffic, otherwise the theme of their conversational interaction would have been drowned in the general mix of what ought to have been no more than a background accompaniment to that theme. In this context, the word 'above' has four senses: (1) *louder* than the ambient noise; (2) *higher* in fundamental pitch; (3) *sharper* in timbre and (4) *closer* to the ears of their interlocutor. I suggested that there was a struggle between them and the ambient noise as to who or which would gain the sonic upper hand (by being 'above'). How does this work?

The two psychotherapists were in a socially constructed sonic environment (the soundscape of a city street) and had to modify their sonic behaviour if they wanted to enter a different mode of social construction (talking to each other and hearing each other). Now, the social construct of the city soundscape can, of course, be interpreted in many different ways, depending on the hearer's relationship to the various activities giving rise to the soundscape's constituent elements. To illustrate this point, imagine first that you play a positively active and audible part in the soundscape – for example, that you enjoy the discrete engine hum of the expensive car you drive to a well-paid and satisfying job or that you switch on the lighting (with its white noise) and ventilation (with its lo-fi hum) of your successful shop in an up-market mall. Next, imagine yourself as young and unemployed, without your own wheels, without anywhere to go, out there on foot amid the noise of city traffic or the ventilation rumblings of a shopping mall. These two relationships to urban soundscapes might well result in diametrically opposed affective interpretations of their constituent noises, interpretations linked to each individual's power over those noises. In the first instance, the everyday sounds of the city are part of you because you help to make them and because their sources are part of what make you happy and successful, whereas in the second case you are debarred from the whole world that makes those sounds because you cannot afford the goods you might want to buy from the shops, let alone a fancy car and, worst of all, you have no working part in the whole system: you are quite simply disqualified as an adult and unlikely ever to become a full member of the club and the sounds it produces. In this comparison, it is clear that different 'readings' of the same sounds are also due to differences of class within the same general culture and economy: they are not solely contingent on differences between different general cultures and economies. It is also clear that we are dealing with the social construction of subjectivity, an important factor in understanding how music relates (groups of) individuals to the environment they populate. The question here is how music interprets and expresses different readings of different soundscapes.

Heavy metal figure and ground

Heavy metal accompaniment (backing, ground) is loud, metrically and periodically quite regular, and full of constant broadband sounds in the bass and middle register. In this way it resembles the ambient noise of postwar traffic, electric motors, ventilation, machines in processing industries, etc. Now, the relentless timetabling of events, constant traffic and electric hum, etc. can all be experienced as the sounds of an inexorable societal machine over which we have little or no control. Still, if you *are* subjected to those noises and rhythms that seem to symbolise real power in your environment, they might be made a little less overpowering if you appropriate them, re-create them and 'intone' them in your own image. This does not mean that heavy metal accompaniments resulting from such appropriation *are* the said soundscape any more than Clint Eastwood *is* Dirty Harry or Coca-Cola *is* 'it': to undergo such appropriation, re-creation and intonation, the soundscape passes, as suggested earlier, through technological and cultural filters and is both stylised and resocialised. In this way, Iron Maiden's music may sound more like power drills or motorbikes and less like digital watches or bar code cash registers than the music of Laurie Anderson but, to my knowledge, direct citations of any of the sounds just mentioned are rare in the music of both artists.

Similar observations can be made about rock's famous 'wall of sound'. With the acoustic horizon brought closer to our ears in the urban soundscape, there are few sounds that seem to reach us from afar. This is not because the city street contains no reverb. On the contrary, if you were to stand alone in the same street, to empty it of sounds and to shout, the acoustic space would be very large. Now fill the soundscape with traffic again. Since the noise is once more loud and, more importantly, constant, by the time the sound of a car has had the chance of being perceived as reverberation, it has been almost instantaneously drowned by more of the same (louder) original continuous noise from the same or from a similar source. This process impedes the perception of large acoustic space. By drowning discrete reverb in this way, the overall impression of acoustic space in a busy city street is crowded and close. Shouting to a friend on the other side of the street becomes impossible because there is an impenetrable wall of sound between the two of you. This wall now becomes the acoustic horizon, much closer than its visual counterpart and far closer than the acoustic horizon in the same space devoid of traffic.

This aspect of urban soundscape is intoned in heavy metal accompaniment, not only by creating the sort of loud broadband sounds mentioned earlier, but also by adding considerable amounts of reverb to a recording or performance. The effect is similar to that of 'actual' reverb on the busy street. This effect of crowding and homogenisation is further enhanced in heavy metal by compressing accompanying instruments, individually and/or en masse. In this intonation process, the relative quiet of decays is brought up to the higher dB level of the same tone's envelope, this 'filling in the holes' of the sound wall. Moreover, since decays are intrinsic determinants of the unique character of individual sounds, using compressors (along with noise gates and limiters) helps to create that characteristically urban heavy metal sound – loud and close-up but full of different elements that can be hard to distinguish. Add to this timbric and registral re-creation of the soundscape its temporal aspects of collective subjectivity (too lengthy a topic to be discussed here) and you have the rehumanised background of heavy metal against which the foreground figures can be musically painted.

On top of ('above') or in front of all this heavy metal backing comes the melodic line, usually delivered by lead vocalists or guitarists. Their melodic statements (phrases) contain divergences from the clock time already reappropriated and subverted by backing instruments. At the same time, since the musical 'environment' (accompaniment, backing) is so heavily loaded with loud bass and middle-range sounds, soloists must raise the volume, pitch and sharpness/roughness of their voice or instrument to be heard. Even though microphones, which bring the singer nearer to our ears, have been in use since the advent of rock, the male heavy metal vocalist raises his voice to an average pitch at least one octave above what he uses for normal speech, while the loudness and grain of his voice also bears greater resemblance to shouting and screaming than to talking or whispering. Whether the vocal expression be one of despair, disgust, celebration or anger, the dominant character of vocal delivery in heavy metal is one of effort and urgency.

Heavy metal guitarists act similarly to the vocalists, except that they cut their way through the throbbing broadband wall of sound by raising the volume and/or fundamental pitch and/or transient values of whatever comes out of their instrument, effects and amps. Just as the motorbike weaves in and out of traffic, the heavy metal lead guitar can cut in and out of its ambient movement and sound, as if transcending the (already subverted and stylised) restrictions laid down by the backing. Of course, such 'guitar distortion = motorbike' sounds are even more common as the heavy accompanying riffs of metal music, this adding a rough but relatively constant accompanimental roar which is as exciting as the noise of the bike as you drive it (while singing?) rather than a series of individual motorbikes passing you (lead guitar).

The heroes of heavy metal have tended to be guitarists or vocalists. It is they who make the most noticeable din and who make themselves heard above it, cutting through all the other noise and movement by using loud and frequently garish gestures of sound and vision. When fans at a heavy metal concert stretch their arms into a huge 'V', it is their victory too. At least in that moment you can feel what it might be like to win the battle against all those sounds and rhythms that seem to represent control over the rest of your life. It is a moment of true magic in the anthropological sense of the word because the heavy metal soloists have stuck loud and highly connotative sonic pins into the caricatured bogeymen of normality and they have emerged victorious.

However, unlike baby's ability to dominate the domestic soundscape, the particular relationships just described between musical sounds, motorbikes and the urban soundscape are in no way constant or universal; they merely illustrate one way in which certain young males were able to exploit the new technical possibilities of a certain instrument developed under a certain set of historically determinable material, cultural and social circumstances in a certain part of the world to enact a drama symbolising in sound the taming and defeat of an inimical system over which they in 'real' life felt they had little or no control and in which they had to survive. Through re-creating a *musical* version of that struggle for survival and controlling the struggle in that form, another solution, though unattainable in real social or political terms, was nevertheless imaginable because heavy metal demands by definition that you make yourself *heard* as well as seen.

However, since the mid 1970s, by which time the majority of the heavy metal connotations just discussed were clearly established, much has happened to music, to sounds, to technology, to society and to the subjective strategies of young people – and it is not just a question of crash-helmet legislation and motorbike insurance.

The post-biker era

Since Steppenwolf sang 'heavy metal thunder' we have had to suffer two decades of Reaganomics, Thatcheritis or whatever you want to call the sort of political disease whose symptoms are greed as a virtue and the destruction of collective conscience by perverted notions of non-cooperative individualism. Since *Easy Rider*, in the post-AIDS era of work-outs and Californian-style body cult, the corporeal has been promoted from division four to the premier league of capitalist culture. The rebellious illusion of lone bikers associated with rock and distorted guitar has become part of the brave 'new' individualism to the extent that young US-Americans are no longer recruited into the forces by Sousa marches but by Van Halen's 'Iron Wings' and the 'Top Gun' anthem. Vauxhalls and Opels are sold to the tune of 'Layla' and Fords to ex-Queen guitarist Brian May's 'Driven By You'. Three decades after the emergence of guitar distortion in pop and rock, we have seen yuppies jogging in designer track-suits, aerobic women doing hysterical physical jerks in pastel-shaded leg-warmers, steroid-inflated men on dubious vendettas, Madonna exposing herself, and a drastic rise in unemployment, especially for young people. We have also seen the sadomasochistic acrobats of all-star wrestling, Aryan males with Hitler haircuts in synth pop videos or Calvin Klein adverts, anorexic female cat-walk executives washing-and-going, the rise of video and of computer games (including a computer game war), the demise of the world socialist system and more unemployment, especially for young people. It would indeed be strange if young people ready to take their place in this brave new world needed the same sort of socialisation expressed through the same sort of music on the same sorts of instrument and through the same sort of attitude to both body and emotions that rockology and the heavy metal canon seemed to find useful.

It should be clear that our own generation's monopolisation of the 'learned' aesthetics of youth culture, through the romanticisation of rock rebellion and emancipation is unlikely to help much, not least because that aesthetics may well have contributed to the reactionary ideology of the Thatcher and Reagan years. I am suggesting that a musicology of society needs to develop models that help us to understand the relationship between different structurations of music and different collective subjectivities. I am also suggesting that the two notions described in this article – (1) sonic anaphones that relate musical structures to the soundscape, and (2) the sonic, including musical, figure-ground dualism symbolising individuals in relation to their environment – , if historically contextualised with some care, can contribute to such an understanding. In short, if babies know instinctively how to assert themselves in their own acoustic environment, it is about time adults gained at least some *intellectual* control over the sounds, both in and outside music, of our society.

PART TWO

Making music

Introduction to Part Two

■   Barry Shank

I N ITS EARLIER STAGES OF DEVELOPMENT, popular music studies often
avoided the topic of music-making itself. This was seen as the province of journalism or hagiography. Since the late 1980s, however, much more attention has been
paid to the areas of creating, starring and performing – in other words, the enormously varied range of functions undertaken by music makers. A new theoretical
sophistication has developed in this area too, evidenced in by the attention to the
vexed questions of musical authenticity and the agency of the performer; who is it
who is performing, what are the agentive effects of performance, and how is this
performer constructed in music and the discourse which surrounds it? This part on
making music addresses these questions from a variety of perspectives.

First we explore the complicated question of the agency of the performer
in two articles that examine the agencies of recognised stars, indeed artists, of
popular music whose agency is both an effect of their social positions and which is
profoundly constrained by those social positions: Jimi Hendrix and Janis Joplin. In
Chapter 6, Alice Echols's 'Little Girl Blue' focuses on the contradictory questions
of agency and authenticity that arose when Joplin fired her first band, Big Brother,
and established the Kozmic Blues Band, an act that would emphasise the black
origins of Joplin's singing style. With this move, Joplin took responsibility for the
choices that shaped the musical aesthetics of her act. Her attempts to function as
the band leader, and not simply the most visible member of the band, were made
more difficult by Joplin's lack of formal training, but even more by the general
sexism of the period, by the assumption that she should simply remain the chick
singer. Further complicating Joplin's efforts to move in this new direction was the
fact that at the moment she chose to emphasise rhythm and blues styles, tensions
deriving from the slow progress of the Civil Rights Movement in the United States
were heating up questions of racial authenticity in musical performance. Joplin's

attempts to pay tribute to her influences were not always heard as legitimate by the portions of her audience that she most wanted to reach. Echols's article carefully describes the tensions and contradictions that placed severe constraints on Joplin's ability to function agentively and authentically while performing the music she loved the most.

Jimi Hendrix struggled at the same historical period with similar conjunctions of race and gender. Hendrix's guitar playing, technically virtuosic and performatively phallic, both enabled and constrained his claims to artistic agency and racial authenticity. Steve Waksman's careful analysis shows the ways in which Hendrix's sonic advances were mapped onto traditional blues structures to produce a specific form of blackness that Hendrix hoped could be heard as such over and against the near minstrel-like conditions under which he performed. Ironically, the very eroticism that powered Hendrix's performance styles and drew large and adoring white audiences reinforced stereotypes of the over-sexed black male as it drew upon a long a complex history of racial representations and cross-racial desire. Steve Waksman argues in Chapter 7 that Hendrix came to feel trapped by this history and that his explorations of the sonic limits of blues tonalities, a set of explorations that were enabled by a mastery of advanced technology, became a strategy of self-definition, a desire to reclaim a certain artistic agency in a heavily overdetermined field.

Jason Toynbee extends the argument for collective agency and performative authenticity to the 1950s jazz performances of Charles Mingus. In Chapter 8, Toynbee asks, 'In what sense might creativity emerge from the very social relations which perpetuate domination?'. He shows us how Mingus functioned as a 'social author,' who was engaged in a political project. Mingus's composition style, like that of Duke Ellington, sought to highlight the individual voices of his band members while constructing a black diasporic context within which those voices could be heard. Mingus's bass served as a narrative voice that introduced, quoted, and summarised the musical moments offered by his fellow musicians. His work was enabled by the social conditions and collective energies of not only these musicians but the structures and practices of his everyday life. Toynbee argues that Mingus's compositional and performance styles cannot be fully grasped as forms of romantic self-expression, but must be seen as truly processive, collective, and historically grounded. Toynbee also offers us a vocabulary for analyzing different performance styles. As a result of Mingus's self-conscious understanding of his musical history, his performance style is 'transformative,' not 'expressive.' It is not concerned so much with truth to self as it is in producing a creative variation of what has come before. Musicians like Mingus who are profoundly aware of the weight and value of these traditions tend to reject the 'direct' mode of performance, whose chief value is sincerity, and replace it with a 'reflexive' mode of performance where the transformation of tradition is foregrounded in order to cue the audience's awareness of the traditional and, therefore, of the transformative elements in the performance. In this way, the artist can function both agentively and authentically within and against the tradition.

In Chapter 9, Simon Reynolds shifts the questions of authenticity and agency away from individual performers, away from rock, and away from the 1960s. Reynolds's discussion of innovation in the production of jungle remixes locates authenticity, not as a relation to a set of social conditions outside of the musical performance, but instead as a devotion to and an understanding of the genre itself. Agency in rave culture, of which jungle was an important subset in the 1990s, is collective, not simply the result of individual choices but rather an effect generated when specific sounds selected by particular producers and DJs, interrogating the sonic foundations upon which the genre is based, are received and endorsed by a dancing raving crowd. Reynolds argues provocatively that the authenticity that is produced through this agentive collaboration results in a real that is the product not of a miming of the social but rather of the death of the social. Reynolds uncovers the seemingly dark, cold, inhuman core of jungle, where the technological origins of the sounds are not masked but highlighted in order to invite industrial creativity and produce a liquid metallic groove. Reynolds's piece closes with a description of a visit to AWOL, a club whose name indicates its efforts to recruit the most committed members of the jungle scene. For these individuals, jungle is a way of life, not simply a set of style decisions. And indeed, the producers who intuit the connections between jungle's sonic foundations and the structures that construct this way of life are those who create the coldest, meanest sounds – war in the jungle. Thus, authenticity remains a value that reinforces the collective agency of the scene.

Finally, Philip Auslander asks us in Chapter 10 to rethink our assumptions that link authenticity to live performance and inauthentic moments to the impact and influence of mediated performances (i.e. recordings). Auslander argues that the live and the mediated should not be thought of as binary opposites, but as mutually constituting possibilities, constructed in relationship with each other. Similarly, production and reproduction have been woven together in standard pop concerts where huge screens display close-up camera shots of the performers for those sitting at the rear of the auditorium. Auslander focuses on the Milli Vanilli scandal, where it was revealed that the Grammy-winning pop duo were not responsible for the vocals on their recordings and, indeed, had lip-synched to recordings during their performances. The uproar that accompanied this revelation was an effect of the industry's need for the value of liveness and traditional understandings of authenticity. The industry repackages the 'same' performance in numerous commodities, requiring the notion of the original to which all these iterations can point. Milli Vanilli pulled the carpet out from under the set of assumptions that linked live performance to the fundamental original and therefore had to be policed and disciplined, even though live and mediatised performance are inextricably imbricated with each other. Live performances now are judged by reference to previously heard recordings; remixes of hit songs can become more popular than initial releases.

In each of these articles, the relationships among performance, authenticity, and artistic agency are shown to be fluid, historically determined, and mutually constitutive. Making music is a technological process that involves representation as well as presentation. Agency is historically enabled as well as socially constrained.

Authenticity is not simply a matter of romantic self-expression or a faithful devotion to a strict interpretation of tradition, but rather is a result of a thoughtful self-reflection on one's own conditions of possibility. Artistically successful popular musicians lay claim to authentic agency through the mediatised performance practices that constitute making music.

Alice Echols

LITTLE GIRL BLUE

ON DECEMBER 21, 1968, just three weeks after her last show with Big Brother, Janis and her new soul band made their debut in Memphis, Tennessee. The band had not been named and the players – ex-Big Brother guitarist Sam Andrew, Brad Campbell, Terry Clements, Bill King, Roy Markowitz, and Marcus Doubleday – had been hurriedly assembled, yet the opportunity to perform at the second annual Stax-Volt Yuletide Thing seemed too good to pass up; it was the ideal place to unveil Janis Joplin's new group. Although Stax Records, the sponsor, had lost its star, Otis Redding, and most of his backup band, the Bar-Kays, in an airplane crash a year before, the label was still 'Soulsville, USA.' Stax was it, the real thing. To smug San Franciscans who thought their music scene was the hippest of all, Janis declared that Memphis was 'where it's at!'. Like Jimi Hendrix, Janis didn't have many black fans, but, banking on her crossover appeal, Stax nevertheless invited her to play their big year-end bash. Janis was the only non-Stax artist to appear and she received major billing, ahead of the Staple Singers, Booker T. and the MGs, Albert King, and everyone else except Johnnie Taylor, whose megahit 'Who's Making Love' earned him the coveted closing spot.

Even with the tightest band, Janis would have been up against very stiff competition. But Janis didn't have a tight band; she barely had a band at all. Her friends Nick Gravenites and guitarist Michael Bloomfield, who had left the Electric Flag, a horn-based soul band similar to the one she wanted behind her, and Elliot Mazer, the record producer, had helped pick the musicians, but the group had not begun to rehearse until a week before the Memphis show. It was all very unnerving – Gravenites and Bloomfield, who went to Memphis to lend his support, would not be available forever, and this was supposed to be Janis's group. She had never fronted a band of professional musicians. How could she tell them what to do when she didn't even have the vocabulary to describe what she wanted to hear? 'It was her constant fear that she'd look bad behind a bunch of good musicians,' explains Mazer.

'None of us thought the band was ready,' he says of the Stax show, 'but they had the gig and they wanted to go.' Moreover, her manager, Albert Grossman, had advised Janis against letting too much time elapse before hitting the road with her new group.

As she and the musicians stood backstage watching the other acts, they began to comprehend the enormity of their mistake. Memphis, it turned out, was a lot more like Las Vegas than San Francisco, where everyone but music impresario Bill Graham of the Fillmore collaborated in the fiction that what they were doing was not show business. Bay Area audiences wanted realness, not slick displays of showmanship. Janis's group realized the extent of the chasm separating them from the other acts when the re-formed Bar-Kays came out wearing 'zebra-striped flannel jumpsuits.' Janis was dressed up, too, wearing a cherry-red jersey pantsuit with matching red feathers at the cuffs. But she and her band didn't know the dances. And there were the Bar-Kays doing the sideways pony, followed by the boogaloo, and much, much more. Stanley Booth of *Rolling Stone* looked on as Michael Bloomfield's eyes became very large and members of the new band shook their heads in disbelief. Booth observed, 'It was the first sign of the cultural gap that was to increase as the evening progressed.'

Janis was the next-to-last performer. In San Francisco's electric ballrooms everyone assumed bands would take forever setting up their equipment and getting in tune. Not so in Memphis, where the salt-and-pepper audience turned cold as Janis's band spent ten minutes putting their act together. Janis decided to save 'Piece of My Heart' and 'Ball and Chain' for the encore and opened with 'Raise Your Hand' by Eddie ('Knock on Wood') Floyd, who had performed right before her, and 'To Love Somebody' by the Bee Gees. The only people in the stands at the coliseum who had heard of Janis Joplin, however, were white teenagers there to hear her big hits. Both opening songs fell flat, and by the third unfamiliar tune the crowd was so unmoved that it was obvious there would be no encore call. 'At least they didn't throw things,' she muttered backstage after it was over. Worst of all was the fact that *Rolling Stone* was covering the event. For Janis, the magazine was rapidly assuming 'the significance of the military-industrial complex,' as David Dalton puts it. She knew her defeat would be painstakingly chronicled in its pages, and, true to form, the paper proclaimed, 'Janis Joplin died in Memphis.' The problem, Stanley Booth conceded, was not Joplin's singing but the band, which he found both ragged and soulless. Janis was stunned – all the agony she had experienced quitting Big Brother, only to get the same review yet again. To her ex-bandmate, Dave Getz, Janis's Memphis misadventure confirmed Albert Grossman's fallibility and arrogance: 'He thought he knew everything.' To Sam Andrew, the show

> was sheer insanity. Janis wanted to emulate Aretha and Otis, but before we even had the repertoire down, we were going to play in front of one of the most demanding audiences in the country, our heroes from Stax . . . It was intimidating, playing the blues for black people . . . How dare we get up there and play their music? Naturally, we were kind of nervous. We just blew it.

Of course, Janis had received negative reviews before, but she had rarely faced an indifferent audience. Memphis was her first defeat since she had reinvented herself as a rock singer back in the summer of 1966, and of all places, Janis hated bombing at Soulsville. She had always feared that one day people would wake up and realize she was an impostor, a talentless girl whose powerful voice fooled people into thinking she could sing. As she lay awake at Memphis's Lorraine Motel less than a month before her twenty-sixth birthday, Janis worried that she was all washed up. Her failure at Memphis, however, was not the result just of the band's raggedy performance or even of the soul-acid rock schism. The Stax-Volt show signaled a decline of the interracialism that had marked popular music during the mid-1960s and the opening of a divide that would only widen in the years to come as black-and-white music diverged. In the waning days of the decade, white artists like Janis, who had 'traded off the black,' and black artists like Jimi Hendrix, who had 'traded off the white,' as Lou Reed put it, would find it harder to cross the racial borders of popular music. Hendrix found himself confronted by Black Panthers demanding he be blacker, while Janis was scolded by white critics for trying to sing 'black' music. Martin Luther King's assassination at the same Lorraine Motel only months earlier had ended all sorts of possibilities, including the cultural hybridity that Janis Joplin and Jimi Hendrix represented. The appeal of a white girl singing the blues like no white girl had ever before would quickly become Janis's ball and chain. R. Crumb had unknowingly captured this shift in his *Cheap Thrills* cartoon of Janis as a sweaty prisoner struggling across a barren landscape with a heavy black ball (marked 'Big Mama Thornton') chained to her ankle.

Janis encountered plenty of resistance when she tried to front a soul band. Had Janis pursued straight-ahead rock, her new group might have succeeded. Mickey Hart of the Grateful Dead had approached Janis about joining him, Jerry Garcia, and the Airplane's Jack Casady in a supergroup, but she had turned him down. She wanted to sing soul, and her timing could not have been worse. King's assassination destroyed the dream of interracialism as black power and its critique of integration gained greater support and credibility within the black community – a shift that reverberated culturally as well as politically. 'Everything changed at Stax,' maintains June Dunn, the wife of Donald 'Duck' Dunn, the white bassist with Booker T. and the MGs. For the first time, writes Peter Guralnick, an 'undercurrent of racial division' threatened the 'surface harmony of the Stax family.' Blacks began questioning the racial hierarchy whereby 'blacks made the music, blacks made the audience, but the ownership was white,' as Homer Banks, a Stax songwriter, put it. Whites, who were accustomed to feeling as though they existed in a racial twilight zone where race was irrelevant, learned otherwise. 'All of a sudden people are noticing that we're white,' recalled one Stax musician, Wayne Jackson. By the early 1970s, many of the whites involved in Southern soul music – most notably, Jerry Wexler, Rick Hall, and Phil Walden – left the field rather than be attacked for making money off black people.

Janis dealt with all the criticism by arguing that blues music was universal and by bending over backwards to credit and promote black singers. Moreover, she differentiated her blues from traditional blues. Hers were the 'Kozmic Blues,' spelled with a 'K' because, she explained to David Dalton, life was 'too down and lonely a trip to be taken seriously; it has to be a Crumb cartoon . . . It's like a joke on itself.' She went on to distinguish between traditional blues and her blues.

> I don't know if this is grossly insensitive of me, and it may well be, but the black man's blues is based on the 'have-not'—I got the blues because I don't have this, I got the blues because I don't have my baby, I got the blues because I don't have the quarter for a bottle of wine, I got the blues because they won't let me in the bar. Well, you know, I'm a middle-class white chick from a family that would love to send me to college and I didn't wanna. I had a job, I didn't dig it. I had a car, I didn't dig it.

For a white woman like her, Janis seemed to be saying that the blues were not about material privation or, in the end, even about lost lovers, but about existential loneliness and despair – 'waking up in the middle of the night blues,' as Sam Andrews puts it. 'One day, I realized in a flash, sitting a bar, that it wasn't an uphill incline, you know, that one day everything was going to be all right,' he said. 'It was your whole life.' Janis's protest – 'No, it just can't be' – would turn up in more than one of her songs.

Janis's second band was reason enough for her to sing the blues. For months people had urged her to dump Big Brother. Although she had done this, she had gone nowhere. Nobody, Albert included, seriously considered the possibility that the second band might fall flat on its face. Nobody thought about the country's shifting racial politics and no one had prepared Janis for the burdens of being a band leader. She was expected to take charge and make the group work, all by herself. Initially, Janis's friend, Michael Bloomfield, whose Super Session with Al Kooper and Stephen Stills was one of 1968's biggest albums, agreed to help her – perhaps with encouragement from Albert Grossman, who managed him, too. Bloomfield had an encyclopedic knowledge of the blues, but he also had certain ideas about Janis's band that clashed with hers. Janis had hoped to hire him as her musical director but, according to Nick Gravenites, 'Michael was so headstrong . . . and it just conflicted too much with Janis's ego, even though she wanted him to work on her music.' So Janis was without anyone to lean on when her trumpeter, Marcus Doubleday, left the group and her organist, Bill King, was drafted several weeks after the Memphis show. 'She's doing the hardest thing you can do – carrying a whole band on her shoulders,' Nick Gravenites said.

By April 25, Clive Davis, the head of her label, Columbia Records, was reportedly anxious that Janis should begin recording her next record, 'I Got Dem 01' Kozmic Blues Again Mama!' Proving once again he was not omniscient, Albert Grossman chose Gabriel Mekler to produce the album. Mekler was best known for his work with Steppenwolf, which had scored Top 10 hits with the biker-rock songs 'Born to Be Wild' and 'Magic Carpet Ride.' Before Janis set foot in the studio there were problems. Mekler didn't like Janis's band and wanted to hire his own musicians. Although he didn't prevail, he succeeded in replacing the trumpeter, Terry Hensley, with Luis Gasca and, halfway into the recording, the drummer, Lonnie Castille, with Maury Baker. Still, when recording began on June 16, he was far from satisfied and he let it show, which didn't endear him to Janis or the band.

Even before Mekler's intervention, the band's personnel was constantly shifting, one reason the group never quite gelled. Only one musician – Terry Clements, the alto saxophonist – had been with the group from its beginning in December 1968. The bassist, Brad Campbell of the Paupers, a Canadian group Albert managed, joined the band after the Fillmore East gig, replacing a temporary bassist, Keith Cherry. Both the organist, Richard Kermode, who took over from Bill King, and the baritone saxophonist, Cornelius 'Snooky' Flowers, were with the group almost from the start. But the band went through three drummers – Roy Markowitz, Lonnie Castille, and Maury Baker – and four trumpet players – Marcus Doubleday, Terry Hensley, Luis Gasca, and Dave Woodward. John Till came on board as guitarist in July 1969. 'Everyone felt as if tomorrow could be the last day,' Sam Andrew says. Appropriately, the band remained nameless until after it was disbanded in December 1969, at which point it came to be known as the Kozmic Blues Band, after the album.

Some of the band members resented being treated like mere employees, but Sam claims he 'kind of liked that idea. I kind of got caught up in the romance of it all. We were really idolizing a lot of Stax-Volt players and Aretha and B. B. King, and they all had big bands,' he says, referring to musicians who remained anonymous. 'And I could do that. I've been in bands where everyone's reading from the sheet.' Maury Baker claims Janis was 'very friendly with all the guys. She was the biggest-loving person I'd ever known.' A number of the players, however, 'would talk shit about her,' claims their roadie, Vince Mitchell. There was never a family feeling in the group. Sam didn't feel as connected to the others, because they were professional musicians who simply 'weren't as interesting to be with' as Peter, Dave, and James, his fellow bandmates in Janis's previous band, Big Brother.

The mediocre concert reviews, the revolving personnel, and Gabriel Mekler's habit of ignoring the players' suggestions shot the band's morale to hell. 'We were musicians and we knew how to play,' claims Snooky Flowers, still testy after all these years. 'We weren't just a bunch of hippies running around playing three chords. Luis Gasca had left the Count Basie Band to play with Janis Joplin. And I had played with all the known R & B bands that came through the Bay Area.' Flowers believes Janis was uncomfortable with the group because she realized the 'band was better than she was, musically beyond her.' Sam doesn't entirely disagree with Flowers, but 'Snooky could upstage anyone,' he says. 'He upstaged Janis and he did it a lot. She probably finally just lost patience with it.'

The recording sessions lasted only ten days, but they were chaotic, according to the bassist, Brad Campbell. 'Everybody was putting down everybody else. It was a mess, a total mess.' Mekler was a hands-off producer, the opposite of John Simon, who produced 'Cheap Thrills'; and Sye Mitchell, the new album's engineer, remembers 'saying more and doing more' than Mekler. Janis was very involved in the making of the record, too. In fact, Clive Davis installed Mitchell after Janis became so abusive with the first engineer, Jerry Hochman, that he quit. Mitchell had witnessed Janis's reaming of Hochman – complete with many choice four-letter words – and wasn't anxious to relieve him. He told Davis he would quit if Janis became belligerent with him, and he warned Janis, 'If I hear any of that from your mouth, I'll walk out the door.' Janis agreed and behaved, says Mitchell, like a 'pussycat, always polite, courteous, and hardworking.'

Janis was dynamic, but too often the band lagged behind her as it had four months earlier at the Fillmore East. To make matters worse, Snooky Flowers says, 'We never got a chance to finish the album. We had to go on the road. We were supposed to come back to the studio and finish the record, but we never did.' Under other circumstances, the bad notes would have been remedied before the album hit the stores, but there was a bigger problem plaguing the album. As Janis's father would later point out, 'the brass in her second group didn't suit her. Her voice was an orchestra in itself.' Janis found herself competing with the horn players whose playing rarely approached the subtle work heard on most Stax records. As a consequence, *Kozmic Blues* finds Janis at her screechiest.

Still, the record has some sublime moments. 'Maybe,' Janis's radically reworked version of the 1957 girl-group hit, and the bluesy 'One Good Man,' co-written by Janis and Sam and powered by Michael Bloomfield's scorching guitar, both really soar, in part because of the uncluttered arrangements. The album's showstopper, though, is Janis's version of 'Little Girl Blue' from the Rodgers and Hart Broadway show *Jumbo*.

Like Nina Simone, who recorded a haunting cover in 1958, Janis dispensed with the song's opening verse, where the middle-aged heroine sings of how the circus dazzled her as a youngster. But in contrast to Simone and every other vocalist who has tackled the song, Janis sings from a position of empathy and identification. Instead of the line 'What can you do? Old girl you're through,' Janis sings, 'I know you feel that you're through.' And Janis's kozmic version makes no wistful mention of a tender blue boy coming to little girl blue's rescue. 'Go on, sit right back down,' she sings in the final verse, as if she is exhorting herself to rely on her own strengths and keep going: 'Count your fingers,' as the song puts it. Janis added and discarded so many lines that the woman administering the Rodgers and Hart estate refused Myra Friedman's request to publish the song's lyrics in her biography of Janis. 'She just hated Janis's version,' Myra says laughingly.

Although *Kozmic Blues* went gold, it generated a mixed critical response and no Top 10 singles. The band's lone African-American, Snooky Flowers, insists that the rock press trashed the album because the group was playing R & B – black music. 'Big Brother represented the Sixties, and they thought Janis was in her purest form in that band. We had horns and sounded more like a polished R & B band, and they weren't accustomed to that.' In truth, the band had two strikes against it: first, it was predominantly white at a time when soul music was supposed to be played by blacks; second, it confirmed the prevailing stereotype of white musicians sounding uptight and stiff, too 'white.' Most reviewers of the album faulted its cumbersome arrangements and the band's sluggish playing. *Rolling Stone* ran two reviews: one was lukewarm, while the other raved about Janis's singing but indicted the group for sounding 'lumpier than a beer hall accordion band.'

At concerts, the audience's reception was sometimes cool, too. Janis had always derived enormous pleasure from performing, yet with her new band either lagging behind her or overpowering her she was connecting only sporadically with the audience. 'They didn't get me off,' she told David Dalton. 'You know, I have to have the umph. I've got to feel it, because if it's not getting through to me, the audience sure as hell aren't going to feel it either.' Performing, one of Janis's many drugs, was failing her. She worried all the time about her singing now that critics were no longer quite so keen. 'Janis would go, "You know, some day they're gonna find out the truth,"' her sometime lover Peggy Caserta recalled. 'I said, "Being?" And she hesitated for a long time and we kept looking at each other. 'Being that I can't really sing,' she said. 'Oh Jesus, is that what you're worrying about today?' I asked, because each day would be a new problem. I think she knew after a while she had developed something she'd captivated the audiences with, but she didn't really believe she was good.'

One night at the Fillmore East, a critic caught a glimpse of Janis in the wings just after she had finished her encore. As the audience called for another song, Janis 'stood back there, pulling herself together for one more time, and her evident exhaustion was raw and frightening. I'd like to forget that look, but I won't for a long time.' As Toni Brown of the band Joy of Cooking observed, 'For Janis it was never enough to have all this applause and to have all these strokes. She needed it all the time. There was this big hole, and it was, 'something come in here and calm me down, take care of me.' What did this woman do when she didn't have this scene around her?' Brown wondered. 'Onstage I make love to twenty thousand people,' Janis once said, 'then I go home alone.' She was rich, she was famous, and she was little girl blue.

Chapter 7

Steve Waksman

BLACK SOUND, BLACK BODY
Jimi Hendrix, the electric guitar, and the meanings of blackness

A world of sound

DURING THE LAST YEAR OF HIS LIFE, Jimi Hendrix opened a world of sound. Electric Lady, it was called, a state-of-the-art thirty-two track recording studio where the guitarist could pursue all the sounds running through his head. And they were plentiful, those sounds, maybe too much for one guitarist to handle:

> Most of the time I can't get it on the guitar, you know? Most of the time
> I'm just laying around day-dreaming and hearing all this music. And you
> can't, if you go to the guitar and try to play it, it spoils the whole thing,
> you know? – I just can't play guitar that well, to *get* all this music together.

Over the course of his brief career, recording studios assumed a special significance for Hendrix as the sites where he could enact his wildest fantasies of sound, and where he could work to exert the greatest amount of control over the sounds he produced with his guitar. By the accounts of his ex-bandmates, his attention to detail in the studio verged on obsessive, laboring for hours over a single effect, manipulating the various technologies at his disposal past their limits, exploring every parameter until he found the sound that was just right for the song, or the song that was just right for the sound.

Electric Lady was Hendrix's effort to move his control over sound one step further, to actually own the means of musical (re)production. It was also his attempt to create a 'total environment' in which physical design and visual appearance segued into the overarching purpose of making music. According to Curtis Knight, a musician and Hendrix biographer, Electric Lady was 'designed to give an atmosphere of being in space,' and featured 'every electronic innovation that could be conceived.' With the opening of the studio in 1970, Hendrix had achieved a degree of artistic control inaccessible to most African-American musicians of the time, including the many players who populated the Chess studios in Chicago. At the same time, though, this physical embodiment of Hendrix's desires was as much a product of the mounting pressures on the artist as it was a result of his musical vision. The sound-buffered underground laboratory of Electric Lady studios was also a sanctuary where Hendrix could escape the burdens of performing according to a set of expectations that he had helped to foster and yet had no ability to manage, expectations that came with the position of being a black hipster artist playing amid the predominantly white counterculture of the late 1960s.

It might seem a bit perverse to begin a study of Jimi Hendrix, a musician widely remembered as one of the most compelling live performers in the recent history of popular music, with an evocation of his attachment to the recording studio. Setting aside quibbles about the problematic opposition between live and mediated perform-ance in popular music, however, I want to posit Electric Lady, and the recording studio more generally, as a crucial supplement to the more spectacular, better docu-mented dimensions of Hendrix's performing identity. If Hendrix on stage was a near-mythic presence who both drew upon and signified a complex history of racial representations, Hendrix in the studio was someone else, an almost insular figure who could lose himself in the seemingly endless sound possibilities afforded by elec-tric technology. In neither case do we find a more authentic Hendrix, but rather in the sum of the two we find a story of the contradictions he embodied. The most public of African-American performers, he surrounded himself with a world of sound, which seemed more and more an attempt to escape the trap of his celebrity.

When asked by Albert Goldman, 'What is the difference between the old blues and the new?' Hendrix replied, 'Electricity.' Hendrix's answer mocks the notion that there is any significant difference between blues old and new. The music is the same, his one-word response seems to imply, it only sounds different. Yet for Hendrix and for 1960s rock in general, that sound had significant transformative power in itself. Discussing the experience of playing at 'little funky clubs,' for instance, Hendrix observed that 'Everything is sweating. It seemed like the more it got sweaty, the funkier it got and the groovier. Everybody melted together, I guess! And the sound was kickin' 'em all in the chest. I dig that! Water and elec-tricity!'. Here the physical atmosphere of the club blends with the physicality of the sound to create a realm of intense sensation that, in Hendrix's mind, worked to bring people together.

Can electricity be the basis of difference? It is a strange concept and one that definitely leans too far to the side of technological determinism. Nonetheless, to understand Hendrix's simple answer to the question of the difference between the old blues and new is perhaps to understand at once how far he had come from the old blues and how much he remained rooted in its language. Hendrix's use of electronic sound significantly expanded the musical vocabulary of rock. Indeed, his array of bent, distorted notes teetering over the edge of tonality and feedback shrieks struggling to avoid the inevitability of sonic decay introduced sounds that had really never been heard before in any musical setting. In doing so, he took advantage of two keys of technological innovations that came about during the 1960s. First, in amplifier design, a British drummer and music-shop owner named Jim Marshall and his partner; electronic engineer Ken Bran, responded to the demand among young

British guitarists for adequate amplification with an amplifier that was inspired by the popular Fender Bassman (favored by many electric blues performers), but made with some significant changes in electronic components. Marshall amplifiers soon set a new standard for rock guitar amplifiers, with greater gain and more output power than their American counterparts, as well as a tone rich in harmonic frequencies. Hendrix took to visiting the shop regularly during his tenure in London, and had Marshall design for him some custom amplifiers with added gain so that he could more readily reach his equipment's output limit and move into the distortion- and feedback-filled realm of the clipped signal.

To facilitate further his use of an overdriven electric sound and his general desire to expand the sonoric range of his instrument, Hendrix also drew upon a range of sonic effect devices that began to appear during the 1960s. Often referred to colloquially as 'stompboxes,' these were small metal boxes containing transistor circuits that, when connected between the line that ran from guitar to amplifier; altered the electronic signal delivered to the amp, changing the sound. The most common such device was the distortion-inducing fuzzbox, a staple of Hendrix's sound. Also prominent were the Octavia (which generated octaves of the note being played at higher frequencies, to give added dimension to the sound) and the wah-wah pedal (named for the way it abruptly shifted the tone of the guitar from low to high, creating a 'wah'-like quiver in the sound). For many of his effects, Hendrix turned to another British electronics specialist, Roger Mayer, who custom-designed effects boxes for many of the leading guitarists on the British scene. Mayer shared with Hendrix a fascination with the many faces of distortion and sound modification, and once described his work as

> an exercise in knowing what to do wrong . . . Once you deviate from a perfect amplifier, which, in essence, does nothing except make the signal larger, you are doing something incorrect in terms of theory. Designing electronic sound devices . . . becomes an exercise in knowing exactly what to do wrong, because when you design a circuit and something is incorrect about it, there are an awful lot of complex changes that occur.

With Mayer's effects pedals in tow, Hendrix could more readily enact his own willful deviations from the norms of electronic sound design and capitalize upon the accidents made possible by amplification to push the sound of his guitar in new directions.

However innovative the *sound* of Hendrix's music may have been, its form typically stayed close to standard blues models. Moreover, the sounds themselves had their roots in the playing of earlier blues guitarists such as Buddy Guy and Muddy Waters. Although he had more resources at his disposal, many of the effects that Hendrix sought to achieve, and that electronic engineers such as Jim Marshall and Roger Mayer incorporated into their products, were extensions of the effects achieved a decade earlier by blues guitarists who were testing the limits of their own equipment. Thus, Hendrix recalled in a 1968 interview that

> the first guitarist I was aware of was Muddy Waters. I heard one of his old records when I was a little boy and it scared me to death, because I heard all of those sounds. Wow, what is that all about? It was great.

Hendrix himself sought to tap into a similar strain of musical expression, defamiliarizing standard song forms through the power of electric sound combined with his own disfiguring brand of virtuosity. With respect to Hendrix's interpretation of the blues, this combination of innovative style applied to traditional form was perhaps nowhere more apparent than in his recording of the song 'Voodoo Child (Slight Return),' the final cut from his 1968 double album, *Electric Ladyland*.

In 'Voodoo Child (Slight Return),' Hendrix's guitar *is* the song; the accompaniment by drummer Mitch Mitchell and bassist Noel Redding, however frenetic, is all but submerged beneath the presence of the guitarist's electrifying performance. The song begins with Hendrix's lone guitar. At first there are no notes, only the sound of Hendrix picking at his muted strings, a sound altered by a wah-wah pedal, which he uses to alter the timbre and place rhythmic accents. After a brief melodic statement also inflected by the wah-wah, the bass and drums enter the song while Hendrix's guitar assumes a harsh distorted tone that slashes and burns its way through the other instruments.

The basic musical figure of 'Voodoo Child (Slight Return)' is a rather simple assemblage of bent notes and a droning E note bass string (actually an Eb, as Hendrix tended to tune his guitar down half a step). Between virtually every repetition of the figure, Hendrix plays some high-pitched improvisatory variation that transfigures the basic structure into something very different. The lyrics are closely tied to the first version of the song, continuing the singer's exploration of surrealistic blues imagery.

> Well I stand up next to a mountain
> Chop it down with the edge of my hand
> I pick up all the pieces and make an island
> Might even raise a little sand.

Having declared his cosmic power, Hendrix plays a searing solo on the upper registers of his instrument, his guitar shrieking and crying like a witch burning at the stake. Long sustained notes melt into rapid runs that verge on chromaticism, while the sound of his guitar is electronically processed to shift in and out of earshot, composing a rhythmic alternation of sound and silence. The solo ends, the song quiets, and Hendrix sings a cryptic verse in which he bends the limits of space and time, and envisions some sort of other-worldly reconciliation: 'I won't see you no more in this world/I'll meet you in the next one – So don't be late.' Another restatement of the chorus is followed by an apocalyptic guitar solo in which Hendrix's guitar emits sheets of sheer electronic noise, once again alternating between excess and virtual silence until, with a last fleet tremolo-bent trip across the fretboard, the song fades away to its end.

Scholars such as Paul Gilroy, Greg Tate, and Charles Shaar Murray locate in Hendrix the most radically revisionist of tendencies, and at the same time value him because even in his most innovative moments, Hendrix maintained a strong sense of musical roots. Perhaps Murray is right that 'Voodoo Child (Slight Return)' stands as Hendrix's foremost articulation of blackness, that the song stands as a sort of space-age blues in which the tradition gains strength even as it is denaturalized and technologized. I want to suggest, however, that Hendrix's articulation of blackness in this song can also be read as a disarticulation, that the savage guitar rites of 'Voodoo Child (Slight Return)' disfigure more conventional blues sounds to such an extent that blackness itself is left as an empty category. Hendrix may indeed be asserting his blackness, but only if he can live it according to his own rules; and blackness therefore becomes a matter of individuality rather than a social condition. Hendrix proclaims he is a 'Voodoo Chile,' and one can only wonder what these lines might have meant to his audience; for Hendrix, the space-age bluesman, played his innovations to a mass of star-gazing white children.

Bodily sights/bodily sites

On June 18, 1967, at the Monterey Pop Festival, Jimi Hendrix enacted one of rock's most visceral moments with his performance of 'Wild Thing.' After playing the first half of the song relatively straight, the guitarist brings it to a prolonged, intense climax. 'Wild Thing' descends into a fit of electronic noise as Hendrix turns away from the crowd to simulate intercourse with his guitar and amplifier, aggressively thrusting his hips at his 'equipment.' He then moves back toward the audience and, after straddling his guitar for a moment, retrieves a can of lighter fluid from the back of the stage, which he proceeds to 'ejaculate' onto his instrument. And next comes a match – the guitar is on fire at the foot of the stage, and Hendrix, kneeling over it, flicks his tongue and motions with his hands to conjure the flames higher. Picking up the tortured, still-burning instrument, he smashes it to pieces, and proceeds to fling its scorched bits into the crowd before stomping off the stage, amplifiers still squealing with feedback.

Add to this scene a still image of Hendrix in the most obviously phallic of poses: his body arched slightly backwards as he plays the guitar behind his back, the neck of his instrument protruding through his legs like a surrogate penis, surrounded by his large black fist. In such instances, which were by no means isolated within the context of Hendrix's career, he specifically and intentionally manipulated his guitar so that it took shape as a technological extension of his body, a 'technophallus.' The electric guitar as technophallus represents a fusion of man and machine, an electronic appendage that allowed Hendrix to display his instrumental and, more symbolically, his sexual prowess.

Hendrix's overtly phallic style of performance was just as crucial to his rock persona as his sound. Yet to say that Hendrix's appeal was sexual as well as musical is only to begin to understand the meaning of his sexuality for his audience. The bodily gestures that constituted Hendrix's performance style, and the ways in which those gestures were perceived, can only be understood when judged within the broad set of cultural meanings and discourses surrounding black male sexuality. Hendrix's music cannot be considered as separate from his physicality: his style of virtuosity was itself highly phallocentric, and his combination of musical and bodily flamboyance was perceived by many of his white guitar-playing peers to offer a unique challenge to their own talent and, by implication, their masculinity. But did Hendrix's performance style pose a similar challenge to stereotypes of black male potency and hypersexuality? Or did it simply represent his success in tailoring a 'caricature' to fit the 'mythic standards' of his audience?

To begin to understand how this field of racialized desire affected the career of Jimi Hendrix, I turn again to Frank Zappa, rock 'n' roll pundit. In an essay that attempts to explain 'The Jimi Hendrix Phenomenon' to the readers of *Life* magazine, Zappa describes Hendrix's sound as 'very symbolic' with its 'orgasmic grunts, tortured squeals, lascivious moans . . . and innumerable audial curiosities . . . delivered to the sense mechanisms of the audience at an extremely high decibel level.' Ultimately, though, the source of Hendrix's appeal lay elsewhere. Despite the intensity of his sound and manner of performance, suggests Zappa,

> the female audience thinks of Hendrix as being beautiful (maybe just a little scary), but mainly very sexy. The male audience thinks of him as a phenomenal guitarist and singer . . . The boys seem to enjoy the fact that their girl friends are turned on to Hendrix sexually; very few resent his appeal and show envy. They seem to give up and say: 'He's got it, I ain't got it, I don't know if I'll ever get it . . . but if I do, I wanna be just like him, because he's really got it.' They settle for vicarious participation and/or buy a Fender Stratocaster, an Arbiter Fuzz Face, a Vox Wah-Wah Pedal, and four Marshall amplifiers.

Zappa creates a dichotomy between Hendrix's sexual appeal and his musical appeal: girls like him because he is sexy, and boys like him because he is a great musician. Yet as his description proceeds, the categories begin to collapse. The boys actually 'enjoy' the fact of their girlfriends' excited response to Hendrix, they acknowledge their own deficiency at the same time as they long to approximate Hendrix's unique blend of musical and sexual prowess. Hendrix becomes an object of desire for the boys as well as the girls, an object 'maybe just a little bit scary' in his ability to cross over both race and gender lines in his appeal.

Zappa displaces the suggestion of homoeroticism only to readmit tacitly the possibility of white male desire for black male sexuality. Hendrix's appeal is not simply a product of his flamboyance, but is intrinsically tied to cultural perceptions of black masculinity, as articulated by Frantz Fanon in his book, *Black Skin, White Masks*. But Zappa's words should also force us to deal with what is generally absent from Fanon's account: the problematic role of white women's sexuality in this scenario. (Black women are strikingly and distressingly absent from all accounts.) For Fanon, the colonial relationship was at its root homosocial, being a relationship between men. Thus did he all but overlook the ways in which the white female body, as the primary object of white male desire, became the screen upon which were projected the various fears and desires associated with black masculinity. Zappa's description of the white male fascination with their girlfriends' excited response to Hendrix suggests that the white man is reduced to a voyeur forced to recognize his own impotence – unless he is somehow able to possess the black man's tools, as Zappa's boys seek to do with their purchase of Hendrix-related merchandise. Commodification as castration? Perhaps. Just as significant, though, is the way in which white women's imagined sexual gratification is taken as the true measure of black male potency.

If this scenario has a ring of familiarity, which I hope it does, it is because I have tried to describe a situation that is essentially a form of minstrelsy. Gone, perhaps, is the blackface, but so many symbols of black masculinity, and specifically of Hendrix's masculinity, are visible that the process of literally 'blacking up' is no longer necessary. I would further suggest that this particular example is indicative of a much broader trend during the 1960s. Scores of white guitarists in the United States and Great Britain, many of whom had only come into contact with black music through recordings, became infatuated with the blues and they found in Hendrix a living model for their own attempt to transgress racial boundaries. Hendrix's presence on the white blues-rock scene had a double-edged effect: on the one hand he lent white musicians an air of legitimacy, on the other hand, he threatened their own claims to authenticity. The threat posed by Hendrix was both sexual and musical, and on each count took shape on the contested terrain where race and masculinity intersect.

Some have chosen to locate a liberatory or deconstructive potential in Hendrix's style. Hendrix himself, though, ultimately came to feel somewhat trapped in his own definition of blackness. He came to realize, gradually, that it was in many ways a role already defined for him. For Hendrix, as for Fanon, the sight of blackness in the eyes of others had become oppressive, and so he expresses a desire to be heard, not seen; listened to, not watched. The most 'visible' of black performers, he yearns for a sort of invisibility. He wants to remove himself from the demands of his public into a realm of pure music where both he and his audience can lose themselves in the power of sound.

Somewhere amid the words and the music of Hendrix lies a vision of utopia, an imagined transformation of the world into an 'electric church' where all differences would submerge beneath a wave of electronic sound. Somewhere, but not here; someday, but not today: as much as Hendrix might have wanted the black kids to realize the spiritual potential of music, he realized that utopia was far from an achieved state, and that blackness stood to separate people from one another. He was continually striving to push against the boundaries of both music and race, boundaries that were inextricably tied within his outlook. Yet through this process he was also perhaps forced to recognize that certain boundaries can be intransigent, that to imagine alternative realities is not to bring them into being. A tragic lesson, as one can only imagine, for someone who seemed to live through his music. Tragic, but maybe necessary. Had Hendrix lived, would he have moved his art to a whole other level of commitment? This we can never know, but we can continue to draw our own lessons from Hendrix, to keep our own imaginations alive, and realize that to do so can never be enough.

Chapter 8

Jason Toynbee

MAKING UP AND SHOWING OFF
What musicians do

M USICIANS ARE EXEMPLARY AGENTS who, through their creative practice, demonstrate how one might act differently, and in so doing, rebut, at
least to some extent, the exigencies of the capitalist system. The question is, though,
how can this happen? In what sense might creativity emerge from the very social
relations which perpetuate domination?

> You, my audience, are all a bunch of poppaloppas . . . All of you sit
> there digging yourselves and each other, looking around hoping to be
> seen and observed as hip. You become the object you came to see, and
> you think you're important and digging jazz when all the time all you're
> doing is digging a blind, deaf scene that has nothing to do with any kind
> of music at all . . .
>
> (Charles Mingus, quoted by Dorr-Dorynek,
> 1987: 16–17)

Running to more than two pages in its edited form, this diatribe delivered to a noisy
nightclub audience in 1959 has a curiously contemporary ring. It is the sound of the
heroic gripe, the characteristic tone of the popular music *auteur* railing against a
world that will not acknowledge him. Mingus chastises the audience for having
misrecognized its own function – namely, the appreciation of 'any kind of music at
all'. Of course, the inference is that his music is very much more, that it constitutes, as he says later, 'another language, so much more wide in range and vivid
and warm and full and expressive of thoughts you are seldom able to convey' (ibid.
18). Now it seems to me that this judgement carries precisely the post-Romantic
rhetoric of expression and genius that Barthes (1976) finds so intolerable. Yet at
the same time there is the kernel of something else. When Mingus says he deals in
'language . . . wide in range and vivid' a weaker, more demotic author is suggested,

an organizer of voices rather than an expressing machine. We might say that the condition of possibility of Mingus's individualism as a musician is dialogue.

This use of dialogue can be heard in the voices of other jazz players to varying degrees. But what makes Mingus so significant as a social author is that from the mid-1950s he uses the bass as a *narrative* voice, making it unfurl each episode in the extended pieces that he then started to write. During such announcing moments, the bass often takes on the characteristics of other instruments. A good example of this can be heard on the first studio recording of 'Hatian Fight Song' from 1957. The piece begins with a bass solo consisting of a string of 'blues guitar lickes'. There are leaps into the upper register of the instrument and copious note-bending before Mingus introduces, tentatively, a four-bar riff that builds in volume and sure-footedness over three cycles, until trombone and alto sax present an answering riff with a skittering 12/4 feel. During the solos from the lead instruments that follow, Mingus keeps on interjecting one or other of these riffs into the standard walking bass line, alternately urging the soloists on or pulling them back. Finally, in his own solo towards the end, Mingus cites blues guitar again before introducing a climactic ensemble coda consisting of the two riffs heard in the introduction.

In effect, then, the role of narrator is enacted in the voices of others. Either the bass adopts an accent from outside the ensemble – that of blues guitar – or it anticipates and parodies the voicings of the band's own brass section by playing 'their' riffs. Yet all the while timbre and rhythmic attack carry the signature, *Mingus*.

If much of Mingus's own playing is concerned with citation, the same principle seems to be at work in the selection and direction of instrumentalists. Above all, he wants to hear distinctive voices. The kind of innovation that Mingus wanted from his musicians had much less to do with formal avant-gardism than with their finding an idiom – that is to say, a voice already heard. The sour tone of Jackie McLean, the acerbic and even more harmonically wayward style of Eric Dolphy, or the smeary legato of trombonist Jimmy Knepper constituted quite particular, locatable voices. Like Duke Ellington, Mingus was always trying to construct a soundscape out of the characteristic dialects of his instrumentalists. Perhaps the major compositional method of both these jazz *auteurs* was the organization of a dialogical environment in which the musicians were obliged to speak as 'themselves'.

Beginning with 'Hatian Fight Song' a group of tunes ('Better Git It In Your Soul', 'Slop', 'Wednesday Night Prayer Meeting', 'Eclusiastics') summon up the sound of the Holiness churches that he had attended as a child. In these pieces the bass player calls out to the band or audience in the manner of a preacher: sometimes he shouts 'Jesus!' or 'I know!' as though testifying to a strong and certain faith. Hand claps 'from the congregation' over stop time or as a sole accompaniment to riffs and solos intensify the impressions of church. On 'Folk Forms No. 1', Dannie Richmond knocks out a snare drum figure modelled on a tambourine pattern used by gospel choirs. Taken together, these tropes have a powerful effect. This is partly a matter of intertextuality – we hear snatches of sacred music – but it also has to do with the production of presence, not so much an 'authentic' realization of a church as a staged one.

It is clear, then, that dialogue and citation abound in the Mingus oeuvre. There is a constant sense of field beyond the text, of voice as place and as historical moment.

The references are both musical — to genres, authors, instrumental voices — and extramusical — they gesture towards locale or to political events.

Mingus can be considered an ideal (if not typical) example of the social author. There are two aspects to this. First, he is engaged in a political project. By incorporating black genres from the past he helps to construct a history of African-American music-making that maps, at one and the same time, a black American 'structure of feeling' (Williams 1965). The cycle of church songs, for example, does not testify to the immanent presence of God so much as call on the audience to witness the social reality of black oppression on earth. And yet, at one and the same time, these numbers are joyous, affirmative, hard swinging. They propose a utopia beyond domination.

As a musician, the techniques of musical diaolgism that Mingus develops enable him to produce a pan-diasporic utopian imaginary in which flamenco, European cabaret and Mexican table dancing are spoken through a black American voice. In effect, he listens out across a global field of musical works to construct a cosmopolitan network of possibility, and in so doing centres himself. That is one reason why Mingus is such an important author, an African-American who constructs a grand union of musical otherness in opposition to white and monoglot culture.

The second aspect of Mingus's social authorship has to do with forms of design and production in popular music. Crucially, Mingus arranges collective and individual voices in a new synthesis that anticipates the mid-1960s revolution in thinking about how music might be put together.

Mingus began to write and arrange for his own bands under the shadow of be-bop in the mid-1950s. Be-bop was, of course, pre-eminently improvised music. But unlike early jazz in which improvisation was mainly collective, or swing where soloists were circumscribed by the constant intervention of the ensemble, in post-war jazz players are heroic individualists. In the work of musicians such as Charlie Parker, Dizzy Gillespie, or Bud Powell, technical virtuosity and improvisatory stamina are elevated to a central position. Obliged to go on ringing the creative changes for chorus after chorus, there is even a sense of desperation about bop soloists: they fly in the knowledge that they might fall back to earth at any moment.

Mingus establishes himself as an *auteur* in opposition to such a tendency. The problem he faces is a double one — how to renew the ground of improvisation while moving beyond the now restrictive form of the standard or blues. What distinguishes Mingus from other musicians confronting this problem is his social approach to the problem of innovation in mid-century jazz. As a composer/arranger his prime technique is to elicit a collective surplus from his musicians — in other words, more than they could be expected to give within the terms of the solo-over-rhythm-section mode of bop. It is worth examining what this means because Mingus's working methods pave the way for rock production, and therefore increasingly for popular music in general. He makes two related innovations here. He insists on working out quite complex arrangements orally, and he makes use of tape editing to overdub, lengthen and rearrange pieces in the post-production stage.

Mingus generally rehearsed his musicians without using a score. The extent to which he initially wrote down compositions remains unclear, but in any case he would introduce them to the band by singing or playing the melody line for each instrument. Musicians had to learn their parts by ear without even a chord chart to refer to. In an important sense, composition, improvisation and recording are elided in the Mingus method. Not only does the process of writing go on during perform-ance, but it also continues at the recording stage. Mingus is unusual among jazz auteurs in his free use of tape editing, a technique realized most completely on *The Black Saint and the Sinner Lady*. Yet what is interesting is that the editing aesthetic is already implicit in Mingus's earlier work. As Gunther Schuller (1986) points out, so-called 'extended form' on the *Pithecanthropus Erectus* and *Clown* albums depends on the repetition of one part of a chord pattern until 'the soloist or the 'composer' feels that the development of the piece requires moving on to another idea' (ibid. 21). An associated trope, the introduction of riffs during a solo to produce a drawn-out, antiphonal tension, also has this aspect of improvised composition. As a composer, then, Mingus improvises dynamics and plays with time, stretching the faculties of his players as much as the form of a piece. Musical dialogue between voices is in a crude sense a correlate of the social dialogue that Mingus supervises during production.

What conclusions can we reach about Mingus as a social author? Most import-antly, I think we need to abandon the idea of expression from within, which has become a commonplace among popular musicians, fans and critics, especially in jazz and rock. Mingus, a putatively self-sufficient creator, in fact works with colloquial voices. Even the voice of his own instrument is employed as part of a dialogue. We might say, then, that authorship consists in the selection and combination of what is 'out there' – that is, possible voices, more or less difficult to hear, in the field of works. Conceived in this way, authorial intention certainly persists. Partly it is an effect of the Mingus habitus; partly it derives from the exigencies of the jazz scene. Most of all, we can hear it pushing forwards in the gap between these two. But whatever its source, the crucial point is that intention will now be refracted as it jostles its way through the social data of voices, players and techniques en route to the realization of the work.

This makes social authorship much more complex than expression. Charles Mingus not only has to select voices but also to integrate them, even as they are reverberating one against another. At times, such integration appears spontaneous; it is done quickly and without much time for reflection. At other moments, it is a more studied process. But in either case, what counts is the ability to collate voices in a chorus that is redolent with utopian possibility. Above all, the method is historical. Hearing backwards, the Mingus oeuvre affirms both continuity and vari-ation, suffering and the transcendence of suffering, in the African-American musical tradition. Blowing forwards, it projects a cosmopolitan alliance of Other voices into the future.

So far, I have not made a distinction between authorship and performance, for in an important sense it is the elision of these moments that distinguishes popular music's mode of production. Mingus makes such a good example of the popular creator for that reason. It is difficult to separate thinking-up from sounding-out in his practice – they run together. Still, I would argue that performance is central to the aesthetics of pop. There are two aspects to it. First, the term can refer to process, the ongoing nature of musical production. From this perspective, performance hints at the uncompleted nature of pop – the fact that there tend not to be great works so much as versions, mixes and shifting genres. In short, performance refers to creation-in-progress. Second, popular music-making has a theatricality about it. There is a self-conscious awareness on the part of musicians and audience of the gap between them, a gap that even the most naturalistic of performers in the most intimate of environments have to confront. From this perspective, creation includes the struggle by musicians to *get across* to an audience. So performance mediates creativity and pushes authors into taking account of it.

Above all, modern popular music, including rock, is *processive* music. It is constructed in a sequence of multiple takes, overdubs and editing, and is then distributed across different kinds of media. The result is that there tend to be many manifestations of a song-performance. Some involve recombination with other types: recording played at home; radio broadcast of recordings; radio broadcast of specially recorded session; music video; live concerts; live concert recording; live concert broadcast; club record-play by DJs as part of a long mix. While some scholars, such as Theodore Gracyk, would have it that these are all 'instantiations' of a primary work, this requires positing an original and stable *idea* of the work. In pop, musical ideas have a temporary and fluid existence. They are always being abstracted from a concrete sounding, only to be sounded again in different but connected ways in the next recording, remix or other performative context.

Now I want to turn to the theatrical aspect of performance. Indeed, I argue that the relationship between the processive and the theatrical is central to popular music aesthetics. By the theatrical I mean the way that music-making is staged as something performed by musicians for an audience. What counts here is the knowledge that music is not only being made, but being made to be heard, and sometimes to be seen too. To put it another way, the theatricality of popular music performance derives from performers conceiving themselves as performers and audience members thinking that they are members of an audience.

Now in one sense there is a tension between the theatrical and the processive. Theatrical performance represents a punctuation in the continuum of production-mediation-distribution. There is an implicit injunction that runs, 'Stop, and listen to us making these sounds!' This is clearly true of live performance, but it also applies to recordings that should, ideally, arrest the listener and impose a theatrical relation of audiencehood even in the banal and comfortable setting of the home. We might say that the recording is congealed performance. However, on another plane, inside the radius of creativity, the two aspects of performance converge. For here, even as the music-maker begins to identify and select possible voices, s/he is anticipating how they will sound. In other words, social authorship of the kind I described earlier also includes an element of performance to the self (as other).

Performers in popular music may or may not see it like this, though. Sometimes artists reflect on their own performativity, but in other cases what counts is 'just doing it'. In fact, what makes the short twentieth century of popular music so interesting is the sheer diversity of performance strategies that have emerged. Each has handled the question of the nature of performance and the extent to which this should be foregrounded in quite a different way. These strategies range from the mediated sincerity of the radio crooner in the 1920s, 1930s and 1940s, through the virtuosic showmanship of the heavy metal guitarists to the reserved shamanism of the contemporary club DJ. Now at one level such diverse approaches to performance represent adaption to new music media. However this is never a matter of simple response to changing technology. Different performance aesthetics are also strongly axiological. Each makes exclusive claims to performative validity, each criticizes other modes of performance.

One banal but vitally important point to keep hold of is that musicians continue to believe in the possibility of getting across to an audience. Audiences continue to be believe in the possibility of being touched. Yet both have reason to doubt how far this authentic relation (in which real communication takes place) can be completely realized in performance – whether live or mediated, naturalistic or camp as anything. This is partly a matter of competence. Performances may simply not be good enough in the sense of reaching a notional threshold of accomplishment. As Simon Frith suggests, 'performers always face the threat of the ultimate embarrassment: *the performance that doesn't work* (1996: 214, original emphasis). The point is that there seems to be something about the performance relationship that is fundamentally volatile, given to interruption and undecidability.

The question is, how do performers cope with all this? The short answer is through a range of different strategies, several of which we have encountered already. To understand their rationale and the relations between them, I want to set up a model of popular music performance types. The *expressionist* mode of performance is concerned with truth to the subject, a full issuing out of music from the inner being. Expressionists believe, above all, in asserting presence. To put it more concretely, rather than expressing himself, the singer can only sing in an expressionist style. Nonetheless, this does not prevent performers from trying to transcend the rhetorical dimension of music and to *truly* express themselves. Indeed, the desperation of this attempt defines expressionist practice.

Peter Wollen (1992:113) suggests that expressionism was imported into be-bop at mid-century via the abstract expressionist art scene in America. However, it is only with the advent of rock that it gets taken up in mass-mediated music. This comes partly as a diffuse legacy of romanticism, but also in Britain through the art school education of musicians. As I have implied, expressionism is a self-deluding and ultimately reactionary performance strategy. Most importantly for the present argument, expressionism represents an attempt to suppress citation and present pure emotion. In this sense, it is a profoundly anti-creative doctrine because it denies that creativity consists in an encounter between the musician-subject and objects in the field of works, or social relations more generally. Instead, it proposes a kind of subjective supremacism – everything comes from within. Yet expressionism cannot be discounted because it encapsulates, albeit in an excessive and fetishized form, a necessary urge in any act of performance, that is to give voice with present intent. Besides, it is often redeemed through being corrupted by other performance modes.

At the other end of the performance spectrum lies the *transformative* mode. Performance here is concerned not with truth to source so much as variation of that which has already been played and sung. The transformative mode of performance always includes a 'listening backwards' in the direction of tradition or Origin. The key point is that Origin will, in almost every case, be a collectivity, a historical moment or geographical place rather than an individual subject or the feelings of the performing artist (as in the expressive mode). The transformative then involves mediation between this source and the ongoing now of performance. Because it is premised on vicissitude, the transformative constitutes the performance mode *par excellence* of diasporic music cultures. It seems to me that the tranformative represents the utopian imperative of pop in its most developed form. Those features that mark it – versioning, bifurcation, repetition/variation – testify to solidarity and the redemption of human agency, but also to a notion of the past that teaches change.

So far, we have been examining that axis of performance that extends from expression to transformation and that focuses on the actions of the performer. However, as we have seen, performative acts always include an audience, that is an Other subject with whom the performer would communicate. The first mode of address to the audience that I would like to consider is the *direct* mode. This was the dominant mode of popular music performance before rock and roll; its key value is sincerity. Sincere address involved the performer giving her/himself over to the audience with both charm and conviction. It emerged partly as a way of compensating for the loss of signs of presence brought about by the advent of mass communication.

In rock, though, this kind of mediated sincerity, or being on the side of the audience, became highly suspect. In fact, it seems that successive movements to renew rock, including various neo-punk tendencies, have all tried to get rid of signs of deference to the audience. One way has been through facial expression. The range of looks used by rock musicians in videos, publicity shots or live performance typically extends from the sneer to the emphatically blank. It is as though rebuffing the audience with an angry and aggressive posture provides the only guarantee of being true to it.

Outside of rock, and indeed in parts of what remains of it, the direct mode of performance has been supplanted more and more by the *reflexive*. Performance here is still oriented towards the audience, but includes a strong awareness of its own, iterative nature. The key aspect of reflexive performance is the *display* of voice by means of an (unspoken) announcement that accompanies it like, 'that's the sound of it' or 'now we're doing it like this'.

Reflexivity has become increasingly important in popular music and has encroached more and more on the other modes of performance. It is perhaps tempting to read this as a symptom of postmodernism. However, I would argue to the contrary that reflexive performance is the continuation of agency in a period when other modes of performance have been exhausted. Furthermore, reflexivity has enabled the recovery of other modes of performance. In fact, almost all expressive or direct performances have an aspect of the reflexive or transformative about them. For without such an inflection, monstrous pomposity and self-indulgence (in the case of expression) or grotesque sentimentality (in the case of the direct mode) become all too palpable. By the same token, the reflexive and transformative can only be obtained from one of the other modes.

Performance can neither be wholly pure nor wholly impure. It is an interrupted act that appears in four fragmented modes: expressionist, direct, transformative, reflexive. These represent performance positions that may be adopted and even combined by musicians. They have distinct political and aesthetic implications that arise from the way that each denies or accommodates the impossibility of performance. While creative acts can be considered in isolation for analytical purposes, this only defers the issue of performance. For it is in performance that acts of creation are realized.

Chapter 9

Simon Reynolds

WAR IN THE JUNGLE

WHILE THE DOYENS OF INTELLIGENCE seemed to have forgotten what had originally made jungle more invigorating than trance or armchair techno, other producers – DJ SS, Asend/Dead Dred, Deep Blue, Aphrodite, DJ Hype, Ray Keith/Renegade – honed in on the genre's essence: breakbeat-science, bass mutation, sampladelia. Their work proved that the true *intellect* in jungle resided in the percussive rather than the melodic. Whether they were white or black, these artists reaffirmed drum and bass's place in an African musical continuum (dub, hip-hop, James Brown, etc.) whose premises constitute a radical break with Western music, classical and pop.

Roni Size and sidekick DJ Die were exemplars. This duo is often regarded as pioneers of jazz-jungle, on account of their early '94 classic 'Music Box' and its sequel, 'It's a Jazz Thing.' Listen again to 'Music Box,' though, and you realize that the sublime cascades of fusion-era chimes are only a brief interlude in what is basically a stripped-down percussion workout. Size's late '94 monster 'Timestretch' was even more austere, just escalating drums and a chiming bass line that together resemble a clockwork contraption gone mad. And the Size and Die early '95 collaboration '11.55' was positively murderous in its minimal-is-maximal starkness. What initially registers as merciless monotony reveals itself, on repeated plays, to be an inexhaustible forest of densely tangled breaks and multiple bass lines (the latter acting both as subliminal, ever-modulating melody and as sustained subaural pressure), relieved only by the sparest shadings of sampled jazz coloration. Forcing you to focus entirely on the rhythm section – which in normal pop is seldom consciously listened to – '11.55' clenches your brain until it feel like a knotted mass of hypertense tendons. Size and Die's fiercely compressed, implosive aesthetic recalled bebop, insofar as it is a strategy of alienation designed to discover who's really down with the program, by venturing deeper into the heart of 'blackness.' Articulating this 'it's a black thing, you wouldn't understand' subtext, and giving a gangsta twist to the music's glowering malevolence, was the soundbite at the beginning of '11.55' – 'you could feel all the tension building up at the convention/as the hustlers began to arrive' – sampled from Hustlers' Convention, a solo album by a member of the Last Poets.

Young producer Dillinja was, like Size and Die, renowned for fusion-tinged masterpieces like 'Sovereign Melody' and 'Deep Love,' with their softly glowing electric piano and flickers of lachrymose wah-wah guitar. But this tended to obscure Dillinja's real claim to genius: the viciously disorientating proper ties of his beats and B-lines, which he convoluted and contorted into grooves of ear-boggling, labyrinthine complexity. 'Warrior' places the listener in the center of an unfeasibly expanded drum-kit played by an octopus-limbed cyborg; the bass enters not as a B-line but a one-note detonation, an impacted cluster of different bass-timbres. On these and other Dillinja classics – 'You Don't Know,' 'Deadly Deep Subs,' 'Lionheart,' 'Ja Know Va Big,' 'Brutal Bass' – the jolting breaks trigger muscular reflexes and motor impulses, so that you find yourself shadow-boxing instead of dancing, tensing and sparring in a deadly ballet of feint, jab, and parry.

If Dillinja and Size and Die were developing drum and bass as martial art, Danny Breaks's work as Droppin' Science is more like a virtual adventure playground, where collapsible breakbeats and trampoline bass trigger kinesthetic responses, gradually hot-rodding the human nervous system in readiness for the rapid-fire reaction time required in the info-dense future. On tracks such as 'Long Time Comin'' and 'Step Off,' bass fibrillates like muscle with electric current coursing through it, hi-hats incandesce like fireworks in slow-mo, beats seem to run backward. Throughout, melody limits itself to minimal motifs where the real hook is the eerie fluorescent glow of the synth goo.

The year of jungle's mainstream breakthrough in Britain and critical recognition in America, 1995 saw jungle torn every which way in a conflict between two rival models of blackness: elegant urbanity (the opulence and finesse of fusion/garage/jazz-funk/quiet storm) and ruffneck tribalism (the raw, percussive minimalism of dub/ragga/hip-hop/electro). Lurking beneath this smooth/ruff dialectic was a covert class struggle: upwardly mobile gentrification versus ghettocentricity, crossover versus undergroundism.

On one side were artists such as Reece, Photek, and Bukem who equated 'progression' with making drum and bass sound more like other genres (house garage, Detroit techno). By the end of 1995, most of them had deals with major labels. On the other side were the purists who wanted jungle to advance by sounding ever more intensely like itself, and therefore dedicated themselves to achieving hard-won increments of polyrhythmic intricacy and sub-bass brutalism. This strategy had the beneficial side-effect of fending off outsiders because it involved plunging ever deeper into the antipopulist imperatives of the art's core (that is to say, all the stuff that happens beneath/beyond the noninitiate's perceptual thresholds). Most of these artists stuck with independent labels or put out their own tracks. Meanwhile, caught between intelligent's serenity and the ruff-stuff's moody minimalism, the idea of jungle as frisky funquake seemed to have simply dropped away altogether.

By 1996, 'jungle' and 'drum and bass' were *the* words to drop. Everybody from thirty-something jazz-pop duo Everything But the Girl to free-form improv guitarist Derek Bailey was dabbling with sped-up breakbeats, as were techno types such as

Underworld and Aphex Twin. LTJ Bukem launched a campaign to bring breakbeat rhythms to Britain's mainstream house clubs. Despite having played a big role in the gentrification process with his crusade for 'jazz-step,' Fabio railed against the reduction of drum and bass to mere 'wallpaper fodder' by its use in TV links and commercials. One of the most bizarre examples of this syndrome is Virgin Atlantic's use of Goldie's ghetto-blues ballad 'Inner City Life' as tranquilizing muzak to steady passengers' nerves before takeoff.

Just as the commercial success of hardcore in 1992 had prompted the first wave of 'darkside' tunes, so the hipster vogue for 'intelligent' inspired a defensive, back-to-the-underground initiative on the part of the original junglists. 'Intelligent' suddenly became an embarrassing term. Even those who had most profited from major-label interest in 'intelligence,' such as Goldie and Bukem, renounced the term, erroneously and rather disingenuously decrying it as a 'media invention' designed to divide the scene. Meanwhile, other producers started talking again about 'darkness' as a desirable attribute.

During 1993's darkside era, when jungle was banished from the media lime-light, AWOL had been *the* hardcore club. Especially after the demise of Rage, AWOL was where the scene's inner circle would gather late on a Saturday night to hear DJs such as Randall push the music to new heights of ruff-cut intensity. After being dislodged from its location at Islington's murky Paradise Club, AWOL settled late in 1995 at the SW1 Club in Victoria, re-establishing its former role there. While some of the drum and bass elite had moved on to Goldie's Metalheadz Sunday Sessions at the Blue Note, the core jungle audience were still attending AWOL or similar nights like Club UN and Innersense at the Lazerdrome (later renamed Millennium) – havens for those who refused the lure of 'intelligence.'

AWOL is not an acronym for 'absent without leave' but for 'a way of life.' If you are not involved in the scene, this article of faith – that buying records at specialist shops, going to clubs on the weekend, wearing MA2 jackets, and smoking a lot of spliff constitute a set of tribal folkways – can seem a tad overstated. But the frequency and conviction with which the claim 'jungle, it's a way of life' is restated suggests that, for the true disciple, something massive has been invested in this music. It was precisely this question – what's at stake for the fans?– that began to haunt my mind when I went to AWOL.

Ethnological research was not on my mind; fun was. I'm not sure if I found any, at least in the conventional sense, but the visit was a reaffirmation of flagging faith, a confirmation that jungle was alive and kickin' despite the surfeit of pseudo-jazzy tracks. It was also a reminder that, for all the success of album-length, home-listening drum and bass, jungle's meaning is still made on the dance floor. At massive volume, knowledge is visceral, something your body understands as it is seduced and ensnared by the paradoxes of the music: the way the breaks combine rollin' flow and disruptive instability, thereby instilling a contradictory mix of nonchalance and vigilance; the way the bass is at once wombing and menacing. AWOL is a real Temple of Boom; the low-end frequencies are so thick and enveloping they are swimmable. Inside the bass, you feel safe, and you feel dangerous. Like cruising in a car with a booming system, you are sealed by surround sound while marauding through urban space.

The odd thing is how subdued the atmosphere is. Smiles are rarer than hen's teeth and even among groups of friends, conversation is minimal. Nobody seems to be having fun. But 'fun' doesn't seem to be the reason every one is here. AWOL's resident crew of DJs – Randall, Mickey Finn, Kenny Ken, Darren Jay – sustain a mercilessly minimalist and militaristic assault, all ricocheting snares and atonal, metallic B-lines that bounce joylessly like ball-bearings in a pinball machine. The night stays at a plateau of punitive intensity, no crescendos or lulls, just steady jungalistic pressure.

By about 4 a.m. the dancers are jiggling about with a kind of listless mania. One girl twitches and bounces mechanically, her limp limbs inscribing repetitive patterns in the air, as if she is animated by some will other than her own. For a Saturday night out, the compensatory climax of a week's drudgery, this seems like hard work. I start to wonder if, like me, she got sucked in by 1991–2 'ardkore's explosive euphoria, its manic, fiery-eyed glee, then got carried along by the music's logical evolution only to wind up at another place altogether. Maybe that stunned, dispirited expression on her face comes from finding herself in the midst of an entirely new cultural formation, a 'way of life' that can no longer offer release, let alone a redemptive vision.

In 1996 a new subgenre of jungle coalesced called 'techstep,' a dirgelike death-funk characterized by harsh industrial timbres and bludgeoning 'butcher's block' beats. The term was coined by DJ/producers Ed Rush and Trace, who shaped the sound in tandem with engineer Nico of the No U Turn label. The 'tech' stood not for Detroit techno, dreamy and elegant, but for the brutalist Belgian hardcore of the early 1990s. Paying homage to R & S classics such as 'Dominator' and 'Mentasm,' to artists such as T99 and Frank de Wulf, Trace and Ed Rush deliber-ately affirmed a crucial white European element that had been written out of jungle's history.

The other important source for techstep was the first era of 'darkside,' as pioneered by Reinforced artists such as Doc Scott and 4 Hero. This was when the teenage DJs Trace and Ed Rush cut their production teeth with sinister classics such as 'Lost Entity' and 'Bludclot Artattack.' The name 'Ed Rush' sounds like a take on 'head rush,' early rave slang for a temporary whiteout of consciousness caused by too many Es. There was a big difference between dark-side 1993 and techstep, though. The original dark-core had still oozed a sinister, sickly bliss on the border between loved-up and fucked-up. In 1996, with Ecstasy long out of favor, techstep was shaped by a different mindfuck of choice: hydroponically grown marijuana, aka 'skunk,' whose near-hallucinogenic levels of THC induce a sensory intensification without euphoria and a nerve-jangling paranoia perfect for jungle's tension-but-no-release rhythms.

If Belgian brutalism and early breakbeat 'ardkore resembled Sixties garage punk, techstep is like Seventies punk rock, insofar as it's not a simple back-to-basics maneuver, but an isolation and intensification of the most aggressive, non-R & B elements in its precursor. As the No U Turn squad honed their sound-and-vision, they accentuated the selfsame 'noise annoys' elements that punk exaggerated in garage rock: headbanger riffs and midfrequency blare. Where intelligent drum and bass suffers from an obsessive-compulsive cleanliness, techstep production is deliberately dirty, all dense murk and noxious drones. The defining aspect of the

No U Turn sound was its bass – a dense, humming miasma of low-end frequencies, as malignant as a cloud of poison gas-achieved by feeding the bass riffs through a guitar distortion pedal and a battery of effects. Another stylistic trait was the way techstep shunned the nimble fluency of jazzy-jungle's breakbeats in favor of relative simplicity and rigor. Although the breakbeats are still running at jungle's 160-and-rising beats-per-minute norm, techstep *feels* slower-fatigued, winded. In tracks such as Doc Scott's 'Drumz 95,' the emphasis is on the 80 bpm half-step, making you want to *stomp*, not sashay.

Techstep is a sadomasochistic sound. Edrush declared bluntly, 'I want to hurt people with my beats,' and one No U Turn release had the phrase 'hurter's mission' scratched into the vinyl. This terrorist stance is in marked contrast to the rhetoric of intelligent drum and bass artists, with their talk of 'educating' the audience, 'opening minds,' and 'easing the pressure' of urban life. Sonically, techstep's dry, clenched sound could not have been further from the massaging, muscle-relaxing stream of genteel sound oozed by DJs such as Bukem and Fabio, with its soothing synth washes and sax loops alarmingly reminiscent of Kenny G.

While the intelligent and jazz-step producers prided themselves on their 'musicality,' the techstep producers veered to the opposite extreme: a bracing 'antimusicality.' Incorporating atonal, unpitched timbres, nonmusical sounds, and horror movie soundtrack dissonance, the new artcore noir was simply far more avant-garde than the likes of Bukem. In an abiding confusion about what constitutes 'progression' in electronic music, the intelligent drum and bass producers were too deferential to traditional ideas about melody, arrangement, 'nice' textures, the importance of proper songs, and hands-on, real-time instrumentation.

By 1997, producers such as Nasty Habits/Doc Scott, Dom and Roland, Boymerang, and Optical had joined No U Turn on their 'hurter's mission.' Techstep got even more industrial and stiff-jointed, at times verging on gabba or a syncopated, sped-up update of the Swans. Above all, the music got *colder*. The Numanoid synth riff on Nasty Habits' awesome 'Shadow Boxing' sears the ear with its glacial grandeur, while the trudging two-step beat suggests a commando jogging under napalm skies with a rocket launcher on his hip. No U Turn themselves reached something of a pinnacle with the dark exultation of Trace/Nico's 'Squadron' whose *Carmina Burana*-gone-cyberpunk fanfares slash and scythe like the Grim Reaper.

Where did the apocalyptic glee, the morbid and perverse *jouissance* in tech-step stem from? Nico described the music-making process-all-night, red-eye sessions conducted in a ganja fog as a horrible experience that poisoned his nervous system with tension. Ed Rush talked of deliberately smoking weed to get 'dark, evil thoughts,' the kind of skunkanoia without which he could not achieve the right vibe for his tracks. Like Wu-Tang-style horror-core rap, techstep seemed based on the active pursuit of phobia and psychosis as entertainment, which begged the question: what exactly were the social conditions that had created such a big audience for this kind of music?

If rave culture was a displaced form of working-class collectivity, with its 'love, peace, and unity' running counter to Thatcherite social atomization, then jungle is rave music after the death of the rave ethos. Since 1993 and hard-core's slide into the twilight zone, debates about 'where did our love go?' convulsed the UK break-beat community, with grim tales of muggings outside clubs, of fights and 'crack' vibes inside. Disenchanted ravers sloped off to form the happy hard-core scene. Others defended the demise of the euphoric vibe, arguing that jungle's atmosphere was not moody, it was 'serious.'

In the absence of Ecstasy, jungle began to embrace an ideology of *realness* that paralleled the worldview of American hard-core rap. In hiphop, 'real' has a double meaning. First, it means authentic, uncompromised music that refuses to sell out to the music industry. 'Real' also signifies that the music reflects a 'reality' constituted by late-capitalist economic instability, institutionalized racism, and increased surveillance and harassment of youth by police. Hence, tracks such as T. Power's 'Police State' and Photek's neurotic 'The Hidden Camera', lyric-free critiques of a country that conducts the most intense surveillance of its own citizenry in the world (most UK city centers now have spy cameras). 'Real' means the death of the social; it means corporations that respond to increased profits not by raising pay or improving benefits but by downsizing.

Gangsta hardstep shares Wu-Tang Clan's neomedieval vision of late capitalism, as influenced by martial arts and Mafia movies whose universe revolves around concepts of righteous violence and blood honor. Techstep is more influenced by dystopian sci-fi movies such as *Blade Runner, Robocop, Terminator, et al.* which contain a subliminally anticapitalist message, imagining the future as a return to the Dark Ages, complete with fortress cities and bandit clans. Hence, No U Turn tracks such as 'The Droid' and 'Replicants' and Adam F's 'Metropolis.' 'Here is a group trying to accomplish one thing . . . *to get into the future'* goes the sample in Trace/Nico's 'Amtrak.' Given the scary millennial soundscape techstep paints, why the hurry to get there? The answer: in a new Dark Age, it is the 'dark' that will come into their own. 'Darkness' is where primordial energies meet digital technique, where it gets scientific. Identify with this marauding music, and you define yourself as predator, not prey.

What you affiliate yourself to with techstep is the will-to-power of technology itself, the motor behind late capitalism as it rampages over human priorities and tears communities apart. The name No U Turn captures this sense that *there's no turning back*. The pervasive sense of slipping into a new Dark Age, of an insidious breakdown of the social contract, generates anxieties that are repressed but resurface in unlikely ways and places. Resistance does not necessarily take the 'logical' form of collective activism (unions, left-wing politics); it can be so distorted and imaginatively impoverished by the conditions of capitalism itself that it expresses itself as, say, the anticorporate nostalgia of America's right-wing militias or as a sort of hyperindividualistic survivalism.

In jungle, the response is a 'realism' that accepts a socially constructed reality as 'natural.' To 'get real' is to confront a state of nature where dog eats dog, where you are either a winner or a loser, and where most will be losers. There is a cold rage seething in jungle, but it is expressed within the terms of an anticapitalist yet nonsocialist politics, and expressed defensively: as a determination that the underground will not be coopted by the corporate mainstream. 'Underground' can be understood sociologically as a metaphor for the underclass, or psychologically as a metaphor for a fortress psyche: the survivalist self, primed and ready for combat.

Jungle's sound world constitutes a sort of abstract social realism; when I listen to techstep, the beats sound like collapsing (new) buildings and the bass feels like the social fabric shredding. Jungle's treacherous rhythms offer its audience an education in anxiety. 'It is defeat that *you* must learn to prepare for' runs the martial arts movie sample in Source Direct's 'The Cult,' a track that pioneered the post-techstep style 'neurofunk' – clinical production, foreboding ambient drones, blips 'n' blurts of electronic noise, and chugging, curiously inhibited two-step beats that don't even sound like breakbeats anymore. Neurofunk is the fun-free culmination of jungle's strategy of 'cultural resistance': the eroticization of anxiety. Immerse yourself in the phobic and you make dread your element.

The battery of sensations offered by a six-hour stint at AWOL, Millennium, or any 'nonintelligent' jungle club induces a mixture of shellshock and future shock. Alvin Toffler defined F-shock as what happens when the human adaptive mechanism seizes up in response to an overload of stimuli, novelty, surprise. Triggering neural reflexes and fight-or-flight responses, jungle's rhythmic assault course hypes up the listener's adaptive capability in readiness for the worst the twenty-first century has up its sleeve. If jungle is a martial art form, clubs such as AWOL are church for the soul-jah and killah priest, inculcating a kind of spiritual fortitude.

All this is why going to AWOL is serious bizness, not 'fun.' Jungle is the living death of rave, the sound of living with and living through the dream's demise. Every synapse-shredding snare and cranium-cracking bass bomb is an alarm call saying 'wake up, that dream is over. Time to get *real*.'

Chapter 10

Philip Auslander

LIVENESS
Performance and the anxiety
of simulation

I N HIS BOOK ON THE POLITICAL ECONOMY of music, Jacques Attali offers
a useful description of the cultural economy in which performance currently takes
place. He distinguishes an economy based on representation from one based on
repetition:

> Stated very simply, representation in the system of commerce is that
> which arises from a singular act; repetition is that which is mass-
> produced. Thus, a concert is a representation, but also a meal a la carte
> in a restaurant; a phonograph record or a can of food is repetition.
>
> Attali, 1985: 41

In his historical analysis, Attali points out that although 'representation emerged
with capitalism' when the sponsorship of concerts became a profitable enterprise
and not merely the prerogative of a feudal lord, capitalism ultimately 'lost interest
in the economy of representation.' Repetition, the mass-production of cultural
objects, held greater promise for capital because whereas 'In representation, a work
is generally heard only once – it is a unique moment; in repetition, potential hearings
are stockpiled' (Attali, 1985: 41). By being recorded and mediatized, performance
becomes an accumulable value, a commodity.

Before engaging these issues, I want to problematize the binary logic of traditional theorizations that place the live and the mediatized in a relation of opposition:
an antagonistic relation in which virtuous live performance is menaced by evil
mediatization. Liveness is depicted as engaged in a life-and-death struggle with its
insidious Other – from this point of view, once live performance succumbs to
mediatization, it loses its ontological integrity. This agon of liveness and mediatization is the ideologically charged binary opposition that authorizes the privileging
of the live in these theorizations.

I would argue that the live and the mediatized exist in a relation of mutual dependence and imbrication, not one of opposition. The live is, in a sense, only a secondary effect of mediating technologies. Prior to the advent of those technologies (e.g. photography, telegraphy, phonography) there was no such thing as the 'live,' for that category has meaning only in relation to an opposing possibility. Ancient Greek theater, for example, was not live because there was no possibility of recording it. (I would suppose that the concept of 'liveness' as we understand it was unthinkable by the Greeks for this reason.) In a special case of Jean Baudrillard's well-known dictum that 'the very definition of the real has become that of which it is possible to give an equivalent reproduction' (Baudrillard, 1983: 146), the 'live' has always been defined as that which can be recorded.

Recent developments have problematized the traditional assumption that the live precedes the mediatized by making it obvious that the apparatus of reproduction and its attendant phenomenology are inscribed within our experience of the live. Straightforward examples abound in the use of video screens at sporting events and rock concerts. The spectator sitting in the back rows of a Rolling Stones or Bruce Springsteen concert, or even a Bill Cosby stand-up comedy performance, is present at a live performance, but hardly participates in it as such since his/her main experience of the performance is to read it from a video monitor. The same is true for the spectators at major league baseball games and other sporting events who now watch significant portions of the games they are attending on giant video screens. The rhetoric of mediatization, such as the instant replay, the 'simulcast,' and the close-up, at one time understood to be secondary elaborations of an originary live event, are now constitutive of the live event itself. The games – their scheduling, the distribution of time within them, their rules, and so forth – have themselves been molded by their entry into the economy of repetition which demands that the form of the games as live events be determined by the requirements of mediatization.

The net effect of these developments is that live performance now serves to naturalize mediatized representations. Roger Copeland has pointed out, for example, that 'on Broadway these days even nonmusical plays are routinely miked, in part because the results sound more 'natural' to an audience whose ears have been conditioned by stereo television, high fidelity LP's, and compact disks' (Copeland, 1990: 29). (The use of the headset mike to generate an amplified voice invisibly would be another example of this phenomenon.) As the personnel involved in staging Madonna's tours freely admit, the goal of their productions and of many rock and pop concerts today is to reproduce the artist's music videos as nearly as possible in a live setting on the assumption that the audience comes to the live show expecting to see what it has already seen on television.

The pop concert as re-enactment of the music video is, in effect, a new performance subgenre. One could say that because the music video sets the standard for what is 'real' in this realm, only a re-creation of its imagery can count as 'realistic.' Reciprocally, the fact that images from Madonna's videos can be recreated in a live setting enhances the realism of the original videos. Live performance thus has become the means by which mediatized representations are naturalized, according to a simple logic that appeals to our nostalgia for what we assumed was the immediate: if the mediatized image can be recreated in a live setting, it must have been 'real' to begin with. 'What irony: people originally intended to use the record to preserve the performances and today the performance is only successful as a simulacrum of the record' (Attali, 1985: 85). This schema resolves (or fails to resolve) into an impossible oscillation between the two poles of what had seemed to be a clear opposition: whereas mediatized performance derives its authority from its reference to the live or the real, the live now derives its authority from its reference to the mediatized, which derives its authority from its reference to the live, etc.

All of these instances exemplify the way mediatization is now explicitly and implicitly conjoined to live experience. The paradigm that best describes the current relationship between the live and the mediatized is the Baudrillardian paradigm of *simulation*: 'nothing separates one pole from the other, the initial from the terminal: there is just a sort of contraction into each other, a fantastic telescoping, a collapsing of the two traditional poles into one another: an IMPLOSION . . .' Baudrillard states, with typical insistence, about such implosions: '*this is where simulation begins*' (*Simulations*, 1983: 57; original emphasis).

In the case of live and mediatized performance, the result of implosion is that a seemingly secure opposition is now a site of anxiety, an anxiety that infects all who have an interest in maintaining the distinction between the live and the mediatized. It is manifest in some performance theorists' assertions of the integrity of the live and the corrupt, coopted nature of the mediatized. Anxiety is also manifest in the response of capital to the collapse of this distinction. Simulation occurs at the moment a cultural economy is thoroughly saturated with repetitions. It threatens to undermine the economy of repetition by imploding oppositions on which that economy depends: in order to render performance in a repeatable form, there must be an 'original' performance to reify. In the remainder of this essay, I will analyze the crisis surrounding the implosion of the opposition between live and mediatized performance by examining an event that crystallizes the issues I have been discussing here. The event is the Milli Vanilli scandal of 1990, which occurred at the contentious intersection of discourses of liveness, mediatization, capital, and technology in the realm of popular music. I want also to suggest that Baudrillard's contention that the triumph of simulation means the end of power as it is has been traditionally understood is problematic. In Baudrillard's schema, when the binary implodes, when it is no longer possible to distinguish between the two terms, ideological opposition, indeed the whole concept of ideology itself, is voided of meaning. While I find Baudrillard's paradigm of simulation persuasive as a description of the situation of performance (and many other) discourses in a mediatized culture, I am not convinced that the advent of simulation necessarily implies a voiding of the existing structures of power and ideology.

In the spring of 1990, the German pop singing and dancing duo Milli Vanilli was awarded the Best New Artist Grammy for 1989. The award preceded six months of speculation and commentary in the media concerning performers, including Milli Vanilli, who allegedly lip-synched to pre-recorded vocals in concert (Madonna, Michael Jackson, Paula Abdul, and many others were similarly accused). Legislators in many states followed the lead of those in New York and New Jersey in introducing bills mandating that tickets and posters promoting concerts during which performers lip-synch state that fact; stiff fines were to be levied against violators. The legislators claimed to see the lip-synch question as a consumer issue.

In November, Milli Vanilli's producer admitted that the duo had not in fact sung on the recording for which they were awarded the Grammy, which was then rescinded, much to the embarrassment of the National Academy of Recording Arts and Sciences (NARAS).

The whole lip-synching controversy inspired a great deal of commentary across the country, prompting a spate of newspaper articles with titles such as 'That Syncing [sic] Feeling' (Detroit News, July 31,1990). Most of the commentary was adamantly opposed to the practice, though virtually all of it also admitted that the main audiences for the performers in question, mostly young teenagers, did not seem to care whether their idols actually sing or not. (My own younger students, polled in the fall of 1990, felt precisely that way.)

Jon Pareles, a New York Times popular music journalist, inveighed against the use of both lip-synching and computer-programmed musical instruments in concert, upholding the value of traditional live performance. 'I'm not ready for the new paradigm . . .' he wrote. 'The spontaneity; uncertainty and ensemble coordination that automation eliminates are exactly what I go to concerts to see' (Parales, 1990: 25). The new paradigm to which Pareles refers is the paradigm of simulation which has usurped the paradigms of representation and reproduction in popular music and, arguably, in the culture at large. The performances he discusses are simulacra in the strict Baudrillardian sense: like the recordings they incorporate and the music videos they emulate, they are re-creations of performances that never took place, representations without referents in the real.

With the award to Milli Vanilli, the Grammies could be said to have entered the age of simulation, an age the music industry itself had entered long before. The process of which Milli Vanilli had been a part is quite typical of the way that popular music has been produced since at least the early l960s: there are many well-known cases of groups being formed by producers specifically to exploit recordings made using other voices. It is also the case that rumors that Milli Vanilli did not sing live and had not sung on their album were in circulation as much as a year before the Grammy vote. In fact, one member of the NARAS voted for Milli Vanilli even though he had specific knowledge that they had not sung on the record (Britt G4). He knew this because he was their vocal coach (though exactly what he coached is not clear). The award to Milli Vanilli constituted the recognition of a particularly impressive simulation by an industry devoted to the creation of simulations. How, then, do we explain l'affaire Milli Vanilli?

I propose that we begin by recognizing, as Baudrillard says of Watergate, that the Milli Vanilli 'scandal' was not a real scandal at all but rather a scandal effect used by agencies of power and capital to 'regenerate a reality principle in distress' (Simulations, 1983: 26–7). As Baudrillard points out, power requires for its working a matrix of significant oppositions and 'capital, which is immoral and unscrupulous, can only function behind a moral super structure . . .' (Simulations, 1983: 27). Simulation threatens the structures on which power and capital depend by implying that moral, political, and other distinctions are no longer meaningful: the Right is the Left, the Mediatized is the Live. 'When it is threatened today by simulation (the threat of vanishing in the play of signs), power risks the real, risks crisis . . .' (Simulations, 1983: 44).

I am arguing that a scandal effect had to be created around Milli Vanilli because the music industry and the concentric rings of power that attend it (including music critics) could not afford to admit that it is an industry devoted to simulation. If the distinction between live and mediatized performance were to be revealed as empty, then the ability to sell the same material over and over again – as a studio recording, as a music video, as a live performance, as a video of the live performance, as a live album – would disappear. The Grammies' ideological procedure of awarding the prize to performers as though they are the authors of their recordings and not merely as Deyan Sudjic puts it, 'the tip of an elaborate commercial network of investors, managers agents and publishers' (Sudjic, 1989: 143), would be exposed. And what of critics such as Pareles? On what basis will they discriminate among recordings and performances once it is acknowledged that all are simply different articulations of the same code, recombinant variations on the same genetic material?

Consider two phenomena that confirm the industry's interest in maintaining the value of liveness as a marker of the real: the recently renewed emphasis within pop music on acoustic performance, of which MTV's 'Unplugged' program is the apotheosis, and the multiple awards given to Eric Clapton at the 1993 Grammy ceremony. These two phenomena overlap significantly, since the recording for which Clapton won his awards was the live album derived from his acoustic performance on 'Unplugged.'

That the lauds heaped on Clapton in the spring of 1993 were based in nostalgia for a pre-Milli Vanilli time when pop musicians could actually play and sing is obvious. Both Clapton's *Unplugged* album and the television series that generated it are overloaded with signs for reality and authenticity that are conventional within the realm of rock music. At least since the early 1960s, acoustic playing has stood for authenticity, sincerity, and rootsiness; hence, the dismay that greeted Bob Dylan's use of an electric guitar at the 1965 Newport Folk Festival. Live performance, too, has long been understood as the realm of the authentic, the true test of musicianship undisguised by studio trickery. It is clear that the MTV show 'Unplugged,' which takes acoustic performance and liveness as its twin imperatives, ironically for consumption as television, is a veritable cornucopia of signs of the real as that category is articulated within the context of the rock and folk-rock music of the 1960s.

The fact that Clapton's *Unplugged* album is largely given over to performances of venerable blues numbers is another bid for authenticity and also an evocation of myths of origin: both rock music's ancestry in the blues and Clapton's own personal history as a rock music legend who launched his career in the mid-1960s as a faithful devotee of American blues guitar styles and who, despite various changes in his music over time, has never fully abandoned that original commitment to the bedrock of the music. These two strands intertwine in one of the most popular selections from the record, Clapton's new acoustic rendition of his song 'Layla.' Thus, both the myth of the blues as rock's progenitor (and rock's consequent mythological claim to authenticity as folk expression), and Clapton's own authenticity as a blues-educated rock legend, are brought into play.

At the risk of seeming cynical, I will also suggest that the song singled out for particular Grammy recognition from Clapton's *Unplugged* album, 'Tears in Heaven,' itself contributes greatly to the real-effect sought by the music industry in the wake of Milli Vanilli. The song is a memorial to Clapton's young son who died in a freak accident. Clearly, this corresponds to what Baudrillard calls 'an escalation of the true, of the lived experience.' As opposed to Milli Vanilli, who won an award for a song they neither composed nor sang, Clapton was rewarded for a song that he not only wrote and actually performed but that also alludes to his personal tragedy. Does it get any 'realer' than this? The song's regret at the death of an individual reinstates the value of the unique that has lost ground in the current cultural moment. In this age of digital cloning, the model is infinitely replicable – death is no longer the ultimate limit, as can be seen from the posthumous performances by musicians and, now, actors cloned from their existing recordings and films. Through the specificity of the personal experience it describes and the personal relationship of singer to song, Clapton's performance returns us to an economy of representation in which the singular event is valorized. By poignantly reinstating death as an unmitigable absence and, thus, apparently recovering the life/death opposition from implosion, the song valorizes living presence and underscores 'Unplugged's' assertion of its own liveness and authenticity. All of this, however, is merely another diversionary tactic intended to mask the fact that the music industry is now fully given over to simulation. Clapton's performance of the song,which took place on television, was designed from the start to occupy a position in the economy of repetition through its many lives as cable show, compact disc, and videocassette. If Milli Vanilli provided capital with the opportunity to stage a scandal-effect, Clapton's meditation on living presence and the abundance of signs insisting on 'Unplugged's' status as live event themselves contribute to the simulation of liveness, the creation of a liveness-effect that also appears to denounce simulation while actually furthering its dominance.

It may be that the implosion of the opposition between live and mediatized performance in popular music from which this discussion departs was actually a *simulation* of implosion created by an agency of capital to consolidate and extend its power by *recuperating simulation itself as one of its strategies*. It seems to be just as possible to see simulation as the latest weapon in the arsenal of capital (or at least as a phenomenon coopted by capital) as to insist that it means the end of the entire system of real power within which capital operates. At the end of a passage I quoted earlier, Baudrillard claims that when power 'is threatened today by simulation . . . [it] risks the real . . . This is a question of life and death for it. But it is too late' (*Simulations*, 1983: 44). But is it, in fact, too late? Or is it possible that simulation can be brought into the system of power to be used by capital to maintain its dominance, as I have suggested in my interpretation of the machinations of MTV?

At the very least, it would seem that the development that Baudrillard treats as a *fait accompli* is actually in the process of occurring. Assuming that we are currently living through such a transitional moment, the problem for cultural criticism is to find ways of identifying sites on which the crises and anxieties that mark this transition occur and to use them as footholds, however tenuous, for critique. This critique, however, must deal realistically with the cultural economy within which representation and reproduction occur, an economy that is, at least in the West and the technocratic East, thoroughly dominated by repetition and mediatization. Cultural criticism must walk a tightrope between uncritical acceptance or cynical celebration of new technologies and cultural configurations on the one hand,

and a nostalgic commitment to categories that are very nearly obsolete on the other. I alluded earlier to the fact that the young audiences for Milli Vanilli and other acts are not concerned with their idols' liveness: simulation does not create anxiety for them in the way it does for the generation of Clapton's earliest fans and for performance theorists. In giving us both Clapton and Milli Vanilli, MTV may be working both sides of the generational street – placating rock's older fans with simulations of authenticity while simultaneously ushering in the new paradigm for the children of those fans. When this latter generation assumes 'power,' the regime of simulation may be in full force, its expansion into the realms of the social and the political may be complete.

Subcultures, scenes and tribes

Introduction to Part Three

■ Andy Bennett

A CRUCIAL ASPECT OF POPULAR MUSIC is its significance as a catalyst for forms of social identity. Collective participation in popular music provides an important sense of belonging and group membership. Since the early 1970s, a number of theoretical models have been put forward by academic researchers as a means of attempting to understand the relationship between popular music, social action and collective identity. Initially, a dominant paradigm in such work was the concept of 'subculture'. Borrowed from the Chicago School by the Birmingham Centre for Contemporary Cultural Studies (CCCS) and adapted for the study of post-Second World War British youth cultures, such as Teddy boys, mods and skinheads, 'subculture' became synonymous with forms of class-based youth resistance in which fashion and music were argued to be key resources. During the 1980s, subcultural theory was criticised on a number of grounds, ranging from the male-centeredness of its subject matter to the rigid interpretation of youth culture as a class-based phenomenon. Criticisms were also raised concerning the lack of empirical evidence to support the claims made by subcultural theorists, the original CCCS work having relied largely on theoretical abstraction and textual analysis. Despite the various shortcomings identified in the CCCS work, however, the term 'subculture' itself remained uncontested, even among those theorists who were most critical of subculture's application in the CCCS work. This changed during the 1990s with the publication of a number of studies that offered new conceptual models for under-standing how audiences appropriate and use music and its attendant resources in strategies of resistance against mainstream society.

The selections presented in this section of the Reader illustrate the new directions in which research on popular music audiences has gone since the mid-1990s. Thornton's work on contemporary dance-club crowds was highly influential in this respect. In Chapter 11, Thornton rejects the CCCS's theoretical model of subculture as unworkable due to the rigid class-based interpretation at the heart of its analysis. She focuses instead on the mainstream/alternative division implied in subculture. Basing her ideas around Bourdieu's work on cultural capital and social status, Thornton argues that 'serious' clubbers acquire authentic status in the club culture environment through the acquisition and display of 'subcultural capital'. This involves creating the right visual image, becoming a proficient dancer, and demonstrating an advanced knowledge of current and past trends in dance music. For Thornton, then, involvement in contemporary 'club culture' is less about class than the possession of the required musical knowledge and stylistic sensibilities, these being essential for acceptance into club culture's inner circle.

Bennett is also critical of the class-based focus of subcultural analysis, arguing in Chapter 12 that if youth cultural groups were ever as structurally defined as the CCCS maintains, this is far less so in contemporary society. However, in contrast to Thornton, who retains the notion of subcultural belonging in her work, Bennett rejects subculture in favour of an alternative conceptual model. According to Bennett, contemporary youth cultural formations exhibit may of the qualities identified by Maffesoli (1996) in his concept of neotribes. For Maffesoli, late capitalist society is characterised by new leisure and consumer-based forms of tribal association, the latter having replaced structural categories, such as class, gender and race, as sites of social bonding. Maffesoli further argues that because social identities are now more reflexive and pluralistic, individuals may identify with and move between a number of tribes. Consequently, tribes are highly fragile and temporal groupings. Bennett applies the concept of neotribe to contemporary dance-music, suggesting that the temporality of the dance music event, together with the opportunities it offers for momentarily engaging with the crowd in a relatively anonymous and arbitrary fashion, closely corresponds with Maffesoli's description of neo-tribal gatherings.

The 1990s also saw the publication of a series of studies utilising the concept of 'scene'. While both 'subculture' and 'neo-tribe' have been used primarily as a means of theorising the process of music consumption, 'scene' is concerned with a far broader spectrum of musical activities which also include performance, production, marketing, promotion and distribution. Originally an everyday term used to describe a cluster of musicalised practices situated in a particular urban or rural location, since the publication of a highly influential article by Will Straw in 1991, scene has been recast to encompass local, trans-local and even virtual activities. Research on popular music scenes has also illustrated the relationship between local and global forces in shaping the ways in which music is produced, performed and received in particular places. Important in this respect is the work of Shank on the music scene in Austin, Texas. In Chapter 13, Shank focuses on a local punk rock venue in Austin, examining how the venue became a space in which the reactionary message of punk rock was rearticulated to satirically address prevalent Texan sensibilities and attitudes towards a range of issues, including politics, gender and sexuality.

Scene studies have also demonstrated how, in addition to music and style, a range of other scene-practices are also important to the articulation of collective identities. In his study of the American Alternative Scene in Chapter 14, Tsitsos focuses on slam dancing and moshing, two aggressive contemporary dance forms in which the participants slam into one another. As Tsitsos explains, although from the perspective of an external observer the violent motions of slam dancers and moshers appear uncontrolled, they are nevertheless encoded with particular rule systems that participants must observe. Moreover, according to Tsitsos, every dancer understands the embodied significance of slam dancing and moshing as a form of resistance against society, and as a means of releasing tension and aggression without resorting to acts of actual physical violence.

Although punk, alternative and other popular music scenes have initially developed at a local level, global flows of music, musicians, DJs, publications, together with the electronic communication made possible by the internet, has produced trans-local connections between similar scenes in different parts of the world. In his description of 'Death' and 'Black' metal in Chapter 15, Kahn-Harris examines the interplay between the local and trans-local with reference to Brazilian Death Metal band Sepultura. Beginning with a look at the band's roots in Brazil, Kahn-Harris considers how Sepultura's transformation into a globally successful performing and recording act was facilitated through an established trans-local network of Death Metal promoters, record labels and touring circuits. At the same time, observes Kahn-Harris, Sepultura's global success served to distance the group from their native country, with the result that in their later work Sepultura attempted to return to their roots – to articulate through their music a sense of Brazilianness.

Chapter 11

Sarah Thornton

UNDERSTANDING HIPNESS
'Subcultural capital' as feminist tool

'**C**LUBLAND', AS MANY CALL IT, is difficult terrain to map. Club nights continually modify their style, change their name and move location. Individual clubbers and ravers are part of one crowd, then another, then grow out of going out dancing altogether. The musics with which club crowds affiliate themselves are characterized by a fast turnover of singles, artists and genres. Club culture is faddish and fragmented. Even if the music and the clothes are globally marketed, the crowds are local and segregated and subject to distinctions dependent on the smallest of cultural minutiae. For these reasons, many clubbers would say that it is impossible to chart the patterns of national club cultures. Nevertheless, they constantly catalogue and classify youth cultures according to taste in music, forms of dance, kinds of ritual and styles of clothing. They carry around images of the social worlds that make up club culture. These mental maps, rich in cultural detail and value judgement, offer them a distinct 'sense of their place but also a sense of the other's place' (Bourdieu, 1990a: 131).

In trying to make sense of the values and hierarchies of club culture, I have drawn from the work of the French sociologist Pierre Bourdieu, particularly his book *Distinction* (1984). Bourdieu writes extensively about what he calls 'cultural capital' or knowledge that is accumulated through upbringing and education which confers social status. Cultural capital is the linchpin of a system of distinction in which cultural hierarchies correspond to social ones and people's tastes are predominantly a marker of class. For instance, in Britain, accent has long been a key indicator of cultural capital, and university degrees have long been cultural capital in institutionalized form. Cultural capital is different from *economic capital*. High levels of income and property often correlate with high levels of cultural capital, but the two can also conflict. Comments about the 'nouveau riche' or people who are 'flash' disclose the frictions between those rich in cultural capital but relatively poor in economic capital (such as artists or academics) and those rich in economic capital but less affluent in cultural capital (such as business executives and professional football players).

One of the many advantages of Bourdieu's schema is that it moves away from rigidly vertical models of the social structure. Bourdieu locates social groups in a highly complex multidimensional space rather than on a linear scale or ladder. His theoretical framework even includes discussion of a third category – *social capital* – which stems not so much from *what* you know as *who* you know (and who knows you). Connections in the form of friends, relations, associates and acquaintances can all bestow status. The aristocracy has always privileged social over other forms of capital, as have many private members' clubs and old boys' networks. The notion of social capital is also useful in explaining the power of fame or of being known by those one doesn't know, particularly when the famous consolidate their social capital in heavily publicized 'romances', weddings and break-ups.

In addition to these three major types of capital – cultural, economic and social – Bourdieu elaborates many subcategories of capital that operate within particular fields such as 'linguistic', 'academic', 'intellectual', 'information' and 'artistic' capital. One characteristic that unifies these capitals is that they are all at play within Bourdieu's own field, within *his* social world of players with high volumes of institutionalized cultural capital. However, it is possible to observe subspecies of capital operating within other less priviledged domains. In thinking through Bourdieu's theories in relation to the terrain of youth culture, I have come to conceive of 'hipness' as a form of *subcultural capital*.

Subcultural capital confers status on its owner in the eyes of the relevant beholder. In many ways it affects the standing of the young like its adult equivalent. Subcultural capital can be *objectified* or *embodied*. Just as books and paintings display cultural capital in the home, so subcultural capital is objectified in the form of fashionable haircuts and well-assembled record collections (full of carefully selected limited edition, 'white label', twelve-inches and the like). Just as cultural capital is personified in good manners and witty conversation, so subcultural capital is embodied in the form of being 'in the know', using (but not over-using) current slang and looking as if you were born to perform the latest dance styles. Both cultural and subcultural capital put a premium on the 'second nature' of their knowledges. Nothing depletes capital more than the sight of someone trying too hard. For example, fledgling clubbers of fifteen or sixteen wishing to get into what they perceive as a sophisticated dance club will often reveal their inexperience by over-dressing or confusing 'coolness' with an exaggerated cold blank stare.

It has been argued that what ultimately defines cultural capital as capital is its 'convertibility' into economic capital (Garnham and Williams, 1986: 123). While subcultural capital may not convert into economic capital with the same ease or financial reward as cultural capital, a variety of occupations and incomes can be gained as a result of 'hipness'. DJs, club organizers, clothes designers, music and style journalists and various record industry professionals all make a living from their subcultural capital. Moreover, within club cultures, people in these professions often enjoy a lot of respect not only because of their high volume of subcultural capital, but also from their role in defining and creating it. In knowing, owning and playing the music, DJs in particular can be positioned as the masters of the scene.

However, sometimes the club organizers who know who's who and gather the right crowd can be perceived as top dog.

Although it converts into economic capital, subcultural capital is not as class-bound as cultural capital. This is not to say that class is irrelevant, simply that it does not correlate in any one-to-one way with levels of youthful subcultural capital. In fact, class is wilfully obfuscated by subcultural distinctions. For instance, it is not uncommon for private-school educated youth to adopt working-class accents during their clubbing years. Subcultural capitals fuel rebellion against, or perhaps escape from, the trappings of parental class. The assertion of subcultural distinction relies, in part, on a fantasy of classlessness. This may be one reason why music is the cultural form privileged within youth's subcultural worlds. Age is the most significant demographic when it comes to taste in music, to the extent that playing music in the family home is the most common source of generational conflict (after arguments over clothes) (Euromonitor, 1989). By contrast, the relation between class and musical taste is much more difficult to chart. The most clearly up-market genre, classical music, is also the least disliked of all types of music by most sectors of the population, hence its abundant use in television commercials to advertise products of all kinds, from butter and baked beans to BMWs.

One reason why subcultural capital clouds class backgrounds is that it has long defined itself as extra-curricular, as knowledge one cannot learn in school. As a result, after age, the social difference along which it is aligned most systematically is, in fact, gender. On average, girls invest more of their time and identity in doing well at school. Boys, by contrast, spend more time and money on leisure activities such as going out, listening to records and reading music magazines (Mintel, 1988a; Euromonitor, 1989).

But this doesn't mean that girls do not participate in the economy of subcultural capital. On the contrary, if girls opt out of the game of 'hipness', they will often defend their tastes (particularly their taste for pop music) with expressions such as: 'It's crap but I like it'. In so doing, they acknowledge the subcultural hierarchy and accept their lowly position within it. If, on the other hand, they refuse this defeatism, female clubbers and ravers are usually careful to distance themselves from the degraded pop culture of 'Sharon and Tracy' (widely evoked synecdoches of an uncool 'mainstream', see p.102).

A critical difference between subcultural capital (as I explore it) and cultural capital (as Bourdieu develops it) is that the media are a primary factor governing the circulation of the former. Several writers have remarked on the absence of television and radio from Bourdieu's theories of cultural hierarchy (Frow, 1987; Garnham, 1993). Another scholar has argued that they are absent from his schema because 'the cultural distinctions of particular taste publics collapse in the common cultural domain of broadcasting' (Scannell, 1989: 155). I would argue that it is impossible to understand the distinctions of youth cultures without some systematic investigation of their media consumption. For, within the economy of subcultural capital, the media are not simply another symbolic good or marker of distinction (which is the way Bourdieu describes films and newspapers vis-à-vis cultural capital), but a network crucial to the definition and distribution of cultural knowledge. In other words, the difference between being *in* or *out* of fashion, high or low in subcultural capital, correlates in complex ways with degrees of media coverage, creation and exposure (see Chapter 4 on 'The Media Development of Subcultures' in Thornton, 1995).

The idea that concern for cultural value and status is common in popular cultures seemingly devoid of them is one which, once stated, seems obvious. However, the many ramifications of the idea are less clear and little explored. A great deal of extant research on youth subcultures has both over-politicized their leisure and at the same time neglected examining the subtle relations of power at play within them. I found the imagined social worlds of the youth who regularly attended dance clubs to be impossible to ignore. They bore witness to fantasies of classlessness where leisure (not work) and age (not income) were key sources of self-esteem. They also relied heavily on denigrated feminine others to elevate, or rather distinguish, themselves from a projected lumpen mass.

When I began my research in 1988, hard-core clubbers of all kinds located the mainstream in the 'chartpop disco'. 'Chartpop' did not refer to the many different genres that made it into the top forty singles sales chart as much as a particular kind of dance music that included bands such as Erasure and the Pet Shop Boys, but was identified most strongly with the music of Stock, Aitken and Waterman (the producers of Kylie Minogue, Jason Donovan, Bananarama, Kim Appleby and other dance-oriented acts). Although one was most likely to hear this playlist at a provincial gay club, the oft-repeated, almost universally accepted stereotype of the chartpop disco was that it was a place where 'Sharon and Tracy dance around their handbags'. This crowd was considered unhip and unsophisticated. They were denigrated for having indiscriminate musical tastes, lacking individuality and being amateurs in the art of clubbing. Who else would lug around that uptight feminine appendage, that burdensome emblem of adulthood – the handbag? 'Sharon and Tracy' were put down for being part of a homogeneous herd that was overwhelmingly interested in the sexual and social rather than musical aspects of clubs. Many clubbers spoke of 'drunken cattle markets'; one envisioned a scene where 'tacky men drinking pints of best bitter pull girls in white high heels and Miss Selfridge's miniskirts'.

Towards the middle of 1989, in the wake of extensive newspaper coverage of acid-house culture, clubbers began to talk of a new mainstream – or rather, at first, it was described as a second-wave of media-inspired, sheep-like acid-house fans. This group was said to be populated by 'mindless ravers' or 'acid Teds'. Teds were understood to travel in same-sex mobs, support football teams, wear kickers boots and be 'out of their heads'. Like Sharon and Tracy, they were white, heterosexual and working-class. But unlike the girls, the ravers espoused the subterranean values proper to a youth culture (like their laddish namesakes, the Teds or Teddy boys of the 1950s) at least in their predilection for drugs such as Ecstasy.

However, when the culture came to be positioned as truly 'mainstream' rather than just behind the times, it was feminized. This shift coincided with the dominance of house and techno in the compilation album sales charts through 1990–1. By the end of this period, talk of 'acid Teds' was superseded by disparagement of 'techno Tracys'. The music genre had even come to be called 'handbag house'. As one clubber explained to me, 'The rave scene is dead and buried. There is no fun in going to a legal rave when Sharons and Tracys know where it is as soon as you buy a ticket'.

Some clubbers and ravers might want to defend these attitudes by arguing that the music of Stock/Aitken/Waterman, then acid house-cum-techno, respectively dominated the charts in 1987–8, and again in 1989–91. But there are glaring problems with this reasoning. First, the singles' sales chart is mostly a pastiche of niche sounds that reflect the buying patterns of many taste cultures rather than a monolithic mainstream (Crane, 1986). Second, buyers of the same records do not necessarily form a coherent social group. Their purchase of a given record may be contextualized within a very different range of consumer choices. They may never occupy the same social space. They may not even be clubbers.

Third, whether these 'mainstreams' reflect empirical social groups or not, they exhibit the burlesque exaggerations of an imagined other. 'Teds' and 'Tracys', like 'lager louts', 'sloanes', 'preppies' and 'yuppies', are more than euphemisms of social class and status, they demonstrate 'how we create groups with words' (Bourdieu, 1990a: 139). So the activities attributed to 'Sharon and Tracy' should by no means be confused with the actual dance culture of working-class girls. The distinction reveals more about the cultural values and social world of hard-core clubbers because, to quote Bourdieu again, 'nothing classifies somebody more than the way he or she classifies' (ibid: 132).

It is precisely because the social connotations of the mainstream are rarely examined that the term is so useful. Clubbers can denigrate it without self-consciousness or guilt. However, even a cursory analysis reveals the relatively straightforward demographics of these personifications of the mainstream. First, the clichés have class connotations. Sharon and Tracy, rather than, say, Camilla and Imogen, are what sociologists have tended to call 'respectable working class'. They are not imagined as poor or unemployed, but as working and aspiring. Their problem is not so much that they are beneath 'hip' clubbers but that they are classed full stop. In other words, they are trapped in their class. They do not enjoy the classless autonomy of 'hip' youth.

Age, the dependence of childhood and the accountabilities of adulthood are also signalled by the mainstreams. The recurrent trope of the handbag is something associated with mature womanhood or with pretending to be grown-up. It is definitely *not* a sartorial sign of youth culture, nor a form of objectified subcultural capital, but rather a symbol of the social and financial shackles of the housewife. The distinction between the authentic original and the hanger-on is also partly about age – the connoisseur deplores the naive and belated enthusiasm of the younger raver or, conversely, the younger participant castigates the tired passions of the older one for holding on to a passé culture.

Young people, irrespective of class, often refuse the responsibilities and identities of the work world, choosing to invest their attention, time and money in leisure. Parsons argues that young people espouse a different 'order of prestige symbols' because they cannot compete with adults for occupational status (1964: 94). Having loosened ties with family but not settled with a partner nor established themselves in an occupation, youth are not as anchored in their social place as those younger and older than themselves. By investing in leisure, youth can further reject being fixed socially. They can procrastinate what Bourdieu calls 'social ageing', that 'slow renunciation or disinvestment' which leads people to 'adjust their aspirations to their objective chances, to espouse their condition, become what they are and make do with what they have' (1984: 110–11).

The material conditions of youth's investment in subcultural capital (which is part of an aestheticized resistance to social ageing) results from the fact that youth, from many class backgrounds, enjoy a momentary reprieve from necessity. Without adult overheads such as mortgages and insurance policies, youth are free to spend on goods such as clothes, music, drink and drugs. In this way, youth can be seen as momentarily enjoying what Bourdieu argues is reserved for the bourgeoisie – the 'taste of liberty or luxury'. British youth cultures exhibit that 'stylization of life' or 'systemic commitment which organizes the most diverse practices' that can only develop at some distance from real economic necessity. (Bourdieu, 1984: 55–6).

This is true of youth from all but the poorest sections of the population, perhaps the top 75 per cent. While youth unemployment, homelessness and poverty are wide-spread, there is considerable discretionary income among the bulk of people aged 16–24. The 'teenage market', however, has long been dominated by the boys. In the 1950s, 55 per cent of teenagers were male because girls married earlier, and 67 per cent of teenage spending was in male hands because girls earned less (Abrams, 1959). In the 1990s, the differential earnings of young men and women have little changed – a fact that no doubt contributes to the masculine bias of subcultural capital.

Although clubbers and ravers loathe to admit it, the femininity of these representations of the mainstream is hard to deny. In fact, consistently over the past two decades, more girls have gone out dancing than boys. This is particularly marked amongst the 16–19 age group because girls start clubbing at a younger age. Dancing is, in fact, the only out-of-home leisure activity that women engage in more frequently than men. Men are ten times more likely to attend a sporting event, twice as likely to attend live music events and marginally more inclined to visit the cinema (Central Statistical Office, 1972–86). When it comes to preferences rather than the practices, gender is again decisive; the first choice for an evening out for women between the age of 15 and 24 is a dance club whereas the most popular choice of men of the same age is a pub (Mintel, 1988b).

Girls and women are also more likely to identify their taste in music with pop. Over a third of women (of all ages), compared to about a quarter of men, say that pop is their favourite type of music. Women spend less time and money on music, the music press and going out, and more on clothes and cosmetics (Mintel, 1988b; Euromonitor, 1989). One might assume, therefore, that they are less sectarian and specialist in relation to music because they literally and symbolically invest less in their taste in music and participation in music culture.

In their American study, Christenson and Peterson found marked gender differences in attitudes to the 'mainstream'. Men regarded the label *mainstream* as 'essentially negative, a synonym for *unhip*', whereas women understood it as 'another way of saying *popular* music' (1988: 298). Women respondents were more likely to say that they used music 'in the service of secondary gratifications (e.g. to improve mood, feel less alone) and as a general background activity' (ibid: 299). These American findings about women's use of music correlate with British clubbers' assumptions about the mainstream.

The objectification of young women, entailed in the 'Sharon and Tracy' image, is significantly different from the 'sluts' or 'prude', 'mother' or 'pretty waif' frameworks typically identified by feminist sociologists (Cowie and Lees, 1981; McRobbie, 1991). It is not primarily a vilification or veneration of girls' sexuality (although that is), but a position statement made by youth of both genders about girls who are not culturally 'one of the boys'. Subcultural capital is a currency that correlates with and legitimizes unequal statuses.

These mainstreams also point to the relevance of Huyssen's (1986) arguments about how mass culture has long been positioned as feminine by high cultural theorists, but here the traditional divide between virile high art and feminized low entertainment is replayed within popular culture itself. Even among youth cultures, there is a double articulation of the lowly and the feminine: disparaged *other* cultures are characterized as feminine and girls' cultures are devalued as imitative and passive. Authentic culture is, by contrast, depicted in gender-free or masculine terms, and remains the prerogative of boys.

The refusal of parental class and work culture also goes some way towards explaining why young people borrow tastes and fashions from gay and black cultures. Savage (1988) has argued that camp and kitsch sensibilities of gay male culture have been repeatedly taken up by British youth. More often noted (and arguably more relevant to club cultures in this period) is British youth's habit of borrowing from African-American and African-Caribbean culture, often with a romantic, 'orientalist' appropriation of black cultural tropes (Hebdige, 1979; Said, 1985).

Subcultural capital is the linchpin of an alternative hierarchy in which the axes of age, gender, sexuality and race are all employed in order to keep the determinations of class, income and occupation at bay. Interestingly, the social logic of subcultural capital reveals itself most clearly in what it dislikes and what it emphatically is not. The concept of 'subcultural capital', as outlined here, is a useful feminist tool for giving fuller representation to the complex strata and politics of popular culture. It has been essential to prising open the wilful obfuscation of sexist hierarchies and the persistent denial that hip cultures are anything other than happily 'equal'.

Chapter 12

Andy Bennett

SUBCULTURES OR NEOTRIBES?
Rethinking the relationship between youth, style and musical taste

DURING THE 1970S AND EARLY 1980S, sociological explanations of the relationship between youth, style and musical taste relied heavily upon the subcultural theory developed by the Birmingham Centre for Contemporary Cultural Studies (CCCS). Since its publication, the CCCS work has been subject to a number of criticisms, ranging from its emphasis on style-based youth resistance as class-based to the male-centred nature of its accounts. Interestingly, however, the term subculture survives in such counter-analytical discourse. Indeed, such is the variety of analytical perspectives in which subculture is now used as a theoretical underpinning, that it has arguably become little more than a convenient 'catch-all' term for any aspect of social life in which young people, style and music intersect. This chapter examines some of the problems associated with the concept of subculture and argues that an alternative theoretical framework needs to be developed that allows for the pluralistic and shifting sensibilities of style that have increasingly characterised youth 'culture' since the post-Second World War period. Drawing upon Maffesoli's (1996) concept of *tribus* (tribes), it is argued that those groupings traditionally theorised as coherent subcultures are better understood as temporal gatherings characterised by fluid boundaries and floating memberships. This argument is supported with empirical evidence drawn from an ethnographic study of the urban dance music scene in Newcastle upon Tyne, north-east England.

The CCCS subcultural theory

Using the original Chicago School premise that subculture provides the key to an understanding of deviance as normal behaviour in the face of particular social circumstances, the CCCS argued that the deviant traits of post-Second World War youth cultures such as Teddy boys, mods and skinheads constituted a collective reaction by working-class youth to structural changes taking place in British post-war society. According to the CCCS, this collective 'subcultural' reaction took a number of forms. Cohen (1972) argued that youth subcultures attempted a 'magical recovery' of community following the break up of traditional working-class neighbourhoods due to urban redevelopment during the 1950s and the relocation of families to 'new towns' and modern housing estates. John Clarke's study of skinhead culture echoes Cohen's view in arguing that the skinhead style represents 'an attempt to re-create through the "mob" the traditional working class community as a substitution for the real decline of the latter' (1976: 99). Alternatively, Jefferson's examination of the Teddy boy style argues that the latter reflected the Ted's '"all-dressed-up-and-nowhere-to-go" experience of Saturday evening' (1976: 48). The relative affluence of the Teddy boys allowed them to 'buy into' a middle-class image – the Edwardian suit revived by Savile Row tailors in 1950 and originally intended for a middle-class market. Jefferson argues that the Teddy boys' 'dress represented a symbolic way of expressing and negotiating with their symbolic reality, of giving cultural meaning to their social plight' (1976: 86). Similarly, Hebdige claims that the style of the mod was a reaction to the mundane predictability of the working week and an attempt to compensate for this 'by exercising complete domination over his private estate – his appearance and choice of leisure pursuits' (1976: 91).

Problems with the CCCS approach

The CCCS observation that working-class youth were at the centre of the new style-orientated post-war youth culture is difficult to dispute. During the post-war period working-class youth were the social group with the largest amounts of disposable income and thus the first 'specifically targeted and differentiated consumers' (Bocock, 1993: 22). By contrast, middle-class teenagers were at this time still 'constrained in their spending' (Benson, 1994: 165). More questionable, however, is the CCCS's contention that such styles were uniformly used by working-class youth in a strategy designed to resist the structural changes taking place around them. This contention rests on the rather tentative notion that, having gained an element of freedom to pick and choose between an increasing range of consumer items, working-class youth was somehow driven back to the fact of class as a way of articulating its attachment to such commodities. It could rather be argued that post-war consumerism offered young people the opportunity to break away from their traditional class-based identities, the increased spending power of the young facilitating and encouraging experimentation with new, self-constructed forms of identity (Chambers, 1985). The problems inherent in the CCCS work become increasingly evident with the attempt to include later stylistic innovations, which were clearly not instigated purely by working-class youth, into the resistance thesis. This point is convincingly made by Gary Clarke in his critique of Hebdige's (1979) analysis of punk which is characterised, according to Clarke, by a distinct air of contradiction between its 'metropolitan centeredness' and the emphasis on 'working class creativity' (1981: 86). Clarke suggests that 'most of the punk creations which are discussed [by Hebdige] were developed among the art-school avant-garde, rather than emanating "from the dance halls and housing estates"' (ibid.).

The concept of 'subculture'

While the essential tenets of the CCCS subcultural theory have been variously criticised and largely abandoned, the concept of 'subculture' survives as a theoretical
model in much sociological work on the relationship between youth, music and
style. Arguably, however, even when wrested away from theoretical context of the
CCCS work, the term 'subculture' remains deeply problematic due to its imposition of rigid lines of division over forms of sociation which may, in effect, be rather
more fleeting, and in many cases arbitrary, than the concept of subculture, with its
connotations of coherency and solidarity, allows for. Pondering a similar point, Fine
and Kleinman argue that the attempt to reify a construct such as subculture 'as
a corpus of knowledge may be heuristically valuable, until one begins to give this
corpus physical properties' (1979: 6).

   This problem is clearly illustrated in the work of Cagle (1995) which takes issue
with the CCCS conceptualisation of subculture as existing outside the mainstream.
According to Cagle, youth groups discounted by the CCCS – for example, glitter
rock fans – could also be counted as 'subcultures' despite their mainstream tastes
in music and style. In certain respects Cagle has a very good point in that the CCCS
did indeed discard a great deal of music and style-centred youth activity, which, in
addition to glitter rock, also included 'Rollermania' and heavy metal, presumably
on the grounds that the mainstream centredness of such youth cultures somehow
removed their potential for counter-hegemonic action which the Centre so readily
associated with mods, skinheads and punks, etc. However, while Cagle is right to
criticise the CCCS on these grounds, his argument has considerable implications
for the term 'subculture' in that it is left meaning everything and nothing. Thus,
if we are to accept that there are both *mainstream* and *non-mainstream* subcultures,
what are the differences between them, and how do we go about determining
such differences?

Neotribes: an alternative theoretical model for the study of youth

In critically evaluating 'subculture' as a framework for the sociological study of
youth, music and style, two main issues arise. First, the problem of objectivity as
subculture is used in increasingly contradictory ways by sociological theorists.
Second, the supposition that subcultures are subsets of society, or cultures within
cultures, such an approach imposing lines of division on youth, music and style
which are very difficult to verify in empirical terms. Indeed, there is little evidence
to suggest that even the most committed groups of youth stylists are in any way as
'coherent' or 'fixed' as the term 'subculture' implies (Frith, 1981). On the contrary,
it could be argued that so-called youth 'subcultures' are prime examples of the
unstable and shifting cultural affiliations which characterise late modern consumer-
based societies. Shields writes of a 'postmodern "persona"' which moves between
a succession of 'site-specific' gatherings and whose 'multiple identifications form a
dramatis personae – a self which can no longer be simplistically theorized as unified'
(1992a: 16). From this point of view the group is no longer a central focus for the

individual but rather one of a series of foci or 'sites' within which the individual can live out a selected, temporal role or identity before relocating to an alternative site and assuming a different identity. It follows, then, that the term 'group' can also no longer be regarded as having a necessarily permanent or tangible quality, the characteristics, visibility and lifespan of a group being wholly dependent upon the particular forms of interaction which it is used to stage.

Clearly, there is a considerable amount of difference between this definition of a group and that which prefigures subcultural theory. Indeed, this definition of 'group' corresponds more closely with Maffesoli's concept of *tribus* or 'tribes'. According to Maffesoli the tribe is 'without the rigidity of the forms of organization with which we are familiar, it refers more to a certain ambience, a state of mind, and is preferably to be expressed through lifestyles that favour appearance and form' (1996: 98). Developing Maffesoli's argument, Hetherington suggests that tribalisation involves 'the deregulation through modernization and individualization of the modern forms of solidarity and identity based on class occupation, locality and gender . . . and the recomposition into "tribal" identities and forms of sociation' (1992: 93). This view is in turn supported by Shields who argues that tribal identities serve to illustrate the temporal nature of collective identities in late modern society as individuals continually move between different sites of collective expression and 'reconstruct' themselves accordingly. According to Shields: 'Personas are "unfurled" and mutually adjusted. The performative orientation toward the Other in these sites of social centrality and sociality draws people together one by one. Tribe-like but temporary groups and circles condense out of the homogeneity of the mass' (1992b: 108).

Neotribalism and urban dance music

The processes of neotribalism in contemporary youth culture are highlighted by the current urban dance-music scene, particularly the musical and stylistic fluidity that underlies this scene. I will now illustrate this with reference to ethnographic research on the dance-music scene in Newcastle upon Tyne. In many studies of urban dance music there is an implication that its style is symptomatic of a 'postmodern' world of fragments in which the arbitrary incidence of signifiers is taken for granted (Muggleton, 1997; Polhemus, 1997). While such references to postmodernism indicate in part a general shift in sociological thinking during the early 1990s, it is arguable that they have also been inspired by urban dance music itself, or rather the way in which the music is created. Through its use of digital technology urban dance music has facilitated new approaches to musical composition. An important development in this respect is 'sampling' which allows for sound sources to be captured electronically and stored in a computer memory (Negus, 1992). By means of sampling, natural and recorded sounds can be removed from their original contexts and reworked into new pieces of music (Frith, 1990). Thus, as an amateur urban dance-music composer and producer explained to me:

> When I start to write I try to get a rhythm track down first and then
> work from there. Sometimes I can get something together myself and

sometimes I just take someone else's drum loop. For example, the thing that's playing in the background at the moment is taken from a Black Sabbath song. So, I'm using that drum loop to trigger some of my own samples. Then I'll programme in my own bass line. After that I might add some brass stabs into the track, let's say for argument's sake from an old Motown track. Then I might sample some pan pipes or a good sixties' guitar break from somewhere and use that a couple of times in the track as well.

Significantly, when the first urban dance-music tracks appeared there existed a ready-made audience who displayed no apparent objections to the music's transcendence of conventional style boundaries. Indeed, as the following interview extract demonstrates, a major aspect of urban dance music's continuing appeal revolves around the consonance of its blatant appropriation and reassembling of stylistically diffuse hooks, riffs and melodic phrases with the musical sensibilities of those who listen and dance to it:

AB   Dance music DJs put snatches of well-known pop songs into
        their mixes, don't they?
John   Yeah, such as they'll be playing something quite hard and then
        they'll put something like Michael Jackson in . . . you know
        what I mean . . . and it's not like people think 'Oh no', you
        know, 'Michael Jackson', and clear the dance floor . . . it's like
        'Oh yeah . . . I recognise that, it's Michael Jackson'.
Susan   If it's done well, if it's chosen well [by the DJ] and it fits in
        with the music, then it's really excellent.

To return to the concept of neotribalism, what comments such as these begin to reveal is that musical taste is a rather more loosely defined sensibility than has previously been supposed. The nature of musical taste, as with music itself, is both a multifaceted and distinctly fluid form of expression. Music generates a range of moods and experiences that individuals are able to move freely between. Urban dance music, because of the style mixing involved in its production, serves to provide a series of 'snapshot' images of such shifting sensibilities of musical taste being exercised by consumers. Indeed, in many of the larger dance-music clubs, different rooms or floors are used as a means of staging a number of parallel events, with clubbers free to move between these events as they please. Consequently, the nature of the urban dance-music event is becoming increasingly a matter of individual choice, the type of music heard and the setting in which it is heard and danced to being very much the decision of the individual. This in turn has a marked influence on the way that clubbers talk about the actual process of clubbing. Thus, clubbing appears to be regarded less as a singularly definable activity and more as a series of fragmented, temporal experiences as individuals move between different dance floors and engage with different crowds. This is illustrated in the following discussion extract in which a group of regular attendees of a particular urban dance-music clubnight in Newcastle are asked to describe an event:

AB   How would you describe 'Pigbag'? What kind of an event is it?

Diane   Well, I would say, um, it's a different experience depending upon . . .

Shelley   Upon what's on . . .

Diane   What music's on and what floor you're on as well.

AB   I know there are different things going on on each floor.

All   Yeah

Rob   There's three types of thing going on actually. There's like the sort of cafe room which plays hip hop and jazz, and then downstairs there's more singing sort of house music . . . and upstairs there's, eh . . . well, how could you describe that?

Debbie   Well, it's quite sort of, eh . . . the more housey end of techno music, with son of like trancey techno . . . the sort of easier, comfortable side of techno.

Diane   Yeah, and then you'll get people moving between all three floors and checking out what's going on.

Such fluid sensibilities of music consumption are not restricted to white urban club culture. While researching the cultural response of Asian youth in Newcastle to bhangra, a style described as underpinning a new 'Asian culture' in Britain (see Baumann, 1997 and Sharma *et al.*, 1996), I discovered that responses to bhangra were actually very mixed with a number of young Asians claiming it was 'good music [only for] certain occasions'. This view was elaborated on by a young female interviewee who explained:

> '[Bhangra] is really suited to events where there's dancing . . . and celebratory events like the Mela. On occasions like that it's great. At other times I don't listen to it, I listen to chart music and stuff like Prince. I don't really like bhangra that much at other times'.
>
> (Bennett, 2000: 111)

Bhangra is thus acknowledged as an important aspect of the celebration of 'traditional' Asian identity along with other cultural images and resources, such as traditional dancing and style of dress. As such, the music's appeal becomes fixed within the context of those occasions on which this identity is celebrated. At other times these young Asians' musical preferences and style of dress adheres more closely with the Western styles with which they are familiar.

Style tribes

Neotribalism forces a similar questioning of the relationship between musical taste and visual style. Willis has argued that visual style and musical taste are bound together in a homological relationship, homology being 'the continuous play between the group and [those items] which [produce] meanings, contents and forms of consciousness' (1978: 191). In noting the visual style mixing which occurred at some of the early raves, several theorists suggested the demise of such homological relationships as young people were seen to become far less concerned with the fit between visual style and musical taste. Redhead, for example, observed a 'mixing [of] all kinds of styles on the same dance floor . . . attracting a range of previously opposed subcultures from football hooligans to New Age hippies' (1993: 4). Alternatively, however, it could be argued that rather than signal the end of the subcultural 'tradition', urban dance music opens up entirely new ways of understanding how young people perceive the relationship between musical taste and visual style which negates the notion of a fixed homological relationship between musical taste and stylistic preference by revealing the infinitely malleable and interchangeable nature of the latter as these are appropriated and realised by individuals as aspects of consumer choice. While this is not to dismiss completely the idea that a form of symmetry can exist between an individual's image and their taste in music, what it does serve to illustrate is that the relationship between musical taste and visual image is much less rigidly defined than was once thought. Indeed, as is evidenced by the following account, rather more fluid notions of musical taste and attendant visual image were in place long before the appearance of contemporary urban dance-music forms. Thus, explains the interviewee:

> . . . in the town where I grew up we were all rockers. We were leather clad, we were rockers. But it was during the punk thing and I used to like the Clash . . . eh and I clearly remember Donna Summer's 'I Feel Love' being one of the best songs of '76 or whenever it was and really, really liking it . . . and a lot of my friends liking it a lot as well, although it was actually still a bit weird to admit it . . . because we were all into Zep [Led Zeppelin] and Sabbath [Black Sabbath] and Thin Lizzy and all the rest. But now you've got people like Leftfield or the Chemical Brothers who are quite happy to pick up very heavy metal guitar riffs and throw that into a dance mix . . . or Primal Scream come along and they do a rock album and then other people get hold of that and remix that stuff and eh, people will go and listen to it and they're quite happy to dance to it . . . I think dance music culture has allowed people to be quite open about the fact that they actually quite like a lot of different stuff. I've never been able to understand the divisions in music. I'm quite happy to go from Orbital to Jimi Hendrix.

As the above extract serves to illustrate, the relationship between musical taste and visual style, rather than assuming a quintessentially fixed character, has typically been understood by young people as a rather more loosely formulated sensibility. In consuming popular music, the individual is free to choose not only between various musical styles and attendant visual images, but also how such choices are lived out and what they are made to stand for. Moreover, in choosing certain musical styles and visual images, the forms of association and social gatherings in which young people become involved are not rigidly bound into a 'subcultural' community but rather assume a more fluid, neotribal character.

Conclusion

This chapter has argued that the concept of 'subculture' is essentially flawed due to its attempt to impose a hermeneutic seal around the relationship between musical and stylistic preference. A new theoretical framework for studying the cultural relationship between youth, music and style was put forward using Maffesoli's concept of neotribalism. It was suggested that neotribe provides a more effective theoretical framework as it allows for the shifting nature of youth's musical and stylistic preferences and the essential fluidity of youth cultural groups. Such characteristics, it is argued, have been a centrally defining, if developing, aspect of consumer-based youth cultures since the establishment of the post-war youth market. In the final part of the chapter, this argument was substantiated using ethnographic research on the urban dance music scene in Newcastle upon Tyne. It was illustrated how urban dance-music and its attendant sensibilities of consumption, although appearing to have inspired a new chapter in the history of post-war youth culture, are actually the product of neotribal sensibilities that have characterised young people's appropriation of popular music and style since the immediate post-war period, such sensibilities being an inevitable aspect of late modern consumer society.

Chapter 13

Barry Shank

PUNK ROCK AT RAUL'S
The performance of contradiction

L IKE FOLKSINGING IN THE EARLY SIXTIES, punk was a musical practice that differentiated among Austin's university students. Throughout the progressive country era, music in Austin either succeeded or failed in attracting students. Among club owners, students were conceived of as a monolithic audience bloc that could mean the difference between a night that made money or one that went bust. Raul's was the first club in ten years (since the closing of the Vulcan Gas Co.) that presented music designed to attract only a subgroup within the students. One ritual of audience participation at Raul's marked this distinction. It involved screaming the names of hated popular musicians and requesting the most despised songs. Despised music was commercially successful music, hated because it was the music favored by the undifferentiated mass of college students. Punk at Raul's constructed a pop culture elitism. Many punk fans at Raul's were college students who believed themselves to be smarter than most college students (that is, more culturally adept), and the evidence for their superiority was their appreciation of this 'smart' music that most college students could not stand. Within this discourse of distinction, common college student musical taste was associated with the social groups that made up the memberships of fraternities and sororities – the dominant social groups on campus. Thus, as punk repeated many of the strategies utilized by Austin's folksinging students fifteen years before, it revived the honky-tonk setting as a site for musicalized critique.

That summer Phil Tolstead and Dan Puckett, both students enrolled in the College of Communications, began to plan their own band. Tolstead and Puckett were fans of punk rock. They had been following the movement in the press and listening to the music on the records, and they were frustrated by the absence of 'real punks' in Austin. When they began seriously to put their band together, they were joined by Manny Rosario, a tough-talking Puerto Rican guitarist, and Tom Huckabee on drums. Together, the Huns wanted to combine some of the elements they had been reading about in their courses in the university with the music and the fashions of punk, and to create a band that would perform all of the relevant contradictions at once. It seemed to Huckabee as though 'the Sex Pistols had established an audience for what we wanted do. They gave it a name -punk rock.'

The Huns's first show was scheduled for September 19, at Raul's. This perform-ance was designed for a specific audience. Just as McLaren had aimed the Sex Pistols at art students in the UK, the Huns were conceptualized as a spectacle for the punk rock fans who were students at the University of Texas. They printed up and distrib-uted posters derived from Jamie Reid's Situationist-influenced work for the Sex Pistols. The posters were not nearly so sophisticated as Reid's record covers, carrying slogans such as, 'Legalize Crime' and 'No Police.' But the word spread throughout the communications school that this show was not to be missed. This band was to be Austin's answer to the Sex Pistols and all of punk rock.

In a manner derived from the Sex Pistols, the Huns wanted to confront and negate the expectations of their audience. Many of their efforts at negation led them into standard punk rock conventions: the attempted *détournement* of Nazi regalia and the German language; the almost ritualized displays of antagonism between the band and the audience. But the local context dominated the meaning of these symbolic gestures. Instead of Marcia Ball's searching out the eyes of her fans, striving to sincerely communicate heartfelt emotions and construct a communion of dancing souls, the Huns were working to display contradiction and antagonism. In contrast to progressive country's pastoral poetry, punk rock was a means to express strong negative feelings about their world. 'We had real fantasies about blowing it all up. We definitely wanted to stir the shit,' says Huckabee. The Huns wanted to create within Raul's a vortex of symbolic destruction that would disable communication, reach beyond the basic conventions of musical performance, and involve their audi-ence in a ritual of self-hate. By piling antagonism on antagonism, through a constant disruption of expectation, the Huns intended to create an overwhelming sense of negativity that would transform all who experienced it.

But their audience was hip to the show. They got it. They knew what was expected of them and they wanted to participate in this mutual construction of nega-tivity. Like the good sports they were, this already knowing audience proudly, self-consciously acted like punks – throwing paper cups and beer at the performers, screaming obscenities, rushing the stage – joyfully performing their assigned role in this deconstruction of the traditional musical experience. It was good fun. When Tolstead sang a few bars of 'Puppy Love,' members of the audience knew that they were supposed to throw ice. During the third song, fans rushed the stage and carried parts of the drum-kit out onto the dance floor, rendering obvious the point that this performance involved so much more than the people on stage. Two songs later, a group of fans dumped a full garbage can onto the stage, spewing smashed and torn paper cups, broken bottles, and a spray of stale beer across the performers. Meanwhile, the Huns played songs such as 'I'm Glad He's Dead', about the assassination of John Kennedy, and 'You Bores Me', an attack on the Skunks.

During the next song, 'Eat Death Scum,' City of Austin police officer Steve Bridgewater entered the club, ostensibly answering a noise complaint. He stood by the door for a few moments, observing the appearance of chaos around him. In the middle of the song, Tolstead spotted Bridgewater, pointed his finger at him and, improvising a new line, chanted, 'I hate you, I hate you.' Slowly, Bridgewater made his way through the crowd, approaching the stage as if drawn there by Tolstead's pointing finger. Tolstead continued to chant 'I hate you, Eat Death Scum' at the police officer, while Bridgewater stood two feet away from the singer, leaning in closer and closer toward him. From Huckabee's perspective, the two appeared to be nearly nose to nose, as if performing an odd duet: Tolstead singing the authority of the performer, the police officer silently representing the authority of the state. Inching closer together on the stage of Raul's, these clashing frames of interpretative authority could not remain in perpetual equilibrium.

Bridgewater screamed over the music, ordering Tolstead to stop. With the cop only inches from his face, the singer leaned over and, in another gesture of disrupted expectation, kissed the cop on the lips. This disturbance of gender rules was more disorder than the officer could stand. He snatched at the singer's wrist and slipped one handcuff on him. The singer grabbed the microphone with his left hand and shouted out over the PA, 'Start a riot. Start a riot'. Two men dressed in polo shirts and gimme caps jumped up from the audience onto the stage to help the cop subdue the singer. The second handcuff was attached as both of the singer's arms were forced behind his back. Other members of the audience jumped onto the stage platform to help their friends who had gotten into a fight with these strangers. The club's bouncer, Bobby Morales, tried to pull the strangers off the stage. The drummer, bass player, and organist continued to play. The police officer pulled out his radio and called for assistance. Manny Rosario, the guitarist, echoed the gesture of Sid Vicious at Randy's Rodeo and swung his guitar over his head, smashing the radio out of the officer's hand. The officer whirled around and, with one punch, sent Manny flying through the air. The instant he hit the ground, the guitar player was up and running out the back door. Uniformed police officers swarmed into the club, the music came to a halt, and the audience stood around in shocked dismay, as the performance was finally completely disrupted.

Three weeks later, in a judicial act of interpretation, Phil Tolstead was convicted on a charge of disorderly conduct. Judge Steve Russell based his verdict on the opinion that 'Tolstead displayed assaultive behavior toward Bridgewater.' The decision of the court was that Tolstead's gestures, his singing, and his kiss constituted assault, justifying the closing down of the performance and the handcuffing and jailing of six persons from the club. The Huns had indeed given a powerful performance, far different from the traditional display of moral authority or the communication of shared feelings. Obviously, punk could not represent merely a contrasting choice in the marketplace of Austin music. The response of the criminal justice system declared that the Huns and their fans had rudely violated the boundaries of legitimate expression. This rock 'n' roll truly challenged people. It was not safe to like it; you could get beat with a billy club; you could get arrested. The ability to derive pleasure from punk rock gave an instant aura of danger, independence, and power to any individual. Clearly different from a taste for any other music, liking punk rock seemed to produce momentary experiences for middle-class Anglo-Texans akin to the everyday life of Blacks or Hispanics. Soon Raul's was packed every night with students longing for that identity streaked with power and danger.

Punk rock at Raul's might have been 'performance art,' but it was also music, a music that generated the physical energy that distributed erotic charges throughout the chambers at the heart of the scene. Young people picked up guitars and drums, and keyboards and microphones, and played songs. The songs had chords and melodies, and beats and words. However important an underlying concept or a theatrical component was to any band's performing style, the core of this signifying practice was music; the participants were music fans and musicians.

The musical aesthetic at Raul's operated on principles of transgression and inversion derived from the critical function of this practice in the very construction of the scene itself. The professional musician, able to provide disinterested renditions of popular songs, was despised. It was absolutely essential for the punk performer to provide some evidence that he or she was risking some component of his or her being, was negating their identity in an interplay with the abject, was questioning in some way the construction of the position from which they performed. For some, merely daring to sing a song with no obvious musical training was risk enough. The much-vaunted musical virtuosity displayed in the progressive country and white blues scenes was not valued; in fact, musical simplicity was emphasized as a means of opening the path to the stage. But this simplicity remained the quality of a music powerful enough to carry the lyric, rhythmic, and harmonic expressions of an underlying semiotic disassociation and, at the same time, to produce a 'freeing situation' capable of sparking the recombination of repressed elements of the human in a search for new identities. In the scene that germinated at Raul's and soon spread into other venues, the performance of rock 'n' roll music in the carnivalesque arena of the honky-tonk again became available as an organizing frame for the pleasurable display of the negativity and contradiction that derive from the semiotic production of the subject.

A close look at two songs from this period will map out the range of the musical and lyrical construction and deconstruction of subjective possibilities in this scene. The Huns' 'Glad He's Dead' was performed at their first show and became a regular part of their repertoire. They released it on their own label, God Records, in 1979. The recording displays the stylistic debt the Huns owed to the Sex Pistols, and in many ways this song is the 'God Save the Queen' of the Raul's era. It begins with eight notes on the kick-drum setting a rapid pulse that does not vary throughout the duration of the song. A distorted rhythm guitar and bass enter, stabbing on an off-beat at a D chord, and then pounding the remainder of the bar on an A, before beginning the harmonic structure of the verse: an alternation of measures between the tonic E and an odd G sharp major. The harmonic tension produced in this chord structure, playing off the expected transition to the subdominant A, is a relatively common trait for a great deal of punk rock, owing at least partially to the simplicity of its execution. Dan Puckett's voice screeches the first lines in a generic Johnny Rotten sneer. 'He sold us all the Bay of Pigs. 'He gave our schools up to the nigs.' 'Nigs' receives an additional emphatic marker as Puckett squeezes a half-note rise out of an extension of the vowel sound. While the guitars shift between the subdominant (A) and the dominant (B), the other members of the band chant the chorus in a monotone background to Puckett's scream: 'I'm glad he's dead, the fucking red. I helped Lee Oswald shoot him in the head.' Three verses attack John Kennedy for his Catholicism, the Cuban missile crisis, the death of Marilyn Monroe, Vietnam, as well as the Bay of Pigs and the integration of southern schools. The final verse describes the assassination scene and declares, 'Lee Harvey Oswald,

America's friend.' The song ends with laughter resounding over the whine of guitar feedback, while the pick-up switch clicks off and on.

Musically, the song is generic punk rock, from its opening drumbeat, distorted guitar tones, and rhythmic accents to its closing feedback. Lyrically, the song stumbles through an unsubtle assault on the Kennedy myth. Not particularly clever, 'Glad He's Dead' appears on the surface as only so much outrageous noise. But by imaginatively returning this song to its more common performance context within the scene at Raul's (where, undoubtedly, the musical and vocal execution would become more haphazard than the recorded version), we can begin what subject positions arc produced within 'Glad He's Dead.' How does this musical text help to establish a structure of identification for its fans?

From the stage of Raul's, surrounded by fans throwing ice and dumping garbage pails, Puckett sings the beliefs of the red-blooded, right-wing, white Texan male – that traditional identity which punk in Austin refuses. However, the first response upon listening to this song is not revulsion but laughter. The inversion of the moral and social order (the working-class, racist, reactionary Texan celebrating the murder of the privileged, progressive, east-coast president) along with the grotesque image of the Kennedy myth produced in the lyrics (including descriptions of the president on his knees before the pope, of the extent of his sexual urges, and finally of his brains on Jackie's coat), creates so powerful a shock that the immediate response can only be laughter – that bodily recognition of the 'contradictory and double-faced fullness of life.' When Puckett laughs at the end of the song, he enunciates that same laughter which the song provokes. Constructed between a laughing audience and a laughing singer, the identifying structure is neither the hallowed myth of Kennedy righteousness, nor the cracker who claims to have helped Oswald with the assassination, but instead has become the subject of laughter, 'an interior form of truth . . . that liberates from the fear . . . of the sacred, of prohibitions, of the past, of power.' Thus, 'Glad He's Dead' is not so much a depiction of Kennedy, Oswald, and the events in Dallas than it is a critique of cultural authority in two of its most effective local forms: the regional authority of the cracker father and the national authority of the generation that claims the myth of Camelot and the slain president. Both are laughingly dismissed over a scream of electronic feedback.

A similar critique of power and authority is maintained in an otherwise quite different song by the Reversible Cords, 'Big Penis Envy.' The Re*Cords performed on the sidewalks and in the capital, as well as in the clubs of Austin. Displaying their musical ineptitude like a badge of honor, the Re*Cords embodied more completely than any other band in Austin the belief that you do not have to be a musician to play punk. As many of their performances were with acoustic instruments, often they were not even loud. Rather than promulgating danger and negativity like the Huns, the Re*Cords set themselves up as the 'court jesters' of the scene. 'Big Penis Envy' was first performed at the 1206 Club in Austin and was released in 1980 on the band's only album.

The song begins with a fragile, tentative guitar line that searches for its notes, in an immediately evident inversion of the masculine power chords common to punk. It then flows into a descending chord change (A–G#–F#–E), played to a rudimentary shuffle rhythm weakly tapped out on a snare drum. The recording features alto and tenor saxophones slithering through their ranges, in uncanny imitation of the atonal vocalizings of the singer who begins the song with a rising wail. 'Sometimes when we make it, I'm scared I'm going to fall right in. I've got big penis envy, Da-da, da-da, da-da, da.' 'Da-da' indeed, the singer bemoans his diminutive penis, the size of a twig, smaller even than the three-inch tool of those experts who insist that size is not important. Throughout this inversion of the stiff, assertive model of masculine authority, vocal lines waver and tremble, the guitar limps through its licks, the drums seem incapable of regular rhythms. The sole lyrical passage stated with any sort of assumed authority is the bridge: 'I wish I had a penis the size of Alcatraz. People would bow below it, and it would have pizzazz. I know that this is not my fate, I'm destined to be razzed. Don't say I'm inadequate, uh-uh, I know it.'

It does not take a great deal of Lacanian training to interpret this description of the prison house of the phallus and its effects, but it is worthwhile to point out the direct lines the Re*Cords draw between their send-up of patriarchal power and their parody of punk rock's musical aggression. The song constructs a musical arena of weak boundaries, easily permeated. The verse slides into the chorus, vocal lines overlap, the tonalities of the saxophones imitate the whimpering voice while constructing tangential melodies. When the bridge arrives and all the instruments begin to play in time, the audience affirmatively shouts along, 'Don't say I'm inadequate, uh-uh!' In 'Big Penis Envy' the Re*Cords perform their own and their audience's placement in a Symbolic still constituted by unequal gender relations, where power remains visible, quantitative, phallic. The overt humor of the song, though, deflects the thrust of the critique displayed in the inversion of the standards of musical power, enabling any audience to sing along, to laugh along, again the 'double-faced fullness of life,' without assuming any identity mirrored back to them. Nevertheless, the positions constructed in the song, although doubled through parody and therefore necessarily unstable, enable a questioning of the discursive links among power, the phallus, loud guitars, and the construction of an autonomous subject with these symbolic associations.

'Glad He's Dead' and 'Big Penis Envy' mark the poles of one axis of differentiation in the Raul's era of Austin punk. The wicked aggression of the Huns stands in stark contrast to the self-effacing humility of the Re*Cords. But both performances are united by the laughter they each evoke from their audiences. This open-throated response marks a contradictory relation to the traditional construction of performing and responding. Throughout the coming decade, the most committed Austin fans will question why they care what songs are being sung, why they continue to go out. The best bands that Austin produced throughout the Eighties will share this conflicted attitude toward their own roles as producers. They will not be able to assume unquestioningly the center of moral authority constructed within traditions of Texan music. They certainly will not imagine themselves to be autonomous business agents operating within a free market. Instead, they will distance themselves from the traditional markers of staged authority and perform in a self-effacing manner that many critics will call unprofessional.

The scene at Raul's marked a burst of creative activity that lasted for almost three years. Bands formed, magazines were founded, record companies started, movies were made. This cultural explosion was both similar to and different from the initial progressive country moment. As with the earlier period of intense activity, musical performance at a specific site was the central activity within a number of overlapping cultural practices that mutually reinforced each other. Musicians, artists, film-makers, and writers, drawn to this liberal oasis in the middle of conservative Texas, worked to make sense out of their feelings of alienation from the contemporary condition. The magazines that formed wrote about music and music-related activities. The movies that were made shared themes with and featured actors involved in the music scene. Artists designed posters and record covers. The Austin audience continued to demand that its musicians speak directly to them.

Chapter 14

William Tsitsos

RULES OF REBELLION
Slamdancing, moshing and the American alternative scene

SINCE 1993, POPULAR MUSIC MAGAZINES in the US have reported the outbreak of an alternative music 'revolution', as bands such as Green Day achieved large-scale popular success. The news media have focused their attention on the dancing known as 'slamdancing', or 'moshing', which is associated with this newly popular music. Slamdancing and moshing are two different, albeit similar, styles of dance in which participants (mostly men) violently hurl their bodies at one another in a dance area called a 'pit'. The media attention paid to this music and its associated violent audience-behaviour paint them as emerging threats to public safety. In this chapter I present a different interpretation, arguing that slamdancing and moshing mirror the ideologies of rebellion that exist in the scene by emphasising individual and communal motion in ways that reflect a desire among dancers for the elimination of all rules (in slamming) or for ordered control (in moshing).

The study is based upon participant observational research conducted during the summer of 1995, when I lived in San Francisco, California, a city with a thriving alternative music scene. In the San Francisco Bay area, I attended numerous concerts in order to observe band and audience behaviour (especially slamdancing and moshing). In addition, I interviewed twelve individuals who either at one time or still considered themselves members of the scene. I spoke with these interviewees (six men and six women, ranging in age from 14 to 32) about their experiences in the scene.[1] These interviews allowed me to gain insight into the meaning of the scene to its members.

Slamdancing and moshing

Slamdancing is a style of dance that originated in the US in the punk rock subculture of the late 1970s and early 1980s. Associated in the US primarily with the apolitical 'drunk punk' scene, slamdancing is a modification of the early punk 'pogo' dance, bringing increased body contact to the original pogo. Moshing emerged during the mid-1980s from the New City straight-edge scene as a variation on slamdancing. Although slamdancing and moshing are so similar that many people use the two terms interchangeably, there are specific distinctions between the two dance styles to be pointed out, and I distinguish between them in my analysis throughout this chapter. In my interviews, though, I used the terms interchangeably, largely because many in the scene do so; indeed, some do not call them by either name, referring to their actions as 'just dancing'.

Although people occasionally slamdance and mosh to recorded music, it is far more common for it to be done at live music shows. Both are aggressive dances that are performed mostly by males in a roughly circular area called the 'pit'. Naming this area the 'pit' designates it as the site of some type of battle. Being part of the scene is about being rebellious, and the term 'pit' suggests that this is a main site of rebellion. The pit is not an explicitly marked off area, but pits usually form in front of the stage where a band is playing. Occasionally (usually at shows in larger venues), more than one pit will break out in various parts of the crowd. The formation of a pit is generally a reflection of the crowd's affection for a band, so if a crowd does not like a band, a pit will not form. Otherwise, pits tend to 'break out' when the energy of the band's performance causes the energy of one person or a few people in the crowd to build to a point at which they move to the front-and-centre pit area and begin agitating like excited atoms. If other people in the crowd are not as excited as these individuals, no one joins them, and the 'proto-pit' usually dies. If the rest of the crowd is excited, though, people join the initial dancers, and the pit forms, clearing a space in the pit area as non-dancers in the crowd shrink away from the dancers.

Inside the pit, certain moves are associated with moshing and slamdancing. Although many of the moves are similar in the two styles, there are unique characteristics of each, too. Slamdancing involves fast movement. Often, this movement takes the form of everyone in the pit running counter-clockwise, occasionally slamming into each other. The dance involves some arm-swinging, but it is usually just one arm (most often the right one) in motion. When dancers are running counter-clockwise, the swinging of the right arm serves a double function. On the one hand, it allows dancers to slam into people and then quickly push them away, and on the other, it helps dancers to gain momentum while running in a counter-clockwise circle. Sometimes, however, slamdancers do not run in a circle, but rather move in a more 'run-and-collide' fashion, simply throwing themselves into the part of the pit where the most people are gathered, slamming into each other. Most slamdancers are not actually trying to hurt each other. Traditionally, when a dancer falls to the floor, the dancers in the near vicinity stop and pick up the fallen dancer.

Whereas slamdancing is more frenetic in its movement, the body movements (such as arm swinging) involved in moshing are slower and more exaggerated. Moshers keep their bodies more bent over and compacted, and they swing either both arms or just one (usually the right) arm around across in a move that one of my interviewees called 'the death swing'. This swinging of the arm(s) in moshing is far more theatrical and exaggerated than in slamdancing. If a mosher swings only one arm, the non-swinging arm is kept ready to provide some guard against collisions with other moshers. The dancers often stand in a stationary position while performing these moves, but sometimes they run into other people inside and on the edge of the pit. To do so, dancers generally just move to where other dancers are clustered and colliding with each other, and join in the collision. In recent years, new moves, such as jumping karate kicks, have been introduced into the repertoire of moshing. The picking up of fallen dancers is a tradition that was sometimes ignored by moshers when the dance first emerged, but it is followed more often nowadays.

Slamdancing and the apolitical punk ideology of rebellion

The moves involved in slamdancing reflect the balancing of individuality and unity that punks undertake in formulating their ideologies of rebellion. On the one hand, the fundamental elements of the dance, including the violent collisions with other dancers and the arm-swinging, are assertions of individual presence and autonomy in the pit. On the other hand, there are elements to slamdancing which create and reinforce unity in the pit, often in the form of a concern for the well-being of other dancers. These elements include the counter-clockwise group motion of dancers and the traditional picking up of fallen dancers. Simon, too, recognises the tension between individual and communal expression that exists in the dance (1997: 166). Slamdancing also mirrors punk ideologies in the symbolic breakdown of order that seems to occur in the pit. The fast, counter-clockwise motion of dancers turns the pit into a swirl of seemingly chaotic motion. Although slamdancers themselves do follow customs that prevent the pit from degenerating into actual chaos, the pit, when viewed from the outside, looks like a lawless realm. The enemy for punks is the mainstream, and slamdancing allows punks to present the threat of chaos while still maintaining unity among themselves within the pit.

Most explanations of the motivations behind slamdancing focus on the energy of the dancing. When I asked one of my interviewees, Dave, why he slamdances, he first played a song for me on a cassette player that he carried with him. Then he answered my question:

> It's about the pump of the music. Did you hear that tempo? It's a certain tempo that really gets me rolling, and metal's like way too fast and stuff. There's just a certain tempo that makes me want to dance, you know, and that's the whole thing. Isn't disco about dancing? Isn't everything about dancing?

For Dave, there is a definite element of enjoyment in the energetic display of slamdancing. Along similar lines, other slamdancers say that they do it because of the adrenaline rush that the music and dancing give them, as this passage from my interview with Jerry demonstrates:

Q   Why do you mosh?
A   Adrenaline.
Q   Adrenaline? Does that pretty much say *how* you feel while you're moshing?
A   Yeah.

Beyond their shared emphasis on the energy involved in the dancing, the above explanations for slamdancing are similar in that they stress the role of the dancing as an individual display. For these punks, punk rebellion is primarily about individual expression, and slam dancing reflects this rebellion. In portraying the dancing as such an intensely individualised activity, all the scene members cited above give the impression that slamdancing is just an adrenalised dance with no rules at all, in which impulsive urges drive dancers to act out spontaneously in any way they desire. The idea of the lawless individual in the pit reflects the vision of rule-breaking individuality that is such a large part of being a punk, especially a drunk punk.

Moshing and the New York City straight-edge ideology of rebellion

In contrast to slamdancing, moshing lacks the elements, such as circular pit motion which promote unity in the pit. The development of moshing in New York City in the 1980s even saw the partial breakdown of the convention of picking up fallen dancers, as pit violence increased. New York City straight-edge shows became legendary for their brutality. One writer to *Maximumrocknroll* noted:

> This is a letter to let people know about what has been happening in N.Y. in the past few months. Please print this – it is very important that word of this gets out. Blood is being shed and lives are being taken, by crews of sell-glorified skinheads and bad-ass little boys. One night they fucked so badly with this one guy at a Prong/Warzone show, that he later *died* while in the ambulance to the hospital.
>
> Anonymous, *MRR* 85, June 1990

Compared with slamming, the fundamental body movements of moshing, such as the more violent swinging of the arms, the more violent body contact, and the lack of group motion place even greater emphasis on individual territoriality over (comm)unity. Whereas the bodily motion of swinging arms and high-stepping legs has remained the traditional motion of slamdancing since it first emerged, moshing has seen the introduction of new moves such as jumping karate kicks. Tim, an avid mosher, writes:

> If you pay attention, you'll notice that some people actually dance and have moves . . . with punches and jumpkicks added in. Running around in a circle and bumping into other people holds no appeal for me because dancing with some sort of style and flow is very important to me, as is it is for a lot of other people at the shows.
>
> Personal correspondence, August 1995

This desire to experiment with new moves on the part of moshers demonstrates their concern with individual expression in the pit, and this reflects the emphasis on individual lifestyle concerns over scene-wide unity which exists in the branch of the scene that spawned moshing. In my research, I encountered no explanation for the motivation behind moshing which emphasised the feeling of unity that it gives participants. Rather, moshers' explanations for their dancing tend to focus more on the venting of individual aggression. In her interview, Rebecca stated that she moshes largely to vent frustration and anger:

A   I'm actually a very violent person, and that's a good way for me to take it out because I don't go around picking fights or anything like that. I've never really been in a fight, but I have a lot of violence. That's something that's very interesting. I didn't realise it in high school, because everyone thought I was this happy-go-lucky person, or whatever. I was like, 'If you knew the thoughts that went through my head'. And they were just like, 'Yeah, yeah, whatever'. And I'm just like, 'No, if you knew' (laughs). But I didn't realize until college just how much anger I have had in me.

Q   Like general anger?

A   Yeah, I thought I wasn't really rebelling against anything, but I realised I was. A lot of it had to do with my stepmother at the time, my now ex-stepmother – yeah! So I think a lot of it had to do with her, and I knew most of it had to with mainstream society at my high school and in the area.

Q   Suburbia?

A   The suburban, the closed-mindedness.

Rebecca was the only mosher I interviewed in person for this study, in part because metal-influenced, straight-edge hard-core is not common in the Bay Area. However, based on my own experiences in the mosh-intensive environment of Albany, New York, as well as correspondence with my high school friends, I believe I gained an accurate sense of the motivations behind moshing. Rebecca and I are both from Albany, and we went to the same shows in high school. She was always one of the first people in the pit, easily noticed because she was one of the more theatrical, aggressive moshers. Although she was unsure of the source of her aggression in high school, this aggression was definitely present, and the moshpit provided the site to vent it. In letters to *MRR,* other people on the scene cite the outlet for aggression which moshing gives them (anonymous, *MRR,* 118, March 1993).

Despite such accounts of moshing as an activity centred on the individual, however, moshing, like slamdancing, could not take place if not for the formation of a moshpit. As I described earlier, the formation of a pit is a communal activity, and as such it requires some sense of unity with other dancers. If one person starts dancing but no one joins, then chances are that the 'proto-pit' will die out. Considering that pit formation requires a united, communal effort, the fact that few moshers point to the dancing's potential to reinforce and create community as a reason why they do it clarifies the way in which the ideology of the New York straight-edge hard-core scene and its contemporary descendants emphasises individual concerns in its ideology of rebellion. However, straight edgers *do* value communal rebellion, albeit to a lesser degree than they do individual rebellion. New York straight-edge bands like Bold called for straight-edge unity in their songs, and these calls are echoed by contemporary bands who are influenced by bands such as

Bold. With this in mind, why did the New York straight edgers phase out elements of slamdancing that promote pit unity, such as circular pit motion and (to some degree) picking up fallen dancers, in developing moshing? Why did they not just slamdance like the drunk punks who also emphasise individual over communal rebellion?

The answer to these questions resides in the different goals of rebellion of New York-influenced straight edgers and drunk punks. Drunk punks see rebellion as individuals showing themselves to be different from the mainstream by breaking rules and breaking down control. For straight edgers, meanwhile, rebellion is an individual battle to gain control and strength. Originally, this 'control' in straight edge was primarily self-control, but since the emergence of New York City straight edge (and moshing) in the 1980s, this has also meant control over others. The sloweddown dance of moshing, like the slowed-down, heavy metal-influenced music of these straight-edge bands, reflects their increased focus on gaining control. The straight edgers who developed moshing were less interested in preserving the traditions of circular pit motion and picking up fallen dancers *not* because they opposed the unity for which they stood, but because these are also the elements of slamdancing that support disorder, a lack of control, and/or weakness – all qualities that the New York City straight-edge ideology of rebellion denounces. Circular pit motion, although it may promote unity within the pit, also increases the level of chaos by moving dancers around the pit in frenzied motion. New York straight edgers were rebelling against the lack of control and order, so they developed moshing as a slower, more stationary dance. Picking up fallen dancers would seem to increase order in the pit, but it also gives support to dancers who are too weak to fend for themselves in the pit. In developing moshing, the New York straight edgers could have maintained the elements of slamdancing that promote pit unity, but doing so would have come at the expense of demonstrating power and control. Forced to choose between strength and unity, they chose strength, even though that meant sacrificing pit unity. This reflects the primacy of individual control in their ideology of rebellion.

For these straight edgers, the moshpit is a sort of proving ground in which those who are too weak must be forcibly eliminated. Straight edge has always been about being strong enough to stay in control. In fighting for control, these straight edgers are also rebelling against punk, which positions itself against outside control. The New York City straight edgers, who developed moshing, often did not consider themselves to be punks at all. So they took slamming, which was part of a subculture with which they did not identify, and attempted to impose control and order on it through moshing. The exaggerated, violent gestures of moshing can be seen as attempts to beat some order into the pit, to purge the pit of its chaotic, anarchic (i.e. punk) elements. Ironically, with so many dancers in the pit attempting to use aggression to impose some sort of order, moshing ends up more chaotic and violent than slamming. While there are drunk punk slamdancers who, like moshers, dance to release aggression, their dancing is not as violent as moshing because the primary object of aggression for drunk punks is the mainstream, an entity not identified with the pit. However, for straight-edge moshers, the object of aggression is the disorder and chaos symbolised in part by the pit itself, and this disorder must be purged.

Conclusions

In this chapter I have examined the three main subgroups of the alternative scene: the political punks/the apolitical/drunk punks, and the straight edgers. Each subgroup subscribes to its own distinctive ideology or set of rules, of rebellion, which addresses the best means and ends of rebellion. These ideologies of rebellion also influence the attitudes towards slamdancing and moshing adopted by members of the scene's subgroups. Political punks advocate communal rebellion over more individualistic action, and their goal is the elimination of imposed rules in favour of a self-imposed order. These punks often reject slamdancing and moshing because aspects of these dances clash with both the means and the ends of political punk rebellion. On the one hand, the bodily motions involved in slamdancing and moshing favour individualised, rather than group-oriented, action, so violating the political punk emphasis on communal action. On the other hand, the symbolic breakdown of order in the pit is not the self-imposed order desired by political punks. Slamdancing and moshing serve as a physical rejection of the values of political punks, so these scene members denounce the dances in return.

Apolitical punks, on the other hand, find in slamdancing a reflection of their ideology of rebellion. The individualistic bodily display in the pit mirrors the apolitical punk emphasis on rebellion through individual, instead of communal, action. The seemingly chaotic atmosphere in the pit, moreover, is a small-scale realisation of the apolitical punk goal of a society without rules. The straight edgers who developed moshing as an outgrowth of slamdancing also value personal over group rebellion. However, these scene members do not aim to eliminate all rules. Rather, they rebel in order to impose their rules on others. This desire for control and strength brought about moshing, a dance with greater emphasis than slamming on individual dancers controlling the pit. Slamdancing and moshing reflect the ideologies of rebellion which exist in the American alternative scene and, through their participation in (and rejection of) these dances, members of the scene pledge allegiance to the rules that govern their rebellion.

Note

1. Among the twelve individuals I interviewed for this study, there were five apolitical drunk punks (four male, one female) and one male apolitical hard-core punk, all six of whom slamdanced. I also spoke with five people (four female, one male) who had associated themselves with the political punk scene, Only one of these five still slamdanced, and three of them did not consider themselves part of the alternative scene any longer. The twelfth interviewee, a woman, was the only mosher interviewed directly for the study, which is otherwise based on personal experience and correspondence.

Chapter 15

Keith Kahn-Harris

'ROOTS'?
The relationship between the global and the local within the Extreme Metal scene

USIC'S 'MALLEABILITY' (TAYLOR, 1997) has always facilitated its export and import from one location to another. Indeed, such processes are central to the creation and dissemination of new musical forms. Yet in our contemporary globalised world, such processes occur ever more extensively and are rapidly giving rise to *new* forms of appropriation and syncretism. Record companies from the developed world find new audiences in the developing world (Laing, 1986). Musicians from the West appropriate non-Western music, sometimes collaboratively (Feld, 1994; Taylor, 1997). Non-Western musicians and musicians from subaltern groups within the West create new syncretic forms that draw on both Western and non-Western music (Mitchell, 1996; Lipsitz, 1994, Slobin, 1993). The resulting 'global ecumene' produces considerable 'cultural disorder' (Featherstone, 1990: 6) whose results cannot easily be summarised.

Yet while there is no privileged standpoint from which to make an overall judgement on the results of the globalisation of music, it is important to attempt to find an analytical perspective that would enable us to relate particular cases to global processes. Certain global musics may produce so many knotty paradoxes that analysis may lose site of the general picture within the complexities of the particular. This study examines one particular paradox, that of the career of the Brazilian Death Metal band Sepultura. I want to show how analysing their career through an examination of the 'scene' through which they travelled allows us to appreciate the unique way in which they responded to globalisation, without losing site of the global flows of capital that structured their career.

In using 'scene' as an analytical framework, I am drawing on both academic and everyday uses of the term. In its academic context, 'scene' is closely related to 'subculture'. However, while 'subculture' connotes a tight-knit, rigidly bounded, implacably 'resistant', male-dominated, geographically specific social space, 'scene' connotes a more flexible, loose kind of space within which music is produced;

a kind of 'context' for musical practice. It assumes less about the homogeneity and coherence of its constituent activities and members (Straw, 1991; Shank, 1994; Olson, 1998). In everyday usage, 'scene' is used in a variety of ways. In Extreme Metal practice, the most common use of it is to refer to local, face-to-face contexts of music-making and consumption (e.g. 'The Gothenburg Death Metal Scene').

Sepultura and the Extreme Metal scene

The Extreme Metal scene emerged in the 1980s out of an interconnected musical and institutional rejection of Heavy Metal. Influenced by punk, bands such as Venom began to develop more radicalised forms of Metal that eschewed melody and clear singing in favour of speed, down-tuned guitars and growled or screamed vocals. From a very early stage, the Extreme Metal Scene was always highly decentralised. Many of its participants never met face to face. Moreover, bands from countries outside the traditional Anglo-American 'core' of the recording industry – for example, Chile, Malaysia and Israel – were influential in the scene's development. While the Extreme Metal scene is characterised by a far greater level of decentralisation than Heavy Metal, local scenes have also been important in its development. For example, in the 1980s the San Francisco 'Bay Area' scene was crucial in the development of Thrash, while in the late 1980s and early 1990s Death Metal was popularised via strong local scenes in Stockholm and Tampa, Florida. Similarly, during the mid-1990s Black Metal was popularised through the Norwegian scene.

Sepultura's early albums, however, are not representative of a uniquely Brazilian Extreme Metal style. Their crude form of Thrash/Death Metal has strong similarities to early Thrash and Death Metal bands such as Sodom and Kreator. The fast drumming dominates everything and gives the guitar riffs an indistinct feel. The gruff vocals are heavily treated with reverb and brief phrases are spat out rather than sung. The lyrics, written in basic and ungrammatical English, deal with topics such as Satanism and war. It would be easy to conclude that in their early career Sepultura simply copied more prominent Extreme Metal bands from elsewhere in the world. However, from a very early stage Sepultura were not only connected to the global scene, but also contributed to it. Thus, Sepultura should rather be seen as one of many bands from throughout the world involved in the decentralised process through which the emerging genre of Death Metal was created out of Thrash Metal. At the same time, however, Sepultura's location in Brazil was not insignificant. Certainly, the Brazilian scene from which Sepultura emerged never popularised a particular style in the way that more famous local scenes did, but it did have its own unique characteristics. For one thing, the early Brazilian scene was not only marginal to the global Extreme Metal scene, but Western-style rock was at that stage in a non-hegemonic position in the country as a whole (Schreiner, 1993). Indeed, the scene was largely confined to São Paolo and a few other cities (Sepultura were from Belo Horizonte), and it interacted closely with the punk scene. The unique Brazilian praxis that the band helped to fashion was different from other local praxes worldwide. Moreover, writing Extreme Metal lyrics in English was no easy task. The language barrier was considerable, at least at first. The Portuguese names of early Brazilian bands such as Sarcofago and Holocausto (Sepultura means 'grave') testify to their greater familiarity with their native language. It was difficult to purchase good equipment and foreign records due to high import taxes. Brazil's lack of prosperity was also highly significant, with the band coming from struggling lower middle-class families. The Brazilian scene, while having its own embryonic institutions, was thus extremely limited in scope in the early to mid-1980s, with only a few shops catering for Metal and a handful of tiny record labels.

Scenes are never static but are constantly in movement, following particular 'logics of change' (Straw, 1991). By the time Sepultura released *Schizophrenia* in 1987, the global and Brazilian scenes had begun to change. In Brazil, rock music was becoming more popular, partly due to the annual 'Rock in Rio' festivals. Sepultura now had a predominant position within Brazilian Metal. On the *Schizophrenia* tour they played to at least 2,000 people every night and sold 10,000 copies of the album (as much as established bands such as Slayer and Anthrax). Globally, Death and Thrash Metal had emerged as standardised genres within a rapidly solidifying set of scenic institutions. Whereas previously the global extreme metal scene had been sustained by a few hundred people linking up isolated local scenes through communication by tape, letter and the occasional record or fanzine, more people were now involved and there were increasing numbers of bands, record companies, fanzines and distribution services. *Schizophrenia* was widely circulated within the global scene and greatly facilitated the band's international reputation, resulting in their 1988 signing to New York-based Roadracer Records (now Roadrunner). Sepultura's decision to leave Brazil physically in order to further their career is revealing. Interviews at the time and since saw the band talking of 'escaping' Brazil and expanding to the global. As Max Cavalera said in an interview with *Kerrang* in 1989:

> It's very difficult because there's almost no chance for a HM band to get on a major label here and also because the Metal crowd is mostly poor people . . . Then if you happen to come into some money and want to produce a big show or something like that, the poor people can't afford to pay to come to the show!

The work of Pierre Bourdieu provides a way of linking an analysis of the phenomenology of how decisions are made with an appreciation of the constraining force of structure and capital. For Bourdieu, all practice occurs in 'fields' (1989), a concept with a certain similarity to scene, in which certain forms of capital circulate. The positions that individuals take within fields are guided by their 'habitus' (1993), through which they understand what possibilities are open and closed to them. In this way we can see that the scene limits or opens possibilities to follow particular trajectories. These possibilities are not simply drawn on by individuals or groups, but are continually being reformulated, negotiated and contested. The questions to ask when looking at the career of Sepultura are: what possibilities opened up to them at various times in their career? how did they create their own possibilities? how did these decisions link to the forms of capital available to them? In avoiding the 'why' there is a danger of writing a cultural history that is entirely without agency or motivation. Yet the 'why' may reveal itself indirectly through an appreciation of the 'how'.

From this perspective the most revealing thing about Max Cavalera's observations in the *Kerrang* interview is the assumption that signing to a major label and putting on a 'big show' would be both desirable and possible. While such sentiments would have been contested by some who valued staying small and 'underground', global success was not problematised within the Extreme Metal scene at that pivotal moment in Sepultura's career to quite the same extent as in other scenes. Sepultura's 'subcultural capital' (Thornton, 1995), their prestige and status within the scene, was convertible into other kinds of capital, capital that could bring them financial and institutional support. The career of Sepultura up until and after their signing to Roadrunner was dominated by a particular scenic logic that enabled local scene members to interact within the global underground. However, the possibility of financial rewards and a full-time career in music-making was only possible if a band focused more single mindedly on the global scene.

From 1989 onwards, Sepultura rapidly became one of the most successful Death Metal bands in the world. In 1991 the band recruited experienced Extreme Metal act manager Gloria Bujnowski and relocated to Bujnowski's hometown of Phoenix. In that period Sepultura were musically and physically at their most distant from Brazil. The Metal press quickly stopped mentioning Sepultura's Brazilianness and treated them like any other prominent Metal band. In most respects, Sepultura had become a leading global Metal band whose connections to Brazil had become less and less salient. Sepultura's trajectory reinforced the trajectory of a global scene within which local scenes produced very similar sounding music and within which place was not musically attended to.

As the 1990s progressed, the hegemony of Death Metal within the Extreme Metal was eroded by the development of Doom and Black Metal, each of which placed more emphasis on place, cultural origin and nationhood. The musical construction of place also began to find a voice in Extreme Metal, notably the 'Oriental Metal' of the Israeli band Orphaned Land and the 'Salsa Metal' of the Venezuelan band Laberinto. Sepultura also contributed to this trajectory. The band had occasionally used 'Brazilian' elements such as the 'um, dois, um, dois, tres, quatro' introduction to the song 'Troops Of Doom' on *Morbid Visions* and a percussion introduction to the title track on *Arise*. There were also occasional lyrics dealing with Brazilian political issues in veiled terms, such as 'Murder' from the album *Arise*. But it was in the 1996 album *Roots* that the most concerted attempt to signify Brazilianness was made. Whereas previous albums had focused on oppression within Brazil, *Roots* wields 'Brazil' as a positive musical and symbolic resource. As Max Cavalera is quoted as saying on the press release accompanying the album: 'I wanted to show some parts of Brazil that were artistic, rather than just songs about street kids and government corruption.'

The demands of extremity and heaviness are refracted through the idea of *Roots*. It is an idea that draws on the power of tradition and community as well as the pain and oppression of Brazilian history. The lyrics speak of constant struggle, but struggle through which strength and unity can be achieved. The music has also changed from their earlier speed-obsessed Thrash with clean guitar sounds. On *Roots*, heavily down-tuned guitars (low E tuned to B or D) create an oppressive, almost drone-like effect over Igor Cavalera's drumming that is pushed high in the mix and relies on the toms as much as bass, snare and hi-hat. Max Cavalera's vocals are often distorted, underlining the oppressive feeling. To this claustrophobic mixture on various tracks is added Brazilian percussion instruments and on one track ('Attitude') the 'Berimbau' – a stringed instrument of Afro-Brazilian origin. These instruments are deployed in such a way that they do not jar. Rather, they create a pummelling, reinforcing effect that adds to the extreme mixture.

Roots refracts the concerns of a global music scene through the lens of a particular construction of Brazilianness. The 'roots' returned to are not tokenistic incorporations of an exotic 'other' to prop up a moribund music, but a resource to be learned from that is part of Sepultura who are also part of a wider, global scene. Nor are roots seen as autochthonous and bounded, but multi-ethnic syncretic and complex:

> . . . we're showing some of the best parts of our country, the colours, the culture and music of the Indians, the African influence with all the percussion and things like that. So we've shown some of those roots, the music of Brazil, and our own roots too – the big cities where we come from, the urban metal style.
>
> Interview with Andreas Kisser, Terrorizer 37,
> November 1996

In many ways, Roots has much in common with the work of other Brazilian musicians, such as Chico Science, who have attempted to syncretise various Brazilian musics with contemporary rock music (McGowan and Pessanha, 1998). Like all such projects, Roots has its problems. While the native Xavante musicians featured on the album appear to have been treated with respect and receive royalties, it is unclear how they understood the project and what they will get out of it. Neither can Sepultura ensure that those who purchase their albums will not exoticise the Brazilianness in the project. Nonetheless, Sepultura did approach Roots in a spirit of discovery that avoids many of the pitfalls that other artists have fallen into in such projects.

There are no easy explanations as to why Sepultura began to experiment with Death Metal, and particularly why they began to use Brazil as a musical and lyrical resource. What is clear is that Sepultura's success in the early 1990s in producing 'placeless' Death Metal left them with the capital to be able to experiment widely with whoever and whatever they wished. The more success that Sepultura have achieved, the more removed they have become from the Brazilian scenic infrastructure, but also the more able they have been to play with new musical possibilities. So global success enabled experimentation with new 'local' and other syncretisms as much as it distanced them from the brute facts of location.

The potentials and problems of the Extreme Metal scene

I began this chapter by arguing the importance of understanding the processes of globalisation in music in ways that allow us to appreciate the specificities and paradoxes of particular cases, while relating them to general global processes and structures. As we have seen, the concept of the scene allows us to examine the ways in which Sepultura's trajectory was produced *by* and productive of particular global-local relations. The case of Sepultura resists simple global-local dichotomies. Instead, at particular points in their career, their position within the scene enabled different ways of responding to their position within Brazil and the world. What might Sepultura tell us about the potentials and problems of the globalisation of music?

Music is deeply implicated in the construction of place, and individual and group identities are tied into this construction. Martin Stokes has shown how music in various locations 'evokes and organises collective memories and present experiences of place with an intensity, power and simplicity unmatched by any other social activity' (1994: 13). Industrialisation and globalisation have made available an increasingly large range of musical resources that have enabled a growing range of groups and individuals to use them in the construction of identity and location.

The very mobility and malleability of music that makes it such a potent tool in empowering people to respond to their location in the world is of course the result of 'flows' (Lash and Urry, 1994) of various forms of capital. These flows result in severe inequalities in the ability of groups to appropriate and distribute music. However much people may feel that a particular music is essentially 'theirs', any exclusive sense of musical ownership is permanently under threat. Western artists may appropriate non-Western musics in ways that trivialise or exoticise them in the dilettante search for new musical materials. Global musical flows are facilitated by multinational corporations that are able to wield substantial financial and other resources. The international state system also affects global flows of music. This can work either through straightforward means such as censorship, or in more complex ways such as the uneven implementation of copyright law. What is intertextuality to some, is straightforward stealing to those who do not have recourse to copyright and capital. Of course, subordinate groups do often appropriate music themselves and sometimes do penetrate other musical markets, but in broad terms the interlinkage of musical and capital flows is highly problematic.

Thus, a vision of what sort of musical texts we would like to see in a world in which processes of globalisation are inescapable must bear in mind both the ability of music to enable people to 'penetrate' their locations in the world *and* the inability of music to transcend global flows of capital and power. It is important to try to envisage a global musical practice as free as possible from large differentials of capital that would reconcile the deep emotional investments in ideas of ownership stemming from the musical construction of place with the fact that music can and *will* travel. This practice should enable the circulation of music and yet still allow for the penetration of locality, identity and ownership in unique, but non-essentialising ways.

An examination of the career of Sepultura within the Extreme Metal scene provides one way of assessing whether the scene might provide a model for this global musical practice. Their Brazil is more than a crudely deployed signifier or a rigidly policed 'authentic' discourse. It is rather a hybrid and flexible concatenation of the discursive and the real that continually links the global and the local. Yet the position from which they are producing this music is, in the last analysis, a highly privileged and capital-rich position. Although they have made concerted attempts to retain Brazilian connections, the connections are those of privileged migrants who can leave whenever they wish. The global Extreme Metal scene enabled them to achieve this position through its exceptional decentralisation in the 1980s and early 1990s. It remains unlikely today that a Brazilian Metal (or indeed rock) band could achieve global prominence in any other way than through such a scene. Yet at the time, the scene was accompanied by a musical practice that did not treat place as a musical resource. Although today place is a musical resource within the scene, it is generally constructed in essentialist, sometimes racist ways. For all its global decentralisation, there is intense ambivalence within the scene towards more complex and ambiguous penetrations of the global and the local. *Roots,* together with Sepultura's subsequent work, was made possible by a more unencumbered position within a wider Metal scene that challenged global flows of capital far less. Moreover, the widening gap between the resurgent Metal scene and the Extreme Metal scene means that the latter is becoming ever less willing and able to learn from Sepultura's musical example.

All that said, the Extreme Metal scene is far closer to the global musical practice we are looking for than are many other scenes. At its best, it allows bands such as Sepultura to galvanise musicians and fans across the world yet still attend to local specificity. As Regev (1997) has argued, such 'reflexive communities' (Lash and Urry, 1994) have the potential to provide temporary resolutions to the apparent contradiction between participation in the field of (global) popular music and the field of local/national identity. The scene also enables members across the world to interact on a fairly equal basis. The scene has the potential to avoid both the tight restrictions of traditional musical subcultures and the anomie of isolated musical occurrences facilitated by large multinationals.

In a similar way, a 'scenic methodology' recontextualises musical texts, institutions and practices within the social spaces in which they are enmeshed. It provides an alternative both to atomising forms of research that ignore wider contexts of music production and consumption, and to forms of research that overdetermine those contexts in 'subcultural' frameworks. The concept allows us to build ideal types in the search for models for a global musical culture. The theoretical and methodological moves involved in developing the concept of the scene can thus provide new ways of thinking about globalisation and music.

Popular music and everyday life

Introduction to Part Four

■ Andy Bennett

DURING THE 1970S AND 1980S, popular music studies was largely concentrated around issues of production, performance and text. Although some research on audiences did exist, this was largely carried out by theorists associated with subcultural theory or youth cultural studies that were more broadly defined. The more mundane significance of popular music for that majority of individuals who were not involved in its production and performance, or associated with a subcultural group, remained largely unexplored. In the 1990s, an increasing awareness on the part of academic researchers of popular music's significance in a range of everyday settings gave rise to a new body of literature. Such work examined the significance of popular music in a variety of hitherto uncharted contexts, including the relationship between music and memory, and music and biography. Similarly, the invention of new devices such as the Sony Walkman, and the various upgrades in personal stereo that followed, led to an interest among researchers concerning issues of musical ownership as it became clear that personal stereo users often compiled their own collections of music to suit their particular tastes and moods. Other developments in digital technology, notably sampling, provided music composers with new possibilities for the juxtaposition of previously different music genres and also for the use of everyday sounds, such as traffic, birdsong, flowing water, etc., in their work. Such new compositional sensibilities in turn led to new understandings of music, not as something defined by specific genres, nor even governed by beats and time signatures, but as tones and textures of sound that could be used to create soundscapes. The studies featured in this section of the *Reader* illustrate the developing awareness among researchers of popular music's significance in a variety of everyday life contexts.

DeNora's empirical study of the relationship between music and self-identity examines how particular pieces of music are appropriated by the individual in such a way that they effectively become part of his/her biography. As DeNora explains, this process can operate at a variety of levels. A typical response of those individuals who took part in DeNora's research was to claim that music functioned as a link to the past, reminding them of a particular place or person that had once been important in their lives. Such is the power of music in evoking these sorts of memories, argues DeNora, that it could elicit very powerful emotions in individuals as the lyrics of particular songs, or the flow of musical passages that vividly reminded them of holidays, previous relationships or close relatives who had since passed away. DeNora further considers how music is also instrumental in the facilitation of individual identities in the here and now. According to DeNora, individuals are able to 'find themselves' in music, the ways in which particular songs and pieces of music are structured – their rhythmic elements, harmonic sequences and tonal textures – bringing out particular aspects of an individual's personality. Indeed, suggests DeNora, the use of music in this way allows the listener to move beyond the notion of a single personality. Through listening to and absorbing the moods inherent in different styles of music, individuals are able to express a range of personalities to suit different everyday contexts.

Bull's work on the use of the personal stereo takes the relationship between music, everyday life and self-identity in a somewhat different direction. A major aspect of Bull's work is a consideration of how long periods of immersion in the individual soundscapes created through personal stereo use informs the phenomenological experience of the listener. In the selection from his work featured here, Bull examines how personal stereo users often describe the experience of listening to music as they pass through their normal everyday surroundings as 'cinematic'. In other words, the everyday life scenarios observed by the personal stereo user are compared with the experience of watching a film. As Bull explains, in describing this experience, personal stereo users adopt a range of aesthetic positions. In some instances, they place themselves in a particular part or role in the film, using the music playing in their headset as a means narrating their interactions with other 'actors' they encounter in the street, the park or on the bus during their journey to work. In other cases, they assume the role of a detached observer, placing others in the role of actors using the music to create imaginary roles for them. Bull further considers how listening to music through the medium of the personal stereo in certain locations can create other kinds of cinematic experience, the style and mood of the music corresponding at a phenomenological level with the physical appearance and atmosphere of a place to create a personalised form of spatial narrative.

The increasing part played by popular music in the creation of everyday soundscapes has also been facilitated by new developments in digital recording and sound production. One particularly significant development in this respect has been the rise of 'ambient', a musical genre characterised by sweeping chords and tone textures, giving it a dreamy, floating quality. As the featured extract from David Toop's highly influential book *Ocean of Sound* examines, 'ambient' has produced new understandings and everyday uses of music. From its function as 'chill-out' music at dance events to its use in the home environment as relaxing background music, ambient facilitates transgression from the mundane routine of everyday life, offering the individual a space for spirituality and reflection.

Another genre of music that has also played its part in defining an alternative soundscape to the more rhythmic styles of rock, dance and so on, is Easy-Listening. Significantly, although more loosely defined than ambient, Easy-Listening has been far more systematically marketed in ways designed to reach target audiences. As the selected piece from Joseph Lanza's book *Elevator Music* explains, in the US Easy-Listening periodically took its place along other more mainstream styles of music with the establishment of radio stations dedicated purely to the broadcasting of music considered to fall within the Easy-Listening category.

Chapter 16

Tia DeNora

MUSIC AND SELF-IDENTITY

IN THE LIGHT OF RECENT SOCIAL THEORY, the concepts of self-identity, personality and biography have undergone major redevelopment. No longer conceptualized as a fixed or unitary entity – as something that is an expression of inner 'essence' – identity has been recast conceptually as a product of social 'work' (Garfinkel 1967; Giddens 1991; DeNora 1995). A great deal of identity work is produced as presentation of self to other(s) – which includes a micro-politics – through the enactment of a plethora or mini 'docu-dramas' over the course of a day (see Garfinkel 1967). But the 'projection' of biography is by no means the only basis for the construction of self-identity. Equally significant is a form of introjection, a presentation of self *to* self, the ability to mobilize and hold on to a coherent image of 'who one knows one is'. And this involves the social and cultural activity of remembering, the turning over of past experiences, for the cultivation of self-accountable imageries of self. Here music comes to the fore, as part of the retinue of devices for memory retrieval (which is, simultaneously, memory construction). Music can be used as a device for the reflexive process of remembering/constructing who one is, a technology for spinning the apparently continuous tale of who one is. To the extent that music is used in this way it is not only, in Radley's sense, a device of artefactual memory (Radley, 1990; Urry 1996); it is a device for the generation of future identity and action structures, a mediator of future existence.

'The song is you' – identity and relation through music

One of the first things that respondents used music for was to remember key people in their lives – for example, loved family members who had died. Monica says:

> There's a piece of music that my grandad used to like very much and
> sometimes I'll be feeling a bit reminiscent about him because we were

very close and I'd listen to that to remember him, but it wouldn't make me sad, it doesn't make me happy either, it's just sort of, 'I've just remembered you today', sort of thing, you know.

Similarly, Lucy describes how, shortly after her father had died:

> I was coming home from choir practice one evening, and I had the car radio on, switched it on as soon as I got going, and it was playing the [Brahms] *Double Concerto* and I just had to stop, and some friends were coming behind, you know, and I was just in floods of tears and they said, 'Why don't you turn it off' and I said, 'I can't' and that it was ages before I could listen to that or anything like it without thinking of him, it's only in the last year or so, because I know now that it meant so much to him and it means so much to me and I realize now how much like him I am. That's not to say my mother didn't have an important role in music as well . . .

The most frequent type of relationship that respondents described in relation to music was romantic or intimate. Music helped them to recall lovers or former partners and, with these memories, emotionally heightened phases or moments in their lives. Diana, for example, described her listening habits and her tendency to listen to biographically key music in the 'late evening . . . I'm on my own with peace and quiet in my study and I'm often up till two in the morning. I regard this time as my own space'.

> Diana   . . . I had an affair with a Londoner and we used to go out in the evenings, about twice a week. I don't know how I managed it. Oh, I know, because my husband was [working at home] and I would just say I was going out and we used to go to a [London] pub . . . and [there singers] used to sing to pop music of that era and 'A Whiter Shade of Pale' was our tune and I just loved it, and I suppose that affair went on for about two years, two and a half years.
>
> Q   Can you tell me about how it came to be your tune? You heard it in that bar did you?
>
> Diana   Yes, and of course it was on the radio all the time. Yes, we just sort of were absorbed in each other, or we'd hold hands or look at each other intently, something like that.

For many of the respondents, such as Diana, music was linked to a 'reliving' of an event or crucial time, linked often to a relationship. Even within the confines of the small, exploratory sample of 52, certain works appeared more than once:

> Lucy   There's the whole pop music of the Sixties and all those hits which can instantly bring back memories . . . 'A Whiter Shade of Pale' . . . I can say it's [German university town] *Hauptbahnhof*, in August 1967, you know! . . . [It] was the hit

in summer '67, and I spent a semester in Germany as a student, and being there in the station, I was just leaving there to go to France, in fact, to meet up with [her future husband] . . . and we spent the summer, well, a couple of weeks, in France and that was the big record then, and . . . I suppose that was the start of our – just before we got engaged or whatever . . . but it was just, just culminated the Sixties I think, there were a whole lot of songs like that . . .

Q   Do you ever listen to that song now?

Lucy   Well I just heard it the other day. I was in a shop, buying something, and there was a woman about the same age as me [fifty-two] and I said, 'That takes you back, doesn't it?' and she said, 'Yeah' [laughs] and in fact, it was a CD, hits of the sixties, that they were playing in that shop.

Q   How did you feel, you said, 'It takes you back'?

Lucy   I just felt happy, you know, reminded me of [things] . . .

As Deborah puts it, 'I have relationship songs, everyone has their relationship songs, and then years later when I talk to somebody I go, 'Oh my God, I totally related that with us, with you.' Maria, for example, describes an outdoor concert she heard on holiday:

Now every time I hear a certain kind of new age music, I think of the sky that night and the moon. It was a hot summer, the tall trees, and standing there, arm next to arm with David, feeling electric, like part of a chain of being with him and our environment.

For Maria, Diana and Deborah, music reminds them of who they were at a certain time – a moment, a season, an era – and helps them to recapture the aesthetic agency they possessed (or which possessed them) at that time. Reliving experience through music is also (re)constituting past experience; it is making manifest within memory what may have been latent or even absent the first time through (Urry, 1996) and music provides a device of prosthetic biography (Lury, 1998). Indeed, the *telling* about the past in this way, and of music's ability to invoke past feelings and ways of being is itself part of this reconstitution. The telling is part of the work of producing one's self as a coherent being over time, part of producing a retrospection that is in turn a resource for projection into the future, a cueing in to how to proceed. In this sense, the past, musically conjured, is a resource for the reflexive movement from present to future, the moment-to-moment production of agency in real time. It serves also as a means of putting actors in touch with capacities, reminding them of their accomplished identities, which in turn fuels the ongoing projection of identity from past into future. Musically fostered memories thus produce past trajectories that contain momentum.

At the most general and most basic level, music is a medium that can be and often is simply paired or associated with aspects of past experience. It was part of the past and so becomes an emblem of a larger interactional, emotional complex. A good deal of music's affective powers come from its co-presence with other things

– people, events, scenes. To stop at this point, however, is to fail to appreciate the extent of music's semiotic powers in relation to the construction of memory and, indeed, to the experience that comes to be lodged and is 'retrievable' within auto-biographical memory. These two issues are related. They need to be developed because they lead into the matter of how, as it is sometimes put, 'the music itself' is active in the constitution of the shape of subjectivity and self-identity.

Musical memories and the choreography of feeling

Music moves through time; it is a temporal medium. This is the first reason why it is a powerful *aide-mémoire*. Like an article of clothing or an aroma, music is part of the material and aesthetic environment in which it was once playing, in which the past, now an artefact of memory and its constitution, was once a present. Unlike material objects, however, music that is associated with past experience was, within that experience, heard over time. And when it is music that is associated with a particular moment and a particular space, music reheard and recalled provides a device for unfolding, for replaying, the temporal structure of that moment, its dynamism as emerging experience. This is why, for so many people, the past 'comes alive' to its soundtrack.

But there is yet more to it. For the women described above, the soundtrack of their action was not mere accompaniment. It did not merely follow their experience, was not merely overlaid upon it. True, the particular music may have been arbitrarily paired with the experiential moment – indeed, Diana, Maria and Lucy all describe how the music that 'brings it all back' was music that 'happened' to be playing, that was simply part of the environment or era. But the creation of that 'moment' as a heightened moment was due in part to the alchemy of respondents' perceived or sensed 'rightness' or resonance between the situation, the social relationship, the setting, the music, and themselves as emerging aesthetic agents with feelings, desires, moods such that the music *was* the mood, and the mood, the music. To the extent that music comes to penetrate experience in this way, it is informative of that experience. Music thus provides parameters – or potential parameters because it has to be meaningfully attended to – for experience constituted in real time. It serves, as was discussed in the previous chapters, as a referent for experience. It is no wonder, then, that on rehearing music that helped to structure, to inform experience, respondents describe how they are able to relive that experience. The study of human–music interaction thus reveals the subject, memory and, with it, self-identity, as being constituted on a fundamentally socio-cultural plane where the dichotomy between 'subjects' and 'objects' is, for all practical purposes, null and void.

Music may thus be seen to serve as a container for the temporal structure of past circumstances. Moreover, to the extent that, first time through, a past event was constructed and came to be meaningful with reference to music, musical structures may provide a grid or grammar for the temporal structures of emotional and embodied patterns as they were originally experienced. Music is implicated in the ways that, as Urry observes with poignant reference to Proust's famous phrase, 'our arms and legs . . . [are] full of torpid memories' (Urry, 1996: 49); it is a mediator of, in Proust's sense, the aesthetic, memory-encrusted unconscious (Lash and Urry, 1994: 43).

Finding 'the me in music' – musically composed identities

The sense of 'self is locatable in music. Musical materials provide terms and templates for elaborating self-identity – for identity's identification. Looking more closely at this process highlights the ways in which musical materials are active ingredients in identity work, how respondents 'find themselves' in musical structures. It also highlights some of the ways that music is attended to by its recipients, how music reception and the units of meaning that listeners find within music differ dramatically from musicological and music-psychological models of music reception and their emphasis on the perception of musical structures. Consider this example from the interview with Lucy:

Q	Have you ever adjusted the volume of music that's playing in your home, either to turn it down or turn it up?
Lucy	I would sometimes turn it up if something was playing, if it was coming to something I really liked, a nice juicy chord, or a bit that I liked, I'd say, 'Oh turn it up' or I'd go in and listen.
Q	'A bit that I like' – you've touched on that a couple of times earlier, that's something that's very interesting. Could you give me an example of some 'bit' of some piece of music, some chord or . . .
Lucy	Well, usually because it's just *a juicy* chord.
Q	What do you mean by 'juicy'?
Lucy	Well – a lot of notes, and, usually perhaps a lower register. I sing alto and I tend to like cello music and lower register music, you know, really punchy sound and, well, 'juicy' is the word, huge chords or just, I don't know, just a phrase, I can't think of a particular bit of music but, I think probably in the *Pastoral Symphony*, come to think of it, or there's lots in Vivaldi, Vivaldi has a good – and Brahms. There's certain things, that you just *wait* for that bit and you really enjoy it.

Lucy goes on to explain how these things may be highly personal: 'I don't know whether they're there for anyone else. I really don't know because they're gone in a second.' At the end of the interview, we returned to the topic of these 'juicy' musical moments, ones that feature the lower register sounds (she describes how she does not like soprano solos) and chords:

Q	You said, you're an alto, and you like music that brings out the lower sounds. Why *is* that? [laughs]
Lucy	I have no idea! [laughs] Maybe because it's sort of *meatier or* something and a sort of more intense experience.

When pressed further, Lucy says that she thinks she likes the lower sonorities:

Lucy	[they are] part of the background. I think it's more being in the background rather than being, because the soprano tends to have

> the tune, even if it's not a solo soprano, whereas we [altos] provide the meat – it's the sopranos and the tenors that carry the song, if you like, and the basses and the altos that *fill out* to make it a sort of – [she stops and looks at me questioningly]
>
> Q   A sonic whole?
> Lucy   Yeah. And I think that maybe that characterizes me in life, that I don't like being in the limelight, I like to – [pause]
> Q   I'm an alto too [laughs].
> Lucy   [Laughs] Yes.
> Q   So, not being 'in the limelight' but being?
> Lucy   Being part of a group. And, you know, pressing forward and doing my bit but not – [pause]
> Q   Filling in, as it were, the needed middle?
> Lucy   Yeah. Seeing what needs doing and doing it but not being spotlighted and being 'out front' sort of thing.

Here Lucy makes a link between a preferred type of musical material ('juicy' chords), a concept of self-identity (the 'me in life') and a kind of social ideal ('doing my bit but not . . . being spotlighted'). She 'finds herself, so to speak, in certain musical structures that provide representations of the things she perceives and values about herself. In that sense, listening for (and turning up the volume on) the 'juicy' bits is a form of self-affirmation. Simultaneously, these bits provide images of self for self. Here, the music provides a material rendering of self-identity; a material in and with which to identify identity.

Using music in this way as a mirror for self-perception (locating within its structures the 'me in life', as Lucy puts it) is a common practice of identity work in daily life. Additionally, different styles of music can be used by the same person to articulate different identities. For example, Elaine, when asked to account for her self-identity, defines it in terms of its multifaceted character; she is a person with many dimensions, and her musical tastes and practices demonstrate this diversity, this range of personae that make up her 'self'. Indeed, Elaine was one of the most musically explosive respondents in the study, engaging in a great deal of 'bursting into song':

> I'm always singing. My kids – one thing I know this is something I always do, somebody says something I say, 'Oh, that reminds me' because it will remind me of a song and I'll say, 'Oh there is a song about that' and then I insist on singing a few lines so they – it's kind of a little joke thing that I do. 'Oh, Mom always knew a song about that'. It can be rather loosely related, but it's just a fun thing that we do, or that I do.

Elaine describes a diverse array of music in relation to her self-identity and its social cultural situation, but she does not describe any examples of lapsed or dropped music in relation to identity. For many respondents, though, identity work is achieved in and through the music to which they have *stopped* listening. Vanessa, for example, describes how she no longer listens to Brian Ferry: 'I haven't played him for years. But I was obsessed with him . . . I'm not interested at all now . . . I think that's a phase of life that's over and – I simply lost interest, I think . . .' At the end of the interview, she elaborates in more detail why she no longer listens to the music (her current favourite at the time of the interview was George Michael's 'Older'):

> I think they had a certain style which you wanted to try yourself. Maybe that's why I liked Roxy Music at that particular time. The high heels, the siren look, the diva vamp – you know, that type of thing. Roxy Music conjured up all that type of thing. I think you go through, you know. Now I like jazz – because of my age [52] maybe – I don't know.

Like Lucy, Vanessa was able to locate the 'me in life' musically. Unlike Lucy, that location took as its semiotic particle the complex of music and performer image. Also unlike Lucy, Vanessa can be seen to have dropped a particular musical mirror or representation of self when it no longer seemed tenable, when it no longer reflected the terms with which she could engage in self-description. Thus, in turning to different musics and the meaningful particles that 'reflect' and register self-identity, that provide a template of self, individuals are also choosing music that produces self-images that are tenable, that seem doable, habitable.

In this chapter, music has been portrayed as a temporal structure, as offering semiotic particles, as a medium with attendant conventional or biographical associations – in action as a device for ordering the self as an agent, and as an object known and accountable to oneself and others. Music may be understood as providing a container for feeling and, in this sense, its specific properties contribute to the shape and quality of feeling to the extent that feeling – to be sustained, and made known to oneself and others – must be established on a public or intersubjective plane. Music is a material that actors use to elaborate, to fill out and fill in, themselves and to others, modes of aesthetic agency and, with it, subjective stances and identities. This, then, is what *should* be meant when we speak of the 'cultural construction of subjectivity', and this is much more than an idea that culture underwrites generic structures of feeling or aesthetic agency, as is implied in so many poststructuralist writings and by musicologists trained in semiotic analysis of texts. Such structuralist perspectives remain distanced from the heart of the matter, from how individuals not only experience culture, but also how they mobilize culture for being, doing and feeling. Anything less cannot address and begin to describe or account for the mechanisms through which cultural materials get into social psychological life.

Chapter 17

Michael Bull

FILMIC CITIES
The aesthetic experience of the personal-stereo user

THE AESTHETICIZATION OF THE URBAN is well documented in the literature on urban habitation. Indeed it is one of the central motifs of much work that concentrates on the visual nature of aesthetic appropriation. Richard Sennett's work (1990, 1994) illuminates the visual prioritization of much urban experience which he contrasts to the decline of speech and touch in urban culture. Bauman (1993) also discusses the aesthetics of urban looking, while others focus on this mode of experience through a reappropriation of Benjamin's account of *flânerie* (Tester, 1994). In the following pages I interrogate the meaning and variety of 'aesthetic looking' through personal-stereo user accounts. In doing so, I produce a systematic analysis of urban aesthetic looking that contests existing accounts which position personal-stereo users as technologized *flâneurs* (Chambers, 1994; Hosokawa, 1984). Such accounts are firmly rooted in visual epistemologies of experience, and discount the specifically auditory nature of experience in general and looking in particular. In analysing auditory forms of the aesthetic, I question existing accounts of the everyday significance of such behaviour.

Personal-stereo users often refer to their experiences as being cinematic in nature. Users describe filmic experience in a variety of ways. An initial distinction can be made between specific recreations of filmic-type experience with personal narratives attached to them and more generalized descriptions of the world appearing to be like a film. However, to investigate the variety of meanings attached to descriptions of 'cinematic' experience, it is necessary to analyse in depth specific examples. In order to do this, I provide five re-created narrative examples. Each account is re-created in the spirit of the text with no content material added, but merely a situating narrative reconstructed directly from the interview material.

Five personal stereo stories

Mags's story

It's two o'clock in the morning. It's raining heavily in the street. Mag looks out of her window and decides she would like to walk; she likes the rain at night. The street is deserted. She hears the sound of the rain on the pavement. She takes a tape from a pile scattered randomly on the floor, puts her coat on, picks up her personal stereo and walks out the door. As she closes the door, she turns the volume up using the switch on her headphone lead. She keeps her finger on the volume control and starts walking, ready to change the volume if she sees anybody approach. She's relieved; the music on the tape is U2; she knows it well. She turns the volume up till the music seems to wash through her, and walks:

> It heightens. Everything becomes filmic. When you see things and when you have music on you hear a sound. I know that when you put music on to an actual image it becomes part of it. Actually, what I do is go out for a walk when it's pouring with rain with a Walkman on.

She can no longer hear the sound of the rain, but she feels it and can see it. The music transforms the scene in the following way:

> It makes it filmic. It seems more like a scene and you can imagine your- self as the tortured heroine from this film walking along in the rain and all this score . . . music blasting! You're the heroine. You can see your- self as if on the screen. You see what's in front of you.

The music on her personal stereo isn't film music. It's just a tape she knows well. She uses the music to construct her own scenario with herself in it:

> You hear it and you try to apply it to your surroundings. A tape you've listened to a lot. That you know really well. Lyrics that you've heard lots of times but you might decide that night to apply some importance to them when you play the scenario.

So she walks down the empty street, the tortured heroine to her own movie. Is she the heroine or is she mimicking someone else being the heroine?

> Both I suppose. I don't have a film in my head that I relate to.

The image is not specific, it doesn't necessarily remind her of a scene but is rather her own creation taken from a stock of memories of heroines from films half- forgotten, scenes barely remembered or scenes from the multitude of pop videos watched distractedly, or maybe even a trace from childhood novels of romance read from under the bedclothes deep into the night.

Dorinda's story

Dorinda rushes out of the flat. She's late again. It's a bright summer's morning. She switches on her personal stereo, clips it to her belt and gets on her bike. The streets are busy and she decides to take her normal detour through the park. The music swells up. It's her favourite personal stereo tape. Violins, Spanish guitar:

> I listen to *1492* a lot, which is the Conquest. Christopher Columbus, which says it all really. It's very much about journeys and it builds. It gives your journey more significance.

As she cycles, her body appears to lose its weight, the bike appears to be moving on its own to the music, but with her guiding it. It's just amazing. It has its prime moments, has it's tranquil moments. She's cycling quite fast. She just has the sound of the sweeping violins in her ears. She faintly hears the siren of a police car or ambulance. She turns into St James's Park and cycles on the footpath. Everything seems more vivid to her:

> On the bike you're very visually dependent. You're so visually dependent and here you are being provided with music to go with it and it's music you've chosen, and it can alter your perspective on things . . . It's a park. It's nicer than going on the road when you've got music to go with it. It will highlight certain things that you see, or it can do. I think it lends significance to what you're seeing, depending on what you're listening to.

She picks her music carefully. It has to fit, to be in tune with her mood and her surroundings. She constructs imaginary scenarios to what she sees while she cycles. She cycles past two people walking in the park. She imagines them as lovers, making up after a quarrel. She cycles along, constructing her own script. When she does this, she is focusing on outside. She doesn't think so much about herself, her own problems:

> Without the Walkman, you wouldn't, you might not even wonder. It's no significance. Suddenly, you're listening to 1492 and it's like 'Are they lovers?' You get caught up. You look at things differently – the pond, the flowers become more flowery. Things are enhanced, moments are enhanced . . . When there's music I think less. It becomes more my journey. It becomes more emotional. It becomes more of a sensory experience and it's lovely.

Yet while she's constructing her scenario in tune to the music, she doesn't see it as her own creation, her own direction:

> It's weird, isn't it? It's happening around me. No, I'm a viewer. I'm a viewer and I'm assimilating what I see. So it's more like watching a film, but it's my life.

Dorinda constructs a fleeting narrative out of her journey. This imaginary narrative she reflectively sees as a form of control:

But the fact that I'm seeing two people and imagining they're lovers. It's not about them. It's about me. It's my relationship to them. It brings it back to me. It's very self-indulgent to be riding a bike with a Walkman. Total control.

The control only works if the music is right though. Cycling in the evening and not wishing to play fast, moving music Dorinda says:

It just doesn't suit the films, the night-time film soundtrack that's my life. Not the soundtrack. You know what I mean.

Catriona's story

Catriona wears her personal stereo a lot; she often daydreams with it on. She likes going to movies. Just recently she has gotten very interested in the Quentin Tarantino movies *Reservoir Dogs* and *Pulp Fiction*. She has gone out and bought both soundtracks and she plays them repeatedly on her personal stereo. The music from these films makes her feel happy, confident. She likes the music to be loud. The fact that it is film music means that it has a different significance for her than if it was her normal listening music:

Because you can remember the scene. Two of the songs from *Reservoir Dogs*. I can remember exactly the scenes, so I think about that. It's funny because the opening scene, this first song, this soundtrack. They're all walking down the street. They've all got their suits on. I was listening to it the other day when I was walking down the street and the first track came on. I didn't feel I was in the film, but I could remember the feeling of the film listening to that song.

The feeling of the film remembered makes her feel more confident. She plays the soundtrack loud so that nothing else intrudes on her listening:

A friend of mine had just dropped me at Paddington. I had to walk to the tube stop. I put on *Reservoir Dogs*. This song at the beginning of the soundtrack. I just felt like I was really strutting. I'm sure I wasn't, but that's what it felt like. I was walking in time to the music.

The mood of the film is re-created through the music and becomes a part of Catriona's persona for that part of her journey.

Magnus's story

Magnus likes to enhance his environment and fantasizes to music on his personal stereo. He describes his actual environment as boring. He chooses his music and creates an adventure out of his normal but mundane journey. He describes the wearing of his personal stereo in town as creating a filmic situation in which he is a the central player:

> It's sort of like making my life a film. Like you have the sound, the soundtrack in the back.

Magnus has a certain idea of the type of film he likes to be in. His home town has an old square in it. He creates the image of:

> Something big with a lot of people, a lot of costumes, or sometimes like a Merchant Ivory film. There is this central square and then at the end there are stairs leading to the town. There is an old fortification. When I walk down to the centre of town I have to walk down these stairs and you walk down these stairs with some Beethoven or something. It makes it more interesting. Walking down, you feel like coming down in a film.

So Magnus is placing himself in a period film, the music isn't film music but merely creates the mood to enhance the surroundings as if it were film music. More specifically, he then begins to imagine or to create specific scenarios to go with the general scene, transforming the mundane into an adventure where he uses his imagination to place himself in the centre of a transformed scenario, heightening its significance and creating a world of expectation:

> I like to daydream. Imagine things. What might happen if I go round that corner. What might happen there. What if that person were standing there.

Magnus sees this as a form of perfect control to use his term:

> It enables me to sort of bring my own dreamworld. Because I have the familiar sounds with my music that I know and sort of cut out people. So the music is familiar. I can go into my perfect dreamworld where everything is as I want it.

Magnus's journeying with his personal stereo becomes an attempt to construct an imaginary world, a perfect image of his own fantasy:

> Everything is exactly as I want it. Everybody is nice, everybody happy, everyone is beautiful. The sun is always shining. I can do whatever I like, basically.

Jade's story

The following comes from extracts of the diary Jade kept, describing the use of his personal stereo:

Get on the bus going home. I'm listening to Rap music Thinking about the films I've watched. Trying to find things in *Goodfellas* that I've seen in other films. The journey is so long because of the traffic. I get so tense that I end up becoming a character from *Goodfellas* for fifteen minutes. I reach Our Price. Turn off my Walkman and it's fine to get in character.

I hear a sample from a movie on the song I'm listening to. It's from *A Few Dollars More*. Now I think about the scenes from that film. I then find that my mood has changed at work because whenever I speak to the colleague from Hell, I'm very cold and become a verbal bounty hunter. Whenever he says something, I just shoot him with short cool blasts of verbal abuse and collect the reward, which is a barrel of laughs.

Catch the bus. I'm listening to the soundtrack of *Pulp Fiction* which puts me in a better mood. While I'm listening to it I envisage myself in the film. That's how absorbed the film's got me. Sometimes I wish I was the bad guy in life with all those witty lines that just shuts people up. So I mentally picture myself in *Pulp Fiction* except that there would be a few more murders and that Ingrid Bergman, Liz Taylor, Deborah Kerr were in it. Then I arrive at work in character repeating all the lines from ages past.

The image is visualized and also represents the fantasized re-creation of a role controlled by the person. The mimetic function of music and film is especially apparent in the above example from a respondent's diary where the language also takes on the narrative and tone of the films mentioned.

The above examples demonstrate a variety of meanings given to filmic experience that varies according to the subject and situation. In the first example, Mags attempts to re-create the physicality or atmosphere of a film by physically going out in the dark. She is in the centre of her movie, yet her surroundings are perceived to be real – for example it has to be raining. She doesn't appear able or willing to transform a scene into one where it is raining. This would fit in with her belief that using her personal stereo during the day is not so filmic for her. Her normal day-to-day use does not conjure up these images for her. There is a similarity in Mag's description of filmic experience with the actualexperience of being in the cinema. She is in a darkened space where she looks ahead of herself in isolation and she places herself in the position of being central, and literally she is the heroine in the centre of the movie.

    The second example of Dorinda constructing her scenario on her bicycle is very different. She constructs the experience as one of projection. She looks out and constructs the narrative as if directing it. For her, the environment and the characters in it provide a fragmented, fleeting mode of appropriation. She is, of course, moving faster on her bike. People assume the role of characters in her film; the film essentially being her journey: 'the night-time film soundtrack, that's my life'. For this, she needs film music that is the soundtrack to a film about a journey, like her own in that respect. Dorinda, unlike Mags, does not necessarily place herself as a character in her narrative but as a viewer. The scene is created as a fictional narrative, not as a part of her autobiography. Although she does mention the soundtrack to the 'film of her life', this appears to be generalized.

Catriona's transformation of her world differs from this. She, like Dorinda, uses specific film music, in this case most recently *Reservoir Dogs* and *Pulp Fiction*. She plays the soundtracks repeatedly, liking the music but also re-creating the atmosphere of the actual movie in her mind. She recollects the various scenes from the film, visualizes them while walking. She doesn't attempt to impose herself on to the scene, merely to re-create it in her head. Also, she doesn't try to transform her surroundings, so there is no visual transformation of the meaning of her surroundings. Her filmic experience is totally hermetic to herself and the music. This, however, is translated into her physical movements which represent a greater confidence as she walks in time to the music through the street. Although this appears to be as much a response to the beat of the music as any characterization of herself in the film. The visual element in Catriona's re-experiencing is lacking. The experience is one of internal re-creation.

Jade's diary entries, while appearing similar to Catriona's inasmuch as no visual heightening or re-creation takes place in his filmic re-creation of experience, differ in all other respects. Jade transforms his attitude to social interaction through film characterization bringing the character of the lead into play in his actual dealings with others. While listening to film music, more often than not Westerns, but also *film noir* and gangster movies, Jade puts himself into the leading character role and becomes a Clint Eastwood or John Travolta, mimicking their language or their perceived manner in 'dealing' with situations. He becomes the star who sorts things out; who nobody successfully 'messes' with. He has an omnipotent fantasy in his dealings with others, especially in times of tension or conflict. The film music puts him into 'character' or 'mood'. He listens on his journeys to and from work and so puts himself into character on arrival. While on the bus he re-creates the movie, as does Catriona, but imaginatively re-creates the film, filling it with his favourite screen stars, while always keeping the central character 'in character'.

Magnus's account on the face of it appears to be similar to Mags's, although with a heightened sense of control. His 'dreamworld' might be seen to be structurally similar to hers. However, he seems literally to reimagine his surroundings, placing them into a scene of a movie, thus making it conform to his desires by transforming it into a romantic period piece with music to suit the surroundings. Having the right music is very important in this instance. He, unlike Mags, will populate his scene with others who become the props to his fantasy. Magnus lays great stress on the perfection of his creation. It becomes a function of his need to perceive things in terms of perfect control. He, like Mags, is at the centre of his movie, but he actively constructs possible adventures, such as imagining what might happen to him if he takes a left turn rather than a right, thus creating an adventure out of the normal and mundane.

These five examples have been discussed in detail as they illustrate the varied ways in which the notion of filmic experience manifests itself among personal-stereo users, and draws us into the description of 'filmic' as either being an interior flow of experience, or an aesthetic that imaginatively appropriates or integrates the world into itself. We can see from these examples that filmic experience need not be particularly visual, but might concentrate on the mood of a scene or on a mimic-king of characters from films. When it is visual, the subject might re-create the scene according to some imaginary film or alternatively the people in the actual surroundings are transformed into characters, as extras to the subjective drama as it unfolds. Sometimes, in order for the illusion to be effective, there must be no people present to intrude into the experience. All these examples are based on the active re-creation of some aspect of their journeying and all take place whilst the person is alone.

The use of personal stereos, therefore, does not unambiguously support theo-ries that discuss the visual prioritization of urban experience. Indeed, use appears in significant ways to contradict notions of visuality. Even within the role of aesthetic re-creation, the geographically visual is often not primarily attended to but merely used as a backcloth. The aesthetic re-creation or reappropriation of the urban through the act of looking is mediated through the subjects' desires, stimulated both by desire and music. Sometimes, the physical scene is endowed with new meaning, a background to their imaginary drama; at other times, the drama is redrawn as an interior recollection or mental orientation or mood where the external world isn't really attended to at all. This appears to demonstrate that standard accounts of non-auditory looking cannot be transposed on to forms of auditory looking without loss of meaning. Therefore, the notion that personal-stereo users are engaged in acts of urban *flânerie* are thrown into doubt.

Chapter 18

Joseph Lanza

'BEAUTIFUL MUSIC'
The rise of easy-listening FM

Wouldn't it be great if you could turn down the world?
Advertisement for WDBN's 'The Quiet Island'

LITE FM – HOME TO SUCH WISTFUL VOICES as Karen Carpenter, Phil Collins, and Gloria Estefan – is just one of many mood-monitored soundscapes that radio has offered us through the years. In fact, the latest spate of Adult Contemporary formats stressing original-artist vocals and dispensing with light instrumentals has interloped upon a once-thriving format called 'Beautiful Music'.

Beautiful Music radio was an effort launched in the mid- to late 1960s that provided soft and unobtrusive instrumental selections on a very structured schedule with a minimum of commercial interruptions. Of all existing FM formats, Beautiful Music was the most carefully thought out and disciplined – almost to the point of functioning as a free background music service, with a day-parting regimen designed to please listeners on their way to work or while relaxing at home.

The history of these adventures in mood radio is intimately tied to the advance of FM technology. When Edwin Howard Armstrong discovered the FM (frequency modulation) signal in the 1930s, technicians were already aware of subsidiary communications authorizations, (SCAs) – FM signals that can only be accessed with a special receiver. During World War II, the US Army used SCAs, with some success, to send top-secret messages to troops. Once the military stopped using them after the war, Congress passed the Subsidiary Communications Authorizations Act of 1956, directing the Federal Communications Commission (FCC) to permit radio stations to lease SCAs for commercial purposes. Seeking to replace relatively expensive and inefficient phone lines, companies such as Muzak also leased SCAs from radio stations to get better sound with fewer technical interruptions.

The advent of FM mood-waves is due largely to the efforts of Jim Schulke, the 'Godfather of "Beautiful Music" Radio'. Schulke, a lean and somewhat reclusive man, was the kind of analytical genius who could dissect a ratings book as if it were a lab animal. While working as a director of advertising for Magnavox, he devised a method of buying airtime on FM stations in bulk and then reselling the blocks to interested advertisers. He perceived the FM band as a lucrative frontier and made a deal with the National Association of FM Broadcasters (NAFMB) for FM usage after agreeing to pay annual dues. Upon hiring a ratings service to conduct a ten-market study on FM listening, he not only discovered that the band had a substantial following, but confirmed his suspicion that light instrumental was the most popular mode.

Schulke noticed that a few stations had their own way of juxtaposing songs so that they were mood-consistent or formed a 'matched flow'. According to Schulke, whose ear-opening study eventually led to his becoming NAFMB's president: 'These weren't very scientific methods, but they worked.' Schulke eventually started a firm called QMI (Quality Media, Inc.) to sign up sponsors for FM independents. To help his stations get better ratings and to pull in more agencies, he later formed SRP (Stereo Radio Productions), bringing in Phil Stout as his vice president of operations. Schulke was, in effect, FM's first bona fide 'mood-musicologist', so precise in his philosophy that he concocted a list of 'do's and don'ts' commonly referred to in the industry as 'Schulkeisms'.

Schulke forbade the playing of any songs that contrasted with one another or varied too much in tempo or tone. There were no overbearing voices to draw attention; only the less fevered singing of such performers as Andy Williams and of choruses such as the Anita Kerr Singers and the Johnny Mann Singers were permitted. He likened his science of 'matched flow' to the ebb and flow of tides, in an era when the average radio listener still had an attention span of longer than seven minutes.

Schulke measured his success through direct listener response. Disk jockeys were told not to announce the songs' artists, in order to prevent excess chatter and to avoid alerting listeners to the repetitions in programming necessitated by the small pool of artists in the station's library. His most conclusive finding was that soft strings were the surest guarantor of listener approval in a focus group consisting mostly of women between the ages of 18 and 49. According to Schulke, 'Females have the ability to hear higher frequencies than men. They are better gauges for good fidelity. The gender demarcation was so important that we concluded, if we lost our dynamic range, we lost our females.'

Beautiful Music's other distinction from competing radio formats was the syndicator's centralized control – an arrangement that squelched the whims or quirks in taste of local DJs and general managers. According to Phil Stout, co-pioneer of Beautiful Music with Schulke and a mood-music programmer since 1960: 'It wasn't like there were hundreds of people involved in Beautiful Music. It was a rather incestuous little group that not only knew one another but branched off into other companies.' Stout always made Schulke's programming work best, as he commandeered the backroom studio of Stereo Radio Productions' (SRP's) New York headquarters. His trial-and-error approach to music selections called for up to two days' work to put together a one-hour tape.

SRP did have genre competitors, however. One of these was Marlin Taylor who, in September 1967, started WJIB, the Boston area's first mood-music FM station. After just two months on the air, the station was overwhelmed by letters and phone calls from advertising agencies and newspaper editors lauding the concoction of Percy Faith, Ronnie Aldrich, Andre Kostelanetz, Roger Williams, and various selections from the London Phase 4 series.

In 1969, Taylor convinced the president of a company called Bonneville to bring a similar format to New York City's WRFM, which wanted to outdo a successful mood music 'Gaslight Revue' emanating from WPAT in Paterson, New Jersey. 'They let me be my own program director,' Taylor recalls. 'In seven months, the station jumped [from] number 23 to number 5 in the Arbitron ratings.'

Bonneville, a corporation run by the Mormon Church in Utah, asked Taylor to put his program into a salable package for more of its FM clients. Out of this endeavor came Bonneville Broadcasting System, a syndication firm that listed Taylor as its founder and president from 1971 until 1983. Bonneville spread its FM tentacles from coast-to-coast, relying on its own version of Schulke's 'matched flow' with four quarter-hours of music recorded on reel-to-reel tapes.

The 'Schulke format', which Schulke and Stout soon christened 'Beautiful Music', became very successful. The 'Beautiful Music' label stuck, and the format reigned at such stations as Atlanta's WPCH and Miami's WLYF (the first FM channel to make number 1 in a major market).

Smaller syndicators attempted similar experiments. Al Ham, a former A&R man for Columbia Records, came up with 'Music of Your Life', an AM nostalgia format that commingled instrumentalists such as Frank Chacksfield with vocalists such as Bing Crosby. Ham's knack for putting together the proper balance of singing and music came from his intense involvement with much of Columbia's early mood music fare. He – as both producer and bass player – had worked with Ray Conniff, Percy Faith, Johnny Mathis, the Four Lads, and Mitch Miller.

Avoiding the direct competition it would have faced on the FM dial, Music of Your Life proved to be a successful cottage industry. Radio stations would sign a contract, pay Ham a flat fee per month, and rent reel-to-reel or vinyl recordings all segued with Ham finesse. The only remotely similar AM animal was WAIT, a Chicago AM station that started in 1962 and claimed to be the first format of its kind; but its style was much more like today's Adult Contemporary, with a 1:1 ratio of vocals to instrumentals and announcements every quarter-hour.

Medina, Ohio, was home to WDBN, a Beautiful Music forerunner and one of Schulke's first inspirations. The station styled itself as 'the Quiet Island' ('in radio's sea of noise'). It signed onto the air in October 1960 and was already broadcasting in stereo by November 1961. By January 1970, when an American Research Bureau study of FM listening showed that WDBN commanded the nation's sixth largest FM audience, the Quiet Island tightened its iron-clad music policy. The plan centered on three basic elements. The first of these, Orchestration and Instrumentation, specified the use of pianos, guitars, heavy strings, horns, and even vocals, with no 'improvisational bridges and saxophones' to jar the audience. The second element involved Tempo, which varied according to the time of day: the wake-up hours between 6 a.m. and 9 a.m. required 'Orchestra-Up', consisting of bright and exciting music to enhance that first cup of coffee; from 9 a.m. to 8 p.m., Jack Jones-style 'love tunes' were the main course; and from 8 p.m. to midnight, basic string orchestras with 'only sentimental vocal chorus' were allowed. The third and final element related to Memory or Familiarity, with each quarter-hour containing 'a musical appeal to an age group between 25 and 49 years of age'. Former station owner Bob Miller admits that the quarter-hour division might have been influenced by Muzak's 'Stimulus Progression'.

Thriving until 1988, the Quiet Island not only entertained; it offered punchy manifestos against what it considered rock-contamination:

> Isn't the rattle of your neighbor's garbage can lids enough without having to listen to freaked-out music? Pull yourself out of your old radio routine and get into something nice and sweet.

> They say many young people today will be deaf by the time they're 30. Their own music is doing them in. Life has gotten louder for the rest of us, too. The song bird, the cricket, the soft crunch of snow underfoot are all becoming lost in the roar of the Seventies . . . Fortunately, there's still one place where you can hear something beautiful – WDBN-FM.

The mid-1970s marked a change that had a far greater impact on everyday musical perceptions than most people could ever realize: 'Beautiful Music' evolved into 'easy-listening' – a label that caught on and still sticks, but has been misinterpreted and misused ever since. 'Easy-listening' is not a copyrighted term or a registered trademark, and it has uncertain origins. By the late 1960s, 'easy-listening' was already being used as a Top 40 chart hit category in *Billboard* magazine to designate light instrumentals and vocals – anything from Paul Mauriat's 'Love Is Blue' to the Lettermen's 'Our Winter Love'.

SRP's other major change was its graduation from strictly playing commercial records and other preexisting music to using custom-made instrumental covers. Schulke and Stout made a deal with the British Broadcasting Company to purchase music recorded by some of Britain's best composers, arrangers, and conductors on both sides of the Atlantic.

SRP's first custom recordings were made in London in 1973, under the direction of Leroy Holmes, who sold one million records of the 'Theme from *The High and the Mighty*'. According to Stout:

> The idea behind custom music was to record the very popular or familiar pieces unavailable in string format. The bottom line of my easy-listening programming was familiarity. I would scatter original material by people like John Sbarra with the 'down-homers' – those very familiar pieces.

> While supervising the 1973 London sessions with Leroy, I heard some fantastic instrumental string music on the BBC. So I called them and discovered they had a number of string orchestras on staff. They used material on the air twice and then erased it so they could continue to give work to these musicians. I asked about a deal to sell some of the stuff to us for exclusive use in the US. They agreed and provided us in excess of 200 cuts per year, and we gave them lists of what we wanted them to record. This arrangement went on for seven or eight years.

Compared to most other radio formats, Bonneville and SRP stations followed a strict regimen. Their diligent plan to stroke the public's heart and soul sometimes paid off with fevered responses from overzealous, sometimes loopy listeners. Stout reminisces:

> I got a letter in the late Sixties from a psychiatrist. The doctor was treating a woman who was a huge listener to one our stations. A particular piece of music we had in rotation was a favorite of hers, and when we took it out she went bananas. It prompted her psychiatrist to drop SRP a line, asking why we weren't playing it, and if we could put it back in.

Stout also received another letter, this time a two-pager, from a woman who accused SRP's programmer of wallowing in lost love. Although just about all of the music was instrumental, the woman could not help perceiving that the titles tended to allude to failed romances. Marlin Taylor encountered an even more unsettling situation:

> One horny woman in New York claimed a song we played pushed her 'hot' button. She complained that WRFM was using it and other songs to send her subliminal messages. She'd leave gifts for me as a bribe to stop playing them. After I had long since departed from the station, she took me to court in lower Manhattan because I didn't return her gift. The judge threw it out. He discovered she was loony, but I still had to hire an attorney!

There were also censorship problems with some SRP subscribers in the Bible belt. For example, if the program included a vocal version of 'What Kind of Fool Am I?', Stout would have to cut the song out because of the line 'I don't give a damn'. Among their other cultural contributions, Beautiful Music stations have more than once brought a particular deserving song or artist out of obscurity. Stout, while sifting through old records, retrieved Johnny Pearson's 'Sleepy Shores', a song previously unappreciated by many, despite its frequent appearance in television commercials. The public got to enjoy it all over again, thanks to SRP's faithful airplay. Another Beautiful Music hit attributed to SRP was Caravelli's instrumental recording of Bob Dylan's 'Wigwam'. Dylan's original version was also listed in *Billboard's* 'Easy-Listening' Top 40 in the latter part of 1970.

Taylor recalls other instances of uncovering obscure gems:

> I played a song called 'Dolannes Melody' by Jean Claude Borelly that had a panpipe. People started calling in asking what the instrument was. Nobody ever heard it before. I later picked out 'The Lonely Shepherd' performed by Zamfir with the James Last Orchestra. It was an unfamiliar melody which drove the listeners crazy. We generated as many as 15 to 20 calls a day for a single play. Nobody else was playing it. My peers told me it was nuts, but the listeners loved it. After that, Zamfir sold over 500,000 albums in television promotions alone.

The advent of Beautiful Music coincided with a historically sensitive period in America's demographics: a time when the generation gap was much more apparent than it is today. The music catered to an adult audience that had spending power and tended to shut itself off from the blaring counterculture.

As hippie-oriented underground radio experiments died and the promotion of product (versus art) reasserted its dominion over the airwaves, mainstream FM rock stations resorted more and more to Beautiful Music's entrepreneurial system. AM was also feeling the draft. When the Carpenters segued into the 1970s with 'Close to You' and Neil Diamond went from his gritty 'Cherry Cherry' to the legato 'Song Sung Blue', the music industry was already sneaking Beautiful Music motifs into the pop charts to accommodate the baby boomers' metabolic meltdown.

SRP's influence became so pervasive in the following years that *Billboard* magazine, in the Fall of 1979, issued a front-page encomium, citing Beautiful Music as the number 1 format in the US. About 80 percent of that audience was listening to SRP. Yet Bonneville, under the aggressive entrepreneurship of its head John Patton, had encroached on Schulke's territory to become the biggest Beautiful Music syndicator. Bonneville greatly expanded its music library, launched a satellite transmission system, and hired Lex de Azevedo and his Million Dollar Custom Orchestra to record more music. By the spring of 1980, many of Schulke's customers had been coaxed onto Bonneville's ledger.

Despite selling his SRP to Cox Broadcasting in 1981 for $6 million, Schulke continued to concentrate on the music. But something was happening: despite the optimistic 1979 findings in *Billboard*, Schulke began to realize that the older adults who listened to his stations got older, their spending power weakened, and their incomes became fixed. Schulke describes the unmistakable signs of easy-listening's impending demise:

> Beautiful Music started to slide by 1980, then slipped as its audience got older. Before Lite FM as we know it caught on, I created a format that highlighted original artist vocals. I sold SRP to Cox Broadcasting just before the *Billboard* article proclaimed Beautiful Music as number one. I was accused of selling the oil well before the oil leaked. But I needed something that satisfied a new demand. After a lot of research, I came up with soft vocal programming called Schulke II.

Before Schulke II was implemented, Schulke took the first step in luring clients away from Bonneville by making a phone call to Bill Moyes of the Research Group. He convinced Moyes to finance a $400,000 Comprehensive Music Testing study that would span four years. Schulke's research involved conducting tests in an auditorium where prescreened subjects listened to about fifteen seconds of a particular cut and then wrote down what they liked about it. He found that vocals were their cutting edge. From there Schulke II started broadcasting a nearly all-vocal program, interspersed with occasional instrumentals – the opposite of Beautiful Music and the forerunner of today's Lite FM or Adult Contemporary. 'Lite FM had driven the nail into the Beautiful Music coffin', according to former Muzak programmer Rod Baum. 'Beautiful Music didn't contemporize enough and started sounding schmaltzy.

People started preferring songs sung'. Consequently, few industry observers were surprised when the May 26, 1990, issue of *Billboard* read: 'Fallen on Hard Times, Easy Moves Toward Soft AC.' Even though easy-listening's defenders continued to hope for an imminent comeback, the vocal strains that enticed listeners between ages 25 and 54 were the fashion.

With easy-listening moribund, critics redirected their bile toward Lite FM. Stephen Holden, in another *New York Times* piece, grudgingly admitted that 'lite radio embraces a larger segment of modern pop history than any oilier current radio format'. But he went on to call the format 'an innocuous musical puree'. Notwithstanding its 'original artists' pretense, Lite FM manages to appropriate Muzak's knack for placing ambiance above discrete musical identity, mixing genres and historical contexts with such aplomb that John Lennon's 'Imagine' plays right alongside Perry Como's 'It's Impossible'.

But even as easy-listening withered away on the public airwaves, it found a new niche on private cable radio lines. To re-create Muzak founder General Squier's dream of music-wired homes, companies such as DCR (Digital Cable Radio) had replaced Squier's wires with the wonders of today's satellite down-link. DCR (located in Hatboro, Pennsylvania) sent digital sound to subscriber stereo systems via their existing cable television service ('It's cable for your stereo!').

Phil Stout had overseen six of DCR's easy-listening adult-oriented channels. An ensemble to which Stout currently gives considerable air time is the London Studio Orchestra, alternately titled the Starlite Orchestra. Its intricate, varied, and, at times, impressively eccentric output – Beautiful Music blended with folk, New Age, panpipes, some hints of techno, and an intermittent chorus – is the culmination of several recording sessions conducted in Holland during the mid-to-late Eighties. A single London Studio Orchestra compact disc can contain tracks that fluctuate from a relatively serene cover of 'My Way' to an innovative and haunting rendition of Erik Satie's 'Gnossiennes' – all done in the elevator music tradition of amalgamating arrangements, instruments and styles previously assumed to be incompatible.

Looking back, Stout concludes:

> Beautiful Music generated a hardcore loyalty. The listeners had a private relationship. When the stations started discontinuing it, there was a groundswell of resentment. You ended up with a disenfranchised audience. We are getting a good response from our easy-listening channel. People are saying they're glad to have this music again because they're not getting it on radio.

As Adult Contemporary mollifies a generation of aging former hipsters, the growing popularity of various contemporary instrumental categories threatens to spawn a new breed of programs that blend the old and new. Today, such meditative formats as KTWV's 'The Wave' in Los Angeles and Stephen Hill's syndicated Music from the Hearts of Space come closest to filling easy-listening's void. The fact that New Age music blossomed just as Beautiful Music started to wilt is no coincidence.

Top Ten Beautiful Music instrumentals

(as listed in the April 1983 issue of *Radio Only*)

1   Percy Faith: 'Theme from A *Summer Place*'
2   Henry Mancini: 'You Don't Know Me'
3   Peter Knight: 'Tonight'
4   BBC, Johnny Douglas Midland Orchestra, exclusive SRP Custom-recording: 'Words'
5   Roger Williams: 'Theme from *New York, New York*'
6   Vangelis: 'Chariots of Fire'
7   Hollyridge Strings: 'Theme from *Love Story*'
8   Henry Mancini: 'Evergreen'
9   Living Strings: 'If I Were a Rich Man'
10 Hagood Hardy: 'As Time Goes By'

Chapter 19

David Toop

SCANNING
Aether talk

ambient in the 1990s; Scanner, John Cage, acid house, disco; AMM; Telepathic Fish, Biosphere, Mixmaster Morris, Land of Oz, The Orb, The KLF

Field recordings

ROBIN RIMBAUD SNAKES OUT a cheap television aerial across my sofa and tunes in his hand-held scanner to the invisible, private world. It is private no longer. Somewhere nearby, a man is talking on the telephone to a woman, telling her that he is about to buy a large loaf of bread in a local baker's. The exchange is mundane but then he says: 'I always wear black to match the colour of my car,' and banal talk is revealed as a Trojan horse carrying other levels of communication: status, style and sexual promise.

As well as organising a London club called The Electronic Lounge, Robin makes records based around material snooped, via the scanner, from telephone conversations. Sounds, atmospheres and sometimes beats are added, but the core material is people talking in the mistaken belief that nobody else is listening. Robin explains:

> I've always been interested in field recordings. When I was younger, when I was thirteen or fourteen, I used to hang microphones out of the window of my family's house and used to record what was outside in the street. I've got hours of tape – I don't know what you would call it. A good way of putting it with the scanner stuff is 'mapping the city'. I don't want to sound like I sit in my little palace, picking up all the classes, but it's like mapping the movements of people during different

periods of the day. It's fairly predictable. In the early morning, very quiet, lots of people ringing in saying 'I'll be late for work', or 'goodbye love', all this affection stuff; you very quickly move into the work rota and you're mapping out the system and the way people interact. You get to a lunch period when things lull and people start ringing up their friends, then it's back to work again. Around six to seven it's people ringing home. Then in the evening, that's where the riot happens. That's when it gets really exciting because all hell gets let loose. The phone rates go down and people have the most surreal conversations. A big aspect for me is that it's so random. You never know quite what you're going to pick up. When I do a live gig and I do an improvisational set, I never know whether all I'm going to get is static. That's just as valid. If there's nothing there, there's nothing there.

Orientation

What is ambient music? Calm, therapeutic sounds for chilling out or music that taps into the disturbing, chaotic undertow of the environment? There are two separate, quite different moments in the past twenty years that tend to define interpretations. The first moment is Brian Eno's; the second one, or my, version of it, goes as follows.

Between 1986 and 1989, a number of import 12-inch singles appeared in the UK, almost all of them from either house-music clubs in Chicago, techno musicians of Detroit or garage-house producers from New York; most of them reduced the elements of dance music to a bare minimum in order to explore the new textures and rhythms of machine music. This music contributed to an emergent movement in Britain, now enshrined in popular mythology as rave. Without rave, chill-out rooms and quiet clubs for ambient listening might have remained the pipe dreams of a few solitary explorers.

Two of the key records that helped to shake British youth into a new phase of hedonism, self-belief and communal dissent were 'Acid Tracks' (1987), produced by Marshall Jefferson, and 'Washing Machine' (1986), made entirely by Larry Heard. Both had their origins in the black, predominantly, though not exclusively, gay warehouse clubs of Chicago.

The basic components of 'Acid Tracks' epitomise the principle of less means more: a Roland TB-303 bassline playing patterns that sweep up and down through frequency and filtering as they run; the thudding, dry bass drum, hi-hat, clap and toms playing straight disco beats from a Roland 909 drum machine; the cowbell and whistle from a Roland 727 and some unidentifiable synthesiser swooshes in the background. It is simple, but ferociously effective, particularly if drugs are involved. This was music without narrative; music as function; music as a technical process.

Larry Heard's 'Washing Machine' was even more direct: a repeating, rolling melodic line with unusual intervals, spongy like a rubber ball in texture, bald of recognisable emotion, except for occasional moments of musical tension and a slight suggestion of exuberance. Little touches of reverb introduce fleeting suggestions of physical space around the sounds; there are short silences or a bar of hi-hat cymbal. The drum programming is more eccentric than 'Acid Tracks', perhaps a reflection of Larry Heard's career as a drummer in Chicago bands playing anything from R&B and jazz fusion to rock.

Never happy to be tied down to one style, Heard was capable of writing anything from strange compositions for drum machine, gorgeous mid-tempo ballads, tracks that sounded like Pink Floyd, backdrops for beatnik poetry or electronic jazz-fusion instrumentals that depicted lush environments of the imagination. With the dance frenzy at its height at the end of the 1980s, the potential context for such a broad sweep of quietly non-formulaic music seemed unpromising. Where did Heard envisage people listening to his records? 'In clubs, of course, but maybe real late-night things. Some of the stuff, without the drum beats, I feel could be soundtrack-type stuff. Just for listening, everyday listening.'

When Brian Eno applied the term 'ambient music' to his activities, he switched the emphasis away from making music, focusing instead on the act of listening. Inevitably, the spotlight returns to the creator, if only for expedient reasons of maintaining a career, keeping up magazine circulations or boosting record-company profits. But many forces were chipping away at the hierarchical, separated roles of producers and consumers. Before Eno's theoretical dismantling of this relationship, early disco DJs had also eroded fixed definitions of performance, performer and audience.

Disco mixing, the merging of records by a DJ, denied the musician as performer, denied the integrity of any individual performance, denied the problems of mixing musical styles or cultural difference, denied the conclusion of a work. Communication, the human problem, could take place in the machine: first, record decks and tape editing, then samplers, then hard-disk drives. Gradually, the DJ became the artist. Gradually, the song, the composition, was decomposed. After its first formative years, during which the global soundbanks were plundered for empathetic records, disco began to work on the principle of decomposing songs into modular and interchangeable fragments, sliced and repatched into an order which departed from the rules of Tin Pan Alley. This new order was designed to suit the nocturnal rhythms of a participatory, ecstatic audience, rather than any model of consensual, concise, classic proportions demanded by pop listeners.

Polaroids

The Roundhouse, Chalk Farm, London, 1994: Chantal Passemonde, co-organiser of Telepathic Fish ambient parties, recalls one such event:

> It was cold, that's the best description. It was traveller people like Andy Blockhead, rather than club people, who had this idea that they wanted to do not a Rainbow Gathering, but a Rainbow Gathering sort of thing, if you know what I mean, in the Roundhouse on New Year's Day. What with the Criminal Justice Bill coming up and all that, and they felt it was really a powerful space to do it in.

> We had the owner's permission provided it stayed ambient, because of the potential trouble they thought they'd get if it was a full-on rave,

which they'd had when Spiral Tribe had done stuff there. So that's how the ambient thing came into it. The whole point was for people to gather after where they'd been on New Year's Eve. We were there all night and then it started at six in the morning. By about seven or eight o'clock that night they'd got in a big heater which made a big difference and then everything started going insanely psychedelic and bizarre. Two bands played – really traveller bands. Pan was one – an insane sort of progressive, psychedelic rock thing. There was loads of shamanic drumming, you know the insanity that occurs. Then Mixmaster Morris played and it went right through the night into Sunday.

It looked amazing. Do you know Nick Mindscape, the guy who does Megatripolis visuals? He had these unbelievably huge screens that hung round one half of the circle, like right down, almost to the floor, and they were projected on. Then on the other side, there were these three vertical drops that were hung so that they were in free form, and they just moved, like billowed in the wind. There were projections on that. That was when it was dark. Matt Black was there and he was doing stuff. Everyone was really colourful, wearing jumpers and stuff. And during the day it was really lovely because all the light comes through the roof. I remember at one point we were playing the first track on B12's *Electro Soma* album. It's all very ethereal and people were blowing bubbles. The whole place was full of bubbles. It did look like a really bizarre, post-apocalyptic, insane thing. People got so cold they were lighting fires. It was like something out of *Mad Max*.

. . . to chill out

One of the frequent criticisms aimed at new ambient and electronic music is that the music lacks stars, focal points, magazine-cover fodder, dynamic performers. By definition, a computer-driven, preprogrammed performance is predetermined. Only a few operators can transcend the knowledge that they, along with the audience, are passive witnesses to the computer's blind need to work through a programme from start to cut-off. The only error, or danger, is that the machine may crash.

Saturday night at the Melkweg in Amsterdam and all this is true of Biosphere's set. Have Macintosh Power Book will travel, yet with visuals and a keen sense of how to pace the music, he conjures real excitement, mystery and tension from digital information. From the PA, two children's voices loop round and round, a sample taken from a feature film to form the basis of a Biosphere track called 'Phantasm': 'We had a dream last night . . . we had the same dream'. A nagging two-note ostinato and these two creepy voices build tangible tension in the room. Photographs of earth shot from a space shuttle fill the screen above the stage, and when the bass drum finally kicks in, the crowd goes wild.

Drinking beer with Geir Jenssen, the man behind Biosphere, in the Melkweg café earlier in the evening, I asked him if his home environment in Tromsø, Norway, exerts an influence on the atmospheres in his music. Tromsø, he explains, has no sun for two or three months of every year. Winter lasts for seven or eight months. 'I feel at my most creative when the sun is gone,' he admits. 'When it's a Christmas feeling and it's dark all the time, you can see the Northern Lights. You see the houses with all the lamps inside. It's very cosy.' This picture strikes us as being rather funny, bearing in mind the fact that techno avoids references to community (other than the techno 'community'), security or domesticity, so we talk about signals transmitted across great distances, of technology and isolation and the dramatic image of invisible connections across a void. 'I think it's great to sit in the darkness with computers', he muses. 'I like this combination of desolate areas and hi-tech equipment.'

Before Geir goes on stage to press the first button, he wants to lay one more ambient cliche to rest:

> I hate it if people use my music as a background. When I was listening to Jon Hassell and Brian Eno, I was inspired to know more about the Himalayas or astronomy, Egypt and archaeology. I want people to get inspired to read astronomy or to get another view of the universe. To be curious.

The milky way

In the hunt for a psychedelic skinhead, acid pixie bare-knuckle backstreet fighter to cast in your new computer game, you could do worse than ink a contract with Mixmaster Morris, The Irresistible Force, DJ, recording artist and tireless advocate of ambient music. Morris is not a person to whom questions are addressed. He just rolls out soundbites for the interrogator to gather up in a shopping bag and reassemble at leisure. A typical example: 'We've had sixty, seventy years of making records. That's stage one. Now we sample them.'

Ever since the Land of Oz chill-out nights in 1989, plus rare early sightings of electronic fluffiness from Fingers Inc. and Virgo in Chicago or The Orb and The KLF in London, the oxymoron of ambient house – dance music for sitting still – had become accepted into common usage. Ambient had turned into one of those polysemous glue words that stick wherever they land. Morris, always on the move, saw ambient rise in Frankfurt, Hamburg, Berlin and San Francisco, finally to survey an international movement in the making. Aside from Holland, Belgium and the inevitable Goa, he had found embryonic scenes in Japan, Austria, Finland, even St Petersburg and Chicago.

Ambient had been one symptom of a shift in music production in the UK. Not a revolution like the hippie movement or punk, which had songs about revolution, but a sudden reorganisation of all the pieces into new formations. Despite persistent associations of New Age values, most of the new ambient is fiercely urban and now age. Some clubs double as marketplaces for ineffectual and overpriced 'smart' drugs, tarot readers, luminous jewellery, masseurs, didgeridoos and 'tribal' drumming, but in general these elements seem to denote spiritual hunger, activism stemming from disillusionment, an alternative economy or simple social discontent, rather than a withdrawal into the elite white light of New Age evolutionism.

Networks

For Higher Intelligence Agency, it was all about getting something going in Birmingham. They started their club, Oscillate, in May 1992. According to Dave Wheels:

> The first Oscillates were above a pub, the only place we could find cheap enough to put it on. You know, everyone was unemployed, on benefit. The first one, I seem to recall, two people turned up. Nobody was interested. Twenty people were there. It was so unpredictable.

Then they moved the club to a Friday. Ultramarine played there. Mixmaster Morris played an ambient set and then Orbital, one of the few techno acts to make a successful jump from studio technocracy to outdoor rock festivals, played a one-off to test the computer-age resolve of post-industrial Birmingham. The club was jammed.

And in London, there was Spacetime and Telepathic Fish. Held in a warehouse in Cable Street, London's East End, in 1990–1, the Spacetime parties were organised by techno/ambient musician Jonah Sharp and holographic clothing designer Richard Sharpe. As Jonah explains:

> They were really experimental. We used to have Morris playing all night. The whole idea behind the music was that people would come and talk. It allowed him to try a lot of things out. I used to play live at them. It was people sitting in the corner, tinkling on keyboards. The whole holographic tiling is synonymous with what I've done. Richard is an inventor – he invented this fabric and he's totally into visual art. We used to decorate the entire room with holographic foil. Two hundred people maximum and it was a lot of fun. Good conversations, which was an important thing. Instead of losing yourself in your own little space, there was a lot of interaction. That was what made me aware of the possibilities of the chill-out space. That environment within a big rave was just starting to happen at that time. I think Alex Patterson was playing at Land of Oz but I didn't know about that. For me, the ambient room or chill-out room was a platform for live music.

Telepathic Fish grew from similar origins as a small squat party to a growing public event with its own fanzine, *Mind Food*. Telepathic Fish was started by a group of art students and computer freaks – Mario Tracey-Ageura, Kevin Foakes and David Vallade – who lived together in a house in Dulwich. Later, Chantal Passemonde moved into the house, shortly after the parties had begun. There were no shared musical visions, simply an idea that the environment for listening to music could be different. For the first party, held in the Dulwich house, six hundred people turned up through word of mouth and Mixmaster Morris DJd. Then they planned a May Day tea party. The fliers were teabags. Mixmaster Morris wanted a German ambient DJ, Dr Atmo, to play at the party, along with Richard 'Aphex Twin' James, a recent addition to Morris's wide circle of friends and fellow psychic nomads. Chantel explains:

We realised that the whole party was going to be too big for the place we were going to have it, which basically was a garden, so we rushed around. Morris knew some people and we found this squat in Brixton, which was run by these completely insane people. Just real squattie types, right over the edge. It was from Sunday tea on May bank holiday and people just turned up in dribs and drabs all through the night. That was the first proper Telepathic Fish, May 1st, 1993. Then, there was no such thing. There probably was on a small scale, lots of people chilling out in their bedrooms – the post-clubbing experience when everyone comes round and you play tunes, but we'd never been to anything like that.

Also highly influential in the development of ambient were The Orb, a collaboration between DJ Alex Patterson and Jimi Cauty. The Orb released their first single called 'The Kiss' in July 1989. 'Cross-over potential: nil' predicted the press release, which was true enough for that single, but slightly wide of the mark by the time The Orb became one of the most successful bands in the UK. Credited to Two Fat Belgians – perhaps a dig at the Belgian New Beat craze (dismally slow, sample-heavy dance records that were failing to export Belgian culture with any success) – 'The Kiss' was one of a number of samplemanic, scratch 'n' sniff, blip culture records released at the time: Drummond and Cauty's Justified Ancients of Mu Mu, Coldcut, New York and Miami hip-hop, Bomb the Bass and M/A/R/R/S. The same approach could be applied to club Djing; throwing any possible source into the mix and gluing together the disparity with beats. But what if the beats were taken out, the volume pulled down, the tempo varied or slowed down to stasis, the diversity taken to extremes? This is what Patterson and Cauty started at the now legendary sessions at Land of Oz.

Patterson and Cauty fused the mellow side of house with slow music, ethereal music, hippie music, bioacoustic music and spliff music, feeding them through all available montage techniques. Nothing was sacred. Ear witnesses have reported The Eagles, Strauss waltzes, Brian Eno, BBC birdsong albums, 10cc's 'I'm Not In Love'. Patterson describes their work:

> We'd build melodies up and then take an eight-track, or was it a twelve-track, into Heaven, just linking it up to three decks, loads of CD players, loads of cassettes and this loop, which would then become an eight-hour version of 'Sueno Latino', 'cause there's a loop of it in there. We used to keep it very, very quiet. We never used to play any drums in there. It'd be just like, you know, BBC sound effects, really.'

Ambient music is more a way of listening, an umbrella term for attitude, rather than a single identifiable style. As Patterson has suggested, the DJ came to the forefront of music. As a semi-anonymous *bricoleur,* a cut-up artisan, the DJ could montage any form of music to create a mood, an environment. Records began to appear that reflected this cavalier approach. What had been a process became an identifiable product. The KLF released a drumless mix of 'Madriga Eterna'. Still calling themselves The Orb, Patterson and Cauty released 'A Huge Ever Growing Pulsating Brain That Rules From the Centre of the Ultraworld' in December 1989.

Ambient house for the E generation they called it – a neat marketing phrase that happened to be exactly right for a brief time.

The Orb single was sampladelic, rather than drumless: church bells, babies crying, celestial choirs, relentless arpeggiated synth sequences in the style of Tangerine Dream, a heavy breakbeat and, at the centre of the Ultraworld, the late Minnie Riperton singing her touching but nevertheless rather sickly ballad: 'Loving You.' This was not the first time Minnie had been electronically, unwittingly trans-planted. After her death from cancer, her unfinished vocals were built up through overdubbing and editing into a posthumous album, a reiteration of music's status as a shifting conglomerate of manipulable bits, rather than a finished entity. The dead are no more immune to this process than the living.

PART FIVE

Musical diasporas

Introduction to Part Five

■   Barry Shank

THE GLOBAL POPULARITY OF RAP MUSIC from the mid-1980s on was
due in no small part to the way in which rap connected with the feelings of
displaced communities of African origin in different parts of the world. The highly
charged cultural significance of music in relation to issues of space, place and identity has also been illustrated through the appeal of bhangra and post-bhangra styles
for youth of South Asian origin and the growth in popularity of banda music in Los
Angeles. In this part, we focus on the movements of peoples and cultures, and on
the specific ways in which the 'same music' can change in new political, social and
cultural contexts. Indeed, one of the key concepts that underlies this section is LeRoi
Jones's important insight into the 'changing same'. The consistency and integrity of
popular musical traditions is not an effect of their lack of change, rather that these
traditions are constituted out of change, out of rhythmic or timbral innovation, new
technologies of sound, new engagements with different markets, but especially out
of new social and political contexts that change the meanings of old sounds and
link new sounds back to traditions.

    In the early decades of popular music studies, the musical practices of dias-
poric peoples were considered to be more authentic to the extent to which they
emulated older musical forms. The roots of blues performance styles were traced
to West African musical practices and a hierarchy of value was created that accorded
more worth to sounds that more closely evoked traditional (not pop) African musical
styles. A second common misunderstanding was to link the integrity of musical practices to a type of racialised essence – i.e. if black folks made the sounds, the sounds
constituted black music. In contrast to either of those positions, the chapters included
in this part build upon Paul Gilroy's critical question:

How are we to think critically about artistic products and aesthetic codes which, though they may be traceable back to one distinct location, have been changed either by the passage of time or by their displacement, relocation or dissemination through networks of communication and cultural exchange?

We have chosen to begin this part with a selection drawn from Gilroy's book, *The Black Atlantic*. This article argues that any unilinear tracing of influence from Africa to the West is mistaken. He analyses three musical moments: the early years of the Fisk Jubilee Singers, the career of Jimi Hendrix, and a reggae remake of the Impressions' 'I'm So Proud' to demonstrate the complexity of the musical Black Atlantic. Gilroy argues that the commonality that links these very different moments is not a racialised essence nor is it a narrowly shared musical vocabulary. Instead, the organic unity that holds these moments together is produced out of the social and political particularities that differentiate each articulation and transformation of the tradition.

Jocelyn Guilbault's analysis of Zouk contributes a different articulation of the Black Atlantic. On the former French colonial islands of the Antilles, musicians such as Pierre-Edouard Decimus sought to create a 'technically flawless music with an international sound'. Decimus's band, Kassav, combined Creole lyrics with rhythmic complexity and a combination of traditional and modern instruments to create a sound that was unmistakably Antillean, but which also reached out to a modern global audience. In fact, Zouk's ability to attract this audience was crucial to its political and social meaning. Black Creole-speaking peoples of the Antilles were at the bottom of the postcolonial social order on the islands. When Zouk became an international popular music, an accepted genre of the French recording industry, the meaning of that Antillean identity changed. As Guilbault shows us, this immediately recognisable local sound was far from a backwards-looking celebration of roots. The complex sophisticated sound of Zouk was combined with traditional instruments and Creole lyrics to establish a new ground for musical pleasure. When later in their career Kassav dropped the gwo ka (a traditional drum) and replaced it with a drum machine, they were not diverging from the impulses that had originated their sound. Indeed, the increased danceability that this shift created was in line with the changing same that had generated Zouk in the first place. Kassav's goals were always commercial, always international. And the success of Zouk shows that the musical flows across the Black Atlantic cross Francophone as well as anglophone borders.

Tony Langlois's analysis of the popularisation of Rai demonstrates the interaction of the local and the global, the struggle between East and West as they play out in popular music. A music once known for its strict locality, its reference to individual persons and street corners of Oran, its use of quarter tones and traditional instruments, and its status as a relatively uncommodified style of live dance music, Rai became an international popular form in the mid-1980s. In the process, commercial recording practices changed several of the central musical signifiers. As Rai became more regional and, indeed, global, lyrics ceased to refer to members of local communities, synthesisers replaced many of the traditional instruments, harmonic structures conformed to European standards and melodies became easier to sing. But Langlois does not narrate this as a strict tale of loss. Rather, the success of European Rai prompted Algerian radio stations to air Rai recordings, and the spread of these recordings reinforced and solidified local dialects. This intervention into the local politics of language links Rai back to local issues and feelings, strengthening local traditions. Langlois focuses on the activities in the studio, outlining the aesthetic and commercial decisions made by local producers, called *éditeurs*. Their decisions trace the narrow line that Rai must walk between East and West in the politics of North African identity.

Rupa Huq's discussion of 'Asian Kool' begins at one of Gilroy's crucial critical insights. In the UK, the taste for bhangra and post-bhangra musical styles has become linked to South Asian identity to such an extent that it has taken on the aspect of cliché and stereotype. Huq disrupts stereotypical assumptions about South Asian musicians who work against bhangra-influenced music. She interviews several South Asian musicians, including women, who play aggressive post-punk rock styles and claim never to have listened to bhangra. Their efforts to work within strictly modern styles and with an eye toward success in the recording industry is not an escape from South Asian identity, but instead it is an effort to construct an authentic South Asian identity that is not defined by its connection to a root or essence.

In contrast, Helena Simonett outlines the rise of technobanda as a blend of traditional and modern musical styles that deliberately looks backwards, incorporating aspects of traditional Mexican music for a popular style that had a profound impact on the cultural image of thousands of young Latinos on both sides of the US/Mexico border. Technobanda represents a modernisation of one of the oldest popular dance forms in Mexico – traditional banda music. It grew in popularity at just the moment when politicians began to blame undocumented immigrants from Mexico and Central America for California's economic crisis. The commercial success of banda and technobanda helped to confirm a sense of Latino community that existed on both sides of the border. For generations, Mexican-Americans have lived in Southern California – some families dating back to when California was a part of Mexico. As young people became more sensitive to the growing racial discrimination, they developed a more forceful identification with Mexican traditions. Banda and technobanda constructed pleasurable arenas within which those traditions and a specific cross-border identity could be reinforced.

The final chapter in this part is taken from Tricia Rose's classic analysis of rap, *Black Noise*. In this selection, Rose details the significance of a 'style nobody can deal with'. Key elements in hip-hop style are 'flow, layering and rupture'. These elements can be found in rap, in graffiti, and musical construction. Indeed, the ability to make creative use of rupture is emblematic of hip-hop's political significance. As Rose tells us, 'Hip hop emerged as a source for alternative identity formation and social status when older support institutions had been all but demolished'. Building again on Gilroy's perception that black music is not expressive of some racial essence, Rose tells us, 'identity in hip hop is deeply rooted in the specific'. Some of the signs of this specificity include the representations of neighbourhoods and local communities as well as the presence of the friends or the crew of the musicians in rap videos. But perhaps the foremost expression of the specificity of hip-hop identity lies in the mobilisation of style as an intensely personal and individual enunciation of resistance to the political context in which hip-hop developed. The competition over style remains a forceful means of individuation in a society that still denies full membership to peoples of colour.

Paul Gilroy

"JEWELS BROUGHT FROM BONDAGE'
Black music and the politics of authenticity"

Examining the place of music in the black Atlantic world means surveying the self-understanding articulated by the musicians who have made it, the symbolic use to which their music is put by other black artists and writers, and the social relations that have produced and reproduced the unique expressive culture in which music comprises a central and even foundational element. I want to propose that the possible commonality of post-slave, black cultural forms be approached via several related problems that converge in the analysis of black musics and their supporting social relations. One particularly valuable pathway into this is provided by the distinctive patterns of language use that characterise the contrasting populations of the modern, Western, African diaspora. The oral character of the cultural settings in which diaspora musics have developed presupposes a distinctive relationship to the body – an idea expressed with exactly the right amount of impatience by Glissant:

> It is nothing new to declare that for us music, gesture, dance are forms
> of communication, just as important as the gift of speech. This is how
> we first managed to emerge from the plantation: aesthetic form in our
> cultures must be shaped from these oral structures.

My main concern in this chapter is less with the formal attributes of these syncretic expressive cultures than with the problem of how critical, evaluative, axiological, (anti)aesthetic judgements on them can be made and with the place of ethnicity and authenticity within these judgements. What special analytical problems arise if a style, genre or particular performance of music is identified as being expressive of the absolute essence of the group that produced it? What contradictions appear in the transmission and adaptation of this cultural expression by other diaspora populations, and how will they be resolved? How does the hemispheric displacement and global dissemination of black music get reflected in localised traditions of critical writing, and, once the music is perceived as a world phenomenon, what value is placed upon its origins, particularly if they come into opposition against further mutations produced during its contingent loops and fractal trajectories? Where music is thought to be emblematic and constitutive of racial difference rather than just associated with it, how is music used to specify general issues pertaining to the problem of racial authenticity and the consequent self-identity of the ethnic group? Thinking about music – a non-representational, non-conceptual form – raises aspects of embodied subjectivity that are not reducible to the cognitive and the ethical.

Working on the contemporary forms of black expressive culture involves struggling with one problem in particular. It is the puzzle of what analytic status should be given to the variation within black communities and between black cultures which their musical habits reveal. The tensions produced by attempts to compare or evaluate differing black cultural formations can be summed up in the following question: How are we to think critically about artistic products and aesthetic codes that, though they may be traceable back to one distinct location, have been changed either by the passage of time or by their displacement, relocation or dissemination through networks of communication and cultural exchange? This question serves as a receptacle for several even more awkward issues. They include the unity and differentiation of the creative black self, the vexed matter of black particularity, and the role of cultural expression in its formation and reproduction.

In the face of the conspicuous differentiation and proliferation of black cultural styles and genres, a new analytic orthodoxy has begun to grow. In the name of anti-essentialism and theoretical rigour, it suggests that since black particularity is socially and historically constructed, and plurality has become inescapable, the pursuit of any unifying dynamic or underlying structure of feeling in contemporary black cultures is utterly misplaced. The attempt to locate the cultural practices, motifs or political agendas that might connect the dispersed and divided blacks of the New World and of Europe with each other, and even with Africa, is dismissed as essentialism, or idealism, or both. The alternative position sketched out in the rest of this chapter offers a tentative rebuke to that orthodoxy which I regard as premature in its dismissal of the problem of theorising black identity. I suggest that weighing the similarities and differences between black cultures remains an urgent concern.

The Jubilee Singers and the transatlantic route

I want to illustrate the arguments outlined above by briefly bringing forward some concrete historical instances in which the musical traditions of the black Atlantic world can be seen to have acquired a special political valency and in which the idea of authentic racial culture has been either contested or symptomatically overlooked. These examples are simultaneously both national, in that they had a direct impact on life in Britain, and diasporic, in that they tell us something fundamental about the limits of that national perspective. They are not, of course, the only examples I could have chosen. They have been selected somewhat at random, although I hope that the fact that they span a century will be taken as further evidence for the existence of fractal patterns of cultural and political affiliation. In rather different ways, these examples reflect the special position of Britain within the black Atlantic world, standing at the apex of the semi-triangular structure that saw commodities and people shipped to and fro across the ocean.

The first instance relates to the visits by the Fisk University Jubilee Singers to England, Ireland, Wales and Scotland in the early 1870s under the philanthropic patronage of the Earl of Shaftesbury. The Fisk Singers have a profound historical importance because they were the first group to perform spirituals on a public platform, offering this form of black music as popular culture. The worldwide travels of the Fisk Jubilee Singers provide a little known but nonetheless important example of the difficulties that, from the earliest point, attended the passage of African-American folk forms into the emergent popular-cultural industries of the over-developed countries. At that time, the status of the Jubilee Singers's art was further complicated by the prominence and popularity of minstrelsy. One review of the earliest performances by the group was headlined 'Negro Minstrelsy in Church – Novel Religious Exercise,' while another made much of the fact that this band of Negro minstrels were, in fact, 'genuine negroes.' Doug Seroff quotes another contemporary American review of a concert by the group: 'Those who have only heard the burnt cork caricatures of negro minstrelsy have not the slightest conception of what it really is.' Similar problems arose in the response of European audiences and critics:

> From the first the Jubilee music was more or less of a puzzle to the critics; and even among those who sympathised with their mission there was no little difference of opinion as to the artistic merit of their entertainments. Some could not understand the reason for enjoying so thoroughly as almost everyone did these simple unpretending songs.

The choir initially struggled to win an audience for black music produced by blacks from a constituency that had been created by 50 years of 'blackface' entertainment. Needless to say, the aesthetic and political tensions involved in establishing the credibility and appeal of their own novel brand of black cultural expression were not confined to the concert halls. Practical problems arose in the mechanics of touring when innkeepers refused the group lodgings, having taken their bookings on the assumption that they were a company of 'nigger minstrels' – white. One landlord did not discover that 'their faces were coloured by their creator and not by burnt cork' until the singers were firmly established in their bedrooms. He still turned them into the street.

The choir's progress was predictably dogged by controversies over the relative value of their work when compared to the output of the white 'minstrel' performers. The Fisk troupe also encountered the ambivalence and embarrassment of black audiences unsure or uneasy about serious, sacred music being displayed to audiences conditioned by the hateful antics of Zip Coon, Jim Crow and their odious supporting cast. Understandably, blacks were protective of their unique musical culture and fearful of how it might be changed by being forced to compete on the new terrain of popular culture against the absurd representations of blackness offered by minstrelsy's pantomime dramatisation of white supremacy.

In explicit opposition to minstrelsy, which was becoming an established element in popular culture by this time, the Fisk Singers constructed an aura of seriousness around their activities and projected the memory of slavery outwards as the means to make their musical performances intelligible and pleasurable. The choir had taken to the road seven years after the founding of their Alma Mater to raise funds. They produced books to supplement the income from their concert performances, and these volumes ran to more than 60,000 copies sold between 1873 and the end of the century. Interestingly, these publications included a general historical account of Fisk and its struggles, some unusual autobiographical statements from the members of the choir, and the music and lyrics of between 104 and 139 songs from their extensive repertoire.

The Fisk Singers's texts describe an austere Queen Victoria listening to 'John Brown's Body' 'with manifest pleasure,' the Prince of Wales requesting 'No More Auction Block for Me,' and the choir being waited upon by Mr. and Mrs. Gladstone after their servants had been dismissed. These images are important, although the history of the choir's performances to enormous working-class audiences in British cities may be more valuable to beleaguered contemporary anti-racism which is struggling to find precedents and to escape the strictures of its own apparent novelty. It is clear that for their liberal patrons the music and song of the Fisk Jubilee Singers offered an opportunity to feel closer to God and to redemption, while the memory of slavery recovered by their performances entrenched the feelings of moral rectitude that flowed from the commitment to political reform for which the imagery of elevation from slavery was emblematic long after emancipation.

Almost one hundred years after the Jubilee Singers set sail from Boston for England on the Cunard ship *Batavia*, another black American musician made the transatlantic journey to London. Jimi Hendrix's importance in the history of African-American popular music has increased since his untimely death in 1970. The European triumph that paved the way for Hendrix's American successes presents another interesting but rather different case of the political aesthetics implicated in representations of racial authenticity. A seasoned, if ill-disciplined, rhythm-and-blues sideman, Hendrix was reinvented as the essential image of what English audiences felt a black American performer should be: wild, sexual, hedonistic and dangerous. His biographers agree that the updated minstrel antics of his shows became a fetter on his creativity and that the irrepressible issue of racial politics intervened bitterly in his fluctuating relationships with the English musicians who provided the bizarre backdrop to his blues-rooted creativity. Jimi's shifting relationship to black cultural forms and political movements caused substantial problems when he returned to play in the US and was denounced as a 'white nigger' by some of the Black Power activists who could not fathom his choices in opting to cultivate an almost exclusively white, pop audience that found the minstrel stance a positive inducement to engage with his transgressive persona, if not his music. Charles Shaar Murray quotes the following diagnosis of Hendrix's success by the rival English blues guitarist Eric Clapton:

> You know English people have a very big thing towards a spade. They really love that magic thing. They all fall for that kind of thing. Everybody and his brother in England still think that spades have big dicks. And Jimi came over and exploited that to the limit . . . and everybody fell for it.

Sexuality and authenticity have been intertwined in the history of Western culture for several hundred years. The overt sexuality of Hendrix's neo-minstrel buffoonery seems to have been received as a sign of his authentic blackness by the white rock audiences on which his burgeoning pop career was so solidly based. Whether or not Hendrix's early performances were parodic of the minstrel role or undeniable confirmation of its enduring potency, his negotiation of its vestigial codes points to the antagonism between different local definitions of what blackness entailed, and to the combined and uneven character of black cultural development. The complexity of his relationship to the blues and his fluctuating commitment to the politics of racial protest which had set American cities on fire during this period extend and underscore this point. The creative opposition in his work between obvious reverence for blues-based traditions and an assertively high-tech, futuristic spirituality distils a wider conflict not simply between pre-modern or anti-modern and the modern, but between the contending definitions of authenticity that are appropriate to black cultural creation on its passage into international pop commodification. Hendrix would later rationalise his ambivalence towards both blackness and America through the nomadic ideology of the gypsy that appeared in his work as an interestingly perverse accompaniment to the decision to play funkier and more politically engaged music with an all-black band.

Authenticity is not so hotly contested in my third example of transnational, diasporic cultural innovation centred on London. It is provided by a song that circulated across the black Atlantic network rather than an individual artist or group. It is included here precisely because the right to borrow, reconstruct and redeploy cultural fragments drawn from other black settings was not thought to be a problem by those who produced and used the music. This is also a more contemporary example, although it relates to the piece 'I'm So Proud,' originally written and performed by the Chicagoan vocal trio the Impressions, at the peak of their artistic and commercial success in the mid-1960s. The group's sixties hits such as 'Gypsy Woman,' 'Grow Closer Together,' 'Minstrel and Queen;' and 'People Get Ready' were extremely popular among blacks in Britain and in the Caribbean. In Jamaica, the male vocal trio format popularised by the band inaugurated a distinct genre within the vernacular musical form that would eventually be marketed internationally as reggae.

A new version of the Impression 'I'm So Proud' topped the reggae charts in Britain during 1990. Retitled 'Proud of Mandela,' it was performed in interperformative tandem by the Brummie toaster Macka B and the Lovers' Rock singer Kofi who had produced her own version of the tune closely patterned on another, soft soul version that had been issued by the American singer Deniece Williams in 1983. I want to make no special claims for the formal, musical merits of this record, but I think it is a useful example in that it brings Africa, America, Europe and the Caribbean seamlessly together. It was produced in Britain by the children of Caribbean and African settlers from raw materials supplied by black Chicago, but filtered through Kingstonian sensibility in order to pay tribute to a black hero whose global significance lies beyond the limits of his partial South African citizenship and the impossible national identity that goes with it. The very least that this music and its history can offer us today is an analogy for comprehending the lines of affiliation and association that take the idea of the diaspora beyond its symbolic status as the fragmentary opposite of some imputed racial essence. Thus, foregrounding the role of music allows us to see England, or more accurately London, as an important junction point or crossroads on the webbed pathways of black Atlantic political culture. It is revealed to be a place where, by virtue of local factors such as the informality of racial segregation, the configuration of class relations and the contingency of linguistic convergences, global phenomena such as anti-colonial and emancipationist political formations are still being sustained, reproduced and amplified. This process of fusion and intermixture is recognised as an enhancement to black cultural production by the black public who make use of it. Its authenticity or artificiality was not thought to be a problem partly because it was content to remain inside the hidden spaces of the black cultural underground and also because of the difference made by the invocation of Nelson Mandela.

The name of Mandela became a paternal talisman that could suspend and refocus intraracial differences that might prove difficult and even embarrassing in other circumstances. His release from prison projected an unchallenged, patriarchal voice, a voice rooted in the most intense political conflict between blacks and whites on this planet, the final frontier of white supremacy on the African continent, out across the relay systems of the black Atlantic. The heroic, redemptive authenticity that enveloped the image of Mandela in these locations was nicely deconstructed in a speech that he himself made in Detroit on his first visit to the US. Mandela answered the Africentric expectations of his audience by confiding that he had found solace in listening to Motown music while in jail on Robben Island. Quoting from Marvin Gaye's 'What's Going On?' he explained, 'When we were in prison, we appreciated and obviously listened to the sound of Detroit.' The purist idea of one-way flow of African culture from East to West was instantly revealed to be absurd. The global dimensions of diaspora dialogue were momentarily visible and, as his casual words lit up the black Atlantic landscape like a flash of lightning on a summer night, the value of music as the principal symbol of racial authenticity was simultaneously confirmed and placed in question.

The problem of cultural origins and authenticity to which these examples point has persisted and assumed an enhanced significance as mass culture has acquired new technological bases and black music has become a truly global phenomenon. It has taken on greater proportions as original, folk or local expressions of black culture have been identified as authentic and positively evaluated for that reason, while subsequent hemispheric or global manifestations of the same cultural forms have been dismissed as inauthentic and therefore lacking in cultural or aesthetic value precisely because of their distance (supposed or actual) from a readily identifiable point of origin.

Soul music and the making of anti-anti-essentialism

Critical dialogue and debate on these questions of identity and culture currently stage a confrontation between two loosely organised perspectives that, in opposing each other, have become locked in an entirely fruitless relationship of mutual interdependency. Both positions are represented in contemporary discussions of black music, and both contribute to staging a conversation between those who see the music as the primary means to explore critically and reproduce politically the necessary ethnic essence of blackness, and those who would dispute the existence of any such unifying organic phenomenon. Wherever the confrontation between these views is staged, it takes the basic form of conflict between a tendency focused by some variety of exceptionalist claim (usually, though not always, of a nationalist nature) and another more avowedly pluralistic stance that is decidedly sceptical of the desire to totalise black culture, let alone to make the social dynamics of cultural integration synonymous with the practice of nation building and the project of racial emancipation in Africa and elsewhere.

The syncretic complexity of black expressive cultures alone supplies powerful reasons for resisting the idea that an untouched, pristine Africanity resides inside these forms, working a powerful magic of alterity in order to trigger repeatedly the perception of absolute identity. Following the lead established long ago by Leroi Jones, I believe it is possible to approach the music as a changing rather than an unchanging same. Today, this involves the difficult task of striving to comprehend the reproduction of cultural traditions not in the unproblematic transmission of a fixed essence through time, but in the breaks and interruptions that suggest that the invocation of tradition that may itself be a distinct though covert, response to the destabilising flux of the post-contemporary world. New traditions have been invented in the jaws of modern experience and new conceptions of modernity produced in the long shadow of our enduring traditions – the African ones and the ones forged from the slave experience that the black vernacular so powerfully and actively remembers. This labour also necessitates far closer attention to the rituals of performance that provide prima facie evidence of linkage between black cultures.

Because the self-identity, political culture and grounded aesthetics that distinguish black communities have often been constructed through their music and the broader cultural and philosophical meanings that flow from its production, circulation and consumption, music is especially important in breaking the inertia that arises in the unhappy polar opposition between a squeamish, nationalist essentialism and a sceptical, saturnalian pluralism that makes the impure world of politics literally unthinkable. The preeminence of music within the diverse black communities of the Atlantic diaspora is itself an important element in their essential connectedness. But the histories of borrowing, displacement, transformation and continued reinscription that the musical culture encloses are a living legacy that should not be reified in the primary symbol of the diaspora and then employed as an alternative to the recurrent appeal of fixity and rootedness.

Music and its rituals can be used to create a model whereby identity can be understood neither as a fixed essence nor as a vague and utterly contingent construction to be reinvented by the will and whim of aesthetes, symbolists and language gamers. Black identity is not simply a social and political category to be used or abandoned according to the extent to which the rhetoric that supports and legitimises it is persuasive or institutionally powerful. Whatever the radical constructionists may say, it is lived as a coherent (if not always stable) experiential sense of self. Although it is often felt to be natural and spontaneous, it remains the outcome of practical activity: language, gesture, bodily significations, desires. We can use Foucault's insightful comments to illuminate this necessarily political relationship.

They point towards an anti-anti-essentialism that sees racialised subjectivity as the product of the social practices that supposedly derive from it.

> Rather than seeing [the modern soul] as the reactivated remnants of an ideology one would see it as the present correlative of a certain technology of power over the body. It would be wrong to say that the soul is an illusion, or an ideological effect. On the contrary it exists, it has a reality, it is produced permanently around, on, within the body by the functioning of power that is exercised.

These significations can be condensed in the process of musical performance, although it does not, of course, monopolise them. In the black Atlantic context, they produce the imaginary effect of an internal racial core or essence by acting on the body through the specific mechanisms of identification and recognition that are produced in the intimate interaction of performer and crowd. This reciprocal relationship can serve as an ideal communicative situation even when the original makers of the music and its eventual consumers are separated in space and time, or divided by the technologies of sound reproduction and the commodity form that their art has sought to resist.

Chapter 21

Jocelyne Guilbault

ZOUK AND THE ISLES OF
THE CARIBEES

The legacy of a colonial past

> After geography there is the shaping force of history.
>
> Gordon K. Lewis

Martinique, Guadeloupe, St Lucia, and Dominica share a similar colonial past. All four have been under both French and English rule at various points in their history, and all four have been populated mainly by blacks, descendants of the African slaves brought over by the two colonial powers. All have suffered from class and racial discrimination and linguistic domination.

Zouk is the creation of black, Creole-speaking Antillean musicians. Their positions of prestige and power in the local media and their commercial success on the international market assume great significance for the islands' Creole speakers in a postcolonial society. In countries molded by the plantation system, the prominence of zouk artists on the local and world scene can be viewed, especially in the French *départements*, as a major contribution toward improving the position of Antillean artists in the class and racial power structure.

Eric Virgal is one of Martinique's leading zouk singers. In the following excerpt from a conversation with him recorded in French at Fort de-France in July 1989, I asked him what had attracted him to zouk:

> Why zouk? Because it's truly *me*. The feeling we have about zouk is that it reflects our way of walking, laughing, dreaming, and speaking. All of our Creoleness is in zouk, all of our everyday life . . . In zouk I have had a chance to discover, and to perform, a kind of music that sells well, that helps me to be recognized, that I can identify with, and that I am not *ashamed* to put on stage. For example, when I was using Haitian

'compas direct' in my gigs, I felt ashamed because it was not *my* music. It was the music of Haitians, and I will never be able to put it across the way they do. And when I was singing calypso, I was borrowing that music, too. It's the same with the Latin American music I do. I feel . . . well, you know. But with zouk? . . . Zouk is *our* music. Zouk is all these different people together, everything we have heard, everything we have lived – all brought together in one form, one music. I say bravo to Kassav because it has understood this. It has found a way to make a good synthesis – and it's all there.

The group Kassav to which Virgal refers has been the leading promoter of zouk. Indeed, not only has Kassav been responsible for the profusion of artists who have emerged in the Creole-speaking islands since the early Eighties, but it has also provided all the background information for the many articles and, in once instance, a book about the zouk phenomenon. The zouk movement, or *zouk mouvans*, as the communications media in Martinique and Guadeloupe call it, began with Kassav and continues to be led by Kassav.

The image that popular groups such as Kassav project, the acts they perform, the sound manipulations they make, the tone of voice and the lyrics they use, the language in which they choose to sing, the particular beliefs they profess, and the relationship they cultivate with their fans – all are part of the worldview they bring to their listeners. Music, as many authors have observed, not only reflects people's reality but also 'constructs' or shapes that reality. As we shall see, Kassav's music has accomplished this not simply through the attractive packaging of its product but also through an ideological stance that inspires the responses of its listeners.

Kassav's beginnings, with 'Zouk-la se sèl médikaman nou ni'

The key figure in the story of Kassav is Pierre-Edouard Décimus, a native of Guadeloupe and a veteran of the Antillean music scene. In the years leading up to his founding of the group, Décimus was reportedly dismayed by the predominance of foreign (i.e. from neighboring islands) music and musicians in Guadeloupe. In the Fifties and Sixties, Latin American music was so popular that many Guadeloupean groups took on Spanish names and even sang in Spanish to be in vogue. By the mid-Sixties, with the fading popularity of biguine and mazurka, the Antillean music scene was invaded by Haitian dance styles, cadence-rampa, and compas direct and, finally, around 1974, by music from Dominica, cadence-lypso. If they wanted to be hired for recordings or performances in their own islands, Martinican and Guadeloupean musicians were forced to emulate the Haitian sound. Local groups, such as Perfecta and Selecta (Martinique) and Super Combo and Les Vikings (Guadeloupe), took advantage of this situation and achieved great success in the region, incorporating the Haitian cadence rhythm into their music and using the percussive horn sounds that had worked so well for Haitian music. Les Vikings, for example, the leading Antillean band, recorded nearly twenty albums during their career. In spite of this success, however, Antillean music had not really established itself.

Around that time, Décimus, who was then the bass player in Les Vikings, gradually came to realize that Antillean musicians needed to rethink their goals and artistic focus. While Les Vikings were playing in Guadeloupe at Le Méridien, the luxurious hotel in St François, between 1975 and 1979, tourists expressed surprise at seeing a Guadeloupean group with a non-French-sounding name. Décimus suddenly realized that what they were pinpointing was, in fact, a problem of Antillean cultural identity. A second revelation came to him during the group's numerous tours abroad. He noticed that hardly any Antillean music was played on the radio stations of the countries he visited. The reason, according to him, was that the Antillean sound did not correspond to international norms. He concluded that, to be recognized as *Antillais*, musicians had to emphasize their 'difference' and, to compete on the international market, produce more technically sophisticated music – i.e. they needed to play more conventionally in tune and to produce recordings using up-to-date technology, which meant going to Paris, where the finest recording studios were located.

Décimus's goal for his next group was set. In 1979, with the aid of his brother, bassist Georges Décimus, and guitarist/vocalist/studio musician Jacob Desvarieux who was already established in Paris, he decided to create a rhythmically complex, technically flawless music with an international sound, one that could be identified unquestionably with the Antilles (Jones, 1988). The name of the group and the lyrics of the songs would all be in Creole. The name 'Kassav' was selected for its punchy phonetic effect (*sa consonance a succès*, the 'ring' of success, in Pierre Edouard's words) and also for its interesting folk connotations. In the Antilles, the word *kassav* refers to a cake made of manioc, a dessert that needs to be prepared carefully. If the juice of the manioc is not extracted meticulously and the recipe not followed properly, the result can be toxic. As Décimus explained in several press and television interviews, the use of 'Kassav' for his group refers to the kind of music it plays, a careful blend of musical influences.

With the support of its first producer, music enthusiast and radio programmer Freddy Marshal, the group decided to combine traditional music with contemporary elements. Their first two albums, *Love and Ka Dance* (1979) and *Lagué moin* (1980), were historical landmarks: Kassav made extensive use of the *gwo ka* (a traditional drum from Guadeloupe) and local rhythms, and revived the national pride that had long been suppressed by Europeans. The journalist Gene Scaramuzzo traces the significance of the arrival of this contemporary form based on musical roots by recalling the effects of the islands' colonial history:

> The *gwo ka*, a very important vestige of the African roots of the Antillean people, had become associated by Europeans and locals alike with the undesirable element of the islands. In addition, a prevailing European sentiment that it took no skill to play the *gwo ka* relegated the drums to non-instrument status and a consequent non-musician status to players of the drum. The use of the *gwo ka* on the early Kassav albums signaled the beginning of legitimization, in the eyes of the people, of their roots.
> Scaramuzzo, 1986: 48

But many musicians I interviewed found it ironic, as did Scaramuzzo (1986, 48), that Kassav has today virtually abandoned the use of the *gwo ka*, in both live and recorded performances, since its early success had encouraged a large number of Antillean musicians such as Gazoline and Batako to incorporate *gwo ka* heavily into their music.

Why did Kassav abandon the drum for a machine? To make its music more accessible, less complex, and more 'international' have been the reasons suggested by several Antillean commentators. While these explanations point to the pressures of the international market, and thus the choice of electronic instruments over traditional ones, they fail to acknowledge that, even with the departure of the drum, not all elements of traditional Antillean drumming have disappeared in Kassav's music. The question is whether the object – i.e. the drum – legitimates the roots of Antillean people more than their unique ways of doing things. Is the integration of traditional musical elements in Kassav's music less significant than the use of the *gwo ka* drum in musical exploration and new creations by local groups? Kassav certainly did not think so. Although the group has abandoned the use of *gwo ka* in most of its arrangements, it has undeniably continued to promote its *Antillanité* by featuring Antillean ways of making music in, for example, the structures of its songs, its arrangements, and its particular mix of foreign music.

It took Kassav five years and many attempts to find the characteristic sound that would establish it as a leading group (with the album *Banzawa* in 1983). In 1984, its resounding hit *Zouk-la se sèl médikaman nou ni* invaded the international market, particularly Europe, Africa, and the Antilles. The immense popularity of this song, with its catchy tune and infectious rhythm, won Kassav the first gold record – France's Disque d'Or – ever awarded to an Antillean group. The record sold over 100,000 copies. This accomplishment was even more amazing considering the severe record-pirating problem in the West Indies and in Africa, where it is especially devastating financially, given the size of the population.

Zouk-la se sèl médikaman nou ni became more than a commercial success. Although not implicitly intended to have any political significance, the title of the song, which translates literally as 'Zouk is the only medicine we have,' became the source of public debate in Guadeloupe and Martinique. Reaction to the song was provoked by the image it projected, that, in effect, 'dance is the only solution we have,' and nationalistic intellectuals and other prominent public figures felt insulted that their nation's image was sullied by such a negative message. Other groups refocused the song's message by placing it in a better light – within the context of contemporary politics. As the Martinican linguist Jean Bernabé wrote: 'If, in addition to being a music for dancing and physical contact, zouk is in fact a practice integrating fundamental elements of the Creole *convivialité*, it would be more readily accepted as therapeutic. Such therapy, moreover, would fit in with the belief that the salvation of our countries must first go through a cultural revolution, a decolonization of minds' (Bernabé, 1986: 15). The band's rise to popularity continued to stimulate debate, especially when the press dubbed Kassav 'the ambassadors of the Antilles.' From then on, media coverage focused on the issues of self-representation and identity and, by so doing, forced the group to articulate its position clearly. Given some people's desire for separation and the fear that others felt of losing the security of the French system, Kassav had become of political interest.

A newly strengthened cultural identity

The goals of Kassav, as expressed in interviews in the print and broadcast media, are manifold: to create a new sound, to succeed commercially, to make the Antilles more widely known and recognized, to give Antilleans personal and national pride, and to fight the ghettoization of black music on the European and Antillean markets. Over the years, these goals have become reality. As journalist Frank Tenaille (1987) summarized, Kassav has invented a new sound, fusing high-tech with an intimate knowledge of Antillean and international musics; it has offered a cultural proposal based first of all on Creole traditions (festive feeling, rhythms, language, social themes) as well as on contemporary life (rock influences, fashion, the overall look, dance). The group has put forward an Antillean identity that proudly accepts its mixed heritage. Drawing on hope and rejecting both fatalism and a victim mentality, Kassav has passed on a new dynamism to a new generation confronted with severe economic and social problems.

In my opinion, the Kassav phenomenon does not simply reestablish the meanings of Creole language, culture, and identity in the current political state of the French islands; rather, it gives them new scope. Kassav makes a cultural statement about what it means to be *Antillais*. This it does not solely by emphasizing its African heritage (see Gabali, n.d.; Lafontaine, 1982, 1983; and Lancréot, 1988) at the expense of European-influenced traditions, as some nationalists seem to propose, but by assuming and actually promoting its uniquely hybrid character. This is something new, considering that hybridization in the past has been strongly opposed by blacks as well as by Europeans (see Guilbault, 1990), yet at the same time is totally in line with the wave of 'world music.' By fusing various musical influences and by relying on a multiethnic representation in its membership, Kassav reflects the racial mosaic that is part of West Indian history.

The climb to fame and power

Throughout Kassav's journey to fame and its quest to establish a group identity, two objectives have remained constant, the same as those that Andràs Tokaji attributes to revolutionary music in Hungary: first, demonstrating power; second, recruiting support. As Tokaji explains, 'The latter does not always take the form of political propaganda; on the contrary, as a rule it simply consists of making apparent the fact of belonging to the same group' (1985: 308). Kassav has clearly achieved its first objective by securing a place for itself on the international market and this, as the Antillean journalist Marie-Line Ampigny (1987) has pointed out, without help from the government or any sponsors. Kassav's demonstration of power has revolved around four issues: creating an autonomous space, winning on the 'master's own ground,' forcing changes on the Antillean scene, and making cultural expression a business.

Kassav's success has been achieved gradually, by relying first on the Antillean public and by recruiting Creole speakers from all the islands. In the same way, the group's popularity in Paris has grown out of the support of West Indians in exile, African immigrants, and other minority groups – horizontally, as it were, through the 'small people,' as opposed to vertically, climbing the ladder of success with the help of the 'big people,' those in power – i.e. the French. Kassav has secured its position by creating a relatively autonomous space with minority groups despite the indifference and at times animosity of the French media – a space on which it has focused, in Décimus's words, 'to show that things can happen, outside France's realm of influence.' The promotion of Antillean music by and for 'small people,' the founder of the group added, is a new way to assert itself vis-à-vis the world political and economic powers.

Ironically, the apprenticeship of Kassav's Antillean musicians in the French recording industry – from recording-studio high technology, to marketing techniques, to acquiring the know-how to attract sponsorship and develop a star image – has led them to conquer this same market. Kassav, and eventually other zouk groups and singers, has indeed become such a dominant force in the French music business that it has not only influenced the media to reverse the tide of ghettoization of black music but furthermore convinced French authorities of its competitive strength on the international market. After having been segregated socially, culturally, and economically for years within the French system, Antillean artists not surprisingly felt a sense of victory in the French authorities' choice of an Antillean female artist (Joelle Ursull) to represent France at the 1990 Eurovision competition.

In 1989, ten years after the group's debut, Kassav's twenty-eight albums and its concerts had reached, according to a news release, over 300 million people. As it has acquired power through fame, Kassav has contributed to some significant changes: a revolution in local show business practices and in record production in the French Antilles; the development of ties for the first time with international markets; new collaboration between local and international commercial entrepreneurs and music groups; and a transformation of social consciousness. Not surprisingly, French politicians and many Antilleans consider zouk's strength to be political. Through its success, zouk has helped to change the asymmetrical relations that have always existed in communications between speakers of French, the official language, and speakers of Creole. It has restored confidence in the usefulness of Creole and instilled among Creole speakers and those considered low on the social scale the hope of controlling the development of their own societies, starting with broadcasting their own music on the radio.

Kassav's financial success has led to the recognition that cultural changes brought about through popular music can bring economic changes, that the process of cultural identification awakened by mass-distributed music in general and zouk in particular informs new attitudes, which in turn affect the economy through consumer choices and production methods. Aware of the multilayered implications of music, Kassav's various enterprises aim now at developing viable economic ventures by promoting not only Antillean music but also other Antillean products. A 1988 news release (Anon., 1988) from Kassav asked, 'Is it utopian to want to propose to the world Antillean products, such as gastronomy, cinema, the arts . . . in the manner of Italian pizza, Japanese technology [electronic and automotive]?' Kassav is convinced that it is not. In the same news release, the group announced its collaboration with two companies in launching its own lines of clothing and cosmetics, and discussed ways to incorporate other sectors of the Guadeloupean economy into this venture. On August 25, 1988, Kassav organized

a symposium sponsored by the Conseil Général de la Guadeloupe to explore the
following three themes:

> To make the decision makers from the socioeconomic and cultural
> sectors sensitive to the issues surrounding zouk as a phenomenon of
> society; to examine the possibilities of putting into place the structures
> for a genuine organization of a new (exportable) activity of Guadeloup-
> ean industry; and to examine the possibilities of using the phenomenon
> as a boost for the Guadeloupean economy.
>
> Anon., 1988

In less than ten years, the radical change in the socioeconomic value of Antillean
music through zouk has brought about profound changes in French Antilleans'
rapport with music. To view music in light of the three symposium themes quoted
above contrasted sharply with the traditional way of thinking about music in the
French islands. During the 1988 symposium, many traditionalists and separatists
expressed concern about the use of music as a unit of production and exchange,
such as Italian pizza or Japanese technology, and how this might affect the ways
music is composed, valued, and used. By seeing music primarily in terms of its trade
exchange value, do Antillean artists not run the risk of losing touch with their own
music in their roles as composers and performers, and with their compatriots'
aesthetic values and cultural needs? Was the early abandonment of *gwo ka* in Kassav's
music, for example, not part of the compromises they thought necessary to pursue
their venture on the international market? Will Kassav and other zouk groups and
singers be able to maintain in the long run the delicate balance between making
music that appeals internationally and making music that nevertheless retains
the characteristics that make it Antillean, if not Guadeloupean or Martinican? Can
zouk be treated as 'goods and services' and still promote cultural specificity and
autonomy, and reflect local social and political goals? These are questions that
continue to arise.

Critics question whether Kassav's choice to co-opt its music makes it less
authentically or characteristically Antillean. Kassav's public response to this has been
that there is no such thing as a 'static' Antillean music, a music that is not a mixture
of various musical genres. In Kassav's view, it is precisely by featuring the hybrid
and constantly renewed and renewable character of Antillean music that one can
promote Antillean cultural uniqueness. And the way to legitimate it is by establishing it as a cultural product with commercial value on the international market.

Chapter 22

Tony Langlois

THE LOCAL AND GLOBAL IN NORTH AFRICAN POPULAR MUSIC

R AI IS A POPULAR MUSIC produced originally in urban western Algeria but
which has been transformed by involvement in the world music business. By
describing the creative choices made in recording studios, I will show how developments in the globalised form of the genre have affected the production and usage
of the Rai in North Africa and which influences have been adopted or rejected. I
will also consider the meanings attached to these musical features and how these
meanings are used to construct concepts of identity and locality (see also Cohen,
1994). While the disembedding of a music from its original context and meanings
(which occurs to some degree in all technological mediations) can loosen its ties
with place, time and identity, this very greyness makes it more open to multiple
usage and interpretation in its active consumption. By looking at studio practice, it
is possible to observe the process of encoding style and metaphor; studying consumption (of cassettes, for example) enables one to observe the interpretation and
construction of meanings, not all of which may have been foreseen by the producers.

Rai has undergone considerable change since its transition from the wedding parties and intimate night-clubs of Oran to open-air concerts and MTV. Of the few performers to have survived this transformation, Khaled (until his move to Europe, he
was known as 'Cheb' or 'Kid' Khaled) has most effectively exploited the opportunity to experiment widely, mixing North African with other, Western styles of pop
music. One of the results of his international success, however, has been the increasing stylistic difference between the Rai produced on each side of the Mediterranean.
This is not simply a matter of diverging tastes, but reflects a growing gulf between
the resident and immigrant experience of being a Maghrebian, their attitudes and
perhaps their aspirations. Since the early 1990s, an ideological battle verging on open
civil warfare has been raging in Algeria and, in this increasingly politically polarised
society, musics, and particularly genres that can be associated with immorality and
Westernisation, are far from being culturally neutral phenomena.

Local to global

Throughout the mid-1980s, pop-Rai (musically, if not contextually, an eclectic departure from traditional forms), was produced in the city of Oran for the local market. The bulk of the new and rapidly expanding cassette industry in this region, utilising cheap and relatively simple technology, consisted of pop-Rai. As Peter Manuel has shown in an Indian context (1993), the advent of new, cheap means of musical production can, if only temporarily, enable the cultural expression of regional or minority interests, potentially in opposition to those of dominant political groupings. Historically, Rai has been the music most associated with discrete social domains, single-sex wedding parties, nightclubs and brothels – i.e. arenas where singers could be outspoken and provocative. Pop-Rai of the 1980s maintained this tradition of frankness and social criticism, continued to sing in the regional dialect and referred directly to places in and around Oran. While the music was now played on a combination of electric and traditional instruments, and its largest audience now only heard cassette recordings of the singers, it remained well imbedded in local traditions, both musically and culturally.

Rai was formerly used in wedding celebrations and night-clubs, both intimate domains where singers were expected to improvise lyrics that praised and teased the audience. Although the songs themselves may originally have had a folk religious or patriotic theme, their performance would entail considerable extemporisation, and an aptitude for this was expected from the singers. The language of Rai songs used, reflected and contributed to a lively vernacular. Even though recording 'froze' its development, it gave the local slang a wider listenership and usage than it would otherwise have had, and its quick production rate ensured that the language was always fresh and amusing. Titles and phrases from Rai songs occurred regularly in everyday conversation between young Waharanis. When Rai became primarily a recorded form, its most outspoken lyrics were quickly toned down. The music was not played on Algerian radio stations until 1983. The banning of the genre ended when, first, Rai's 'liberal' and 'modern' associations were thought to be useful to the government to counter the growing Islamic cultural critique of the regime; second, an awareness of considerable international interest in the music changed the local perception of it; and third, the words and topics of the recordings were rendered suitably innocuous for broadcast. By means of this compromise between the needs of state broadcasting agencies and those of the music industry, Rai grew more popular throughout the Maghreb, though, as many Algerians believe, considerably blander.

Studios and production choices

Editeurs

The *editeur* of a studio performs a multiple role, making daily aesthetic and economic decisions that negotiate several significant social discourses. Along with an engineer he records and mixes the music and is usually heavily involved with arranging it. He may also use a synthesiser to overdub the bulk of the instrumental parts, typically added after the vocal track. Furthermore, the *editeur* negotiates all the financial arrangements (first-time performers will have to pay him, while he will have to bid against other *editeurs* for more proven talent). It is he who decides how many cassettes will be produced, and when and how they will be marketed. As there are no binding contracts between performers and *editeurs* in Algeria, and very few in Morocco, each cassette is negotiated separately, and has to make money before another is attempted. In charge of creative decisions, A&R and marketing, the *editeur* holds a pivotal position in the music business and exploits it as best he can, since he rarely owns the studio and would himself be replaced if he failed to make money for the owner.

Musicians

Few 'live' musicians are required for a recording; apart from the singer and a *derbukka* (goblet drum) player, the overwhelming bulk of the music is produced on synthesisers by one or two people. Studio *editeurs* are often themselves highly talented instrumentalists, sometimes with 'classical' training on the *'ud* (lute) or violin, and equally able to play Maghrebian traditional and Western pop music. Several times inexperienced singers were painstakingly rehearsed with the *editeur* accompanying on 'traditional' instruments, yet when at the recording, the *'ud*, for example, would almost invariably be replaced by a synthetic 'Spanish guitar' sound produced on an electronic keyboard.

This sound seemed to lack the tonal colour and subtlety of performance that the indigenous instrument was capable of, so why was this kind of choice made? Perhaps surprisingly, in Rai there was a market preference for the modern sound over the traditional, even if this would not have been to the personal taste of the *editeur* himself. Likewise, Western concert flutes, or pan-pipe sounds were employed in preference to the indigenous *gasbah* or *ney* because the latter sounded 'too close to home' and 'old-fashioned'. Clearly, the synthetic 'voices' were considered more exotic and sophisticated than those with regional connotations.

These 'foreign' voices, however, tend to replace or 'modernise' sounds that were already broadly familiar to the North African listener. For example, what is regarded as the most 'traditional' form of wedding music in this region is played by two *ghraita* (double-reed shawm pipes), which alternate short melodic phrases in a call-and-answer pattern to the accompaniment of a large double-headed drum, the *tabl*. This tradition is maintained in the villages towards the east of Oran, notably in the town of Mostaganem. To the west of Oran and into Eastern Morocco, identical rhythms are played on military-style snare and bass drums, while the same shawm parts are played on trumpets. This example of syncretism is clearly the result of colonial culture contact; instruments have changed, but the role and social context remained largely unaltered. More recently, the same musical features are played on synthesiser and drum machine and, although this is a departure into the exotic in some respects, the musical structure itself and the relationship between the instruments can, to many North Africans, still be somehow evocative of the wedding party context. Possibly, many such stylistic changes brought about through the creative decision-making of local *editeurs* consist of such cosmetic renovations rather than innovations, and that this displays more creative conservatism in the indigenous form of Rai than detractors might claim.

Europe and the Maghreb

The success of Cheb Khaled abroad moved the cultural centre of gravity for Rai. No longer was Rai's authenticity the sole property of one or two cities in North Africa, but its local product was naturally compared with the polished imported form, produced in an environment where star performers were given time to develop their style and encouraged to mix their musical influences to appeal to the widest of audiences. The results of these developments on North African Rai were enormous, and affected not only instrumentation, but also the lyrics. In all earlier forms of the genre, lyrics were principally directed towards a home audience, as was evidenced by the common use of regional language and slang, and frequent specific references to places and quarters in the Oran area. Oran itself has a reputation (often a bad reputation) in North Africa for liberality and Westernism and, rather like the Liverpool sound of 1960s Britain, Rai and Oran are closely connected in people's minds throughout the Maghreb. Songs that describe nursing a broken heart along the Boulevard Front du Mer mean much less to an international audience than they do in Algeria. Likewise, the inclusion of the occasional song in praise of a local holy man, or another from the repertoire of Ahmed Wahby, who has been the most celebrated Waharani singer since before independence, are not likely to stir the imagination of a Franco-Maghrebi youth in a housing estate in Lyon. Song themes changed considerably in European-produced Rai, but they did so rather slowly in North Africa. To the local audience, the music of Khaled was appreciated enormously, but they complained that his songs were no longer about anything. Perhaps, more to the point, people in Oran were accustomed to knowing which town and quarter the singer came from and, although Rai listeners were very proud of the achievements of their own, they found it hard to continue to identify with the global version of their music.

Technology and tradition

Scales and modes (*maqamat*) that include quarter-tone notes feature rarely in Rai, except in vocal melismatic ornamentation, and although historical reasons exist that partly explain this, their absence cannot be completely distanced from the general ideological context in which music is currently practised. Egyptian and Levantine Arab musics, which typically feature such scales and modes, are actually very popular in North Africa, but the indigenous art and folk traditions tend not to be. Quarter-tones *do* exist among the *nubat* (suites) of the Andalouse repertoire, but these pieces are rehearsed and performed less frequently than those with less complex tonal systems. Given that Western Algeria and Eastern Morocco were only relatively briefly incorporated into the Ottoman empire, that Oran itself was a Spanish presidio for most of its existence, and the obstinate resistance of Berber ethnicity to both internal and external hegemony, perhaps it is not surprising that the Maghreb remains culturally distinct from the rest of the Arab world.

Recently, the dominance of electronic keyboards in musical practice and the adoption of some European innovations have no doubt contributed to the declining use of quarter-tones in Rai. However, the only epoch in which *maqamat* were frequently used in Oran was in the late 1950s and early 1960s, when Egyptian Nasserist politics were being appropriated by Algerians for the purpose of rallying against the French. The great *Waharani Orientale* singers of this period, including Ahmed Wahby, fused regional rhythms and expressions with the arrangements and sentiments of Umm Kulthum and Mohammed 'Abd al-Wahhāb in an act that expressed a pan-Arabic identity in opposition to European colonialism. Despite regional traditions, the choice of one form of syncretism over another is ideologically loaded and, in the case of contemporary Rai, the existence of some Western features and the absence of others from the East might well be interpreted as a form of cultural resistance to recent attempts at political Islamification (*integrism*).

Since Wahby's time, it has been Western rather than Eastern musical elements that have been most obviously appropriated in Oranaise popular music, perhaps reflecting contemporary aspirations. Since Rai has become a world music in particular, European chord progressions and simple harmonies have become commonplace, while songs have become shorter. This, of course, fits the requirements of European radio play (although it has no bearing on broadcasting in the Maghreb). *Editeurs* have claimed that these developments were not made consciously, but were merely reactions to local demands.

Language, purity and place

With its blend of traditional, 'modern' and exotic musical elements, Rai is indeed not unlike a patois. As such, it is simultaneously used everywhere in the region, while it is considered a debased version of 'high' musical, linguistic and moral codes. Languages, in the Maghreb as elsewhere, have important political significance. Throughout North Africa, local dialects of Arabic and Berber predominate, with French, Spanish and standard Arabic used for specific purposes, such as education, commerce or official discourse. For communication internationally, literacy and bilingualism are pragmatic necessities, but their usage, especially in state-run institutions and bureaucracy, excludes monolingual Arabic speakers (often the less privileged section of society) from a significant area of political authority. Furthermore, widespread use of the language of the colonial regime, however necessary this may be, severely hampers the project of satisfactorily distinguishing the modern independent state from the colony. Official business is still partly conducted in French and although politicians attempt to use standard Arabic in all broadcast speeches, this is not a language many feel comfortable with.

The patois of the Oran/Oujda region (known as *Derrija*) is much simpler grammatically than standard Arabic, and the vocabulary is shorter, but its very limitations make it well suited to humorous word-play, puns and double entendres. The local language is not simply the most familiar, but that most suitable for the creative and playful construction of experience-near meaning. Like Rai, the dialect is a flexible, universally used, unwritten language that distinguishes the people from this area, but simultaneously denies them inclusion in the broader constructions of national and pan-Islamic community.

Adherence to and respect for tradition is considered a virtue in North African society, an attitude that applies equally to language, religious practice, social values and music. This acknowledgement of the authority of the past is reflected in both formal and informal power relationships, particularly in the deference expected and shown within the family, to religious leaders and between the individual and state representatives. Since independence, such 'traditional' power relationships were largely taken for granted. Emigration northwards served as an alternative for those who dissented; it also masked economic and demographic problems facing the governing FLN (National Liberation Front) party. In the last decade, however, Europe has severely restricted immigration, and the younger generation of North Africa (some 60 per cent of the population are under 30 years of age) have become highly critical of postcolonial regimes. The government of Algeria in particular is seen to have failed to live up to either the Socialist or Islamic principles it has espoused since the early 1960s. It has clearly been unable to provide adequate housing, employment and an acceptable quality of life for all but a select few. Similar criticisms are voiced in Morocco. 'Traditional' relationships of deference to the older generation has been ruptured by the widespread conviction that the governments have failed their people, and before the deterioration of political circumstances in the early 1990s Rai served to express some of this disenchantment.

Conclusion

In the present circumstances in North Africa, Rai often occupies uncomfortable cultural territory. It is not as Westernised as its detractors maintain, and this view is supported by the growing disenchantment with French Rai, as it increasingly comes to resemble mainstream Euro-pop. North African culture, like all others, comprises and is negotiated from numerous, often contradictory strands. The syncretic nature of Rai music, with all its contradictions, can be considered in many ways to be 'typically Oranaise' and has meaningful resonances throughout the Maghreb. However true this may be, this position runs counter to the ideology espoused by Islamic political movements. While Rai has not actively supported the incumbent military regime, it has made compromises in its anti-authoritarian stance in order to achieve broadcast on national networks. As such, it has allowed itself to be partly appropriated by the vehemently anti-Islamic government.

North African Rai has been constructed on an ideological fault-line, exhibiting all the mixed metaphors of a society divided not only by age, class and gender distinctions, but also torn between the attractions of both Western and Eastern globalised configurations of identity. Given the close, if antagonistic, relationship between Algeria in particular and colonial powers, the glossy modernism of 'Westernity' is in many ways the most familiar and desirable discourse. On the other hand, claims to inclusion in the morally correct *Ummah* (the community of believers) are undeniable, even if this ideology effectively denies the value of local and Berber identities, which are more 'experience near' concepts. Rai, which at an important level displays the syncretic reality of all these competing influences, was problematic because this reality is not, in the end, acceptable to those prepared to use violence to erase cultural 'anomalies'. Musicians feel too constrained by current political circumstances to make anything meaningful of Rai, and have turned their attentions elsewhere. Listeners, too, have turned to less contentious and more locally phrased genres. Whatever attractions 'the modern' might have had, 'tradition' is a safer bet.

Chapter 23

Rupa Huq

ASIAN KOOL?
Bhangra and beyond

BRITISH BHANGRA MUSIC – Punjabi folk and Western pop shoved in the rock 'n' roll blender at high speed – provides heaven-sent fodder for cultural critics of both the popular and academic spheres. In its recorded and live forms, it is cross-cultural musical expression, a subculture hailing from the twin sites of turn-of-the-century urban Britain and the subcontinent inextricably bound up with the identities of 1990s UK Asian youth. This chapter will attempt to peel away some of the issues associated with the scene and look beyond bhangra at the music and movement(s) that it has spawned, in particular the so-called 'new Asian kool'.

Un-kool Asians

Despite a short-lived selective flirtation with, and exoticization of, the Indian subcontinent's supposedly mystical side in the 1960s, Asians have simply never assumed a principal place in *Top of the Pops*/MTV youth culture mythology; instead, they have perennially been considered unhip. Western popular culture has long been over-endowed with stereotypical images of Asians as submissive, hard-working, passive and conformist. These deep-seated media representations spanning three decades of mass migration are still crucially important in shaping the perception of contemporary Asian club culture. Black iconography in popular culture contrastingly has always been seen as cool and hard by the youth culture at large: something to aspire to. Hewitt (1986) has shown how this even applies to the ways in which young people use the English language: words from the West Indian vernacular such as 'hard' and 'dread', for example, have entered everyday youth-culture-speak. When Apache Indian duetted with Maxi Priest, the former delivering his lines in patois and the latter in Punjabi, it was seen by Gilroy as an important gesture of mutual cultural respect. Lou Reed memorably sang 'I Wanna Be Black'. Rick Astley,

Jamiroqai and Mick Hucknall arguably made careers out of the same wish, but no one at any time expressed desires along the lines of 'I Wanna Be a Paki'.

Bhangra is a music of very specific derivations, namely Punjabi folk dance, which by definition cannot carry equal appeal to the inhabitants of an entire subcontinent. The group Joi Bangla, of Bangladeshi descent and based in East London, for example, have expressed reservations about bhangra's narrow Punjabi focus and instead use Bengali lyrics, as have the Asian group Dub Foundation. It is something of an over-simplification to see bhangra as the one force uniting the disparate members of Britain's Asian youth. Indeed, an effort to maintain a distance from (old-style) bhangra is one of the defining features of those associated with Asian kool.

Press to play: representations of bhangra

Bhangra has not received much attention from academia but its existence can be detected from popular reports. The musicological, cultural and economic reasons for bhangra's lack of progress all are apparent in its British press coverage, throwing up some interesting questions of representation and the ways in which Asian youth in the UK are viewed by the respectable media. By 1993, the *Face* (August 1993) was calling bhangra 'a scene that parallels the dancefloor revolution of acid house' but it took the British media until 1986 to discover it (Banerji and Baumann, 1990). In March of that year the *Face* itself featured a daytime event, termed by Baumann the 'classic public event for Bhangra music'. However, Baumann despaired of traits in the early reporting of bhangra:

> Not all of this publicity was welcome for apart from its often patron-izing tone, its pictures of a new generation of Asian youth regularly bunking off school to attend live shows created images that did justice to neither parents' attitudes nor to youngsters' aspirations.
>
> (Baumann, 1990: 146)

These tabloid attitudes are still prevalent in many descriptions of bhangra today.

The media focused on the repressed – Asian – youth angle. A *Guardian* article of 1990 was entitled 'Rave of the secret rebels: the clandestine clubbers who do their kicking against cultural restraints on the dance floor'. We are told:

> Normally the girls here would not be allowed near a club; their culture and parents forbid it. Now they had five hours to release their frustra-tion and rebel . . . Asian girls have to be protected from 'Western depravity'. They are kept at home.

It is a cautionary tale including adventure and deception: 'Nazreen quickly dismissed the insane urge to blab all to her parents, the next afternoon was only a month away.' This tone spread to television as well as the press. Benjamin Zephaniah in a BBC documentary in 1993 told the camera at Le Palais nightclub, Hammersmith: 'Raving from 11 a.m. is quite normal in the Asian community. This is a real cultural melting-pot and most Asian parents think that daytime raving is safe.'

Interestingly, the *Independent*'s 1994 commentary on Bombay Jungle, a weekly night-time bhangra rave at the fashionable Wag club in central London, contrasts with the *Guardian*'s report of four years before. In 1990 we were told, 'Hardly anyone smoked, no-one drank, knowing that if the secret was to be maintained they had to arrive home as spotlessly as they had left.' Those attending night-time events it seems are not subject to the same code of conduct. By 1994 the *Independent* notes, 'Couples don't restrain from physical contact and both sexes smoke and drink freely' (24 May 1994). As with other youth culture, bhangra has attracted lay speculative theories. A raver quoted in the *Independent* explains: 'For once Asians can conduct themselves in a way they would never dream of doing in front of their parents. Coming to the Wag reassures me that I'm not the only one suffering an identity crisis.' This quote in particular reinforces dominant representations of Asians who were caught between two cultures, desultory, directionless, confused. It is, however, rather reductive to see Asian youth as perpetual victims of the system when the reality of dual, or indeed multiple, identities is much more complex.

No sell-out: the burden of representation

Much expectation is vested in the executants of the new Asian pop, much more than in their white counterparts who are not subjected to the same continual pressure to supply self-justifications. All those involved are immediately seen as spokespersons for the 'community' and 'their generation', even if their music is not particularly Asian. This has been termed 'the burden of representation' (Mercer, 1994: 233–58; Gilroy, 1988). The burden of representation is intrinsically bound up with media representation because of the mass media's role in the legitimation of cultural production. Many are aware of the restricted frameworks in which they are forced to operate. Gurinder Chudha has said (*The Guardian*, 7 August 1992): 'This burden is very much a noose around the neck, but it also keeps us in check.' Playwright Hanif Kureishi has also met with a critical response from some sections of the Asian community as did Chudha's feature *Bhaji on the Beach*. Kureshi has rejoindered: 'The Asian community is so diverse, so broad in terms of class, age and outlook that it doesn't make any sense to talk of the so-called Asian community' (*Guardian*, 7 August 1992). This shows a self-awareness on the part of artists regarding their positions in Asian cultural production. Cornershop's Tejinder Singh has commented (*Asian Age*, April 1994): 'Other bands are just there. We're not easy to categorise like Transglobal Underground or Apache Indian. We've had to justify ourselves a lot more than anybody else.' The burden is closely interwined with stereotypes and operates on two levels: within the artist's own 'community' itself and outside. In common-sense terms, it can be described as 'not letting the side down'.

Smashing stereotypes 1: Asians with attitude

'Belligerent Paki-fists', *The Observer* stormed (3 November 1993) about Asian rappers Fun^Da^Mental. The well-worn path straddling politics and pop has been documented among others by Denselow (1989) and Frith (1978), but although the purchase of pop as a radicalizing force seemed to be spent by the 1990s, it is interesting to note that at a time when mainstream pop music continued to disengage with the political, many of the new wave of Asian pop groups were addressing two campaigns in particular: the Criminal Justice Bill issue and anti-racism. Tactics for both drew heavily on the Rock Against Racism tradition of the late 1970s. At open-air awareness/fundraising gigs for both causes, Cornershop, Asian Dub Foundation and, most prominently, Fun^Da^Mental were appearing regularly on the bill.

Asian Dub Foundation have played benefits for different factions of the anti-racist campaign. DJ John Pandit, the band's 'political strategist', is a youth worker for a civil rights advice and support group in Tower Hamlets, east London – a major area of Asian concentration and troubled by racist violence in recent years. I asked him: Are you a single-issue band, the issue being anti-racism? He replied as follows:

> We find it difficult to be just entertainment. A lot of groups will have a radical sound and attach themselves to these campaigns because it's flavour of the month, not having been involved in these campaigns. We've done all this, we've been through this, seen it all. Ani from his educational point as a tutor and me being involved in anti-racist work for ten years now. There's no problem working with all of these people but they need education as well. They're front groups, sure, but then all groups are a front for something.

The 'political' side of the new wave of Asian-produced second-generation pop can further be seen from some of its lyrical content, some of whose themes certainly have at least political undertones, tackling old taboos. After all, according to its web page definition, 'Lyrical content of Bhangra songs relates to celebration, or love, or patriotism or current social issues.' Of course, not all Asian pop can be filed under 'political'. Producer Bally Sagoo's trademark is revamping and revitalizing old Asian film-score classics by interweaving thumping Western bass lines among the string-draped sitar and tabla tunes. It is worth emphasizing here the complex inter-textuality and array of musical reference points available to Asian youth. (Aki of Fun^Da^Mental, for example, cut his musical teeth in the early 1980s punk outfit Southern Death Cult). The willingness to subvert convention and tweak about with accepted musical forms is reflected elsewhere. Media analyses of Asian pop always look at it in terms of the 'Other'. However, Asian pop has not been afraid to laugh at itself and be more 'playful' than simple po-faced political posturing. The politically conscious name of the group KK Kings recalls both Guru Nanak's prescribed five Ks of Sikh conduct and the Ku Klux Klan. Their single 'Holidays in Asia' is a bastardization of Cliff Richard's 'Summer Holiday' and the Sex Pistols' 'Holidays in the Sun'. Other bhangra titles recall earlier moments of rock history, such as the 1992 album titles *Never Mind the Dolaks* and *Bomb the Tumbi* from Satrang and Safri Boys respectively, playing on the Sex Pistols *Never Mind the Bollocks* album and on the name of chart dance-outfit Bomb the Bass by substituting the names of two Indian music instruments. This demonstrates conversely the way in which Asian pop can be seen assuming its place at the heart of pop music in Britain rather than at the periphery only to be 'othered' by the media. The cultural producers and receivers of Asian pop do not operate in a vacuum.

Smashing stereotypes 2: sistas are doing it for themselves

If Asians have long been the 'invisible community' in British academic and popular discourse, an important invisible subcommunity is Asian women. The several Asian women DJs, band members and singers – and, of course, audience members – have been largely ignored, despite a slew of journalistic accounts of 'women in rock' published in 1995 (Raphael; Evans). Unsurprisingly, gender has not been uppermost in the few analyses of bhangra that exist, although, perhaps surprisingly, many of those centrally involved in the scene have been women. Outside bhangra, artists such as Sonya Aurora-Madan of Echobelly and Anjali Bhatia of the Voodoo Queens have been outspoken on the subject of Asian women in rock.

Anjali Bhatia is the lead singer with the all-girl punk band the Voodoo Queens, an outfit that musically has more in common with 1970s punks X-Ray Specs than Apache Indian, and was initially labelled as part of the short-lived, US-imported, riot grrrl trend, based on abrasive female guitar rock. She too accepts the notion of a burden of representation, and claims that this is accentuated by being an Asian female via the cliché of East-meets-West 'exoticness'. Anjali described the Voodoo Queens as follows:

> When we first started out we were very pigeonholed. Talking about the press is, I think, wasting time, but I think it has to be said, if you're asking a question like that, that they took up on the fact that 'hey, they're Asians, women as well, what a brilliant press angle' so they just hyped us up to that, one as being Asians and one as being riot grrrls. I think it's detrimental to be pigeonholed and I think the press is very racist and sexist as well.

Was there a difference between what she is and how she has been portrayed?

> I find it sort of an insult, to be a fad. To be Asian is a sort of fashionable thing now whereas when I was growing up it wasn't fashionable to be Asian. I was being called Paki every day. You should know. You get abused for being Asian and suddenly, like, Asian women are the new thing. Even modelling agencies are looking for Asian women as the new cool. I just find that an absolute insult. We've been around for a long time and now they've just discovered that Asian people are cool.

She replied as follows on the possibility that the Voodoo Queens might turn into role models for people growing up now:

> I'm not really into role models myself. I think everyone should aspire to be no one but themself, but no, we have had a lot of fan letters and things from young Asian girls. Before, putting on a guitar was totally alien to them. It's great.

Did she believe that her audience was made up of mainly white indie kids?

Most of it is, yeah, I mean, of course, there's always a few Asians in there but its always like 'spot the Asian,' you know 'token Asian'. There's a few more than before. I think people tend to think that if you're Asian you only like bhangra, which is again a real pain because once again that's pigeonholing people too.

Perhaps the female Asian performer most eager to distance herself from the common associations with bhangra was Echobelly's lead singer Sonya Aurora-Madan who described the intense media pressure of living up to the media hype: 'Everyone expects me to be this Asian-female-escaped-from-an-arranged-marriage freak.' She has never had any interest in bhangra as she grew up listening to Blondie and the Jam.

Conclusion

It is a mistake to assume automatically that all Asian youth will somehow be adherents of bhangra, be it of Punjabi folk-dance tunes or their Nineties legacy. As Annirudha Das of Asian Dub Foundation told the pop weekly news-sheet *Melody Maker*, 'Just because of our skin colour it doesn't mean we have to be into Bhangra' (22 April 1995). Similarly, the audience of a Cornershop or Voodoo Queens gig will be largely white. Within the category of 'Asian kool', a number of noticeable changes can be determined. The more recent wave of clubs, including Outcaste, can be described as 'conscious kool', established to destroy old stereotypes of Asians shipwrecked on 'uncool island'. Such negative stereotypes will not evaporate overnight, but 'Asian kool' should go some way to erode them as long as the new groups' readiness to distance themselves from bhangra does not blind them to their audiences and to their own stated intentions. It must be borne in mind that bhangra takes on a number of forms – unkool bhangra being just one of those.

Bhangra music and all its derivatives have demonstrated a longevity in British pop music; it has outlived many of its Western counterparts since its initial emergence in the mid-1980s. The possibilities of mainstream market penetration present further avenues for commercial opportunism. The argument that all youth culture ultimately submits to the processes of capitalism and market forces has been made throughout its post-1945 history. Much attention has been focused on the alternative economic systems that support the manufacture and distribution of bhangra cassettes (e.g. Baumann, 1990). However, by the mid-1990s more concerted efforts at a mainstream crossover were noticeable. First, Apache Indian was signed to Island Records, then Bally Sagoo went to Columbia in a widely reported £1.2 million deal (*The Observer*, 7 August 1994). Meanwhile Multitone, one of the leading labels in the field, had been licensed to RCA Records, part of the multinational BMG group. As John Pandit of Asian Dub explained:

> The music industry is so important for British capitalism that they need to compartmentalize everything. They have their own markets like the gay market, the pink pound. Now there's the rupee pound, a new Asian audience. It's the history of Western imperialism: let's talk about exotic Asians.

Just as the study of youth is often framed in problem-solving terms, Asian youth are forever examined through the prism of race and racism – the recipients, for example, of 'Paki-bashing' (Mungham and Pearson 1976) – constantly caught between two cultures or suffering multiple identity crises. Asian identity is now, however, more acceptable and more recognized than ever before. Young Asians are in a stronger position to assert themselves positively in ways that were previously unavailable. Awan (1994) claims that 'young Asians are much more interested these days in breaking into the market by producing a sound that appeals outside the Asian community without altogether abandoning their Asian identity'. Perhaps the most critical lesson to be drawn from the burgeoning new Asian forms is that they collectively demonstrate that Asian youth are staking out new territories on the (sub)cultural landscape of 1990s Britain and claiming them as their own, devoid of the baggage of cross-cultural crisis. The fiction of the 'passive Asian' stereotype, an extension of the largely middle-class phenomenon of the 'academically achieving Asian', was further undermined in the public eye in June 1995 when young Asians 'rioted' in the streets of Bradford, Yorkshire (a subsequent review showed that the disturbances were provoked by the police, although no disciplinary action was taken beyond the 're-education' of one officer – *The Guardian*, 11 April 1996). Perceptively reflecting on media marketing, ADF's John Pandit explained at the time, 'There is no Asian kool. The only new Asian kool that's happening is in Manningham, Bradford [district of the disturbances]'.

Until Apache Indian's success of 1993, the nearest to an Asian presence in the charts was Monsoon's quasi-Indian-flavoured novelty hit of 1982 'Ever So Lonely'. By 1996 an Asian had been number one. In many respects bhangra has moved on, but then again this is hardly surprising. Sonic elements of current Asian club culture may represent something of all elite – the 'I've never liked bhangra' chorus of conscious kool – but in the meantime other musical developments have occurred such as the rise of non-bhangra pop. These two strands can be twinned together in a new phase of pop that is 'beyond bhangra'. Yet, for sure, bhangra will remain one of the fragments, one of the many (di)versions through which youth culture manifests itself in the current period.

In the late twentieth century, ethnicity was being used as never before in popular culture. Multicultural babies were being used to sell multi-coloured co-ordinates (United Colours of Benetton), while Michael Jackson assured the world that 'it doesn't matter if you're black or white.' At a time when the mainstream charts were dominated by the Britpop trend, reheating old Sixties and Seventies leftovers with its whiter-than-white selective amnesia view of pop history, bhangra and its spin-offs involving rap, ragga and jungle, reflect the diversities that Blur, Oasis and Pulp deny. *The Times*'s David Toop mused of Bhangramuffin, 'few could have imagined the latest of these unlikely collisions since it seems to cut right across the tight racial divides of inner-city Britain' (15 January 1993). Britpop bleaches away all traces of black influences in music in a mythical imagined past of olde England as it never was, whereas beyond bhangra and jungle are rooted in the urban reality of today's Britain. It is village green versus concrete jungle and we know where we would rather be.

Chapter 24

Helena Simonett

TECHNOBANDA AND THE POLITICS OF IDENTITY

IT IS CERTAINLY NO COINCIDENCE that technobanda popped up in Los Angeles at the same time that politicians began to blame undocumented immigrants from Mexico and Central America for California's economic crisis (1995). Technobanda had a profound impact on the development and expression of the cultural self-image of hundreds of thousands of young foreign- and American-born Latinos during a period of heightened awareness among California residents of large-scale immigration from Mexico and Central America. Since much of contemporary politics is organized around identity, this chapter examines (techno) banda and the quebradita as a site for negotiating identity among Mexicanos in the US.

Wave of ethnic pride

In neighborhoods where Mexicans constitute demographic majorities, many do not regard themselves as members of an alienated and marginalized minority. Los Angeles's proximity to Mexico enables Mexican newcomers, as well as long-term residents, to maintain strong ties to their homeland. Rather than immigrants in the traditional sense, most of these people are transmigrants who remain attached to and empowered by a 'home' culture and tradition. Frequent travel back home and maintenance of multiple relations across the border enable them to cling to their accustomed ways of life. Because of their sheer demographic mass and limited contact with other Angelenos, Mexicanos have not only retained a strong sense of cultural identity, but they also fashion their new place so as to feel at home.

Although the sense of being a 'people' with historical roots was not new to Mexican Americans, Chicano scholars celebrated Latinos' new-found confidence, claiming that now, on the verge of the twenty-first century,

L.A.'s culture comes full circle. Twenty years ago, sociological literature considered ethnic identification a deviant behavior . . . Today
Latinos have begun to value their own norms and ways of life. It is only
the strength of our identity and our multirooted culture that can make
the disaffected among us, particularly the youth, feel like they belong
to the larger society. In fact, we are becoming the mainstream.

Summarizing the ambience at a Los Angeles nightclub when the quebradita craze
was in full swing, Ruben Martinez asserted: 'To say that there is Latino pride in La
Puente tonight would be an understatement. It's more like a cultural revolution.
We're Mexican, speak Spanish, dance quebradita and are damn proud of it.' But
why so much pride? he asked. Why now? And why would American-born Mexicans
proclaim themselves Mexicanos 'on this side of the border'? The quebradita wave,
Martinez argued, fueled a latent feeling that they too had a right to succeed in this
country, where most of them were born. The dimensions of the movement let them
recognize that others too felt the need to belong. Indeed, like other youths of foreign
descent, Mexicanos are often more hurt and troubled by their exclusion from mainstream society than are their parents. Faced with discrimination and a more and
more openly expressed racism, children and young adults have tried more fiercely
to assert their ethnic particularity and to search for a musical voice to state unequiv-
ocally who and what they are.

   Banda music was something new for a generation of Mexicanos who had grown
up listening to mainstream rock and rap music. By the mid-1990s, a large number
of young Latinos had engaged technobanda as a space for cultural affirmation. Instead
of American popular music, the latest banda hits now poured out of open car
windows: this was their political statement. Techno banda was 'their own' voice –
and, a heavily amplified voice at that, not one to be ignored. A young banda
aficionado told me:

Have you noticed that the more that things turn against the immigrants
and the more laws they make against the immigrants, the more they are
coming out? They are dressing more expressive[ly], they like to turn up
their car radios more. They're proud of who they are, they are not intimidated any longer. The banda movement helped young people to address
the issue of being Mexican. To tell who they are or to fight against injustice and discrimination. Definitely . . . I have friends that were ashamed
of their roots, they didn't want to admit that they are Mexican. And
now I see my Cousins' friends, they're going to dance banda: 'Yes, I'm
Mexican!' Young people are aware of a lot of things – at a younger age.

   Identity formation was encouraged by the mass media. KLAX-FM, which had
developed a youth market among the teenage children of immigrants, also reached
a young American-born audience. Committed to strengthening cultural bonds and
to adhering to Mexican traditions and customs, the KLAX DJ Jesus Garcia
announced: 'The banda movement opened my eyes. It is a great thing for the children. It will open their eyes too. Even when they don't dance quebradita any longer,
they will continue to care about their roots. That's the most important thing – the

traditions and the customs – and we encourage to keep them alive' (interview, 1995, Hollywood). Recalling her own experiences, the KBUE DJ Rosy Gonzalez argued that the popularity of banda music was more than just a momentary inclination:

> The reason why it became so strong among the youth is that for a long time young Mexican Americans didn't know much about their roots. I grew up here and I remember going to school and if you were listening to Mexican music, they'd say you are a nerd. Everybody was lying to themselves because they'd go home and what they would listen to at home was Mexican music. But among friends it was not cool to listen to Spanish music. Now, all the youths are enjoying the music, finding out more about their roots, about who they are really. They are proud of their music, of who they are, and I think that's great. At the same time it's a kind of a rebellion against politics here in the United States.
>
> (Interview, 1996, Hollywood)

Graciela Beltrán, a young Mexican American ranchera singer who started to record with banda when 'the movement' was in full swing, asserted that she had never been a victim of the contradictions that affect many children of Mexican immigrants. She never had to hide her cultural preference: 'At this moment, I feel most at ease with the folkloric wave. [Singing Mexican music genres] has allowed me to learn about and to love my cultural roots even more. I have found a way of expression that will be mine for the rest of my life.' The 'banda movement' north of the US–Mexico border will indeed be more than a simple footnote in the history of banda music.

Subcultural affiliation and identification

The cultural backlash generated by the prevailing anti-immigrant climate of the early 1990s reinforced the Latino communities in the southwest. As young people of Mexican descent became more sensitive to racial discrimination and exploitation, they began to take an increased interest in their own and their parents' and grandparents' heritage and traditions. Musical replenishment from south of the border encouraged Mexicanos to reaffirm and bolster their ethnic consciousness and to express their cultural loyalty. People's choices of which particular subculture to affiliate with and belong to are not random, as Slobin (1993) has argued. Songs, sounds, and styles are important features in any subculture because they embody certain values and attitudes that the group members share. Slobin criticizes the tendency in earlier cultural studies to analyze cultural expressions using a single parameter. British scholars in particular tried to map class onto the music of subcultures (see Hebdige, 1979). They tended to see youth culture as a spin-off of a necessary 'parent class,' and style features such as clothing and music as emblems of identity with the parent class (Slobin, 1993: 43). Banda aficionados or 'quebradita people' easily fit the concept of a subculture, and an examination of the dance movements show strong affinities with Slobin's considerations.

While some quebradita participants told me that 'the cowboy outfit is more like a fashion statement,' others insisted on its symbolic value: 'I wear a *tejana* [Stetson hat] because I'm proud of who I am.' Indeed, the Stetson hat, the most conspicuous emblem of the 'banda movement,' mirrors the music's working-class origins and could entice one to analyze banda music as class confined, just as Keil and Keil (1992) and Pena (1985) analyzed the polka and Texas-Mexican *conjunto*, respectively, as working-class phenomena. But in spite of the fact that banda music was mainly nurtured by Mexican low-wage laborers and blue-collar immigrants in Southern California, technobanda was not solely a working-class phenomenon. Musical identities do not necessarily correspond with how people are placed in this world socially. The same music may be meaningful to a range of people who do not share class, nationality, age, or even language. Moreover, a music's connotation to backwardness or upward mobility may be perceived quite differently. For those aspiring to a higher social status, affiliation with 'low-class' music is not desirable, while for individuals who have accommodated to their status in society, such music loses its threatening connotation. Representative of many young banda fans, one told me: 'I'm more into [Mexican music] than my parents are right now. I'm listening to KBUE, while my mom is listening to oldies in English.' Another related: 'I had to defend the music and explain [to] my colleagues and friends that banda is beautiful. I also thought before that banda was low-class music. The music has that stigma.' A Mexican-born interviewee analyzed the status of banda, pointing out the music's different reception:

> Banda music has been around forever. I grew up with banda music. At that time, not very many people liked it. At least in Mexico, only the poor listen to that type of music. The rich do not listen to [banda]. They have Spanish pop-rock music, romantic music such as ballads. You go to a club, and it's divided: the rich and the poor. Even in TV shows and Spanish soap operas, when they make fun of the poor, the poor characters listen to banda. And you have the rich characters that listen to another, more sophisticated type of music. Here in California, it cuts through the classes. Here it doesn't matter.

In the US, (techno)banda was able to leave its marginalized confines and to become the cultural expression of a very diverse people, thus transcending class boundaries. Rather than simply a class marker, music in contemporary America may be 'at once an everyday activity, an industrial commodity, a flag of resistance, a personal world, and a deeply symbolic, emotional grounding for people in every class and cranny the superculture offers' (Slobin, 1993: 77).

For many individuals who felt their ambiguous social position as Chicanos or Mexican Americans in the US, participation in banda events was an alternative musical activity that also affirmed their political standing. As one college-educated young woman asserted:

> I like the music, but it is also political. To me, a lot of it has to do with my parents' history. It is knowing my history. I like a lot of the lyrics, especially the old songs – the older lyrics talking about growing up in a

small town. Banda Machos's 'Sangre de indio' talks about moving away from the hometown, about being an Indian. They're talking of being proud of who you are. I know how it is to live in a small town because of my parents. I feel proud of listening to this kind of music. It reinforces what I was taught to believe. My parents always said: 'You have to be proud of who you are.' That's why my parents always took us back twice a year. When we were little, they would take us [for] the whole summer. [The music] brings back those memories for me, when I was little. I like hearing [the songs]. It's a statement about my parents' history and it validates the history, what they have been through. It also shows, in a political sense, 'Yeah, we're also here and we are proud of being here. We're strong people.'

Emotional grounding

Music embodies imagined worlds. Yet the banda movement has shown that imagination is not simple daydreaming or idle escapism, but rather an empowering force. Because music offers strong images of characteristic identities, it is a source of identity and pride. Richard Middleton has noted that 'popular music has always been concerned, not so much with reflecting social reality, as with offering ways in which people could enjoy and valorize identities they yearned for or believed themselves to possess' (1990: 249). In particular, new compositions addressing the dance style and clothing encouraged banda fans to identify with the new style by participating actively in the dance events, dressed up as vaqueros. One of the dancers remembered the first years of the dance craze:

> Technobanda was very strong. They dressed the music that was playing. Yes, they listened to it, they dressed it, and they drove it. Have you seen the trucks with the hats? That was very in, the trucks with the hats, with the ropes on the mirror.

The music and lyrics of many songs comprise features of a concept called *lo ranchero*. According to Pena,

> To understand the significance of the concept we must first be aware that it is a component of a larger ideology of romantic nationalism that is rooted in Mexican thought on both sides of the border. This ideology has been nurtured for a very long time . . . , but its most recent manifestations can be traced to the Mexican Revolution of 1910 and the intense nationalism it spawned . . . Romantic nationalism in Mexico has exerted a unifying influence by appealing to the glory of the nation's 'unique' heritage. As components of this nationalism, the concept of *lo ranchero* and the symbols that cluster around it – of which *musica ranchera* is one-have contributed to the ideology by ennobling the existence of hacienda and rural life in general, portraying this existence as idyllic.
>
> (Pena, 1985: 10–11)

Technobanda's innovation of adding a vocalist enabled the band to expand the traditional instrumental banda repertory and reinterpret songs from the vast pool of Mexico's lyric genres, notably the ranchera, a melodic and highly emotional song type that developed during the post-1910 revolution period. Although usually associated with mariachi, rancheras are performed by all regional Mexican music ensembles. Rancheras' affective intensity lies in both the sound, including the typical gritos [emotional yells], and in the song lyrics. As 'momentary recreations of a simpler and romanticized folk heritage,' they evoke feelings of nostalgia and patriotism, and therefore of Mexicanness (Pena, 1985: 11).

The ranchera style is particularly suited for romantic songs about love, loss, and suffering. Most often, the subject of the pain and the nostalgic desire of such songs is a woman. Similar sentiments may also be caused by the separation from the beloved *tierra*, the place and, in a broader sense, the nation where one was born. The departure, forced or voluntary, from the purity of the rural homeland and the longing to return 'home' are the theme of many rancheras, both old and new. A typical example is the traditional Canción mixteca [Mixteca song], which nurtures nostalgic longings for the ancestral homeland: 'How far away am I from the land where I was born! What immense nostalgia invades my thoughts! . . . I'd like to cry, I'd like to die of anguish.' In a similar vein, one of Banda Machos's hit songs, 'Los machos también lloran' [Machos Also Cry; original title: 'Los hombres también lloran'], regrets the loss ('I left the land where I was born . . . I left my father to work alone, I left him crying, alone and sad') and expresses the hope of returning.

Like the peaceful rural homeland evoked in the Banda Machos ranchera, the village of El Chante is represented as a sanctified place, an imagined locus of purity, goodness, sharing, and neighborliness. Identifying itself with 'its' village, Banda El Chante encourages the construction of both locality and community, and consciously places itself in a tradition, for, as their names suggest, traditional bandas have always identified with particular localities, enjoying a special association with the public and community life of their own village or town.

The fervent adherence to Mexican regionalism and nationalism may be attributed to feelings of uprootedness and dislocation among Mexican immigrants. Yet, kindled by an anti-immigrant rhetoric that does not distinguish undocumented immigrants from legal ones or from long-term residents and citizens of color, there has also been a noticeable resurgence of regionalist and nationalist feeling among Chicanos. Their participation in banda events may have been an attempt to redefine Los Angeles's cultural space so that they could feel at home in a city and society that favor a policy of rejection and estrangement. Because music is capable of creating a spontaneous collective identity, it serves well as an affirmation of ethnic and/or national difference.

Contemporary and traditional

Technobanda allowed Mexicano youths to experience an attachment to values shared with grandparents and parents and rooted in their 'homeland.' On the other hand, it also allowed them to share social conventions, fashions, and aspirations derived from American youth culture. Like other recent popular musics of large migrant populations, technobanda's syncretic fusion of traditional elements and contemporary features is an expression of its listeners' and participants' own senses of identity. As pointed out by Peter Manuel (1995), cultural expressions of migrant communities often show an inclination toward postmodern aesthetics, while simultaneously retaining ties to premodern ancestral traditions. The coexistence of post- and premodern cultural attitudes in lower-class urban subcultures, though, is not a 'postmodern pastiche' in the sense of a calculated play with elements from disparate discourses and subjectivities as employed by postmodern artists.

> Rather, subcultures are often born into struggles against poverty and discrimination, in which the reconstitution of a sense of personal or collective subjectivity is not a casual pursuit, but rather an urgent task crucial to psychic survival . . . [T]he migrant's search for a sense of identity, like that of modernizing societies in general, is not necessarily a postmodern process, but one which synthesizes traditional and contemporary subjectivities in an often profoundly emotional manner.
>
> (Manuel, 1995: 229, 235)

California's sociopolitical circumstances have contributed much to the power and force of banda music. In its modern garb, technobanda appealed to hundreds of thousands of young people. As a 'traditional Mexican' music, it was a source of pride in one's own culture and race. Moreover, technobanda generated a taste for acoustic banda music and thus helped to release the concealed possibilities of the traditional Sinaloan banda. Banda's modernized version and the dance craze it triggered was a detour on the road to learning about and eventually appreciating Sinaloan banda music. As the KBUE DJ Rosy Gonzalez emphasized, many young people found their roots, their 'home,' in banda music: '*Banda de viento* is a feeling that people have of back home. When I hear *banda sinaloense* I get the chills. That's why banda music, the original banda de viento, will always be around.' Similarly, one young college-educated banda fan told me about her own experience:

> When I was in high school, I wasn't very much into Spanish. I would come back to my parents' country, Mexico, Jalisco, twice a year. I never stopped because that's my roots. I have a lot of family there. Both my grandmothers are there. My father's family is there. My mom's family is also there. What helps is that they're both from the same small town, El Chante. Now, I like the tambora more than technobanda. It's the real stuff.

Another banda fan summarized the tendency among young listeners in the US to go back to their roots, 'to seek out the real thing':

> Technobanda and quebradita are not so hot anymore. Now, the real *banda sinaloense* is strong. They are very versatile – they play anything from que bradita to *tropical* to nortenia. I think when the studios started

to make these techno-mixes, that's what killed technobanda. It was the wrong direction. People wanted to go back to their roots, to hear the real music, played by real musicians – not by synthesizers and computers.

Music often serves as a 'key to our remembrance of things past' (Frith, 1990: 142), an observation that is especially true for the 'banda movement' that swept the southwest in the early 1990s. Triggered by California's particular sociopolitical conditions that increasingly polarized its population, young people of Mexican decent began to take more interest in their Mexican heritage, in their (assumed) traditions. They considered technobanda an intrinsically traditional music – and as such, it helped them to build a consciousness of the past and to forge a vision of the future. Thus, traditional music does not simply belong to the past; rather, it overcomes temporal distance by virtue of its own meaningful presence. The sedimentation of cultural values holds the promise of the continuity of meaning and relevance of a way of life for its people as a distinctive group. Hence, to understand technobanda's power, we ought to consider technobanda a 'popular traditional music'-a traditional music in modern garb whose success is rooted in its capability to transcend spatial, temporal, and social boundaries.

Chapter 25

Tricia Rose

VOICES FROM THE MARGINS
Rap music and contemporary cultural production

H IP-HOP CULTURE EMERGED as a source for youth of alternative identity
formation and social status in a community whose older local support institutions had been all but demolished along with large sectors of its built environment.
Alternative local identities were forged in fashions and language, street names, and,
most important, in establishing neighborhood crews or posses. Many hip-hop fans,
artists, musicians, and dancers continue to belong to an elaborate system of crews
or posses. The crew, a local source of identity, group affiliation, and support system
appears repeatedly in all of my interviews and virtually all rap lyrics and cassette
dedications, music video performances, and media interviews with artists. Identity
in hip-hop is deeply rooted in the specific, the local experience, and one's attachment to and status in a local group or alternative family. These crews are new kinds
of families forged with intercultural bonds that, like the social formation of gangs,
provide insulation and support in a complex and unyielding environment, and may
serve as the basis for new social movements. The postindustrial city, which provided
the context for creative development among hip-hop's earliest innovators, shaped
their cultural terrain, access to space, materials, and education. While graffiti artists'
work was significantly aided by advances in spray-paint technology, they used the
urban transit system as their canvas. Rappers and DJs disseminated their work by
copying it on tape-dubbing equipment and playing it on powerful, portable 'ghetto
blasters.' At a time when budget cuts in school music programs drastically reduced
access to traditional forms of instrumentation and composition, inner-city youths
increasingly relied on recorded sound. Breakdancers used their bodies to mimic
'transformers' and other futuristic robots in symbolic street battles. Early Puerto
Rican, Afro-Caribbean, and black American hip-hop artists transformed obsolete
vocational skills from marginal occupations into the raw materials for creativity and
resistance. Many of them were 'trained' for jobs in fields that were shrinking or
that no longer exist. Puerto Rican graffiti writer Futura graduated from a trade

school specializing in the printing industry. However, as most of the jobs for which he was being trained had already been computerized, he found himself working at McDonald's after graduation. Similarly, African-American DJ Red Alert (who also has family from the Caribbean) reviewed blueprints for a drafting company until computer automation rendered his job obsolete. Jamaican DJ Kool Herc attended Alfred E. Smith auto-mechanic trade school, and African-American Grandmaster Flash learned how to repair electronic equipment at Samuel Gompers vocational High School. (One could say Flash 'fixed them alright.') Salt and Pepa (both with family roots in the West Indies) worked as phone telemarketing representatives at Sears while considering nursing school. Puerto Rican breakdancer Crazy Legs began breakdancing largely because his single mother could not afford Little League baseball fees. All of these artists found themselves positioned with few resources in marginal economic circumstances, but each of them found ways to become famous as an entertainer by appropriating the most advanced technologies and emerging cultural forms. Hip-hop artists use a contemporary crossroads of lack and desire in urban Afrodiasporic communities.

Stylistic continuities were sustained by internal cross-fertilization between rapping, breakdancing, and graffiti writing. Hip-hop events featured breakdancers, rappers, and DJs as triple-bill entertainment. Graffiti writers drew murals for DJs' stage platforms, and designed posters and flyers to advertise hip-hop events. Breakdancer Crazy Legs, founding member of the Rock Steady Crew, describes the communal atmosphere between writers, rappers, and breakers in the formative years of hip-hop: 'Summing it up, basically going to a jam back then was (about) watching people drink, (break) dance, compare graffiti art in their black books. These jams were thrown by the (hip hop) DJ . . . it was about piecing while a jam was going on.' Of course, sharing ideas and styles is not always a peaceful process. Hip-hop is very competitive and confrontational; these traits are both resistance to and preparation for a hostile world that denies and denigrates young people of color. Breakdancers often fought other breakdance crews out of jealousy; writers sometimes destroyed murals, and rappers and DJ battles could break out in fights. Hip-hop remains a never-ending battle for status, prestige, and group adoration, always in formation, always contested, and never fully achieved. Competitions among and cross-fertilization between breaking, graffiti writing, and rap music was fueled by shared local experiences and social position and similarities in approaches to sound, motion, communication, and style among hip-hop's Afrodiasporic communities.

Fab Five Freddy, an early rapper and graffiti writer, explains the link between style and identity in hip-hop and its significance for gaining local status:

> You make a new style. That's what life on the street is all about. What's at stake is honor and position on the street. That's what makes it so important, that's what makes it feel so good – that pressure on you to be the best. Or to try to be the best. To develop a new style nobody can deal with.

Styles 'nobody can deal with' in graffiti, breaking, and rap music not only boost status, but also they articulate several shared approaches to sound and motion found in the Afrodiaspora. As Arthur Jafa has pointed out, stylistic continuities between breaking graffiti style, rapping, and musical construction seem to center around three concepts: flow, layering, and ruptures in time. In hip-hop, visual, physical, musical, and lyrical lines are set in motion, broken abruptly with sharp angular breaks, yet they sustain motion and energy through fluidity and flow. In graffiti, long, winding, sweeping, and curving letters are broken and camouflaged by sudden breaks in line. Sharp, angular, broken letters are written in extreme italics, suggesting forward or backward motion. Letters are double and triple shadowed in such a way as to illustrate energy forces radiating from the center – suggesting circular motion – yet the scripted words move horizontally.

Breakdancing moves highlight flow, layering, and ruptures in line. Popping and locking are moves in which the joints are snapped abruptly into angular positions. And yet, these snapping movements take place one joint after the previous one, creating a semiliquid effect that moves the energy toward the fingertip or toe. In fact, two dancers may pass the popping energy force back and forth between each other via finger-to-finger contact, setting off a new wave. In this pattern, the line is both a series of angular breaks, and yet one that sustains energy and motion through flow. Breakers double each other's moves, like line shadowing or layering in graffiti, intertwine their bodies into elaborate shapes, transforming the body into a new entity (like camouflage in graffiti's wild style), and then, one body part at a time reverts to a relaxed state. Abrupt, fractured yet graceful footwork leaves the eye one step behind the motion, creating a time-lapse effect that not only mimics graffiti's use of line shadowing but also creates spatial links between the moves that gives the foot series flow and fluidity.

The music and vocal rapping in rap music also privileges flow, layering, and ruptures in line. Rappers speak of flow explicitly in lyrics, referring to an ability to move easily and powerfully through complex lyrics and the flow in the music. The flow and motion of the bass or drum line in rap music is abruptly ruptured by scratching (a process that highlights as it breaks the flow of the base rhythm), or the rhythmic flow is interrupted by other musical passages. Rappers stutter and alternatively race through passages, always moving within the beat or in response to it, often using the music as a partner in rhyme.

These verbal moves highlight lyrical flow and points of rupture. Rappers layer meaning by using the same word to signify a variety of actions and objects; they call out to the DJ to 'lay down a beat,' which is expected to be interrupted, ruptured. DJs layer sounds literally one on top of the other, creating a dialogue between sampled sounds and words.

What is the significance of flow, layering, and rupture as demonstrated on the body and in hip-hop's lyrical, musical, and visual works? Interpreting these concepts theoretically, one can argue that they create and sustain rhythmic motion, continuity through layering,and manage threats to these narratives by building in ruptures that highlight the continuity as it momentarily challenges it. These effects at the level of style and aesthetics suggest affirmative ways in which profound social dislocation and rupture can be managed and perhaps contested in the cultural arena. Let us imagine these hip-hop principles as a blueprint for social resistance and affirmation: create sustaining narratives, accumulate them, layer, embellish, and transform them. However, also be prepared for rupture, find pleasure in it, in fact, *plan on* social rupture. When these ruptures occur, use them in creative ways that will prepare you for a future in which survival will demand a sudden shift in ground tactics.

Although accumulation, flow, circularity, and planned ruptures exist across a wide range of Afrodiasporic cultural forms, they do not take place outside capitalist commercial constraints. Hip-hop's explicit focus on consumption has frequently been mischaracterized as a movement into the commodity market (e.g. hip-hop is no longer 'authentically' black, if it is for sale). Instead, hip-hop's moment(s) of incorporation are a shift in the already existing relationship that hip-hop has always had to the commodity system. For example, the hip-hop DJ produces, amplifies, and revises already recorded sounds, rappers use high-end microphones, and it would be naive to think that breakers, rappers, DJs and writers were never interested in monetary compensation for their work. Graffiti murals, breakdancing moves, and rap lyrics often appropriated and sometimes critiqued verbal and visual elements and physical movements from popular commercial culture, especially television, comic books, and karate movies. Black style through hip-hop has contributed to the continued Afro-Americanization of contemporary commercial culture The contexts for creation in hip-hop were never fully outside or in opposition to commodities; they involved struggles over public space and access to commodified materials, equipment, and products of economic viability. It is a common misperception among hip-hop artists and cultural critics that during the early days, hip-hop was motivated by pleasure rather than profit, as if the two were incompatible. The problem was not that they were uniformly uninterested in profit; rather, many of the earliest practitioners were unaware that they could profit from their pleasure.

Hip-hop has always been articulated via commodities and engaged in the revision of meanings attached to them. Clearly, hip-hop signs and meanings are converted, and behaviors are relabeled by dominant institutions. As the relatively brief history of hip-hop that follows illustrates, graffiti, rap, and breakdancing were fundamentally transformed as they moved into new relations with dominant cultural institutions. In 1994, rap music is one of the most heavily traded popular commodities in the market, yet it still defies total corporate control over the music, its local use and incorporation at the level of stable or exposed meanings.

Rap music

Rapping, the last element to emerge in hip-hop, has become its most prominent facet. In the earliest stages, DJs were the central figures in hip-hop; they supplied the break beats for breakdancers and the soundtrack for graffiti crew socializing. Early DJs would connect their turntables and speakers to any available electrical source, including street lights, turning public parks and streets into impromptu parties and community centers.

Although makeshift stereo outfits in public settings are not unique to rap, two innovations that have been credited to Jamaican immigrant DJ Kool Herc separated rap music from other popular musics and set the stage for further innovation. Kool Herc was known for his massive stereo system speakers (which he named the Herculords) and his practice of extending obscure instrumental breaks that created an endless collage of peak dance beats named b-beats or break-beats. This collage of break-beats stood in sharp contrast to Eurodisco's unbroken dance beat that dominated the dance scene in the mid- to late 1970s. Kool Herc's range of sampled b-beats was as diverse as contemporary rap music, drawing on, among others, New Orleans jazz, Isaac Hayes, Bob James, and Rare Earth. Within a few years, Afrika Bambaataa, DJ and founder of the Zulu Nation, would also use beats from European disco bands such as Kraftwerk, rock, and soul in his performances. I emphasize the significance of rap's earliest DJs' use of rock because the popular press on rap music has often referred to Run DMC's use of samples from rock band Aerosmith's 'Walk This Way' in 1986 as a crossover strategy and a departure from earlier sample selections among rap DJs. The bulk of the press coverage on Run DMC regarding their 'forays into rock' also suggested that by using rock music, rap was maturing (e.g. moving beyond the 'ghetto') and expanding its repertoire. To the contrary, the success of Run DMC's 'Walk This Way' brought these strategies of intertextuality into the commercial spotlight and into the hands of white teen consumers. Not only had rock samples always been reimbedded in rap music, but also Run DMC recorded live rock guitar on *King of Rock* several years earlier. Beats selected by hip-hop producers and DJs have always come from and continue to come from an extraordinary range of musics. As Prince Be Softly of P.M. Dawn says,

> my music is based in hip-hop, but I pull everything from dance-hall to country to rock together. I can take a Led Zeppelin drum loop, put a Lou Donaldson horn on it, add a Joni Mitchell guitar, then get a Crosby Stills and Nash vocal riff.

Kool Herc's Herculords, modeled after the Jamaican sound systems that produced dub and dance-hall music, were more powerful than the average DJ's speakers and were surprisingly free of distortion, even when played outdoors. They produced powerful bass frequencies and also played clear treble tones. Herc's break-beats, played on the Herculords, inspired breakdancers' freestyle moves and sparked a new generation of hip-hop DJs. While working the turntables, Kool Herc also began reciting prison-style rhymes (much like those found on *The Last Poets' Hustler's Convention*), using an echo chamber for added effect. Herc's rhymes also drew heavily from the style of black radio personalities, the latest and most significant being DJ Hollywood, a mid-1970s disco DJ who had developed a substantial word-of-mouth following a round the club scene in New York and eventually in other cities via homemade cassettes.

Grandmaster Flash is credited with perfecting and making famous the critical rap music innovation: scratching. Although Grand Wizard Theodore (only 13 years old at the time) is considered its inventor, Theodore did not sustain a substantial enough following to advance and perfect scratching. Scratching is a turntable technique that involves playing the record back and forth with your hand by scratching the needle against and then with the groove. Using two turntables, one record is scratched in rhythm or against the rhythm of another record while the second record played. This innovation extended Kool Herc's use of the turntables as talking instruments, and exposed the cultural rather than structural parameters of accepted turntable use.

Flash also developed the backspin and extended Kool Herc's use of break beats. Backspinning allows the DJ to 'repeat phrases and beats from a record by rapidly spinning backwards.' Employing exquisite timing, these phrases could be repeated in varying rhythmic patterns, creating the effect of a record skipping irregularly or a controlled stutter effect, building intense crowd anticipation. Break beats were particularly good for building new compositions. Making the transition to recordings and anticipating the range of sounds and complexity of collage now associated with sampling technology, Flash's 1981 'The Adventures of Grandmaster Flash on the Wheels of Steel' lays the groundwork for the explosive and swirling effects created by Public Enemy producers, the Bomb Squad, seven years later. Using multiple samples as dialogue, commentary, percussive rhythms, and counterpoint, Flash achieved a level of musical collage and climax with two turntables that remains difficult to attain on advanced sampling equipment ten years.

The new style of DJ performance attracted large excited crowds, but it also began to draw the crowd's attention away from dancing and toward watching the DJ perform. It is at this point that rappers were added to the DJs' shows to redirect the crowd's attention. Flash asked two friends, Cowboy and Melle Mel (both would later become lead rappers along with Kid Creole for Flash and the Furious Five) to perform some boasts during one of his shows. Soon thereafter, Flash began to attach an open mike to his equipment inspiring spontaneous audience member participation. Steve Hager's description of their intertextuality, fluidity, and rhythmic complexity indicates a wide range of verbal skills not generally associated with early rappers:

> Relying on an inventive use of slang, the percussive effect of short words, and unexpected internal rhymes, Mel and Creole began composing elaborate rap routines, intricately weaving their voices through a musical track mixed by Flash. They would trade solos, chant, and sing harmony. It was a vocal style that effectively merged the aggressive rhythms of James Brown with the language and imagery of Hustler's Convention.

> Many early rappers were inspired by the intensity of Melle Mel's voice and his conviction. Kid, from rap group Kid-N-Play, attributed some of this intensity to the fact that Mel was rapping for a living rather than a hobby: 'For Melle Mel . . . he's rapping to survive. As such, his subject matter is gonna reflect that. I go on record as saying Melle Mel is king of all rappers. He's the reason I became a rapper and I think he's the reason a lot of people became rappers. That's how pervasive his influence was.

Melle Mel's gritty dark voice was immortalized on Flash and Furious Five's 1982 'The Message,' voted best pop song of 1982. The power of rappers' voices and their role as storytellers ensured that rapping would become the central expression in hip-hop culture.

The rappers who could fix the crowd's attention had impressive verbal dexterity and performance skills. They spoke with authority, conviction, confidence, and power, shouting playful ditties reminiscent of 1950s black radio DJs. The most frequent style of rap was a variation on the toast, a boastful, bragging, form of oral storytelling that was sometimes explicitly political and often aggressive, violent, and sexist in content. Musical and oral predecessors to rap music encompass a variety of vernacular artists including the Last Poets, a group of late 1960s to early 1970s black militant storytellers whose poetry was accompanied by conga drum rhythms, poet and singer Gil Scott Heron, Malcolm X, the Black Panthers, the 1950s radio jocks, particular Douglas 'Jocko' Henderson, soul rapper Millie Jackson, the classic Blues women, and countless other performers. 'Blaxploitation' films such as Melvin Van Peebles's *Sweet Sweetback's Baadasss Song*, Donald Goines's gangsta fiction, and 'pimp narratives' that explore the ins and outs of ghetto red-light districts are also especially important in rap. Regardless of thematics, pleasure and mastery in toasting and rapping are matters of control over the language, the capacity to outdo competition, the craft of the story, mastery of rhythm, and the ability to rivet the crowd's attention. Rap relies heavily on oral performance, but it is equally dependent on technology and its effects on the sound and quality of vocal reproduction. A rapper's delivery is dependent on the use and mastery of technology. The iconic focus of the rapper is the microphone; rappers are dependent on advanced technology to amplify their voices, so that they can be heard over the massive beats that surround the lyrics.

Hip-hop emerges from complex cultural exchanges and larger social conditions of disillusionment and alienation. Graffiti and rap were especially aggressive public displays of counterpresence and voice. Each asserted the right to write – to inscribe one's identity on an environment that seemed Teflon resistant to its young people of color; an environment that made legitimate avenues for material and social participation inaccessible. In this context, hip-hop produced a number of double effects. First, themes in rap and graffiti articulated free play and unchecked public displays; yet the settings for these expressions always suggested existing confinement. Second, like the consciousness-raising sessions in the early stages of the women's rights movement and black power movement of the 1960s and 1970s, hip-hop produced internal and external dialogues that affirmed the experiences and identities of the participants and at the same time offered critiques of a larger society that were directed to both the hip-hop community and society in general.

Few answers to questions as broadly defined as 'what motivated the emergence of hip-hop' could comprehensively account for all the factors that contribute to the multiple, related, and sometimes coincidental events that bring cultural forms into being. Keeping this in mind, this exploration has been organized around limited aspects of the relationship between cultural forms and the contexts within which they emerge. More specifically, it has attended to the ways in which artistic practice is shaped by cultural traditions, related current and previous practice, and by the ways in which practice is shaped by technology, economic forces, and race, gender, and class relations. These relationships between form, context, and cultural priority demonstrate that hip-hop shares a number of traits with, and yet revises, long-standing Afrodiasporic practices; that male dominance in hip-hop is, in part, a by-product of sexism and the active process of women's marginalization in cultural production; that hip-hop's form is fundamentally linked to technological changes and social, urban space parameters; that hip-hop's anger is produced by contemporary racism, gender, and class oppression; and finally, that a great deal of pleasure in hip-hop is derived from subverting these forces and affirming Afrodiasporic histories and identities.

Developing a style that nobody can deal with – a style that cannot be easily understood or erased, a style that has the reflexivity to create counterdominant narratives against a mobile and shifting enemy – may be one of the most effective ways to fortify communities of resistance and simultaneously reserve the right to communal pleasure. With few economic assets, and abundant cultural and aesthetic resources, Afro-diasporic youth have designated the street as the arena for competition, and style as the prestige event. In the postindustrial urban context of dwindling low-income housing, a trickle of meaningless jobs for young people, mounting police brutality, and increasingly draconian depictions of young inner-city residents, hip-hop style is black urban renewal.

PART SIX

Music industry

Introduction to Part Six

■   Jason Toynbee

ACCORDING TO ONE COMMONLY HELD APPROACH to the music industry, commerce suppresses creativity, giant corporations squeeze out independent companies, and production for the market replaces music making for the people. However, the trouble with this approach is its failure to account for the fact that popular music has thrived as well languished under conditions of capitalist industrial organisation. If capitalism in general is alienating and inequitable, it has nonetheless produced popular music as we know it.

This is Simon Frith's starting point. In 'The Industrialization of Music' he recognises the importance of the profit motive, but beyond this he makes no assumptions about the underlying nature of the industry – except to observe that, historically, popular music has developed in tandem with the music industry. It was in the 1920s, with the advent of the phonograph, music carrying media and businesses built on these technologies, that music came to be made and distributed on a mass scale. Such developments, in effect, inaugurated modern popular music. What is interesting , then, are the strong continuities between the 1920s and the contemporary period.

For instance, as Frith points out, recurring patterns can be found in the introduction of new technologies. The record industry has always been pushed forward by developments in 'hardware', the machinery used for playing back recordings, as new equipment stimulates the production of new 'software' to play on it. This happened in the 1920s when records stopped being a novelty, something you needed to make your gramophone work, and became instead a commodity in their own right. The pattern was then repeated in the 1940s with the arrival of vinyl records playing at two different speeds, and a new marketing divide between pop (45) and classical (33.3 rpm). We might add that the CD has been associated with a similar phenomenon – people have bought back catalogue, and new artists have developed the extended form CD album. Frith's general point is simply that new technology always has consequences, not just for the industry, but for our experience of music – the way listeners use and categorise it. Indeed, the two aspects are inseparable.

Another continuity that Frith points to is the huge effect of oscillation between boom and slump in the capitalist economy. Again, what is interesting is the way in which business *responds* to change. The Great Depression of the 1930s almost wiped out the recording industry, but by the end of the decade a few giant companies had re-established themselves in the market. At the same time, radio stations and film studios were buying into the music business: multi-media pop as we know it today was anticipated before the Second Word War.

It is this very historical moment that James P. Kraft focuses on in his chapter reproduced here. Like Frith, he is interested in how technological change generates deep effects in the way music is made. Drawing on his own detailed archival research and interviews from participants, Kraft explains how thousands of musicians in the US were thrown out of work at the turn of the 1920s as the advent of network radio and the film soundtrack led to the rapid centralisation of music making. A relatively small number of musicians relocated to New York and, more significantly, Los Angeles – centre of the film industry and national radio broadcasting – where they joined a pool of highly skilled orchestral players.

What is particularly interesting about Kraft's study is its attention to music making as a form of labour. We have become used to thinking about popular musicians as somehow located outside the industry, engaged not in work so much as in creation. It is certainly true that rock, hip-hop, dance music or jazz have tended to be produced beyond the direct supervision of the music industry. Artists in these genres make the key creative decisions about what to write, play and record. Yet arguably, we are seeing a return to a much more managed form of production with the rise of 'manufactured' pop acts. Kraft's study has a strong contemporary relevance, then, in that it shows some of the factors at work in a music industry where labour is directly controlled. One such factor is the possibility of union organisation. In the 1930s, Hollywood studio musicians were organised in a branch (or local) of the American Federation of Musicians. This boosted their power to bargain for better pay and conditions in the orchestras that employed them.

In the early twenty-first century, union organisation on this scale is unlikely because labour market conditions are so different. Aspiring stars are happy to gamble on an uncertain future rather than look for steady employment. And session musicians tend to work individually or in small groups across a variety of different studios. It seems there is neither the desire nor the opportunity to get together and assert collective strength. But that does not mean that the contemporary period is without a politics of musical production.

Indeed, in Chapter 28, David Hesmondhalgh shows the potential of the British dance music industry of the 1990s as a 'genuinely democratizing alternative' to the corporate music business. Examining the independent record companies that serviced rave and post-rave subculture, Hesmondhalgh identifies two aspects here. One is decentralisation and the opening up of music production to the many through relatively cheap computer music technologies. The other is a tendency to reject individual authorship or stardom; in its place is a concentration on developments in musical style and subculture. Hesmondhalgh sees this as a radical alternative to the cult of the rock super-star and its associated corporate strategies of marketing and promotion. But he also identifies problems for dance music independents in adopting this model. In order to survive in a competitive environment, companies have two main options. One is to produce cross-over hits that succeed in the mainstream market. The other is to make compilation albums. Often this involves entering a licensing deal with a major company. Each strategy, then, threatens the 'credibility' of independents. The more they cross-over, the more they undermine the democratic principles on which they were built in the first place.

In the final analysis, Hesmondhalgh is not hopeful about prospects for the independent dance sector, for dance music's collective ethos is actually much less political than was the case in punk. Where punk independents had a critique of big capital, the dance labels are ultimately pragmatic and so have succumbed more easily to incorporation.

Dominic Power and Daniel Hallencreutz are sceptical about any such approach. In Chapter 29 they argue that the key challenge facing popular music producers in small countries is how to link into the international music business. On this view, getting involved with the majors means access, not incorporation. In a case study, the writers compare the music industry in Stockholm and in Kingston. They find that although international sales of Swedish music have been modest, the income derived by the music industry in Stockholm from these sales has been high. This is because record companies and publishers based in the city are well integrated into the global music industry and, in particular, its intellectual property system. Efficient copyright monitoring and collection means that fees and royalties are returned to the producers who have created the musical wealth in the first place. Conversely, in Kingston there is an idiosyncratic system of production based on the entrepreneurial prowess of sound-system operators and local record companies. The majors have almost no presence and copyright is hardly enforced. As a result, little money comes back to Jamaica in respect of music exports, which are actually higher in volume than those of Sweden.

Power and Hellencreutz take us full circle, from the commonly held belief we began with whereby the industry is a corruptor of music, to a benign view where the problem is simply one of learning the rules of the game. If Jamaicans took on the business practice of Swedes they would be better off, these writers suggest. The case is well made, but I would suggest another conclusion is possible. Music making in Kingston is different from that in Stockholm largely because it depends on repetition and rampant copying. The version is everything. This deviates from the international music industry model where (apparently) individual authorship and stardom, and a well-policed intellectual property regime are all crucial. Still, it is the Kingston system of production that has enabled the emergence of a specifically Jamaican music and in market terms explains why it has been successful internationally. What is more, as the international music industry heads towards an uncertain future, in which digital copying and filesharing may come to seriously threaten its old business models, it may well be that the decentralised, 'right-less'

Jamaican system of production is actually more appropriate. Kingston may have the lesson on how to survive.

Whether or not this is so, the chapter by Power and Hellencreutz, like the other pieces in Part Six, demonstrates the importance of research into the music industry. Industry and music are intimately related, but they are also linked in highly complex ways. Examination of the economics of music thus has a vital part to play in explaining why we have the music we do, and perhaps also in understanding how we might have a different music in the future.

Chapter 26

Simon Frith

THE INDUSTRIALIZATION
OF MUSIC

Introduction

[. . .]

THE CONTRAST BETWEEN music-as-expression and music-as-commodity defines twentieth-century pop experience. It means that however much we may use and enjoy its products, we retain a sense that the music industry is a bad thing – bad for music, bad for us. Read any pop history and you will find in outline the same sorry tale. However the story starts, and whatever the author's politics, the industrialization of music means a shift from active musical production to passive pop consumption, the decline of folk or community or subcultural traditions, and a general loss of musical skill. [. . .]

What such arguments assume (and they are part of the common sense of every rock fan) is that there is some essential human activity, music-making, which has been colonized by commerce. Pop is a classic case of alienation: something human is taken from us and returned in the form of a commodity. Songs and singers are fetishized, made magical, and we can only reclaim them through possession, via a cash transaction in the market place. In the language of rock criticism, what is at stake here is the *truth* of music – truth to the people who created it, truth to our experience. What is had about the music industry is the layer of deceit and hype and exploitation it places between us and our creativity.

The flaw in this argument is the suggestion that music is the starting point of the industrial process – the raw material over which everyone fights – when it is, in fact, the final product. The industrialization of music cannot be understood as something which happens *to* music, since it describes a process in which music itself is made – a process, that is, which fuses (and confuses) capital, technical and musical arguments. Twentieth-century popular music means the twentieth-century popular record; not the record of something (a song? a singer? a performance?) which exists independently of the music industry, but a form of communication which determines what songs, singers and performances are and can be.

We are coming to the end of the record era now (and so, perhaps, to the end of pop music as we know it) and so what I want to stress here is that, from a historical perspective, rock and roll was not a revolutionary form or moment, but an evolutionary one, the climax of (or possibly footnote to) a story that began with Edison's phonograph. To explain the music industry we have, then, to adopt much wider perspective of time than rock scholars usually allow. [. . .] [T]his means focusing on three issues:

1   *The effects of technological change*. The origins of recording and the recording industry lie in the nineteenth century, but the emergence of the gramophone record as the predominant musical commodity took place after the 1914–18 war. The history of the record industry is an aspect of the history of the electrical goods industry, related to the development of radio, the cinema and television.

2   *The economics of pop*. The early history of the record industry is marked by cycles of boom (1920s), slump (1930s) and boom (1940s). Record company practices reflected first the competition for new technologies and then the even more intense competition for a shrinking market. By the 1950s the record business was clearly divided into the 'major' companies and the 'independents'. Rock analysts have always taken the oligopolistic control of the industry for granted, without paying much attention to how the majors reached their position. What were the business practices that enabled them to survive the slumps? What is their role in boom times?

3   *A new musical culture*. The development of a large-scale record industry marked a profound transformation in musical experience, a decline in established ways of amateur music-making, the rise of new sorts of musical consumption and use. Records and radio made possible new national (and international) musical tastes and set up new social divisions between 'classical' and 'pop' audiences. The 1920s and 1930s marked the appearance of new music professionals – pop singers, session musicians, record company A&R people, record producers, disc jockeys, studio engineers, record critics, etc. These were the personnel who both resisted and absorbed the 'threat' of rock and roll in the 1950s and of rock in the 1960s.

The making of a record industry

The origins of the record industry are worth describing in some detail because of the light they cast on recent developments. The story really begins with the North American Phonograph Company which, in 1888, was licensed to market [. . .] Edison's phonograph [. . .]. They sought to *rent* machines, as telephones were rented, via regional franchises to offices: the phonograph was offered as a dictating device.

The resulting marketing campaign was a flop. The only regional company to have any success was the Columbia Phonograph Company (Washington had more offices than anywhere else!). But even it soon found that the phonograph was more successful as a coin-operated 'entertainment' machine, a novelty attraction (like the early cinema) at fairs and medicine shows and on the vaudeville circuit. And for this purpose 'entertaining' cylinders were needed. Columbia took the lead in providing a choice of 'Sentimental', 'Topical', 'Comic', 'Irish' and 'Negro' songs.

Meanwhile, Emile Berliner, who in 1887–8 was developing the gramophone as a means of reproducing sounds using discs not cylinders, was equally concerned to make recordings – he needed to demonstrate the superiority of his machine over Edison's. He formed the United States Gramophone Company in 1893, and the following year Fred Gaisberg who had started at Columbia as a piano accompanist and thus taken charge of recording, was poached by Berliner to be recording director and talent scout. Berliner, unlike Edison, regarded the gramophone as primarily a machine for home entertainment and the mass-production of music discs, such that 'prominent singers, speakers or performers may derive an income from royalties on the sale of their phonautograms' [Gellatt, 1977:13] and in 1897 Gaisberg opened the first commercial recording studio.

For the next five years there was an intense legal struggle between disc and cylinder. But in 1902 the Victor Talking Machine Company (that controlled Berliner's patents) and the Columbia Graphophone Company (that controlled Edison's) pooled patents. They thus 'controlled every patent bearing on the manufacture of disc machines and records' [Gellatt, 1977: 133].

By 1914, however, the basic patents were expiring and a rush of new manufacturers appeared. [. . .] Their profits (and legality) depended on innovations in the techniques and qualities of sound reproduction, and their record-making activities were an aspect of their marketing of record players.

It is useful at this point to make the usual industry distinction between hardware and software: hardware is the equipment, the furniture, the 'permanent' capital of home entertainment; software is what the equipment plays – particular records and tapes. The invention, manufacture and selling of hardware must, obviously, precede the manufacture and selling of software. What normally happens, then, is that hardware companies get involved in software production simply in order to have something on which to demonstrate their equipment. We can compare the early history of the record industry with the recent history of video: video manufacturers were also confused about what video-buyers would use their machines for. Software was seen at first only as a means of advertising hardware (where the initial profits lay). [. . .]

At a certain moment in the development of a new electronic medium, though, the logic changes. If people begin by buying records, any records (train noises, the first compact disc releases), just to have something to play, as ownership of the new equipment becomes widespread, records are bought for their own sake, and people begin to buy new, improved players in order to listen to specific sounds. Records cease to be a novelty. In the record industry this switch began in the 1920s, the real boom time for companies making both phonographs and phonograph records. In the words of Edward Lewis, a stockbroker who helped Decca become a public company in 1928, 'a company manufacturing gramophones but not records was rather like making razors but not the consumable blades' (Lewis, 1956; *see also* Frith, 1990). [. . .]

[. . .] At this stage, record companies were simply part of the electrical goods industry, and quite separate in terms of financial control and ownership from previous musical entrepreneurs. [. . .] Few companies were interested in promoting new numbers or new stars, and there was a widely held assumption in the industry that while pop records were a useful novelty in the initial publicizing of phonographs, in the long run the industry's returns would depend on people wanting to build up permanent libraries of 'serious' music. Fred Gaisberg, for example, the first A&R man, whose work soon took him from America to Britain and then across Europe and Asia, was essentially, a classical music impresario.

This argument has had a continuing resonance: while each new technological change in mass music-making is a further 'threat' to 'authentic' popular music, classical music always benefits from such changes, which from hi-fidelity recording to compact discs have been pioneered by record companies' classical divisions. The record industry has always sold itself by what it could do for 'serious' music. The important point here is that in the history of electric media, the initial 'mass market' (this was true for radio, TV and video as well) is the relatively affluent middle-class household. The organization of the record industry around the pop record (and the pop audience) was a later development – a consequence, indeed, of the slump.

Slump

For anyone writing the history of the record industry in 1932, there would have been as little doubt that the phonograph was a novelty machine that had come and gone as there was about the passing of the piano-roll. Sales of records in the USA had dropped from 104 million in 1927 to 6 million; the number of phonograph machines manufactured had fallen from 987,000 to 40,000. In Roland Gellatt's words, 'the talking machine in the parlor, an American institution of redolent memory, had passed from the scene. There was little reason to believe that it would ever come back' [Gellatt, 1977: 256]. [. . .]

The 1930s slump was marked not just by an overall decline in leisure spending but also by a major reorganization of people's leisure habits. The spread of radio and the arrival of talking pictures meant that a declining share of a declining income went on records (just as in the recession of the late 1970s and early 1980s, there was less money overall to spend on leisure and more products, such as video recorders and computer games, to spend it on). I will not go into the details of the slump here, but simply note its consequences. Firstly, it caused the collapse of all small recording companies and re-established the record business as an oligopoly, a form of production dominated by a small number of 'major' companies. [. . .] By the end of the 1930s, when EMI and Decca manufactured nearly all the records made in Britain and controlled the process by which they got into the shops, the contemporary meaning of 'a major record company' had been established.

In the USA the development of an oligopoly was equally apparent – by 1938 three-quarters of records sold were manufactured by RCA or Decca, and most of the rest by the American Record Company, which controlled Brunswick and Columbia. But the meaning of a 'record company' was more complicated: the music business was now part of film and radio corporations of a sort that did not yet exist in Britain (where radio was a state monopoly and the film industry feeble).

[. . .] By 1926, RCA was networking shows via its National Broadcasting Company. There was, too, an early broadcasting emphasis on 'potted palm music' (to attract relatively affluent and respectable listeners) which meant that while radio did 'kill' record sales it also left pockets of taste unsatisfied. Early radio stations were not interested in black audiences, for example, and so the market for jazz and blues records became, relatively, much more significant.

As radios replaced record players in people's homes, so the source of music profits shifted from record sales to performing rights and royalties. The basic technological achievement of this period – the development of electrical recording by Western Electric – marked a fusion of interests between the radio, cinema and record industries. Western Electric could claim a royalty on all electrical recordings, and was the principal manufacturer of theatre talkie installations; film studios like Warners had to start thinking about the costs (and returns) of publishers' performing rights, and began the Hollywood entry into the music business by taking over the Tin Pan Alley publishers Witmark in 1928. [. . .]

Decca was [then] the first company to realize that an investment in advertisement and promotion was more than justified by the consequent increase in sales. The peculiarity of record-making is that once the break-even point is passed, the accumulation of profit is stunningly quick – the costs of reproduction are a small proportion of the costs of producing the original master disc or tape. It follows that huge sales of one title are much more profitable than tidy sales of lots of titles, and that money spent on ensuring those huge sales is thus a 'necessary' cost. Decca developed the marketing logic that was to become familiar to rock fans in the late 1960s: promotion budgets were fixed at whatever figure seemed necessary to produce big sales. Only major companies can afford such risks (and such sums of capital) and the strategy depends on a star system, on performers whose general popularity is guaranteed in advance.

In the 1930s the recording star system depended on a tie-up with film and radio (hence the arrival of Bing Crosby – Decca was, again, the first company to realize how valuable he was). [. . .]

[. . .] [A]ggressive selling and the star system meant a new recording strategy. Companies became less concerned to exploit big stage names, more interested in building stars from scratch, as *recording* stars. They became less concerned to service an existing public taste than to create new tastes, to manipulate demand. Electrical recording helped here – crooning stars like Crosby could suggest an intimate, personal relationship with fans that worked best for domestic listeners. His live performances had to reproduce the recorded experience, rather than vice versa. And jukebox programmers offered a direct way to control national taste. But radio mattered most of all. By the end of the 1930s it was the most important musical medium: radio gave record companies a means of promoting their stars, while the record companies provided radio with its cheapest form of programming. Two media which had seemed to be in deadly competition, had become inseparable. Radio, after all, did not kill the record star.

The 1930s marked, in short, a shift in cultural and material musical power – from Tin Pan Alley to broadcasting networks and Hollywood studios, from the publisher/showman/song system to a record/radio/film star system – and the judgement of what was a good song or performance shifted accordingly – from suitability for a live audience to suitability for a radio show or a jukebox. It was in the 1930s that the 'popularity' of music came to be measured (and thus defined) by record sales figures and radio plays. Popular music now described a fixed performance, a recording with the right qualities of intimacy or personality, emotional intensity or ease. [. . .] For the record industry (as for the film industry) the audience was essentially anonymous; popularity meant, by definition, something that crossed class and regional boundaries; the secret of success was to offend nobody.

The technological roots of rock

By 1945 the basic structure of the modern music industry was in place. Pop music meant pop records, commodities, a technological and commercial process under the control of a small number of large companies. Such control depended on the ownership of the means of record production and distribution, and was organized around the marketing of stars and star performances (just as the music publishing business had been organized around the manufacture and distribution of songs). Live music-making was still important but its organization and profits were increasingly dependent on the exigencies of record-making. The most important way of publicizing pop now – the way most people heard most music – was on the radio, and records were made with radio formats and radio audiences in mind (one factor contributing to the replacement of band leaders by singers as pop's biggest 'names').

The resulting shifts in the distribution of musical power and wealth did nor occur without a struggle. The declining significance of New York publishing houses and big city session musicians, the growing importance of radio programmers and record company A&R people, were marked by strikes, recording bans, disputes over broadcasting rights and studio fees, and, outside the USA, such disputes were inflected with the issue of 'Americanization' (and anti-Americanism). The USA's influence on international popular music, beginning with the world-wide showing of Hollywood talkies, was accelerated by America's entry into the Second World War – servicemen became the record industry's most effective exporters. By the end of the War the pop music heard on radio and records across Europe (and South East Asia) was either directly or indirectly (cover versions, copied styles) American. Hollywood's 1930s success in defining 'popular cinema' was reinforced in the 1940s and 1950s by the American record industry's success in defining 'popular music'.

Outside the USA the ending of the war and war-time austerity and restraint meant immediate expansion for record companies (in Britain, for example, Decca's turnover increased eight-fold between 1946 and 1956). In the USA, post-war euphoria was short-lived. By the end of the 1940s TV seemed to carry the same threat to the pop industry as radio 20 years earlier. Resistance to this threat and the subsequent unprecedented profits were due to technological and social changes which, eventually, turned the record industry into the rock business.

The technological developments which began with CBS's experiment with microgroove recording in the late 1940s, and culminated with digital recording and the compact disc in the 1980s, had two objects: to improve recorded sound quality, and to ease record storage and preservation. For the electrical engineers who worked to give their companies a competitive edge in the playback market, the musical aspects of their experiments were straightforward. What they were trying to do was to make recorded sound a more accurate reproduction of 'real' sound – from the start the new processes were marketed in the name of 'high *fidelity*'. But this sales talk of records reaching nearer and nearer to the 'complete' experience of 'live' music is just that – sales talk. Each new advance – stereo discs in the 1960s, compact discs' elimination of surface noise and wear in the 1980s – *changes* our experience of music. [. . .] The increasing 'purity' of recorded sound – no extraneous or accidental noises – is the mark of its artificiality. Pre-war records were always heard as a more or less crackly mediation between listeners and actual musical events; their musical qualities often depended on listeners' own imagination. To modern listeners these old discs (and particularly classical 78s) are 'unlistenable' – we are used to treating records as musical events *in themselves*.

A second point follows from this. All hi-fi inventions (and this includes the compact disc) have been marketed, at first, on the assumption that the consumers most concerned about sound quality and a permanent record library are 'serious' consumers, consuming 'serious' music. The late 1940s 'battle of the speeds' between CBS's 33⅓ rpm LPs and RCA's 45 rpm singles was resolved with a simple market division – LPs were for classical music collectors, 45s for pop. Pop thus continued to be organized in three-minute segments, as music of convenience and of the moment (a definition reinforced by the continuing significance of jukeboxes for pop sales).

Record companies' assumptions about 'true' reproduction, 'serious' consumption and the 'triviality' of pop were, in the end, undermined by the invention that made hi-fi records feasible – magnetic tape. [. . .]

[. . .] Record companies quickly realized tape's flexibility and cheapness, and by 1950 tape recording had replaced disc recording entirely. This was the technological change which allowed new, independent producers into the market – the costs of recording fell dramatically even if the problems of large-scale manufacture and distribution remained. Mid-1950s American indie labels like Sun were as dependent on falling studio costs as late-1970s punk labels in Britain (the latter benefiting from scientific break-throughs and falling prices in electronic recording).

But tape's importance was not just in reduced costs. Tape was an intermediary in the recording process: the performance was recorded on tape; the tape was used to make the master disc. And it was what could be done during this intermediary stage, to the tape itself, that transformed pop music-making. Producers no longer had to take performances in their entirety. They could cut and splice, edit the best bits of performances together, cut out the mistakes, make records of ideal not real events. And, on tape, sounds could be added artificially. Instruments could be recorded separately. A singer could be taped, sing over the tape, and be taped again. Such techniques gave producers a new flexibility and enabled them to make records of performances, like double-tracked vocal, that were impossible live (though musicians and equipment manufacturers were soon looking for ways to get the same effects on stage). By the mid-1960s the development of multi-track recording enabled sounds to be stored separately on the same tape and altered in relationship to each other at the final mixing stage, rather than through the continuous process of sound addition. Producers could now work on the tape itself to 'record' a performance that was actually put together from numerous, quite separate events, happening at different times and, increasingly, in different studios. The musical judgements, choices and skills of producers and engineers became as significant as those of the musicians and, indeed, the distinction between engineers and musicians has become meaningless. Studio-made music need no longer bear any relationship to anything that can be performed live; records use sounds, the effects of tape tricks and electronic equipment, that no one has ever even heard before as musical [Frith, 1983; 1986].

It is, to conclude, a pleasing irony of pop history that while classical divisions of record companies led the way in studio technology, their pursuit of fidelity limited their studio imagination. It was pop producers, unashamedly using technology to 'cheat' audiences (double-tracking weak voices, filling out a fragile beat, faking strings) who, in the 1950s and 1960s, developed recording as an art form, thus enabling rock to develop as a 'serious' music in its own right. It was pop producers, straightforwardly employed to realise raw musicians' ideas as attention-grabbing commodities for the teen mass-market, who developed recording as a new form of communication, thus enabling rock to give its account of 'authenticity'. [. . .]

Chapter 27

James P. Kraft

MUSICIANS IN HOLLYWOOD
Work and technological change in
entertainment industries, 1926–1940

THIS ARTICLE [. . .] DESCRIBES AND ASSESSES the impact of new
technologies on one atypical group of American workers – musicians in Los
Angeles – during a particularly important and stressful time of economic upheaval,
the 1920s and 1930s. Between the two world wars, the 'music sector' of the
economy shifted from a diffused structure to a concentrated, highly mechanized
setting. This shift transformed the musicians' working world. With sound movies
and network radio, business firms reproduced and marketed musical performances
on a far wider scale than was previously possible. The mass dissemination of music
eliminated thousands of jobs in silent-movie theaters and radio stations across
the nation, while simultaneously creating a much smaller number of new opportunities in a few expanding media centers – especially Los Angeles. This article
emphasizes that new opportunities in Los Angeles were lodged in elaborate occupational frameworks characterized by new patterns of hiring, wages, working
conditions, and definitions of skills. It also shows that musicians, like other skilled
workers, rejected the notion that modernization should benefit only entrepreneurs
and their customers and sought instead to influence to their own advantage the
changing work environment.

[. . .]

The story of the recording, reproduction, and harnessing of sound waves to
American entertainment industries encompasses a host of personalities, technologies, and businesses. [. . .] By the early 1920s, however, broadcasters knew that
running telephone wires from radio stations to football stadiums provided new
sources of entertainment, and that programs emanating from one station could be
carried by telephone lines to another station and thus sent to audiences far from the
original broadcast. As a result, broadcasters in small communities 'hooked up' to

powerful stations in large cities to gain access to an assortment of news and entertainment programming not otherwise available to them.

As radio networks crisscrossed the nation, advances in sound technology made headway in the motion picture industry. [. . .] By the end of 1925, Western Electric and Warner Bros had together coupled film technology with high-quality amplifier tubes and slow-turning phonographs to produce the first sound movies. The popularity of *Don Juan* in 1926 and *The Jazz Singer* in 1927 persuaded industry leaders to abandon silent films in favor of 'talkies.' The new technology immediately revolutionized a favorite medium of popular culture, the motion picture. With sound movies, audiences no longer sang along with words on the screen or audibly expressed their opinions of the content of movies.

[. . .]

[. . .] By 1927, more than 500 stations dotted the national landscape, and perhaps 2,000 musicians earned full- or part-time wages in radio. The advent of silent films brought even greater opportunities. Like burlesque and vaudeville, silent films used live orchestras to create appropriate moods. As the popularity of movies soared in the 1910s and 1920s, a new wave of theater construction swept the nation, significantly boosting the demand for skilled instrumentalists. By 1927 approximately 25,000 musicians were working six or seven days a week in theater orchestras at nearly double the wages of skilled workers in the building trades.

Leaders of the musicians' labor union, the American Federation of Musicians (AFM), were confident that these circumstances assured the employment status of professional instrumentalists. [. . .]

Such hopes were illusory. By 1929 theaters across the nation were replacing live musical performances with recordings. In radio, music transmitted from powerful, highly capitalized radio stations gave broadcasters and radio audiences alike cheaper and often superior alternatives to local bands and orchestras. By the early 1930s, entrepreneurs capitalizing on higher fidelity and lower-priced records had created a multimillion-dollar jukebox industry in which coin-operated music machines displaced live performances in cafes and dance clubs. But the march of technology had its greatest imprint in movie theaters. Between 1928 and 1933, the talkies eliminated the jobs of approximately 20,000 musicians, perhaps a quarter or a third of the total of all music employment. The efforts of musicians to prevent the spread of sound movies were futile. The public ignored their calls for boycotts of sound theaters, and strikes against the theaters simply hastened the loss of jobs. The Great Depression provided the coup de grâce [Kraft, 1994].

This plunge in musical employment illustrates how innovations in technology and capitalist organization can quickly alter the patterns of life for workers. In the early twentieth century, technological changes in the entertainment industries had notably enlarged the demand for music labor. Mechanization of those industries in the 1920s disrupted the market for musicians, thereby turning a labor scarcity into a large surplus. Like artisans in other trades, professional instrumentalists discovered that efficient 'factories' in distant places produced cheaper and often superior products. Paradoxically, however, while closing off local job opportunities across the nation, the substitution of capital for labor intensity created a smaller number of new and exceedingly attractive jobs in such places as Los Angeles and New York, where entrepreneurs produced the products that displaced live, local talent.

* * *

[. . .] In the early 1930s Los Angeles was a principal production center for the film, radio, and record industries. The city's eight major motion picture companies produced 85 percent of all American films, and the nation's major radio networks and recording companies relied heavily on their flagship firm in Los Angeles. Anomalies in an era of severe depression, these expanding entertainment enterprises created many new jobs for musicians. By 1935, perhaps 1,000 were working in media industry studios in Los Angeles, the number varying at any one time according to production schedules and other factors. Almost all of these jobs were in the glittering suburb of Hollywood at the foothills of the Santa Monica Mountains, a few miles northwest of downtown [*Overture*, May 1933, pp. 6–9; 1938a, p. 2; 1932b, p. 2].

Local 47 of the American Federation of Musicians struggled to save theater jobs while trying to exploit new opportunities in film and radio. Organized in 1894, the Los Angeles local had long enjoyed a position of strength in the city's labor movement. In a citadel of antiunionism, Local 47 established a virtual monopoly over musical services and negotiated 'closed-shop' hiring policies in theaters, clubs, and other places that hired musicians. This success was largely attributable to the fact that, before the era of recorded music, employers had suffered irretrievable losses whenever musicians went on strike. The union's power in Los Angeles was not unlike that of AFM locals in other big cities. The AFM was an affiliate of the American Federation of Labor. Rules that fined members for performing with non-members and working in establishments on the local's 'unfair list' were especially effective in solidifying union ranks. Like workers in the building trades, musicians worked strictly for small businesses, which had no collective organization strong enough to resist union goals. In other words, employers themselves were largely ununionized. [. . .]

With the advent of sound movies, Local 47 joined carpenters, painters, electrical workers, and stagehands to bring uniform wages and all-union hiring policies to production sectors of the film industry. The 1926 Studio Basic Agreement recognized five unions of skilled workers and set up a joint management-labor committee to explore grievances and arbitrate disputes [Refior, 1955: 172; Bordwell *et al.*, 1985: 312]. Local 47 continued to work closely with other unions to secure satisfactory working conditions in other fields of employment. [. . .]

Good working conditions in the entertainment industry in Los Angeles, coupled with the nationwide decline of theater work, made Local 47 the fastest growing affiliate of the AFM. [. . .]

This growth attracted musicians from across the nation to Los Angeles, which created problems for the local union. Officials realized that the union's future depended on keeping labor supply and demand in equilibrium; the AFM, however, had always recognized the right as well as the need of musicians to travel freely between union jurisdictions. Transfer members therefore expected easy access to local jobs, while resident musicians demanded protection against outsiders. In 1929, Local 47 appealed to the national union for help in dealing with this problem.

In response to the appeal, Weber, the president of the national union, addressed the problem at the AFM's annual convention in 1929: a one-year ban on the employment of newcomers discouraged sonic instrumentalists from moving to Los Angeles. Yet hundreds of Depression-worn musicians were willing to make the sacrifice for a chance to secure work in the studio at a later date. Union rules prohibited newcomers from full-time work as a musician for three months after their arrival in Los Angeles, but many newcomers found part-time work in clubs, hotels, or private engagements. Many of them also worked outside the music business [*Official Proceedings*, 1929; TeGroen and Fisher, 1988].

* * *

After a year in Los Angeles, instrumentalists could seek work from studio 'contractors.' The contractors were usually men with limited musical skills who had agreements with studios to supply orchestras for film production. Through the kind of favoritism this system encouraged, a handful of contractors soon dominated the market, and the musicians they favored had regular employment. [. . .]

The contractors' control over hiring was a major source of dissatisfaction for instrumentalists, whose employment and income depended on a small clique of insiders. Even when composers or conductors requested individual musicians, as they sometimes did, contractors might ignore their requests. Studio musicians therefore carefully nurtured relationships with contractors and kept their complaints about the hiring process to themselves. As one instrumentalist put it: 'You stand a chance of losing a quarter or half the income for a year if a big contractor, like X, becomes cool to you.' Another explained: 'You're on a contractor's list and you can be removed from it in a minute' [Faulkner, 1971: 144–7].

Instrumentalists who benefited from this hiring structure enjoyed some of the best wages and working conditions in the profession. Seated behind music stands with their backs to movie screens and surrounded by hanging microphones and busy soundmen, motion picture musician were the envy of all other instrumentalists. (In the late 1930s, when public school teachers earned less than $3,000 a year, sidemen in movie orchestras might make $10,000 [*Overture*, 1942, p. 21]. [. . .]

[Nonetheless, . . .] film work was stressful. With producers paying for every wasted minute, instrumentalists had to perform with precision and efficiency. That fact put a premium on sight-reading skills, for musicians did not receive even the most complicated music scores in advance. Al Hendrickson, a Texas-born guitarist who worked on perhaps 5,000 films during a remarkable 40-year career, recalled that even the best readers worried on some jobs. Hendrickson remembered arriving at one early morning film session 'just in time for the downbeat' and finding a complicated opening passage written especially for him. 'The first cue was a solo that started on the highest fret on the classical guitar,' he recollected, but after an uncomfortable delay, he 'worked it out, some way. Things like that,' he said, 'happened to all of us' [Obrecht, 1988: 18].

* * *

[. . .]

Throughout the 1930s, the nation's three radio networks (NBC, CBS, and Mutual) maintained powerful flagship stations in Los Angeles. These stations provided lucrative full- and part-time work for a few hundred talented (and fortunate) instrumentalists. A half-dozen smaller stations in the city, each of which occasionally received network programs, also employed orchestras for live broadcasts. In 1935, the radio industry employed about 400 musicians in Los Angeles. Although the international executive board of the AFM handled labor negotiations with the networks, Local 47 required orchestras in network stations to be classified under the rubrics of 'sustaining' or 'commercial' radio programs. This had the effect of prohibiting network instrumentalists from working in both local and network programs, thereby increasing the total number of jobs.

'Sustaining' orchestras, typically of eighteen to twenty-five pieces, contracted to work five or six days a week for forty or fifty weeks a year. These orchestras performed on 'nonsponsored' programs, and their members were called 'staff' musicians. Versatile sustaining orchestras played classical as well as popular music, sometimes backed up well-known singers, and even played 'bridges' and 'cues' for dramatic programs or comedy shows. In his recent study of music in early radio, Philip Eberly noted that staff musicians 'might be called upon to accompany a classical singer, to glide through a lilting Strauss waltz or to perform a rousing Sousa march [Eberly, 1982: 23, Atkins, 1988].

Commercial orchestras worked differently. Usually fifteen-to-twenty-piece groups hired to serve weekly sponsored hour or half-hour radio programs, they played for several shows each week. They also played 'intros' and 'themes' for talk-oriented programs and provided music to back up well-known singers and musicians. Some commercial programs featured celebrity traveling bands that stopped in Los Angeles for weekly radio shows. The Kay Kyser Orchestra played in cities coast-to-coast, for example, but returned to Los Angeles once a week for NBC's 'Lucky Strike Program.'

* * *

Film and radio orchestras in Los Angeles between the 1920s and 1940s included very few blacks or Hispanics. Reedman Art Smith, who worked in both film and radio at that time, said later, 'I would have been shocked to have seen a black musician in the studios' [Smith 1988]. The popular Cab Galloway, emcee of a prime-time network radio show in the early 1940s, and pianist-composer Duke Ellington, whose music graced several Paramount films, were two of the few blacks who worked in film or radio on a regular basis. Minorities generally found studio jobs only in productions made specifically for minority audiences.

Like the rest of America before the civil rights movement of the 1960s, Los Angeles was segregated. In fact, blacks had their own musicians' union there until 1952. With more than 500 members in 1930, the all-black Local 767, a chartered affiliate of the AFM, had its own headquarters and its own staff of business agents who policed clubs and restaurants in which black instrumentalists performed. To protect each other, the two locals agreed to a common wage scale. According to John TeGroen, vice president of Local 47 during the 1940s and president when the two locals amalgamated in the early 1950s, relations between the two unions were always amicable. Local 767, he maintained, never demanded greater access for blacks to studio work. The lack of legslation prohibiting discrimination undoubtedly discouraged complaints [*Overture*, 1956, p.6; Te Groen, 1989].

The absence of blacks in film and radio work was only partly a matter of racial discrimination. It also reflected basic matters of musical skills. Improvisation and individuality of interpretation, musical qualities to which many local black instrumentalists gained national fame, were clearly less important than sight-reading skills. In other words, the technical changes that gave rise to new opportunities in media centers also encouraged specific definitions of virtuosity. Skills that worked to advantage in securing club or theater jobs, or even opportunities for record production, did not necessarily have the same advantage in film and radio work. Still, the absence of blacks and other minorities emphasizes the importance of social acceptability in securing studio employment. The oversupply of instrumentalists allowed bandleaders to be highly selective in choosing members of film and radio orchestras. With so large a pool of talent available, they could and did use personal and social factors in hiring or refusing to hire individual musicians.

Minorities were more visible in the city's expanding recording industry. The deepening pool of talented entertainers in Los Angeles combined with technological developments in record production to spur the growth of this industry throughout the 1930s. Instrumentalists found employment in three major record manufacturers, Decca, Columbia, and RCA-Victor, and in a host of small independent firms as well. Locals 47 and 767 had strict guidelines for the employment of instrumentalists at record companies. The companies hired musicians not on a staff, or full-time, basis, but by the 'session.' In the late 1930s, instrumentalists earned at least $24 for a two-hour recording session according to union wage scales, and at least $6 for each additional half-hour. For radio transcriptions, which were often simply recordings of live broadcasts, they earned $18 an hour [*Overture*, 1938b, p. 2].

[. . .]

During the late nineteenth and early twentieth centuries, when millions of Americans faced technological and other changes in their workplace that reduced the skills demanded of their jobs and thus diminished their bargaining power, the status of musicians had risen steadily. But in the second quarter of the twentieth century, technological changes affected instrumentalists as much as they affected any other group of workers. The introduction of labor-saving machinery in the musicians' workplace did not simply reduce skills and bargaining power. It also swiftly and completely eliminated major sources of employment. New methods of reproducing sound represented revolutionary developments, in terms not only of industrial production but of labor relations as well. The new technology put control of the labor process more firmly in the hands of management and made thousands of working musicians superfluous. Successful entrepreneurs like Warner Bros. grasped the meaning of the new sound technology at once, a fact that encouraged them to welcome other technological advances.

The innovations drastically reduced employment nationwide but created new opportunities in the rising entertainment industries in Los Angeles and other media centers. Talented, ambitious instrumentalists therefore flocked to Los Angeles to promote, and often to save, their musical careers. The fortunate few of them who secured studio jobs (and paradoxically helped to displace their peers in the hinterland) worked in highly structured environments with distinctive patterns of hiring, wages, working conditions, and definitions of skill. The fact that management depended heavily on the skills and reliability of the musicians they employed gave Local 47 considerable clout in industrial relations, and, with astute leadership and close attention to the needs of local musicians, the union gained a measure of control in the workplace.

Within the broader perspective of labor experience in US society, that of the musician between the wars shows that the impact of technological change could be ambiguous and ironic, positive but devastating as well. Although technical innovations underlying capitalist development often served labor's interests, they also narrowed job opportunities, forcing widespread and sometimes painful social dislocations. Entrepreneurs had used technology, not to improve the status of workers, but to minimize labor costs, and thus musicians as a group suffered from the resulting mechanization. Yet in the new world of work that emerged, some instrumentalists, those who were especially talented and well connected, found themselves prospering. Their ability to do so depended on trade-union activity, but it also hinged on the indispensability of particular skills in the production process – a tenuous link in the lives of workers.

Chapter 28

David Hesmondhalgh

THE BRITISH DANCE MUSIC INDUSTRY
A case study of independent cultural production

[T]HE EXPLOSION OF SMALL, INDEPENDENT RECORD companies in Britain since the dance music boom of the late 1980s has been seen as a challenge to domination of the music industry by multinational corporations, and many commentators have compared the intervention of the dance indies with that of punk companies in the late 1970s and early 1980s. Savage (1991: 600), for example, describes post-house dance music as 'punk's access principle fuelled by new technology' (and see O'Hagan, 1987). But do the large numbers of independents, and the intense focus on them in the dance world, add up to the provision of a genuinely democratizing alternative? Has dance music culture substantially affected the structure and organization of the British music industry?

Dynamics of genre and authorship: every man and woman is a star?

[. . . One] distinctive feature of dance music culture which allowed independent record companies to thrive was the focus amongst audiences on shifts in style rather than on the identity of performers. Two dynamics connect producers and audiences in the music industry (and, in different ways, in other entertainment sectors such as film): authorship and genre. Both dynamics have creative and commercial functions. They allow the organization and understanding of codes and conventions of meaning, but they also allow publicity and promotion to offer audiences-as-consumers indications of the potential pleasures and meanings available to them if they purchase a tape, CD or video. Dance music cultures have, over many years, been somewhat less concerned with authorship, with performer identity, than is the case in other music cultures such as rock (see Straw, 1991).

[. . .]

The relative lack of concern with authorship within postwar dance music culture (as compared to that within rock and other forms) perhaps reflected a lack of interest among dance audiences in rock notions of authenticity, sincerity and integrity, and a preference for other values: immediacy and sensuality, but also, as Will Straw (1993) suggests, a pleasure in secrecy and obscurity, in the idea that a sound would not become known to everyone, but would remain the particular province of the dance fan and his/her associates. [. . . In fact] dance musicians often deliberately adopted a series of pseudonyms to create confusion over their identities. Commentators in the dance press often remarked that the lack of a star system was a distinctive and challenging feature of the genre as a production culture. There was a strong implication in such views that the star system represented a fetishization of certain individuals, and dance music culture, like many youth music movements, was based on a celebration of collectivism. Whatever the problems of such views, the association of the corporate entertainment industry with the star system was accurate. This is because, once promotional money has been spent on establishing an artist's name and identity, record companies aim to produce a series of increasingly profitable albums. The artist's name serves as a brand, around which meanings can be attached and varied, in accordance with changing audience patterns.

But in early post-house dance music culture, the concentration on shifts in style far outweighed the importance of individual artists. One reason for this was the tendency, already noted, for dance music audiences to be attracted to obscurity, to secret knowledge about music which kept their culture away from the prying eyes of the mainstream. A second factor derives from aesthetic features of dance music as a genre [. . . where] the 'real' authors were the sound mixers. Only occasionally in the history of popular music has it been possible for record companies to base promotional strategies around the identity of sound mixers, and usually this has been the case only when this function was combined with that of the arranger (e.g. Phil Spector). When rave culture began to construct this lack of authorship as radical, and white labels and performer pseudonyms were seen as a disruption of the authorship categories prevalent in pop and rock culture, the record company came to serve as a brand instead of the name of the performer. And, because dance music culture had inherited the countercultural and punk distaste for the music corporations (though, as we shall see, in a pragmatic and somewhat muted form), it was mainly *independent* record companies that came to serve as the means by which a record could be identified.

Crucially, this lack of a star system meant that small record companies did not have to spend time and money building up a profile for a new artist. There was no need, for example, for the promotional videos and live concert tours that rock and pop artists need to break through into a wider market. Many small dance companies, like the punk 'Xerox' labels of the late 1970s (see Laing, 1985) disappeared, often voluntarily, as soon as they issued a record. But dozens of small and medium-sized dance independents have survived, and many of them are based outside the London hub which dominates rock and pop production. So, there are two features of dance music culture that I think can be portrayed as allowing a democratization of music production: its decentralization, and the rise of an independent sector that was able to co-exist with the majors. I turn now, however, to an analysis of some ways in which dance music can be understood as limited in its ability to provide an 'alternative' to the corporate music industry.

Maintaining the sector: crossovers and compilations

Recording and promotion costs are low in dance music, as we have seen [. . .] But to sustain companies over a number of years is [still] difficult. Inevitably, some records will achieve less success than others, and even though the break-even point may be as low, in some cases, as 1,000 sales, many releases will not achieve this level. These less successful records need to be cross-subsidized by records that make more money. There are two main ways in which such 'serious money' can be made. The first is to have a 'crossover' hit. A record might be picked up by the dance press, by an influential club DJ or by a big radio show. The small record company might then enter into a distribution and marketing deal with a bigger company to ensure that the demand is capitalized upon. However, such crossovers, and the organizational strategies needed to achieve them, raise a key issue within the production politics of dance music culture (and indeed, one common to all contemporary Western popular music cultures widely constructed by their audiences as subversive). This is the presence of contradictory attitudes towards popularity itself. While some sections of a 'subcultural' music believe that they should be heard in the mainstream, others argue that the music's force comes from its resistance to co-optation. But many audiences and producers believe both at the same time.

[. . .]

The danger for an independent in 'crossing over' is, in the terms of dance music culture itself, the loss of 'credibility': gaining economic capital in the short-term by having a hit in the national pop singles chart (or even having exposure in the mainstream or rock press) can lead to a disastrous loss of cultural capital for an independent record company (or an artist), affecting long-term sales drastically [(see Bourdieu, 1993: 75 for a discussion of 'going commercial' in the case of high culture).]

The second main way of making the level of profits that would allow the independents to subsidize risks elsewhere involves a more complex relationship between economic and cultural capital. At the heart of dance music economics are *compilation albums*. These consist either of tracks originally issued by the company as 12-inch vinyl singles, or of a series of tracks licensed from other companies and grouped together under some unifying theme. [. . .] React Recordings, for example, one of the most successful dance music labels specializing in compilations, had substantial success in 1995 with an album called *Artcore*, which consisted of jungle tracks with a sophisticated flavour, a sub-style which some journalists had called 'ambient jungle'. The term 'artcore' is a pun on the subgenre of techno referred to above, hardcore. [. . .] Other methods of uniting the tracks on an album include linking it to the name of a well-known DJ (with the suggestion that the compilation represents a typical set by that DJ). This has the added advantage that, as with a conventional album by an artist, someone is available for publicity interviews and appearances. Some dance commentators have suggested that DJs blur traditional processes of production and consumption in music-making. In fact, as such cases show, they have become the basis of a new star system, in recording as well as in the clubs.

There are a number of commercial reasons why such collections of material are profitable. First, the costs of recording the tracks have already been undertaken when the tracks were released as singles. Second, the cost of a 12-inch single is usually between £4 and £5 at the time of writing, but the consumer can get 10 or 12 tracks on a CD compilation album for about £13. Third, while many of the retail chains do not stock vinyl singles, they are much more likely to take such compilation CDs for a less specialist audience. Most of these compilations consist of tracks licensed from other independents. [. . .] The willingness of the independents to become involved in such licensing deals means that the compilation market acts as the commercial lifeblood of the independent dance sector, and sustains a network of labels which are separate from the ever-increasing ties between large and small companies.

The irony is that the compilation album is a commodity that is looked down upon in the dance world, because of the high prestige attached to obscurity within such subcultures (Straw, 1993). Such compilations have the least credibility among dance crowds, whereas 'white labels' have in the past had the highest (Thornton, 1994: 179). This is because compilation albums release carefully accrued, subcultural knowledge into the mass market. The most important way in which small dance music labels have sustained themselves is felt by many 'underground' insiders to be a debased form – and this reveals the contradictions about popularity faced by entrepreneurs within dance music culture. [. . .]

Major/independent partnership and the 'credibility' problem

Dance independents have inherited the anti-corporate rhetoric of the rock counterculture and of punk. Small record labels generally claim to be more responsive to subcultural trends than major companies, and to offer their artists greater artistic autonomy. Yet dance music has served as the most prestigious indigenous form of subcultural music in Britain and Europe in the 1980s and 1990s during a time of unprecedented collaboration between majors and independents. So how 'independent' is the dance music sector? Many recent commentators have suggested that the independent/major division needs to be dissolved altogether (e.g. Negus, 1992: 16–18). Other writers have pointed out the similarity between such views, and the emphasis in 'post-Fordist' writing on new, supposedly consensual relationships between small and large firms (Longhurst, 1995: 36–9; Hesmondhalgh, 1996). Countercultural discourse clearly overstated the opposition between the two ideal-types, majors and independents. Nevertheless, it is perhaps premature to dissolve the difference altogether. The most important task in an era of unprecedented collaboration between small and large firms in the cultural industries is to specify the relationships carefully and to analyse their implications. The varieties of 'partnership' between corporations and 'independents' include a range of licensing, distribution, ownership and financing deals. Many small companies are distributed through a multinational corporation, although there are many independent distribution companies, offering alternative routes. Some distribution deals involve financing whereby the major company will put money up for development costs, such as touring and recording. The small company can also license its recordings to a particular company for release overseas, and going with a major means that such releases might be better co-ordinated. Increasingly, the majors have been keen to base their financing deals on buying a stake in a smaller company, with the option for either party to withdraw from the deal after a specified period (see Hesmondhalgh, 1996: 474–7 for a more detailed discussion of these relationships). Here I want to examine major-independent interaction in dance music, and to analyse the ramifications of such 'post-Fordist' links for understanding the intervention of dance music in the industry as a whole.

[. . .]

Since rave culture intensified the commitment to an underground ideology in dance music (and therefore led to a much stronger questioning of the intervention of the multinationals in dance music), the corporations have adopted various means of making it look as though dance specialists are autonomous of their parent companies. EMI brought in respected dance specialists from an independent label (XL, part of the Beggars Banquet network) in order to set up a company that has separate offices and a separate name (Positiva), but which is effectively part of the major company. PolyGram's holding company structure has been effective in creating the illusion that acquired large independent companies such as Island are fully separate from the parent. [. . .] The European branch of Sony has taken a distinctive approach, having set up a Licensed Repertoire Division (LRD) to carry out a series of ownership, financing and licensing deals with small labels, including Creation, Network, Nation and others. [. . .] The German-owned multi-national BMG, meanwhile, signs funding and distribution deals with smaller companies on an ad hoc basis. Some (such as Deconstruction, the UK's most successful dance music label in the early 1990s) move into BMG's corporate headquarters, while others such as Dedicated (an indie rock/pop label set up by Doug D'Arcy, formerly of Chrysalis) stay in their own premises. PolyGram and EMI too have sometimes set up this kind of short-term deal with specialist companies. Of the majors, only Warner Music has taken the approach of setting up a specialist dance division under the name of one of its fully owned corporate companies (the East-West Dance Division), but it also has the Perfecto label, run by leading DJ and mixer Paul Oakenfold within its headquarters.

It is vital for the corporations and their connected 'independents' to present the relationship between them as one that allows relative autonomy for the small company. Some popular music researchers have accepted this version of events. Keith Negus, for example, has argued that under the new 'fight-loose' regimes operated by major companies, 'staff within major entertainment companies and the labels connected to them experience a large degree of autonomy in carrying out their daily work' (Negus, 1992: 19). But it is no more true to say that the small labels work autonomously of their parent companies, than to say that musicians work autonomously of the firms they are signed to. [. . .] Of course, some sub-divisions of majors are given considerable autonomy to make prestigious signings, and develop careers for musicians. But this is very much a licensed autonomy, granted only to subdivisions that are targeted towards niche audiences who will be attracted to 'quality' acts.

[. . .]

Such strategies should not be conceived of as examples of corporate 'flexibility' (Hesmondhalgh, 1996), with its connotations of a relinquishing of control. Rather, they can be seen as a pragmatic response by multinational firms to the anti-corporatism inherited from rock and soul mythology that runs through various forms of 'alternative culture' in the late 1980s and early 1990s. They provide the majors with what are effectively specialist dance subdivisions, but with a separate identity so that credibility can be maintained among subcultural audiences and producers. [. . .] In spite of the knowing scepticism of some insiders, the process of pseudo-indification has limited the extent to which dance music has been able to offer channels of production and distribution that are genuinely 'alternative' to the enter-tainment corporations. The majors have worked to assimilate as rapidly as possible the symbolic resonances attached to independent record companies.

The tentative interventions of dance

There are other factors that are limiting the ability and inclination of dance inde-pendents to act as an 'alternative' to the music divisions of multinational enter-tainment corporations. One is the gradual undermining of the politics of anonymity which, I argued above, has sustained low promotional costs in the dance sector. The more established sections of the dance music industry are very keen to see the devel-opment of name artists, and the rise of a star system in the dance world that would run in parallel to that of the popular music industry as a whole. In part, this is simply because, as we have seen, the logic of capital accumulation is in favour of the star system: groups and artists act as brand names for music, and the fruits of promotional work can be transferred beyond one record to a series, as audiences carry certain expectations about sounds and messages from one record to the next. In addition, albums by established stars can be sold as 'back catalogue', a source of income that has become much more significant as the multimedia environment of the late twentieth century offers more and more opportunities for copyright owners.

[. . .]

But the drive to develop recognizable dance acts also comes from the desire on the part of dance audiences to see the music they like have an effect within the main-stream, to take its place alongside the indie, rap and pop acts on MTV, for example. We return here to the issue, introduced above, of discursive splits over the value of mass popularity and clashing definitions of success. The 1990s have seen the growth of an audience for dance music that rejects the values of obscurity and anonymity discussed earlier. Instead, a new crossover dance audience accepts the authorship politics previously associated with rock culture. The hugely successful dance act, The Prodigy, exemplify this: they tour, they make videos, they release singles in order to promote albums. They are a dance act, with the industrial features of a rock act.

[. . .]

While the development of a star dance act will, of course, benefit a particular independent company greatly, the independent dance music sector as a whole can only be disadvantaged by such a move towards a rock-style star system. As the promotional costs associated with such a shift rise, majors and the pseudo-independents linked to them will dominate the market because they are best able to absorb the great risks associated with increased promotional budgets. This risk is especially great in a genre that has such a fast turnover of styles and fashions. So a complicated logic emerges. Dance fans call for recognition for the music they love, but recognition is only granted via the star system. And the star system itself destroys the conditions that allow an independent music sector to thrive and that I outlined above: a committed audience that is prepared to seek out information about new sounds; and the consequent low promotional costs that such an audience helps to bring about.

[. . . True, d]iscourses of collectivism identified among dance music audiences as a whole (see e.g. Redhead, 1993) can be found within the industry, and rave culture appropriated certain technological developments to help bring about an encouraging decentralization of production and consumption. But the independent labels at the heart of the dance music recording industry exhibit a more provisional and less politicized anti-corporatism than the post-punk companies that preceded them. This fact is not merely a reflection of Thatcherism, late capitalism or any other label for the 'times in which we live'. It seems to me that the limited challenge offered by dance music institutions to the British music industry is, at least in part, a function of the lack of attention to such issues which, as I argue elsewhere (Hesmondhalgh, 1997), is characteristic of dance music culture. In spite of a general scepticism about corporations, many dance labels turn very quickly to the multinationals for deals. [. . .] So although the closed-off, subcultural nature of dance music provides a challenge to the majors, it has been a challenge that they have largely succeeded in answering.

My sceptical analysis does not preclude the possibility that dance music culture has had radical impacts in other ways: in making club spaces less oppressive for young women, for example; in providing a utopian, collectivist discourse for youth at a time when the public sphere offered only individualism and the free market; or, at the level of the text, in forging more imaginative and creative visions of a politics of the body. I am sympathetic to all these claims, although they are, of course, often overstated. But, in any attempt to provide a more general assessment of the history of dance music culture than is possible here, all of these innovations need to be set against the limited impact of dance music on the organization of musical creativity.

Chapter 29

Dominic Power and
Daniel Hallencreutz

PROFITING FROM CREATIVITY?
The music industry in Stockholm, Sweden and Kingston, Jamaica

Introduction

[. . .]

T HE POPULAR-MUSIC INDUSTRY has in the last fifty years grown to become an important global industry and a major area of economic activity – one that operates on a variety of intersecting geographical scales. The music industry is, most often, a highly localised cultural-product industry that draws on local creative milieux and cultural forms, and has a tendency to agglomerate in urban areas (Hesmondhalgh, 1996; [. . .] Scott, 2000). [. . .] It is argued in this [chapter] that in the music industry it is not only the quality of the creative milieux that counts towards commercial success but also the links between the local production system and international circuits of capital, distribution, and effective property rights.

This argument is tested here with two of the world's most dynamic and creative musical agglomerations: Stockholm, Sweden, and Kingston, Jamaica [. . .]. The choice of these two cases for comparison rests upon the recognition of the world-class position of both cities in the production of music products. This choice is further validated, we believe, by the fact that this assessment rests to a large extent on the international and export competitiveness of their respective products: in short they are strong competitors in the same global market. The fact that both of the music-production milieux treated here are embedded in relatively small economies, albeit radically different ones, makes the international competitiveness and export of their products more important than they may be for artistes and firms in larger economies where domestic demand is large enough to support a profitable and fully functioning industry that need not necessarily look outside its borders in order to be viable (one may think here of countries such as Brazil, India, or China that have highly productive and profitable music industries despite the fact that the products are not significantly exported to or consumed in international markets). These considerations, we believe, make the two cases more amenable and interesting for comparison than they may first appear.

What is particularly interesting, however, when comparing the two is that, although Kingston's products have a far higher global commercial value than those from Stockholm, it is Stockholm's local production system and urban economy that make the bigger profit in real terms. [. . .]

In this [chapter] we draw special attention to the crucial roles of intellectual property rights (IPR) regimes and attendant industrial and firm structure for the 'profitabilty' of music. [. . .] As we shall see, the absence of an institutional structure to protect copyright and collect royalties, etc. has meant that Jamaican 'investments' and 'product development' have not been protected. This has resulted in actors and firms being forced to turn over their cultural and financial capital as quickly as possible, resulting in a fragmented industrial structure characterised by underinvestment (financially at least) and cut-throat competition. Stockholm, by contrast, can be seen as an example of a musical economy centrally located in the present capitalist IPR regime: an economy where musical products are defended by a strong local regime that allows long-term investments in creative acts to be returned. The two cases therefore serve to illustrate that both the present political economy of place, where different positions within the global economy confer vastly different rewards, and differences in, and the erosion of, the efficiency of IPR regimes can have dramatic effects on industrial and profit structures for cultural-products industries.

[. . .]

The examination of the case studies was based largely upon qualitative fieldwork involving semistructured and unstructured interviewing of industry participants and concentrated on recorded music (as opposed to live performance, etc.).

Stockholm

Despite talk by many music journalists of the existence of a distinctive Scandinavian sound, exemplified by the likes of the Cardigans and Stina Nordenstam, the strength of the Swedish music scene seems to lie in producing Anglo-American music that is often better than the 'real thing'. By singing in English and fitting into well-established rock, pop, and dance genres many Swedish artistes have produced products easily palatable to international markets and have enjoyed considerable commercial success. [. . .]

[. . .]

These 'creators' both attract firms to and are drawn in by Stockholm's position as the centre of the industrial system of music production and sales in Sweden. The region has a large number of local and international music companies: around 200 record companies and approximately 70 music-publishing companies – around

50 per cent of the national total. The most immediately apparent aspect of the firm structure of the city is the extent of its internationalisation; or its exposure to the global majors. All the 'majors' in the global recorded-music industry are active in Sweden through fully owned subsidiaries headquartered in Stockholm. Since the early 1980s these corporations have strengthened their positions by acquiring most of the large independent companies (such as Metronome, Elektra, Sonet, and Polar). When acquiring these companies, the corporations also incorporated their licensing deals and facilities for distribution, as well as affiliated publishing companies. The ten largest record companies (by turnover) in Sweden are now all owned by foreign majors and are all headquartered within walking distance of one another in central Stockholm. Thus the global majors have to a large extent acquired all the central elements of Stockholm's, and Sweden's, record-production and music-publishing system. [. . .] However, research revealed that the local subsidiaries often operate quite autonomously when it comes to Swedish products and projects. Rather than simply following orders from the head office, actors were seen to display high levels of intrafirm or conglomerate entrepreneurship and often attempted to use the global marketing organisation of their parent company to export music produced and recorded in Stockholm (and elsewhere). Furthermore, there is evidence of continuous formation of new firms, manifested by a growing number of independent record companies, publishing companies, production companies, etc. Strong local dynamism and entrepreneurship seem in this case to go hand in in hand with dominant foreign ownership.

[. . .] Firms that produce music videos and music-oriented multimedia firms in Stockholm are likewise an example of associated services that are supportive both of indigenous musical product and employment and of export-driven provision of music services, for example, Åkerlund & Pettersson Filmproduktion and Bo Johan Renck who have received international recognition for their videos for the likes of Metallica, U2, Iggy Pop, and Madonna. An interesting feature of this music-services environment is not only that these production companies have produced songs, multimedia content, and videos, etc for international artistes but also that international artistes have chosen Stockholm as their recording and creative locale. Forss (1999: 107) estimated that sales of music services to foreign clients accounted for just over 12 per cent of Swedish music exports. This has, according to local artistes, strengthened the creative 'buzz' in the city and given many artistes further reasons for staying in the city rather than leaving for global centres such as London or New York.

[. . .]

An important consideration for understanding the general evolution of Sweden's commercial music industry is that a very supportive consumer base exists: domestic demand is very high with a domestic retail market worth around US$322.9 million in 2000 [. . .] and with Swedes ranking as the sixth highest per capita consumers of recorded music (IFPI, 2001 [. . .]). A sizeable proportion of sales are of Swedish artistes (27 per cent of sales in 1998; see http://www.ifpi.se) suggesting awareness of local producers and indicating a high level of quality in the domestic product. [. . .]

Servicing this demand is a large number of retailers, most of which are parts of larger chains or subsections of extensive retail operations such as department-store chains. These retailers most usually source their product through a relatively centralised national distribution system located in the Stockholm region and dominated by the Association of Gramophone Suppliers (GLF) and its ten members – the majors, their subsidiaries, and MNW (MusikNätet Waxholm) Records Group – and their database and ordering system *Grammotex*.

The city's industry is further supported by a high level of technological ability and infrastructure. The existence of the latest facilities for the completion of a project from creation to saleable product has been an important factor in keeping the largest possible part of the value chain and profits of musical products in the country and city. As will be seen in the case of Kingston, it is quite common for the musical exports of smaller centres and countries to consist of only the core idea or track which is then sent abroad for postproduction, pressing, marketing, distribution, etc. Because the largest majority of the profits are to be gained at these later stages it is important for a centre to have the capacity to do as much as possible 'in house'. Stockholm as a city has one of the most advanced media technology and telecommunications infrastructures in the world and can handle all aspects of the production chain. [. . .]

Perhaps the most important factor in securing the 'repatriation' of profits in an export-oriented cultural-products industry is the existence of an effective system for the protection of intellectual property. Without such a system the profits of creativity have a tendency to disappear very quickly. By virtue of a long history of artisan organisations and unions the music industry is well tended by representative organisations and collecting agencies [. . .]. The domestic presence and international surveillance and enforcement mechanisms of many of these organisations, combined with the Swedish state's active international protection of Swedish intellectual property, are important in minimising as much as possible the loss of export revenue within the chaotic maze of international music licensing and consumption, and to a lesser extent to piracy. Furthermore the domination of the majors in the export of Swedish music products and services has meant that Swedish products have enjoyed the majors' extensive powers to protect IPR globally: the majors are the only actors with the resources and manpower to protect (or exploit) copyright worldwide.

All in all, Stockholm seems to be a clear-cut case that industrial competitiveness often develops in a clustered or agglomerated manner; that is, it takes a large number of firms that are both competing and cooperating with each other to trigger growth. The industrial and organisational structure of Stockholm's music industry is at once both highly competitive and highly cooperative and is characterised by a diversity of actors and firms with a relatively high turnover. The pace of structural, organisational, and technical change in the city's industry has been high, and it would seem as though these changes have benefited the exports of Swedish musical products. For us, however, the feature of the Stockholm scene most supportive of export performance is the dense network of interorganisational linkages, voluntary associations, and service organisations that secure both relatively open export and distribution channels and also copyright (and thus indirectly revenues back to the creative milieu). [. . .]

Kingston

[. . .]

Kingston is at once the production and innovation centre for a small but complex and dynamic domestic music market, as well as being a strong global supplier both of music product and of innovation [from music techniques such as those used in dub to entire stylistic genres such as ska, reggae, dancehall, and ragga [. . .] (Chang and Chen, 1998).

The most interesting feature from a comparative perspective of Kingston as a music-production centre is that, unlike almost all other centres in the world, the Kingston case is one where the global majors have almost no direct presence or role. The organisational and firm structure of the city's industry is largely fragmented and overwhelmingly dominated by small-scale A&R and original-creation-driven firms. [. . .]

[. . .] The global majors have shied away from direct involvement, preferring instead to 'cherry pick' already-developed products. This is widely acknowledged by industry actors interviewed in Kingston to have in the past been a rather dubious, and often exploitative or even criminal, process with the majors buying complete master tapes and exclusive rights off whoever could get their hands on them. [. . .]

Links between foreign firms and local firms and artistes have been, and are, put under further strain by cultural differences that have led to an extreme unwillingness on the part of the majors to have dealings with local firms. [. . .]

Despite the lack of direct involvement by the majors it is important to note that foreign firms have in many respects been the most important actors in the history of Jamaican music and its international success. Probably the most important lead firm in the development of Kingston's music industry has been Island Records (bought by Polygram in 1998 and now the Island Def Jam Music Group, a subdivision of Vivendi Universal Group) originally set up and owned by the English-born Chris Blackwell. Blackwell, who spent some of his early years in Jamaica was largely responsible for the rise to superstardom of Bob Marley. Island Records and Blackwell were instrumental in bringing the music of Jamaica first to Britain and then to the world (Chang and Chen, 1998; Salewicz and Boot, 2001). Despite the lead role and success of foreign companies like Island and Columbia in selling large quantities of Jamaican music globally, the fact remains that these lead actors have only a very limited presence at the local level and have, as mentioned above, tended to cherry pick already-developed products rather than invest in new lines.

The dynamism of Jamaican musical output then has largely been a story of endogenous growth in innovative activity. Exact figures on the number of firms and individuals involved in the production of music in Kingston are hard to come by owing to the lack of precise figures for the industry and the informal (often illegal) nature of many firms and individuals involved in the town's music industry. [. . .] What is certain, however, when one reviews histories of popular music, global recorded-music sales, and current international and Jamaican charts is that, at least in terms of professional artistes, a large number of acts – around 2,000 (either single artistes or groups) according to local estimates – currently reside or have their origins in Kingston.

These acts are supported by a large number of independent, most often very small-scale, record companies and labels, such as Tuff Gong, Dynamics, Penthouse Records, Sonic Sounds, and Scorcher Music. A major feature of the system is that it is relatively unique in organisational form and differs from places like Stockholm where record companies, characterised by high degrees of internal transactions, are the central production units. Kingston is characterised by a complex mix of producers (in the music industry sense of the term), record companies, and record labels with high degrees of external transactions. In Kingston, and in reggae music, the 'producers' are more prominent than in other places and genres and tend to control the industry by creating and owning the basic tracks or the underlying 'riddims' (a special combination of a bassline, drum pattern, and an associated melody; similar to the soul and jazz concept of 'grooves' 'riddim' is a commonly used musicological concept in Jamaican music, and indeed rap, and is not to be simply confused with 'rhythm'). The producer books the studio time (many own their own studios) and chooses from a never-ending stream of singers and DJs who want to record; in the hierarchy of the Kingston music industry the producer is on top and his (seldom her) name gets equal or greater attention than the artistes' name. Producers, record companies, and artistes often own multiple record labels which act both as stylistic identifiers and as 'meeting points' for collaborative projects. The owners of 'sound systems' – essentially large, mobile discotheques playing at dances, nightclubs, and house parties – are major actors in the city's music-production system. They act not only as performance venues but also as A&R sites and production centres with some of the systems acting as 'record labels' by recording and releasing the sessions onto the recorded-music market. [. . .]

The complex and fragmented nature of the production system and the multiplicity of actors, most often working on an essentially freelance basis, can be seen to have strengthened the role of interpersonal and informal contacts in the innovation process. In order to survive in the city's industry, firms and individuals realise that constant social and business interaction is important. In contrast to the trust and cooperation that are often pointed to as central to the creative milieus of small firm clusters (compare Scott, 2000), in Kingston this interaction is predominantly competitive rather than cooperative. The diversity of small-scale firms who do not have the capabilities to develop products fully in-house means that the industry is characterised by high levels of external transactions which further embed actors in the system. High levels of external transactions and dense social interaction mean that information flows more fluidly than in many other music-production centres. This means that it is extremely hard to keep products under wraps before release and that new musical ideas and techniques rapidly diffuse (one day is not an uncommon time for new riddims to be widely copied by other artists and made available to the market). Thus agglomeration (of musical activities) in the urban area fosters intensified transactions and interactions that are crucial to commercially successful creative and innovative product development. Furthermore the speed of transactions and information exchange have a definite effect on the way in which products are released. Whereas in European and US markets product release tends to be spaced out over time, in Kingston record companies pursue a policy of flooding the market in an attempt to sell as many records as possible in the shortest possible time. [. . .]

There may of course be considerable benefits accruing to musical innovation in an area with a fragmented firm structure. Some writers have noted that fragmentation and lack of concentration in the corporate organisation of recorded-music production may favour diversity in product type and encourage innovative processes [. . .] (Lopes, 1992; Peterson and Berger, 1975). However, the same writers also note that this process tends to be cyclical: corporate organisation changes as majors exploit diversity, leading to concentration; independents take advantage of niche markets leading to refragmentation. What is interesting about Kingston is that it has largely avoided the extremes of this cyclical process of corporate restructuring that countries such as the US and indeed Sweden have had. Nevertheless, although the process of cycles of concentration and diversification have not been as stark in Kingston as elsewhere, the *international* production and distribution of Jamaican music has been subject to these pressures. For example, the period of Jamaican musical-product diversification engendered by new, Jamaica-focused and international-market-oriented foreign independents – such as the early days of Island Records and later the impact of the UK-based Blood and Fire label – was in turn followed by corporate concentration as the independents were bought up by the majors and product lines were refocused onto a narrower line of large-unit sellers (such as greatest-hits and compilation albums).

However, the level of fragmentation and often disorder in the structure and organisation has important negative consequences. One consequence is that the lack of links to international players and their distribution channels and resources has significantly underlined the lack of capital and financing sources for upgrading and investment in new products (successful launch of new records on an international level involves a substantial investment in stock, marketing, advance-shipping costs, etc that most Jamaican firms cannot finance). [. . .] Furthermore the lack of high-standard equipment and up-to-date techniques means that domestic postproduction, remixing, video production, and related services tend to get exported. It must be remembered that it is often in these later stages of the journey of music products to the market that added value is created and profits made, and as we saw in the case of Stockholm these types of services can draw in business from outside the country that is both profitable and beneficial to the dynamics of the local centre.

Thus firms must rely on the low-tech and impoverished domestic market. Demand in the domestic market for the CD format is extremely low – probably around 10 per cent of unit sales (see IFPI, 2001) – and sales of CDs almost entirely relate to foreign products. Insufficient local demand for CDs and digital quality and the relative poverty of the markets further hinder attitudes and abilities to upgrade; in 1999 the Jamaican music industry on the domestic market generated US$5.4 million, which leaves only seven countries that generate less (IFPI, 2000). Interviews revealed that the average 'hit' tends to sell between 2,000 and 10,000 vinyl copies normally priced at around US $2 per unit. Once the profits are shared out over the entire value chain there remain only very small margins for those involved. [. . .]

Although the domestic market may in terms of cash be relatively impoverished it is one that is dominated and driven by highly 'sophisticated consumers' who are crucial to the innovation and creative dynamism of the industry. Whilst many things go very slowly in Jamaica, others go very quickly and this can be seen to be especially true of music trends and fashions in Kingston. Successful sounds and riddims are copied almost instantly and it is not atypical for a sound or stylistic innovation to be totally overexploited and out of date within a few weeks. The speed of production and release coupled with the speed at which consumer fashions change puts an enormous pressure on even the most-established artists constantly to come up with new sounds to satisfy audiences. A fragmented and sole-trader-dominated retail and distribution system serves the recorded-music needs of the consumers. The intense competition amongst the highly flexible and adaptable distributors and retailers (many often act as both) ensures that the products get to market, often direct from the studio, at breakneck speeds. On the other hand, fragmentation makes marketing and distribution economies of scale hard to achieve, limits reinvestment opportunities, and makes it much easier for pirates and gangsters to be 'involved' in the value chain.

[. . .]

The problem of small returns to high levels of musical creativity in the country's music industry is widely recognised as being in large part a result of the lack of an adequate intellectual-property-protection regime in the country and the lack of effective enforcement of existing legislation and international protocols ([. . .] Kozul-Wright and Stanbury, 1998). [. . .]

The fragmented firm structure, lack of direct links with the majors, and underdeveloped nature of performers' organisations and industry representatives have made it especially hard for Jamaica to enforce existing copyrights internationally and collect revenues. [. . .]

An important part of the intellectual-property environment in Kingston is industry specific, and culturally related to the underground nature of musical creation, propagation, and commercial adaptation. Interviewees frequently referred to the existence of a predominant 'hustler mentality' in the industry:

> piracy is the time-honoured tradition. In dancehall, the rhythm is king: lyrics and melodies – not to mention singers, royalties, DJs and copyrights – are afterthoughts
>
> (*Vibe*, September 1992, page 78; cited in
> Stephens, 1998, page 162)

As Gilroy (1987, page 164) notes, the focus of modern Jamaican dancehall culture is not the cult of personality that drives the commodification and value chains of popular music but rather the blending and creative appropriation of others' music. Interviews further revealed that this lax attitude to musical ownership and property rights, by the standards of copyrighters, was not only a part of the current general cultural norms that operate in the Kingston scene but had also often been part of the religious beliefs that many of the Rastafarian predecessors to dancehall and the like thought of as central to musical expression. Indeed the problems many artistes and firms have had with copyrights (particularly with pre-1980s recordings and compositions) can be related to Rastafarian antiproperty attitudes. The most obvious sign perhaps of this antiproperty attitude is the infrequency with which reggae stars have, or have left, wills and well-managed intellectual-property portfolios, most notably the case of Bob Marley who failed to leave a will. This sort of view of intellectual property is far removed from the view that prevails in the global industry. [. . .]

In conclusion, Kingston has functioned as a world-class innovation centre or creative milieu driven by a fragmented industrial structure that is highly competitive and embedded in a dense interactive and transactional social mode of production. Nonetheless, for a variety of reasons most of the value chain is outside the city and country and the industry faces serious problems in retaining profits and securing the investment necessary to improve its export potential.

Conclusion

It appears from these two different examples [. . .] that the stronger the firm-level and institutional links between localised industry actors and multinational corporations and the better the integration of the country into international IPR regimes, the higher the rate of return (both financially and in terms of technical and innovation resources) to the local production centre. If one were to think these cases worthy of generalisation then it would seem that in the case of the music industry the spreading influence of the global majors should not necessarily be seen as the equivalent of the spread of cultural imperialism and centralised commercial exploitation as is so often the case. The majors are powerful actors in laying the ground for and financing not only musical products but the IPR issues surrounding them. In the case of these two production centres a complex set of relations between local and global scales exists and processes of linking the scales offer very real positive, as well as negative, possibilities for creativity, competitiveness, and profitability. [. . .]

Popular music and technology

Introduction to Part Seven

■ Jason Toynbee

THE STUDY OF TECHNOLOGY has become a major strand in popular music studies. On the face of it, this would seem to be an entirely appropriate development. After all, popular music emerged as a distinct form of culture through mediation – initially via the phonograph. What is more, the subsequent history of pop has been marked by a series of important technological changes at the stages of both production and reception. Now, in the early twenty-first century, not only the sound of music but its mode of distribution are undergoing transformations once again, this time aided and abetted by the Internet and digital technology. Nevertheless, it would be a mistake to jump to the conclusion that technological change shapes popular music and culture in any straightforward way. As Raymond Williams (1974) argued many years ago, social forces (such as the profit motive, entrenched power and imagined use) promote or inhibit technological developments. There is nothing inevitable about technological 'progress'.

All the chapters in Part Seven demonstrate this nuanced approach, although the writers vary considerably in the way they understand the relationship between technology, music and social relations. For Rick Altman, the key issue is the heterogeneity of sound, the fact that it is composed of many elements. What appears to be a single sound – a note struck on the piano, say – is actually multiple, a combination of frequencies, fundamentals and partials. Sounds have a certain biography as well. They begin, reach a crescendo and then die away, and the profile of this sound envelope, as it is called, varies enormously from one case to another. That piano note heard in a bar is completely different from the 'same' note heard in a concert hall. Recording then increases the complexity at stake here. Not only does the recording process make its mark on a recorded sound (factors such as microphone type and angle are crucial), but playback technology impacts on what we hear. Reproduction through a loudspeaker actually *reduces* the heterogeneity of sound by folding 'variables into a single, undifferentiated source'.

Altman's background is in film studies, and he brings a certain scepticism from that field concerning the way technology functions as a means of representation. Just as the moving image appears to present the world in a completely natural way so too, Altman argues, recording seems to carry sound to us directly, without any effect of mediation. That is why we need to analyse recordings critically in order to understand how they have been artificially imbued with meaning and significance even as they convince us by their apparent faithfulness to an original sonic moment.

Where Altman is suspicious of the ideological effect of recording, Andrew Goodwin is cautiously optimistic about the politics of new music technologies. Specifically, he identifies a progressive potential in those electronic music-making systems emerging in the 1980s. If recording tends to disguise its own artificiality, which is Altman's point, then for Goodwin electronic music making 'draws attention to itself'. What is more, it privileges rhythm, rather than the voice (apparently 'human', in fact an artificial construct) which predominates in multitrack, tape-recordings. Above all, Goodwin points to the democratising effect of electronics. It enables a broader interconnectivity between instruments and processors with the result that one musician can control many sounds. Electronic and digital technologies also open up access to the many music makers who have neither the skills nor finances to be able make conventional rock recordings.

In an important sense, Goodwin's essay is a product of its times. The 'new' technologies that he analyses have become, at the start of the twenty-first century, the standard tools of the trade. And electronic dance music and hip-hop which seemed to represent a popular avant-garde at the beginning of the 1990s are now mainstream genres. That does not necessarily reduce the force of his argument, but it does reinforce the point that, in the case of ever-changing music technology, continuity may be as important as radical transformation. This is certainly a key thrust in Paul Théberge's chapter.

Théberge proposes that music technology consists not only of hardware – instruments, recording devices and so on. The term can also be applied to musical techniques ranging from the way that musicians perform through to the coding of music making and listening, via notation, for example. This is a broad definition of technology, but also a useful one. For one thing it enables us to see beyond the split that Théberge points to between music as something conceptual, and music as social and embodied. This division, deeply inscribed in the West, is simply not present in most non-Western cultures. Here the theory and practice of music remain bound together in what the sociologist Pierre Bourdieu calls a 'logic of practice'. Théberge goes on to argue that such a logic actually applies in the case of *all* musical activity. Listening, configuring the body in order to play or sing, and then reflecting on what you are doing are parts of a continuous process. The difference in the case of classical music, the most rationalised of all Western styles, is that the logic of practice has been suppressed as a model for music making. In classical music one doesn't *conceive* of music in a holistic way, but rather one compartmentalises it.

Notation has played a key role here, Théberge argues. Although it began as a technology of description, a means of graphically showing music that was already in performance, from the end of the Middle Ages notation came to be a means of *pre*scription, a method of transmitting the commands of the composer to the performer. Again, in tracing this development Théberge is keen to show how music technology is a broad, social formation – something that organises listeners and music makers, bodies and instruments, social practice and musical theory.

At least implicitly, Théberge approves of the appropriation of technology in folk and popular musics. In Chapter 33, Kodwo Eshun makes this theme explicit in his short piece, 'Futurhythmachine', an elegant argument about the interconnection of black musical culture, technology and rhythm. Suggesting that slavery can be read as a kind of 'alien abduction', he explains the musical culture of the Black Atlantic (Gilroy, 1993; see also his chapter in this volume) in terms of mutation rather than conventional identity theory. Most recently, Eshun argues, in British electronic dance music of the 1990s, and especially the genre called jungle, there has been a co-evolution of people and machines. A new model of robotics – 'local intelligence' – provides the best way of understanding this. The body itself now becomes a 'distributed brain'. Dancing limbs and digits articulate complex polymetric beats. As for the future, Eshun sees a moment when 'DJs will have extremely developed finger tips', a moment when music makers and their machines start to mutate.

Eshun's vision is poetic or, better, he adopts a language to match his themes: music as black science fiction, and technology as a re-enchantment of the body. The work of a journalist, this is not the sort of writing we expect to see in academic papers on popular music. Perhaps for that very reason his essay offers a penetrating analysis of music technology which draws on contemporary cultural theory even while it darts through a dizzying series of interpretive moves.

For an example of how empirical social science can, in quite different ways, reveal the changing significance of music technology, we should turn to Chapter 34 by Marjorie D. Kibby. Kibby examines a Web chat-room and its users, set up by Oh Boy Records in 1996 and dedicated to John Prine. A singer–songwriter located somewhere at the borders of folk and country music, Prine has a loyal group of mainly middle-aged fans.

Kibby begins with the observation that traditional, geographically bounded communities are now being supplemented by new virtual localities, composed of participants who interact using the Internet. In the case of popular music, this trend takes on a special significance. Historically, the commercialisation of music has resulted in a certain privatisation, whereby individual audience members listen alone at home. The institution of the star-and-fans has enabled a degree of reconnection, but it is through the Internet that the renewal of community may be finding its fullest expression. Using a Web survey, semi-structured email interviews and qualititative analysis of the chat-room contributions, Kibby found evidence of a flourishing online fan community, focused on John Prine. As she notes, '[i]t is the ritual sharing of information that binds contacts into communities'.

In fact, the range of topics of chat-room exchange was fairly narrow. Kibby divides them into contact with and sightings of Prine, Prine trivia and speculation about whether Prine would appear in the chat-room. Given these themes, the problem for those involved became one of avoiding repetition. With little new information, and with no participation from the man himself, the chat-room became increasingly, and palpably, redundant. Moreover, in a communication context where anonymity was assured, the antagonism of some participants rapidly escalated, leading quite quickly to abusiveness. Oh Boy's response was to close the room. It seems, then, that even middle-aged fans are unable to manage their own fandom, at least in an online environment. Kibby thus ends on a downbeat note, markedly at odds with the optimism of Goodwin or Eshun.

Read together, the selections in Part Seven suggest the ambiguity of the impact of new music technology. We encounter optimistic readings but also pessimistic ones, an emphasis on change as well as the importance of continuity, the uncovering both of increased alienation and stronger community. Perhaps the conclusion to draw from this is that technology is never a cause in its own right, but always reflects the state of play of social relations. Raymond Williams' observations about this are as pertinent now as they were in the 1970s.

Chapter 30

Rick Altman

THE MATERIAL HETEROGENEITY
OF RECORDED SOUND

[. . .]

IF I ATTEND THREE CONCERTS of Mozart's 'Little Night Music,' one in a
well-upholstered salon, another in a large concert hall, and a third in a city park,
I am in one sense hearing the 'same' music three times, that is, music that is represented by a single, identical score. Yet how different are the sounds that reach my
ears during the three concerts!

Musical notation assumes that each sound is single, discrete, uniform, and unidi-
mensional. Stressing the formal concerns of music's internal, self-referential aspect,
musical notation diverts attention from sound's discursive dimensions, concealing
the fact that sound is in reality multiple, complex, heterogeneous, and three-dimensional. As a concept, middle C exists independently of space and time, in the abstract
notion of a sound of approximately 262 cycles per second. As a reality, however,
no two versions of middle C are identical, because of the different temporal and
spatial circumstances in which they originate and are heard. The middle C located
on the first line below the G clef may be only a concept, but the sound that we
hear with our ears – whether on the street or in a movie theater – is a heterogeneous event that carries its own temporal and spatial dimensions and constitutes a
full-fledged narrative. When we listen to recorded sound, we are therefore always
listening to a particular account of a specific event.

In order to respect the discursive complexity that is characteristic of all sound
events, we can no longer continue to depend on a fundamentally conceptual terminology that remains insensitive to sound's phenomenality. Instead we must have a
terminology capable both of respecting sound's heterogeneous nature and of figuring
the narrative component built into the very process of recording and reproducing
sound. This article proposes such a terminology, based on a schematic but systematic
review of the physical phenomenon that we call sound.

Sound events: the production of sound

What is sound? What happens when a sound is made? While this is hardly a technical treatise, it will nevertheless be useful to recall the manner in which sounds are produced. Three elements are required for the production of any sound. First, there must be vibration, such as that of the vocal cords or a violin string. Second, the vibration must take place in a medium whose molecules can be set in motion, such as air, water, or a railroad rail (sound cannot be transmitted through a vacuum). Third, the transmitting medium must absorb and transmit the original vibrations in the form of changes in pressure. [. . .]

Even taking the three-dimensional nature of sound events into account, however, this description vastly oversimplifies the situation. Whereas an electronic tone generator is capable of producing pure tones, all musical instruments produce notes that combine a fundamental frequency (such as the violin's 196 Hz G string) with a series of partials: harmonics (tones whose frequency is a whole number multiple of the fundamental) and overtones (tones whose frequency is related to the fundamental according to a more complex formula). Depending on the instrument and the way it is played, the combination of harmonics and overtones can vary tremendously. When played in such a way as to emphasize the upper harmonics, for example, the violin sounds harsh and strident, while a mellow tone results from stressing instead the lower harmonics. If the oboe, trumpet, flute, and cello sound so recognizably different, it is primarily because they produce radically different combinations of partials.

[. . .]

For what we call a sound is typically made up not only of multiple frequencies, but actually has multiple different fundamentals produced over a period of time. Think of the following familiar sounds: a refrigerator, snoring, a lawnmower, the wind, a squeaky door. We think of each as a single sound, but none is actually single in the way that an A-440 produced by a tuning fork is unitary. Each of these sounds constitutes an event taking place in time, involving multiple separate sounds organized in a familiar, recognizable fashion. Given the importance of rhythmic and melodic elements for our recognition of each of these sounds, it would be more appropriate to compare them to musical phrases than to individual notes.

Yet even individual notes have a temporal dimension. Returning for a moment to our violin string, consider the difference between plucking and bowing the string. In one case the sound starts suddenly, reaching its full volume extremely rapidly; in the other case the violinist seems to be sneaking up on the note, teasing the molecules into moving rather than suddenly shoving them. Whether violent or peaceful, this initiation of the sound event is termed the attack. It is followed by the sustain. How long is the note hold? How long does it stay at full volume? Finally, the sound fades away. This stage is called the decay, implying not only a temporal measure but also a qualitative one. Compare, for example, the decay of a plucked string that is simply allowed to spend its own energy and the decay of a plucked string instantaneously dampened by a finger.

[. . .]

The production of sound is thus a material event, taking place in space and time, and involving the disruption of surrounding matter. This doesn't mean that we have to be molecular physicists or sound engineers to understand sound, but it does suggest a very precise basis for our description of sound events. It is no longer sufficient to analyze a musical score or a written text to understand the effects of a particular performance event. Recognizing the extent to which sound sets matter in motion – albeit invisibly – we readily see the importance of developing a vocabulary and a methodology appropriate to the comply materiality of sound. Instead of describing just a sound's loudness, pitch, and timbre, we stress the extent to which every sound event includes multiple sounds, each with its particular fundamental and array of partials, each with its characteristic sound envelope, each possessing its own rhythm within the sound event's overall temporal range.

The sound narrative: the story of a sound event

In order to understand sound as it is produced, we need to recognize the material heterogeneity of sound events. Sound production is only part of the story, however, for sound, like the proverbial tree falling in the forest, must be heard in order to take on its narrative and social significance. By offering itself up to be heard, every sound event loses its autonomy, surrendering the power and meaning of its own structure to the various contexts in which it might be heard, to the varying narratives that it might construct. Beginning as the vibration that induces molecular movement, sound is not actualized until it reaches the ear of the hearer, which translates molecular movement into the sensation of sound. Just as the sound event necessarily introduces a temporal dimension into the production of every sound, so the process of perception always guarantees sound's spatial nature.

[. . .]

In other words, the fact that a 'single' sound reaches our ears over a period of time permits us to reconstitute certain facts about the circumstances surrounding the production of that sound. What our ears are doing is a form of narrative analysis. They are analyzing the narrative produced by sound pressure, in all of its complexity, in order to ascertain how, by whom, and under what conditions that sound pressure was produced. To be sure, some people have ears that are better trained in this process of narrative analysis than others, but we have all developed over the years a great deal of expertise in this area. We use the delay between visual information and the first arrival of direct sound to determine the distance of the sound source. The difference in the characteristics of sound arriving at our two ears permits us to locate the sound source laterally. The ratio of reflected to direct sound helps us to decide whether the speaker is facing us or not. Combined with other information, this ratio also helps us recognize the size of the room in which the words are spoken. By noting how long the reflected sound lasts, we refine our conclusions about the originating space.

[. . .]

The fact that we come equipped with two functioning ears each makes still more information available to us. Because all sounds that are not exactly equidistant from both ears arrive at our ears one after the other, and under slightly different conditions, our ears are able to localize sound laterally as well as in terms of distance. Especially when aided by a radar-like rotation of the head, our own personal sonar gives us varied information about our soundscape.

Our ears are so good at decoding sound that it would be a shame to deprive our terminology of our ears' expertise. Without entering the specialized worlds of acoustics, audio engineering, and otology, we must nevertheless find ways of respecting not only sound's material heterogeneity, but also the cleverness of our ears in analyzing the auditory narratives that it constitutes. Constantly delayed, dampened, reinforced, overlapped and recombined, sound provides us with much of the information we need to understand its origins and its itineraries – but the existing terminology clearly does not.

The sound record: recording the story of a sound event

[. . .]

Sound's existence as both event and narrative immensely complicates – and enriches – our understanding. Usually discussed as the most transparent of classical narratives, sound is in fact a *Rashomon* phenomenon, existing only in the separate stories of various perceivers of the original event. Potentially important apropos of any sound and its perception, this fact takes on special significance in all media that make use of recorded sound. For what the record contains is not the sound event as such but a record of a particular hearing, a specific version of the story of the sound event. Every recording is thus signed, as it were, with the mark of the particular circumstances in which it was heard. A recording of the shattering window made next to my father's easy chair will be signed in a different way from a recording of the 'same' event made next to my sister's desk. Every recording carries the elements of this spatial signature, carried in the audible signs of each hearing's particularities. Even when those signs are contradictory or have been tampered with, even when they seem not to match the visual data provided with the sound record, they still carry information that is narrative and spatial in nature.

The situation is immensely complicated by the fact that sound records never convey exactly the same information that a given auditor would experience. Far from arresting and innocently capturing a particular narrative, the recording process simply extends and complicates that narrative. Just as the upholstery of a particular soundscape has an impact on the sound narrative, so the way in which sound is collected and entered into memory becomes part and parcel of the overall sound phenomenon.

Even in the simplest of sound collection systems, decisions regarding the location of the microphone carry enormous importance, especially when the sound is to accompany a related image. Should sound collection take place in the same room as the sound to be recorded? At what distance? Under what acoustic conditions? Or should sound collection be in a remote location, thus reducing volume, dampening certain frequencies, and increasing the ratio of reflected to direct sound? This approach will certainly convince auditors that they are not located in the same sound space as the speaker. In fact, if the reverb level is high enough and the image slightly out of focus, the sound may even appear to have been collected in a time frame different from its production.

[. . .]

Nor is microphone location the only variable available to the sound engineer. The microphone itself makes many choices regarding the type, amount, and source of sound that will be collected. It is perhaps useful, in an image-oriented world, to think of the microphone as a 'sound-camera,' a collection device for sound that shares many of the characteristics of familiar image-collection devices. Just as cameras may have wide-angle or telephoto lenses, changing the angle of image collection and thus the apparent distance of the object filmed, so microphones vary from omnidirectional to narrowly focused, thus changing both the angle of sound collection and the apparent distance of the sound source. In addition, the change in the ratio of direct to reflected sound that accompanies a change in microphone may also affect perception of room size and other characteristics.

Microphones also vary in their sensitivity to specific sound frequencies. The familiar carbon microphone in our telephones has an extremely limited frequency response. Sound heard over the telephone thus always sounds dull and lifeless. Close-miking with a telephone mike (or stripping the sound of appropriate frequencies in postproduction) thus gives the impression that all sounds presented are being heard through a telephone. Since no microphone is equally sensitive to all frequencies, the choice of a microphone fairly assures that some sounds will be boosted, while others will be dampened.

Many other microphone characteristics may come into play as well. It is often assumed that every microphone produces a faithful sound record. Actually, no microphone produces an entirely faithful sound record. Not only does every microphone have its own particular directional characteristics (omnidirectional, bidirectional, cardioid, shotgun and so on), but every microphone also has its own particular frequency response, sound configuration, and power requirements. In addition, many microphones produce unwanted sounds of various types (hum, pop, hiss, buzz, crackle and so on) in a wide variety of situations (loud sound signal, wind pressure, close sound source, vibration and so on).

Recorded sound thus always carries some record of the recording process, superimposed on the sound event itself. Added to the story of sound production we always find the traces of sound recording as well, including information on the location, type, orientation, and movement of the sound collection devices, not to mention the many variables intervening between collection and recording of sound (amplification, filtering, equalization, noise reduction, and so forth). Indeed, the recording system itself provides one of the most important determinants of sound characteristics; as such it not only provides a record of sound, it also participates in the overall sound narrative. Think for example of the differing frequency responses of 78 rpm records and digital compact disks. It is so difficult to compare musical performances recorded on these two radically different technologies that the masterworks of Toscanini and Furtwangler seem diminished without the wonders of digital remastering (which is none other than an attempt to restore the frequencies to which pre-war disk recording was not sensitive).

To record is thus to recall to mind, as the dictionary would have it, but like most mnemonic devices, sound recordings must heighten some aspects of the original phenomenon at the expense of others. So-called recordings are thus always representations, interpretations, partial narratives that must nevertheless serve as our only access to the sounds of the past.

Hearing events: hearing the record of the story of a sound event

But how can we gain access to those sounds? A recording, as we all know, is not a sound. Without some sort of playback device, a recording can only sit silently on the shelf. And as long as it sits on the shelf, it has only one space: the space of the recording of the original sound event. My record of Oistrakh and Rostropovich playing the Brahms Double Concerto with George Szell and the Cleveland Philharmonic Orchestra was recorded in Severance Hall. Once I put the record on my stereo and set the needle down, however, the Concerto becomes very Double indeed. Not only do I hear the fabulous acoustics of the Cleveland Orchestra's home concert hall, but at the same time I have to put up with the less than ideal acoustics of my own living room. Every sound I hear is thus double, marked both by the specific circumstances of recording and by the particularities of the reproduction situation. [. . .] The sound system plays the record of the story of an event. At every point in that chain, new variables enter, new elements of uncertainty. Sound heads, amplifiers, leads, loudspeakers, and theater acoustics all force new auditory data on the audience, just as the recording process itself had earlier introduced an implicit viewpoint.

Just as sound events remain only hypothetical sound sources until they are actualized by a hearer, so the playing of a sound record takes on meaning only in the presence of an audience. Yet the process of hearing a recording differs significantly from listening to a live sound event. [. . .] When attempting to locate a crying child we normally call heavily on our binaural hearing system to provide cues regarding lateral location. When we listen to a recording of a crying child, no such localization is possible. However much we might rotate our heads or change positions, we remain unable to make use of the directional information that was present when the sound was produced, but which is no longer available in the recording (unless it is in stereo, and even then the location of microphones and speakers plays just as important a role as the location of the original sound source). For listening to the sound pouring out of a loudspeaker is like hearing a lawn mower through an open window: wherever the lawn mower may actually be, it always appears to be located on the side of the house where the open window is.

When we listen for a crying child, we are marvelously effective at cutting out extraneous sounds and concentrating on the cries that we recognize as those of our own child. Dubbed the cocktail party effect by Colin Cherry, the process of selective auditory attention is far more difficult when we are listening to recorded material. Whereas live sound provides an extraordinary number of variables, each permitting and promoting selective attention, recorded sound folds most of those variables into a single, undifferentiated source. In a live situation, we easily differentiate among the various sound sources surrounding us, but with recorded sound no such clear distinctions are possible.

Live sound situations reveal the actual relationship between the sound producer and perceiver, while recordings suggest only an apparent relationship. If I sit in an auditorium and listen with my eyes closed to a series of speeches, I remain constantly aware of the speakers' location. I know what direction they are facing, how loud they are speaking, and what tones of voice they are using. When I listen to a recording of the same meeting, I can no longer locate the speakers. Nor can I be sure of their original body positions, volume, or tones. Depending on the type, location, and movement of the microphone(s) used in the recording process, the recorded sound substitutes an apparent sound event for the original phenomenon. Revealing its mandate to represent sound events rather than to reproduce them, recorded sound creates an illusion of presence while constituting a new version of the sound events that actually transpired.

What happens in the course of a hearing event is thus not the expected detective activity wherein the hearer searches the recorded sound track for clues permitting reconstitution of the original sound event. Instead, we follow the trail that has been laid for us all the way to an apparent sound event having all the aural guarantees of reality but only partial correspondence to the original sound event. Indeed, it is the partial nature of the relationship that makes hearing events so fascinating. If there were no connection between the apparent sound event and the original sound source, recorded sound would not have its extraordinary capacity for ideological impact. It is precisely because recorded sound seems to reproduce an original phenomenon that recordings attract and hold audiences so readily. Between the illusion of reproduction and the reality of representation lies the discursive power of recorded sound.

We hear recordings with the same ears we use for live sound. We reach conclusions about the evidence provided by recordings in the same way that we interrogate and evaluate live sound. We constitute apparent sound events just as we directly perceive live sound events. Yet recordings systematically fail to justify our confidence in them. Most listeners have learned to concentrate on the aspects of sound events that are most faithfully rendered by recordings and to pay little attention to the aspects introduced or transformed by the recording process. A proper theory of sound will accept no such selective deafness. It will pay special attention to those very points where confusion is possible, recognizing in such moments of imprecision, indecision, or incoherence the very place where sound seizes the opportunity to take an active role in the definition and exploitation of culture. [. . .]

Chapter 31

Andrew Goodwin

RATIONALIZATION AND DEMOCRATIZATION IN THE NEW TECHNOLOGIES OF POPULAR MUSIC

THIS CHAPTER IS ABOUT THE NEW COMMUNICATIONS technologies that invaded the world of pop production and consumption during the 1980s and early 1990s. It will deal with some of the consequences that these technologies have for the meaning of rock and pop music, and in particular with the important consequences that changes in music-making technology imply for both musicians and listeners. In doing so, I will engage with the classic debates about the rationalization and democratization of modern music first raised by Max Weber, Walter Benjamin, and Theodor Adorno in their very different discussions of the culture industries. [. . .]

From the mid-1960s to the 1980s, 'multitracking' was the dominant practice in professional recording. Here, a multitrack tape recorder (accommodating 4, 8, 16, 24, 32, and even 64 separate tracks) provides individual input for each instrument, so that the parts can be recorded at different times, allowing for an enormous number of possibilities in the 'mixing' of these parts onto a stereo master tape. This is the source for the music we eventually hear, on record, cassette, or CD. The best known early example of this process is The Beatles's 1967 album *Sgt Pepper's Lonely Hearts Club Band*, on which two four-track tape recorders were linked together to create the then revolutionary complexity of eight-track arrangements. [. . .]

This stacking up of elements through multitracking has been subtly but crucially altered by the arrival of samplers [for digitally storing and manipulating sound], MIDI [a system for interconnecting computers and music-making machines], and software that [together] imitate the recording studio. [. . .] Because MIDI manipulates music as digital information, changes can be made to the music (for example, the exact placing of notes in a synthesized or sampled bass-line) without any re-recording. Often the music is stored in one place (a sampler, perhaps) and it is there that changes, additions, and stacking up of elements occurs, not on tape. Clearly this places the record producer in an unusually powerful position. Once the sounds are stored in the sampler, then control of the computer amounts, musically speaking, to control of the entire performance. Any element in the recording (such as drums, guitars, and so forth) can be accessed and manipulated through the sampling computer. One consequence has been that producers can now make records in the absence of the musicians themselves, and, as a result, their role has been made increasingly visible in music criticism and on album sleeves. The shift from *technical* to *artistic* status for sound mixers, engineers, and producers, first noticed by Kealy (1990/1979), is thus accelerated. As I will show, this very recent technological development also has implications for the debate about rationalization in contemporary music.

Looking for the perfect beat

Building his essay on the work of Max Weber, Paul Théberge (1989) has suggested that the technology of multitracking in modern pop increases the trend toward what Weber (1958) terms 'rationalization'. Théberge argues that economic and bureaucratic forces within the music industry favor a shift toward rationalized practices of music production, which are driven primarily by economic (as opposed to artistic) considerations. The need to bring order and cost-effectiveness to musical production has overridden concerns with the act of performing music. Théberge believes that the modern recording studio encapsulates many of these features. In particular, the multitracking process minimizes (and sometimes entirely obviates) interaction between musicians, since the assignment of individual instruments to separate tracks means that each part must be recorded separately (if not in time, then physically so) so that the parts do not 'bleed' into each other. [. . .]

   Théberge sees the process of multitracking, then, as deeply ideological, creating an illusion of community and interaction, where in fact there is only a simulation created by the manipulation of separate, rationalized elements. These elements are apparently fused, partly through stereo imaging and the application of electronic reverberation (which can be used to construct the illusion that the individual parts were recorded in the same acoustic space) in the final mix. I do not agree with Théberge's analysis of multitracking, but nonetheless I want to use his suggestive and insightful essay to build an account of the new technologies of pop production [. . .] that are displacing the tape recorder.

Consequences

Théberge makes an acute point when he describes one effect of contemporary studio techniques:

> Not only are the cymbals and tom-toms spread over almost the entire breadth of the stereo field; they also become a spatial/structural framework within which the sound of the other instruments in the group can be freely distributed. In effect, the entire ensemble appears to play as if inside a drum set of almost mythic proportions – inside the spatialized rhythmic structure of the 'beat itself.
>
> (Théberge, 1989, p. 104)

This radical placement of sounds can be heard very clearly, for instance, on the Terry Lewis and Jimmy Jam produced recording of the song 'Human', performed by the Human League on the Album *Crash*. This song includes, as a repetitive musical anchor, an electronically treated drum fill across the tom-toms that is divided and spread across the stereo field so that it seems to travel through our heads from ear to ear.

This kind of stereo imaging is interesting partly because it dovetails with changes in technologies of consumption. Previously, we might have assumed that few listeners would notice the placing of elements in the mix. On a cassette player it would hardly be audible, and a turntable would only reproduce this accurately if we were situated directly between the loudspeakers. In the past, only audiophiles would routinely recognize such effects. Three developments lead me to speculate that stereo imaging is now more important than before. First, the Walkman. This pervasive piece of technology is nearly always used with headphones, which inevitably place us right inside the stereo mix. Second, car stereos similarly force us to take a position within the field of left–right images, albeit perhaps to a lesser extent than is true for the Walkman. And third, compact discs emphasize ear-to-ear effects because the clarity of digital sound makes the stereo imaging sharper.

This is significant [. . . because] radical placing of musical elements along the lines of the drum part in 'Human' marks a break with the practice of illusionism. No one has ever heard an actual drum-kit sounding like this in a natural (i.e. non-mass-mediated) environment. Even if one were placed accurately enough (which is almost impossible, since the listener would need to be perched atop one of the drummer's cymbals!), the degree of 'bleeding' between the left-hand and right-hand parts would be such that the effect would be lost. In other words, radical stereo imaging of this nature *draws attention to itself*. It is not illusionist, and it does nothing to create the impression of a community of musicians playing in real time. In fact, it undermines it. In Brechtian terms, such aural effects work to 'reveal the machinery' of the acoustic representation.

It is also the case, however, that the drum-kit has not only been dispersed, it has also been dismantled and condensed. As individual parts of the kits are assigned separate tasks in propelling a beat, sometimes parts of the kit are missing. Often they are replaced by other sounds [. . .]. And if multitracking focuses your attention on the singer, placing the voice center stage, the new technologies privilege rhythm. The most significant rhythmic trend has turned out not to be the amplification of the mythic drum kit, but the deployment of other instruments (especially synthesizers) and sounds (including voices) as elements of the rhythm track. In the dance music of the late 1980s and early 1990s, for instance, one might say that almost the entire ensemble, whether human or mechanical, is now a rhythm section. [. . .]

But the relation between these percussive elements is often extremely complex and demonstrates one way in which the new digital technologies imply a profound riposte to the notion of rationalization in the recording process. If multitracking *is* a highly rationalized form of production that substitutes *reaction* for *interaction* between musicians, it can be argued that sampling music computers and virtual tracks fundamentally change this. In the multitracking process, interaction is absent partly because the musicians who record first (usually the rhythm section) are neither able to react to each other's performances, nor to the performance of the players who overdub their own parts later. Sometimes this would be technically difficult – the drum part, for instance, would not be easily rerecorded after the other musicians had laid down tracks based on a prior rhythm. But chiefly this is an economic consideration dictated by studio costs and session fees for musicians.

[. . .] However m]any acts now use their rehearsal rooms or preproduction studios to program drum machines, sequencers, and samplers in advance of the actual recording process, which may then generate virtual tracks that go straight to the master tape. Where this master tape is digital (digital audio tape, for instance), amateur and semiprofessional recordists now find that they can produce professional-quality recordings of great complexity at historically low costs. Major labels also take advantage of these new opportunities: for instance, Mute Records in London for some years operated its own preproduction studio where programming could be done for many of its acts, thus saving the label significant sums of money in studio time.

The relative breakdown between professional and semiprofessional technologies is often seen as *democratizing* pop production in new ways. But it may also be read as more grist to the mill of a Weberian pessimism, in which bureaucratic efficiency triumphs over creativity. It is not. [. . .] Seemingly a tool of still greater rationalization, the new technologies in fact enable the composer/producer to react to other parts and then change the original part in order to take account of the reaction. Alterations can be effected by pushing a few buttons on a computer terminal. This is musical interaction between the parts, regardless of whether or not more than one musician is playing.

Similarly, where the multitracking process can be seen as one that rationalizes temporality in music production, the new technologies achieve precisely the reverse. Now, parts can be programmed out of sync with each other and the tempo itself can be programmed to vary. In other words, the tendency toward rhythmic one-dimensionality that is identified as an effect of multitracking is in fact reversed by machines and samplers.

Clubbing music to death

I want to move toward a conclusion here through a consideration of some of the wider implications of these trends that seem to me to be of an importance that can hardly be exaggerated. In particular, the new technologies can facilitate popular music that runs almost exactly contrary to the predictions of Weberian and Adornian pessimism.

One simple response here follows Walter Benjamin in seeing the new technologies as mediators in the breakup of the division between producers and consumers, where 'the distinction between author and public is about to lose its basic character' (Benjamin [1969]). The sampler, obviously enough, is – like the photocopier – a machine that lends itself to a Benjaminite analysis, since it facilitates and encourages the transformation of the reader into a writer, the listener into a musician, and blurs the distinction between originals and copies (see Goodwin, 1990). The development of sampling clearly suggests an interpretation that stresses the democratizing effect of the new technologies. This is especially the case where samplers are used to recontextualize mass-media texts, as is often the case in rap music. [. . .]

Still, two reservations must be noted here. First, the new technologies are not nearly as classless as they might appear to be. There is a world of difference between a Casio sampler bought in a department store and the hugely expensive sampling computers that sit in preproduction studios. [. . .] Second, there is the issue of gender. Certainly there are one or two established female musicians who are interviewed about music technology and sometimes even pictured with it (Kate Bush, Laurie Anderson). But of the generation of musicians who grew up making music exclusively on machines, this new 'democratizing' machinery seems thus far to have generated only one major female star who appears to operate the technology itself: Betty Boo. [. . .] In other words, it is the boys, still, who are playing with the toys.

A more credible analysis of the new music would look not to Walter Benjamin, but to his colleague (and critic) Theodor Adorno, whose modernist critique of popular music (Adorno, 1990 [1941]) parallels Weber and advocates a deconstruction of musical rationality that has turned out to be extremely prescient. For what is really striking about the recent development of popular music is its progressive shift away from conventional tonality and structural conformity. Rap and hip-hop music is the most obvious source of this trend, where extremely avant-garde sounding recordings that thoroughly challenge the conventions of tonality and song structure have routinely charted, gained status as million-selling albums, and – I would argue – set the terms for the future development of pop. Public Enemy is only the most radical example of this development. Even the more mainstream versions of rap offered by artists such as Run DMC and M.C. Hammer significantly undermine pop conventions to the extent that many rock fans still challenge rap's status as 'music'. In the dance genre of house music, a similar trend is at work, but here it is a radical minimalism and an almost total emphasis on rhythm machines that help to deconstruct notions of what a 'song' is. [. . .]

This musical challenge to the aesthetics of pop is mirrored by [. . . a new form of] professionalism. [. . .] We are now hearing the results of the first generation of musicians who taught themselves computer programming instead of guitar licks. These musicians rarely if ever go to 'band rehearsals', for there *is* no band to rehearse. Rather, they sit down at 'workstations,' monitor radio and television constantly for useful sound-bites, and keep their CD players plugged into their recording equipment, ever in search of new sounds to appropriate. Manipulating a record turntable or programming a drum machine is, for this generation of musicians, the equivalent of learning an instrument. In the words of New Order's Stephen Morris: 'The ones who will succeed are the ones who understand technology. You don't need to be musical; musicality is actually a disadvantage' (1990, p. 80). It is as impossible to imagine what these musicians will do when the full implications of sampling and MIDI have been realized as it would have been for a critic in 1954 to speculate on how rock and roll would eventually sound.

This is because the technology does not, as it is often assumed, dictate the development of pop music. This variant of the technological determinism thesis is mistaken. Certainly, technologies do set pressures and limits on what can be done, but the notion that the technologies now make musical decisions is often simply bad faith. [. . .] Sampling, after all, is often deployed as a high-tech version of an earlier practice – the reappropriation of the record turntable to steal and scratch sounds in the dance club. The drum machine was developed after composers such as Daniel Miller (who went on to found Mute Records) had redeployed the electronic synthesizer to create drum-like sounds. The multitrack tape recorder exists because musicians and producers (such as The Beatles's producer George Martin) improvised recording techniques, using existing equipment, that the manufacturers had not anticipated. The mixing desk, designed to produce the 'best' final mix of a song, was reworked in the 1980s as a place where songs could be remixed, deconstructed, and perhaps destroyed. It is the abuse of technology, rather than its iron rule, that has driven pop forward.

What is clear is that the image of the musician has radically changed, so that Betty Boo and her Portastudio is now a valid mass-mediated star-icon. [. . . T]he new technologies of pop have indeed made the concept of the group obsolete, and rendered problematic the distinctions between musicians, technicians, and publicists. One result of this has been an interesting dislocation of the relation between pop stars and their music. For pure dance acts such as 808 State, the explicit rejection of rock imagery has itself become a promotional ploy:

> We don't think of it as 808 State in the charts, we see it as clubbers in the charts. We're not so much a band as part of a scene . . . Stars? They're the last thing you want when you're in a club, aren't they? Dance music is about the records, not the people who make them.
>
> (Price and Massey, 1990, pp. 38–9)

[. . .] Paradoxically, and as the comments of 808 State suggest, this trend may be undermining the discourses of stardom identified by Théberge (1989) as part-and-parcel of multitracking technology. It is interesting to note, for instance, that the music videos of contemporary dance acts (Soul II Soul, Black Box, C+C Music Factory, Deee-Lite) rarely deploy the degree of personae and characterization that is present in the more narrative-based clips made for rock groups.

Interestingly enough, these trends have prompted some musicians and critics to make arguments that strongly parallel the Weberian critique of temporal and harmonic rationalization, and timbral conformity. Such positions reflect a conservative critical response that pits 'technology' against 'real' musicianship (Rolling Stones's guitarist Keith Richards is one among many of the 'old guard' who bemoan the new technologies – even as they increasingly rely upon them!) and that attempts to cling to a hard-and-fast division between creative and technical roles. As Sarah Thornton (1990) has suggested in her account of critical discourses in popular commentary about rock and dance music, this privileging of the role of the musician, and the idea of the 'group' masks ideological assumptions about the aesthetics of leisure since it marginalizes extremely popular genres (such as disco) and practices (clubbing) that do not conform to romantic and author-centered conceptions of artistic production. Similarly, the idea of 'interaction' and its relation to bureaucratic rationalization needs to be rethought in the light of the empirically founded technological developments noted here, and the reconceptualization of the field suggested by Thornton (1990) and others.

There are clearly dangers in thinking about music as though it were a free-floating mystery, a social practice unconnected to actual conditions of production. As students of pop, we need to know exactly how the means of musical production impact upon the sounds themselves. But in undertaking *that* task, we have to recognize also that definitions of *music* and *musician* can change. The new technologies of pop music have not created new music. But they have facilitated new possibilities, and I have tried to show how that potential differs significantly from the practices of multitracking and the age of the tape recorder. In order to understand these new processes, we must think outside the categories of criticism established for other kinds of music and abandon paradigms that – if indeed they were ever true – are inappropriate to the new technologies of today's pop.

Chapter 32

Paul Théberge

MUSIC/TECHNOLOGY/PRACTICE
Musical knowledge in action

[. . .]

IN THIS CHAPTER, I EXPLORE A WIDE RANGE of issues related to music and technology that will serve to highlight certain continuities and discontinuities in musical practice that have occurred with the adoption of digital musical instruments during the 1980s. The focus, then, is not so much on technology per se as on 'technique,' understood in its broadest possible sense. I refer to the notion of technique not simply in the limited sense commonly employed in music (e.g. performance or compositional technique) but in its full sense as the organization of means–material and social–employed for musical ends.

[. . .]

Instruments and the body in musical knowledge and practice

In the curriculum of the conservatory or the university music program, the study of the techniques of instrumental performance are kept separate from the study of theory, composition, and, to a lesser extent, even history. In this way, the tools and the practice *of* music are thought of as distinct from the discourses of knowledge *about* music. We are thus presented with two systems of 'logic': one concerned with the practical – a world of skill, dexterity, immediacy, expressive action, style, and subjectivity – and the other, with knowledge – analytic, methodical, detached, formal, structured, and objective (cf. Bourdieu, 1990b). To a large degree, this separation is an expression of a more fundamental division in Western culture between the body and the mind (McClary' 1991: 23–5, 53–4, 136–9).

Of course, these divisions are in many ways artificial but, nonetheless, deeply rooted in the history of Western art, music, and thought. Indeed, long philosophical tradition has debated the status of music as a 'language,' an argument essentially idealist in character and neglecting the social and corporeal aspects of music-making. As Bourdieu has pointed out, aesthetic theories from the time of Kant have been based on a notion of purity of form as the primary source of pleasure – 'a pleasure totally purified of all sensuous or sensible interest' (1984: 493). [. . .]

[. . .] Indeed, the reduction of theory and analysis to the task of explicating musical form could be considered the necessary technical support structure (a 'technology') of idealist musical aesthetics (see Kerman, 1985: 64–85). By the turn of the century, Schenker's methods of musical analysis could not only dispense with the performance of music but even the surface details of the score itself. In the twentieth century, music analysis has increasingly turned to abstract mathematical models of explication (Kerman, 1985; Dunsby and Whittall, 1988).

[In contrast] [t]he field of ethnomusicology, its theories and methods, may be useful here in offering a model of how concepts and practices are intertwined in meaningful ways in music-making. For example, in the theoretical research model put forward in *The Anthropology of Music*, Alan P. Merriam [. . .] describes six areas of inquiry for the in-depth study of music in culture ([1964]: 44–8), several of which are of immediate interest to the study at hand. The most relevant is what he refers to as 'musical material culture,' essentially the study of musical instruments, their recognized taxonomy, physical characteristics, techniques of performance, symbolic value, distribution, and the economics of their production ([1964]: 45). However, I see these areas of inquiry to be interrelated to a degree not entirely evidenced in Merriam's work. For example, [. . .] the successful production and marketing of new musical instruments cannot be entirely separated from the training of musicians, which is treated as a separate area of inquiry in Merriam's scheme.

Turning now to the role of musical instruments in the formulation of musical concepts and practices, it is instructive to consider one of the most fundamental problems of music theory: the structuring of pitch materials in the form of modes, scales, and tuning systems. Questions of pitch, and especially tuning, are commonly considered to be among the more abstract areas of music theory, but, although the pitch systems of the West have often been represented in the most mathematical and/or metaphysical of terms (e.g. in the language of ratios or in appeals to 'the music of the spheres'), the origin and the significance of most scales and tuning systems are usually found in musical practice, not in abstract science. This fact is well understood in a number of recent anthropological studies of musical cultures where there appears, on the surface at least, to be relatively little in the way of formalized music 'theory.'

For example, Hugo Zemp's (1979) account of the pan-pipe music of the 'Are'are people reveals a subtle differentiation of pitch relations – differences in the 'interval' between two tones – which are systematically linked to the characteristics of the various pan-pipes in use, to specific performance practices, to the melodic figures and polyphonic organization of the music, and even to the spatial configuration of musicians playing in ensembles. All of this is described by the 'Are'are through an extensive vocabulary that makes frequent use of visual metaphors of distance and movement. The musical concepts of the 'Are'are and the tuning of their pan-pipes are thus closely interwoven into the context of musical practice and constitute a kind of 'system,' but one not easily recognized as such through simple observation or by analysis of the music or the instruments themselves.

According to these insights, it could be argued that, virtually anywhere that drums, pipes, or stringed instruments are found, there will also exist a clearly defined 'logic of practice' (Bourdieu, 1990b), which, even if it only takes the form of distinguishing between different types and sizes of instruments, nevertheless constitutes a kind of musical 'theory':

> Partial as these native theories are, . . . they demonstrate how termi-
> nology and technical theory may well develop where there is an object
> or instrument on which an otherwise abstract system can be observed
> in visible operation; the growth of musical theory and of scale-systems
> also is connected with observations on musical instruments, not on the
> singing voice or on acoustic phenomena in the abstract.
>
> (George Herzog, in Zemp, 1979: 34)

In sharp contrast to these practically based notions of pitch relations, however, scientists and theorists of music in the West have come to study the sounds produced by various instruments quite differently from the manner in which performers might approach the same (or similar) objects. For example, at least since the time of Pythagoras in the sixth century BC, a great many theorists in the West have developed (or justified) their ideas on musical scales and tuning by observing the vibratory characteristics of a string instrument known as the 'monochord'; following Pythagoras, the vibrations are usually classified according to the mathematical ratio of the string lengths that produce them. What is interesting about this practice, for my purposes here, is that the monochord is seldom considered to have been a signifi-cant instrument of musical performance per se. [. . .] [It] was thus a very peculiar form of technology – an instrument of science, not music – and knowledge derived from it was, from the outset, rational, objectified knowledge.

[. . .]

Unlike the monochord, however, the central role of keyboard instruments in musical practice ensured that modifications in the mechanics and tuning of keyboards would proceed, at least in part, in response to the requirements of science, aesthetics, *and* musical performance. The size of the human hand, the need for a common practice among musicians, habit, and training, all contributed to the continued dominance of the twelve-notes-to-the-octave limitation on tuning and to the traditional seven-white-five-black configuration of the keyboard (Partch, 1974: 408). Even today, with few exceptions, these factors continue to exert a consider-able pressure toward conformity on the designers and marketers of new musical instruments.

[. . .]

Ultimately, however, musical instruments, scales, and tuning systems are only the material and conceptual infrastructure onto which musical style is built. They may, in part, determine *what* sounds are played, but they have much less influence on *how* they are played. Indeed, the manner in which you play an instrument can transform both the instrument itself and the nature of the musical sounds produced. You need only compare, for example, the characteristic body postures, hand positions, and bowing styles of the orchestral violin player to those of the folk fiddler to realize that there is more to the difference between 'classical' music and 'folk' music than just the relative complexity of musical form. The folk fiddler neither holds, plays, nor even tunes the instrument in the same manner as the orchestral player. Indeed, as their names imply, there is a sense in which the 'violin' and the 'fiddle' can hardly be considered the same musical instrument, although, in virtually all respects, they are physically identical. For all their superior training, the violinist can seldom match the sense of style that any fiddler acquires intuitively through direct musical experience. Even when the violinist is able to imitate the techniques of the fiddler, it will sound 'wrong' to their ears, and they will tend to adapt the music to their familiar playing technique (Thede, 1967: 14).

For my purposes here, the most important issue concerning musical style is that, for musicians, style is something that is primarily felt; it is an awareness that is as much physical as it is cognitive. Nowhere is this fact more evident than in improvised and semi-notated forms of music, where a sense of the relevant musical traditions and conventions are passed on not through discourse but through practice. In his discussion of jazz improvisation, Howard Becker (in terms reminiscent of Bourdieu) observed that 'conventions become embodied in physical routines, so that artists literally feel what is right for them to do . . . They experience editorial choices as acts rather than choices' (1982: 203–4). Similarly, David Sudnow has described the technique of jazz improvisation as 'the knowing ways of the jazz body' (1978: xiii). Fluent improvisational technique, because it must answer to the needs of performance in 'real time,' demands that the body become accustomed to routines, not simply as a form of acquired technique but as elements of musical style:

> Only after years of play do beginners attain that sort of full-fledged competence at place finding that the jazz pianist's left hand displays in chord execution . . . Through repeated work in chord grabbing, an alignment of the field relative to the body's distancing potentials begins to take place, and this alignment process varies in delicacy and need in accordance with the form of the music. The rock-and-roll pianist's capacities for lookless left-hand reaching differ from the baroque specialist's, and these both from the stride-style jazz pianist's. Every musical style as the creation of human bodies entails correspondingly constituted tactile facilities for its performers.
>
> (Sudnow, 1978: 13)

Similar observations could be made about virtually any group of instrumentalists. For example, drummers know that to move between playing the steady beat of rock to the shifting accents of reggae or to the melodic and polyrhythmic style of jazz requires not simply a knowledge of relevant rhythmic patterns and phrases but a realignment of the body and its balances – a complete re-'patterning' of the coordination of the limbs. Style, then, for the musician, is something that is acquired only through an extended process of learning through practice.

[. . .]

[. . .] [T]hat musical performance, and perhaps especially improvisation, is bound to a set of acquired physical and aural techniques and capacities that are oriented toward action within a particular temporal flow – a flow that places present and future into a relationship of intimate proximity (hence, as noted above, the importance of anticipation even among listeners). The same temporal relationship also characterizes the actions of musicians when they perform together, and, as Bourdieu (1990b) has pointed out, this temporal dimension – the implied 'presence in the future' – may indeed be essential to all forms of practical 'logic'. [. . .]

[. . .]

From the foregoing discussion it is clear that how you learn to make and listen to music cannot be explained solely by the direct physical or cognitive relationship between you and your chosen instrument. Indeed, although Sudnow's perceptive and poetic account of learning to play jazz piano may be revealing, it also portrays the learning process as essentially a personal (even solitary) journey toward both the acquisition of skill and the realization of individual potential. Similarly, when addressing the creative role of new technology in music, music theorists [. . .] often assume that the most important issues revolve around the problems of human/machine 'interaction' (cf. Truax, 1976). In either case, the focus is almost exclusively on the individual whereas, as important as the phenomenological and communicative relationship between individuals and musical instruments may be, other problems of a more collective or social nature are equally significant.

Among those problems are the conventional sociological issues related to race, class, and gender. If learning is, indeed, a *social* process, then the factors influential in determining not only *who* has access to musical knowledge and skill, in the first place, but *how* that knowledge is transmitted need to be addressed. For example, throughout most of their history, keyboard instruments have generally been the province of the middle and upper classes. Compared to other musical instruments, they are relatively expensive, they need to be kept indoors, they must be regularly tuned and serviced by trained technicians, and playing even a simple accompaniment on them might demand considerably more study than is required on an instrument such as the guitar. Not surprisingly, then, the piano was one of the last musical instruments to be mastered by black performers in America and incorporated into African-American musics (Jones, 1963: 90). The early blues and boogie-woogie pianists played in an extremely percussive style, and at least one historian has suggested that this style may not have been simply the result of musical predilection. In his book *The Jazz Scene*, E.J. Hobsbawm has stated that most of the boogie-woogie pianists were 'limited' at best, and, even among the most expressive players, some were 'technically downright bad' (1989: 120). Whether you accept Hobsbawm's harsh (and perhaps inaccurate) assessment of the technical achievement of the early jazz pianists or not, clearly access to particular instruments as well as training will have an impact on any given social group's approach to music.

[. . .]

In more recent forms of popular music, such as rock, the male domination of musical performance and studio recording appears to be equally problematic. Mavis Bayton (1990) has described some of the difficulties encountered by women seeking to enter the world of rock. These problems include not only the issues of deviant lifestyle versus family commitment [. . .] but, also, the very relationship of women to music, instruments, and amplification. Bayton argues that, unlike young male musicians, women are less likely to be proficient on their instruments when they enter a band, or, because of the limited number of females who play rock instruments (especially bass guitar and drums), women often end up playing an instrument other than the one on which they are most familiar. Many female players also have backgrounds in classical, notated music, which can be an impediment to learning songs from records and to adopting rock instruments and playing techniques. Finally, women often feel that it is more difficult for them than for males to become comfortable with both the ancillary technology of rock (amplifiers, mixing consoles, and the like) and the specialized technical terms and abbreviated slang employed in its use (Bayton, 1990: 238–43, 248–9). As regards the latter point, even though the home has become the site of music production through the development of inexpensive home recording equipment, the market for that equipment is still largely male, as high as 94 percent according to an AMC survey (1988).

The problems cited by Bayton, however, extend beyond simply deciding to adopt a certain instrument and becoming comfortable with amplification and recording technology. *How* one plays an instrument is influenced by social stereotypes, teachers (formal and informal), and a variety of other factors. For example, Charlotte Ackerley has described how female guitarists have been systematically discouraged from playing lead guitar. With the exception of only a handful of artists, such as Bonnie Raitt, one of the few female artists in the country/blues tradition who can boast a career as both a singer and a lead guitarist, most women learn to play rhythm guitar or accompaniment-type patterns (1978: 260).

Clearly, then, musical practice, even at the most fundamental level of the relationship between musicians and their instruments, cannot be separated from either the specific contexts of musical style and genre or larger issues of race, class, and gender. In this way, the constitution of individuals as social subjects has at least as large an impact on their relationship to musical technology as the form of the technology itself [. . .].

The role of notation in Western musical practice

It is not possible in the present context to detail the gradual but profound changes in musical culture that attended the development of musical notation, a process that required several centuries to come to full fruition; nor is it possible to describe fully the equally momentous changes in musical production and consumption that have occurred since the introduction of sound recording technology. I will address here, however, a number of specific issues concerning musical notation as they relate to composition and performance to the organization of musical labor and to matters of economy. [. . .]

Although musical notation and sound recording are, in most respects, fundamentally different from one another – both technically and with regards to their modes of production, distribution, and consumption – there are, nevertheless, ways in which notation has prepared the social, cultural, and economic ground for sound reproduction. Both notation and sound recording were initially conceived of as primarily mnemonic or reproductive technologies, but each has, in its own manner, become *productive*; that is, each has become a vehicle for the planning and creation of musical works. Finally, recent computer-based programs, such as sequencers, exhibit characteristics related to both notation and sound recording. I wish to proceed, then, with an eye toward such continuities as well as the discontinuities between these technologies.

[. . .]

What is most interesting in the history of [. . .] notational innovations is the manner in which Western art music began to evolve as a specifically notated art form from about the fourteenth century onward. The increasing trend toward polyphonic vocal music during the latter part of the Middle Ages undoubtedly created the need for greater precision in notation, but by the fourteenth century *composition* – as a form of musical activity separate and distinct from performance – had begun to emerge. The role of notation prior to this time had been primarily descriptive – that is, an attempt to accurately record the essentials of an oral tradition. It now became prescriptive – a set of more-or-less clearly defined instructions written by one individual to be executed by another.

This activity was, from the outset, characterized by a relationship to time that was different from performance; with notation, not only was the musical work preserved in a concrete form, but musical time itself was represented in a spatialized pattern. The 'urgency', anticipation, and shared sense of time characteristic of performance was replaced (for the composer at least) by a detached set of quasi-mathematical calculations and operations executed with little reference to 'real-time' modes of action. [. . .]

[. . .]

[. . .] The evolution of a 'social technology' to realize the work plan embodied in the musical score would eventually culminate, in the eighteenth and nineteenth centuries, with the development of the symphony orchestra, with its balanced, specialized sectional divisions and its highly trained personnel all under the musical/administrative control of the conductor. Before this event could happen another musical role had to be invented: whereas a certain anonymity had accompanied compositional activities prior to the fourteenth century, after that point individual musicians began to achieve public recognition in their new-found role as *composers*, eventually setting themselves apart as 'artists' and 'geniuses' from the rest of the musical world.

[. . .]

Between the sixteenth and the nineteenth centuries, the score gradually became the vehicle for an economic and moral ownership right that ultimately granted status to the composer as the individual creator of the musical work. According to Jacques Attali, music publishers were the first to attempt to exploit copyright as a means of bringing about a capitalist organization of musical production and thereby enhancing their own economic control over it. [. . .]

Composers themselves, however, had few legal rights, but as the feudal system continued to break down and composers began to work outside the confines of court life, they, too, began to wrest control of the score away from, first, the lord, and, then, the music publishers:

> Little by little, as they dissociated themselves from the courts, musicians obtained part ownership of their labor; in other words, they succeeded in separating ownership of the work from the object manufactured by the publisher – even though they sold the right to publish it, they retained ownership of it and control over its usage.
>
> (Attali, 1985: 53)

In this way, the simultaneous ideological and economic valorization of the score – as definitive artistic statement, on the one hand, and object of exchange, on the other-became the source of both the composer's musical status and socioeconomic independence.

It is important to note again the reduced importance of performance within this evolving 'technology' of legal rights and economic entitlement. Performers were given no special rights or privileges with regards to the sounds they made, to their interpretations of the musical score. [. . .]

[. . .]

As already suggested, one reason for the decreasing use of improvisation skills in Western art music is the increasing use of notation in musical training. [. . .]

Learning to play a musical instrument through the mediation of the notated score changes the nature of the learning process itself. Sudnow's account of learning to play jazz piano emphasizes the physical/spatial aspects of execution as well as a certain aural and rhythmic intentionality that relates directly to the music to be played. In the technical training of performers in musical traditions dependent on notation, the acquisition of performance skill is standardized in the form of the étude. Although the piano études of composers such as Chopin and Liszt could sometimes achieve great musical and poetic depth, the vast majority are tedious and banal, giving only the impression of skill and often responding to little more than an 'interest in the simple athletics of piano playing' (Loesser, 1954: 254–6). Musical skill is thus transformed into mere 'technique,' a purely physical phenomenon scarcely requiring, at least in the case of the piano, any aural capacity at all.

[. . .]

Western middle-class values of musical literacy and educational methods organized around notated music have been adopted in most public school systems throughout Europe, North America, and, indeed, many non-Western countries as well. In this way, Western notation has become the dominant system of notating music throughout the world, although that dominance is certainly on the wane (Bennett, 1983: 224–5). It has had an impact on genres of music quite removed from the tradition of Western art music. Christopher Small has argued that, in education, the reliance on the notated score places the student in the position of receiving a product rather than engaging in a creative process (1980: 30–1). He further argues that the producer-consumer relationship characteristic of modern society and the notion that knowledge exists essentially outside and independent of the individual foster a consumer mentality within the entire educational enterprise (ibid.: 182). Though Small does not unduly emphasize the role played by musical notation, clearly it has become an important component in a complex set of objects, rules, and procedures – an 'educational technology' – which, taken together, 'serve to confirm the pupils as consumers of knowledge' (ibid.: 185).

Conclusion

The relationship between musical instruments and the entire process of music-making as analyzed by Merriam – including the conceptualization of music, musical behavior, and sound – is extremely complex and, indeed, can only be separated in theory; that is, through an application of the 'logic' of science, not that of practice. For the performing musician, as I have argued in this chapter, both the relationship to musical instruments and the musical process itself are completely fused so as virtually to defy analysis: While learning to play a musical instrument, the musician develops a sense of style that is intuitive, a sense that is felt as much as consciously understood. Sudnow's reflections on playing jazz piano reveal the degree to which performance practice is dependent upon more than the acquisition of simple 'technique' (in the limited sense of physical dexterity); it relies, rather, on a type of listening that involves a 'directionality of purpose' derived primarily (although, as I have argued, not exclusively) through practice.

Musical skills, attitudes, and a sense of style are not acquired in a vacuum, however. Notably, the social networks of popular musicians, by their very nature, have tended to exclude women. With regards to new technology, this isolation makes for a form of double exclusion. [. . .] [I]t thus becomes difficult for women to gain access to either technical knowledge or practical skill.

The gradual development of a sophisticated form of musical notation in the West made possible the conceptualization and rational planning of large-scale musical works. Only through notation could 'composition,' as a distinct form of activity entirely different and separate from performance practice, exist. [. . .] [H]owever, not all forms of notation (for example, instrument tablature) necessarily lead to the same levels of rationalization. Only through the evolution of a complex social technology – in the form of an educational system, a trained and disciplined orchestral ensemble, and a legal system of rights and entitlements – did notation come to play the role that it has in Western musical culture.

Chapter 33

Kodwo Eshun

FUTURHYTHMACHINE
[An interview with Kodwo Eshun]

[. . .]

WHEN I MOVED INTO MUSIC JOURNALISM I realised you could use music journalism as a form of pop analysis which is being conducted in public, month in month out, in the pages of magazines like *i-D* and *The Wire*. The key thing came when Paul Gilroy made the argument in *The Black Atlantic* that modernity starts with slavery.

The rupture of slavery, the mass transportation of people from Africa to America, constitutes a total break in modernity, an existential, world historical crisis. In 1992, Mark Sinker made the analogy between alien abduction and slavery. He said they're the same thing: the aliens have already landed, they landed in the seventeenth century; they transported a whole series of people and a whole series of genetic mutations took place in America. The implication of this was that we are all descendants of aliens, that we are all mutations of that first mutation.

It opened up a continuum between science fiction, techno theory and music. Black science fiction uses a whole cluster of names which is very important, so there's Black science fiction, Black futurism, Atlantic futurism, international futurism, sonic fiction and phono fiction. It's a possibility space which leaves behind or moves away from traditional notions of Black culture as based on the street for instance, based on traditional notions of masculinity, based on traditional notions of ethnicity. It's a boredom with those ideas. It has left traditional identity politics, traditional cultural studies far behind.

Round about the early Nineties, an inertia, a stasis set in with a lot of these ideas; an extreme predictability emerged from identity theory and cultural studies as it was being theorised. Every time it would be: this is essentialist, that's essentialist, this is reductive, this is appropriation. At this point, terms which are overused become concept toxins. They become poisonous concepts, they literally affect the brain, hence you can see people's bodies getting heavy, that's what a concept toxin does.

Since '95 I've been tracing these science fiction components in each field of music and then simultaneously becomes a tracing of the co-evolution of humans and machines. By which I mean that machines have mutated rhythm, and rhythm therefore to me mutates the body, because my definition of the body dissolves the distinction between mind and body. The body to me is a distributed brain, it's a big brain in the sense that the whole body thinks. I was very inspired by Daniel Dennett (1995) and the things Sadie Plant (1997) has written about in terms of connectionism, in terms of new advances in robotics and the idea that intelligence isn't central anymore. In old robotics they tried to build a central command brain, and then round the Eighties and Nineties robotics totally changed and they started seeing that that's not how intelligence works at all. So, what you have is local intelligence; you don't need a brain telling the hands to move, the hands work by themselves and the arms work by themselves. The complexity of interlinking small systems adds up to a complexity that generates consciousness. We are what we hear and what we see and what we feel and touch as much as what we think.

If there's a perceptual level of information happening at the level of your fingertips, happening with your hips, happening with your groin, happening with your arse, happening with your feet, happening with your elbows, the next step is to listen to what these aspects of the body are saying and to realise that these different sensory levels have been really misunderstood. The DJ goes into a journey of the hands. The whole scratch is like this manual perception. I figure in the future that the DJs will have extremely developed fingertips, because they're super-sensitive, like lily pads, like frogs. Their heads will be fused to their necks, and I think in about twenty years' time their legs may well have withered away, 'cause they never dance.

That's how I think of the body, and that's how I think of rhythm. I think of rhythm as a kind of an abstract machine, which appeals to the entire distributed body, because rhythm is parallel music. The first time I heard Mantronix's Kings Of The Beats I couldn't hear the loop-point, the moment when the rhythm cycled on itself. I thought it was a new rhythm every time. It took me ages to hear the cycle, where the rhythm loops back on itself. To understand rhythm you have to switch from listening to the individual notes and harmonies to pattern recognition. It develops your ideas to listen to parallel systems happening in time. That's why African drum choirs are like parallel systems. They work on simultaneous simple rhythms but they are working in parallel so they accrete. You get incredible levels of complexity as you get the connections across rhythms. This idea of rhythm is this connection machine of small information components, building and building. I think this appeals to the entire body with hyper-rhythmic sense. You get this idea of the whole body being mutated, and that's what jungle [dance music genre of which 'jump-up' is a sub-genre] allowed.

But there's also the idea of bodies composed of different rates of evolution. Jungle may well have increased the level of feet intelligence. Jungle's emphasis is on the stepper and on the steps, like in jump-up where the beat is like a propeller. It's like a trampoline that gives you a spring in your heels and literally sets your steps bouncing. There's a whole attention to the feet there, and it's like the feet coming into their own, throwing off their oppressed status. The body is ranked, the body is hierarchised and organised. But with something like jungle the feet suddenly become extremely important. If I were to draw a picture of the stepper, their head would be a giant foot. It's a big foot with big toes coming out of it. You have to grasp the intelligence of the feet.

This is a kind of re-enchantment of the body which is really crucial, and a lot of music does that. But that's not big P Politics, it's not like marching and protesting Politics. That's sensual/sensory politics. It's just as crucial if not more so, because your hands are you. They're a different kind of politics that has a lot to do with mnemotechnics. Your mother says: don't put your hand like this, don't put it like that. That's social law, which gets inscribed in the body. It becomes muscular, it becomes a gesture, it becomes physicalised. A lot of music is about unlearning the mnemotechnics that have been inscribed by the social world, before you had a chance to revolt against them. Then, when you're ten, you wonder why you seize up when you get into certain moods or why certain gestures grab you like that and that's a politics right there.

Chapter 34

Marjorie D. Kibby

HOME ON THE PAGE
A virtual place of music community

I N 1996 A SMALL INDEPENDENT RECORD company, Oh Boy Records, set
up a 'chat page' on its website where fans of its major artist, John Prine, could
exchange typed messages in close to real time. The page became a place where fans
could 'virtually' meet to get information or exchange experiences and opinions
relating to Prine. Through the chat page a fan community was established, in that
the chat page became a meeting place that could not exist within real-world boundaries [. . .] While music communities are usually associated with 'local' places, 'the
notion of 'communities' or localities as bounded geographic entities increasingly has
been seen as problematic to the study of music in urban settings' (Gay, 1995: 123).
Communities exist through dialogue; through an exchange of past social history and
current social interaction. Developments in communication technology have
contributed to a 'deterritorialization of space within a global cultural economy'
(Fenster, 1995: 85), to a point where 'local' is no longer disconnected from 'global'
and the identity of a specific place is located both in 'demarcated physical space'
and in 'clusters of interaction' (Gupta and Ferguson, 1992: 8). In the absence of a
communal physical space, the Oh Boy home page became the site of a 'local' Prine
community.

The ritual exchange of information online allows fans a feeling of community
between themselves and between them and the performer, facilitating a belief in a
commonality, although they are dispersed geographically and disparate in needs and
experiences. An electronic place in which to 'gather' enables a direct link between
fans, and even makes possible a direct connection between fans and performers.
The link benefits not only the fans, but also the performer and the record company,
in that it provides a connection to a central focus of the performer and the producer,
the marketplace. However, an online community is subject to the interpersonal
dynamics of any face-to-face community, as well as the communicative and social
effects of possible anonymity.

Early in 1998 a small group began to dominate the page with 'off-topic' chat, and someone began making abusive and offensive comments anonymously on the page, resulting in a rapidly escalating exchange of vitriol, which included criticism of John Prine. Oh Boy responded by posting a disclaimer, briefly filtering the exchanges and then closing the chat page.

The place of performers and consumers

The commodification of popular music following the development of recording technology inscribed a division between music producers and music consumers [. . .] The commercialisation of popular music was accompanied by a move in the 'place' of music from the public performance space to the private listening space: increasing the isolation of the consumer from the musician and from other consumers.

Despite the increasing gap between music production and consumption, fans retain a belief in the bonds between themselves and the performers, though these links remain largely illusory: 'Fans have inherited the belief that listening to someone's music means getting to know them, getting access to their souls and sensibilities. From the folk tradition they've adopted the argument that musicians can represent them, articulating the immediate needs and experiences of a group or cult or community' (Frith, 1986: 267). Fans feel that they 'know' the musician and that the musician speaks for them. Music contributes to the way people make sense of their lives, in that it provides symbolic categories into which fans can organise the ongoing stream of events that constitute their personal, social and cultural life. Music's role as an agent of socialisation is partly dependent upon the maintenance of the performer's 'authority' through a direct connection between the star and the fan, which enables the fan's knowledge of the musician and the musician's representation of the listener's experience. When recording technology disrupted the physical line between performer and fan, symbolic links were developed to maintain a sense of commonality between performer and listener, and create a community among fans.

John Prine's music is firmly rooted in a folk tradition and is essentially a 'music of the people': 'The peculiar thing about John Prine's songs is that they're always accessible and always personal . . . . Ultimately they speak about you and me' (Dawson, 1976). Prine plays small venues like clubs and bars; he occasionally plays solo, and when he plays with a band he does at least one segment alone and emphasises audience contact: 'there's a part of the show where it is just me. I let the fans throw songs at me from the audience, and I sing them' (Puckett, 1995: 15). The implied connection between Prine and his fans was born in folk music, fostered by the lyrics of the songs and the musician's style, and actively maintained by both Prine and his audience.

[. . .]

John Prine Chat Page

The study of the John Prine Chat Page involved: a web survey form, the web address of which was publicised on the chat page and linked from the major John Prine fan page; a semi-structured email interview; and a qualitative analysis of exchanges on the chat page over a twelve-month period. Participants were self-selected for the survey, which took the form of multiple-choice questions plus an 'any comment' open question. Respondents clicked on the desired responses, then clicked a submit button to return the survey. Internet provider addresses were automatically attached to identify any multiple responses. Participants who were willing to be interviewed were asked to give their email address. The interview consisted of a series of open-ended questions, plus an option to give additional information or opinions. Forty-seven people responded to the survey, twenty-one agreed to be interviewed, and seventeen responded to the interview questions.

[. . .]

The primary modes of use of the John Prine Chat Page were: socialising (70 per cent of those answering the survey reported using the page for general or social chat); exchanging music related ideas and experiences (41 per cent of respondents); and getting or providing music-related information (34 per cent indicated that they used the chat room as a source of information).

The Chat Page was used as a means of connection for John Prine fans, a minority group in most real-world communities. The chat page gave fans a sense of place, and with it an identity.

> I really enjoy it, where I live most people have not even heard of Prine.
>
> (Survey)

> I have been a Prine fan for 26 years. The Prine chat room lets me share my music tastes with others who agree with me.
>
> (Survey)

> It is good to know there are so many people who appreciate John as much as I have for so long.
>
> (Chat Room, 4 January 1998)

[. . .]

It is the ritual sharing of information that binds contacts into communities. Information sharing on the John Prine chat room was ritualised into a number of repeated exchanges. One category of exchange concerned contact with Prine: stories of how people first heard of his music, when and where they had seen him in concert, and of personal meetings or sightings. A second category was exchanges of Prine media 'sightings' where the man or his music appeared in film, television, newspapers or magazines. Another major category of exchanges was Prine trivia, where chatters asked often rhetorical questions, usually about song lyrics, but occasionally about Prine history or connections. A fourth conversation, repeated to the point of ritualisation, involved speculation about John's appearance in the Chat Room.

Prine stories emphasised the link between the fans and the performer and established that link as the commonality between chatters. Everyone is able to tell the story of when they 'discovered' Prine's music; others have stories of meeting him, or of particular connections with him, and many can exchange common tour or concert experiences.

> I started listening in '74, when my sister introduced me to his music.
> (Chat Room, 31 March 1997)

> In 1973 one of my husband's friends moved into a house where someone left a JP 8 track behind. They had never heard of JP so they listened and the rest is history.
> (Chat Room, 1 April 1998)

> JP fan from Clarksville, Tn since 1972 when John's first album was on WKDF, the rock station in Nashville.
> (Chat Room, 2 March 1998)

> John and Fiona got married on April 6, 1966 [. . .] My friends' friends went to the wedding and had photos.
> (Chat Room, 20 May 1997)

> Got to talk to John Saturday night, after the Bee Cave performance (Austin).
> (Chat Room, 31 March 1997)

[. . .]

Knowledge of Prine's career and especially of his music was a marker of belonging, and the chat so regularly involved rhetorical or multiple-answer questions that they became a ritual part of the exchange.

> Okay, Prine makes a lot of references to alcohol and alcoholic beverages in his songs. Name the drink and the song it came from, and indirect references don't count, i.e. 'melted icecubes in a paper cup'.
> (Chat Room, 19 May 1997)

> John likes to work holidays into his lyrics. What holidays can you find, and the songs they are in.
> (Chat Room, 29 October 1996)

> How many other folks appear on JP's albums . . . ?
> (Chat Room, 11 May 1996)

> TRIVIA!!!! What song and what album was it on, that a song was misidentified . . . It had an accordion in it?
> (Chat Room, 9 February 1997)

> Name three JP songs for, or about, his dad???
> (Chat Room, 10 November 1997)

The Prine Chat Room constituted a community, where community is understood in the sociological sense as meaning a group of people who share social interaction and some common ties between themselves and other members of the group, and who share a defined place or area for at least some of the time. The defined place of the Oh Boy Chat Page allowed people who shared an appreciation for the music of John Prine to engage in social interaction. They formed a virtual community. The constituting core of the community was its invisible member, John Prine, and the chat regularly returned to a discussion of whether John Prine himself visited the chat room.

[. . .]

The success of the John Prine Chat Room lay in the fact that it enabled a virtual community, defined by the place of the web page; connected by implied links to John Prine; and bound by the ritual sharing of information. Its demise can be explained in terms of the particular characteristics of this group and the characteristics of computer-mediated communication generally. One issue to affect the viability of the group was John Prine's cancellation of the remaining part of his European tour in 1997 and the announcement that there would be no new tour dates for 1998. John Prine was undergoing treatment for cancer, it has since been revealed. Furthermore, *Lost Dogs and Mixed Blessings,* released in 1995, was Prine's last 'new' album. The only release since then was the second live collection, *Live on Tour* (April 1997). By February 1998, there was no new information to exchange. By this time the 'regulars' had a well-established social relationship, but had almost exhausted their exchanges of Prine contacts, media sightings and trivia questions. One evening's chat monitored from 9 p.m. to 12 p.m. on 17 February 1998 contained no mention of either John Prine or his music. The absence of Prine as a topic of conversation was noticeable [. . .] That which bound the group, the ritual exchange of information, had declined to a point where it almost ceased to exist.

Another factor, inherent in any medium of communication, is that people have a variety of purposes for using a forum. These purposes may not always be sympathetic and can, in fact, be antagonistic. Some people used the Chat Page as a way of getting information, and some as a place to meet with people they had a great deal in common with other than geographic location. Others used it as a way of validating and sharing their music-related opinions and experiences. Still others found social contact to be the most important element, in that the page was a way of meeting and talking to other people and the topic of conversation was not a primary consideration. As the connection with John Prine declined, the links that bound these disparate users dissolved, and the gaps between their interests and motivations widened.

[. . .]

A related characteristic was the increasing emphasis on a division between 'the regulars' (or the 'regs') and the newcomers. The composition of the Chat group had remained fairly consistent for the first year that it was in existence. Once the page was picked up by search engines, the number of new and one-time visitors increased significantly. Long-term participants can operate as moderators and 'contribute to an increase in the sense of community of a list by reintroducing social dynamics in a medium that does not facilitate it' (Rojo, 1995), but the efforts of moderators to keep discussions to particular topics, to disseminate netiquette conventions, or to promote reciprocal interactivity are not always appreciated by all participants.

[. . .]

> Ain't it strange that the regulars from the daytime and the regulars from the night chats seldom mingle? I've noticed that. Just like shift workers passing in the night. Kind of like . . . this is mine . . . that is yours . . . I'm angry and you guys are Prine freaks . . . and they never meet. The shift workers analogy is appropriate.
>
> (Chat Room, 7 April 1998)

Another characteristic of electronic communication was a factor in bringing about the closure of the Chat Page; namely, that people are more insulting when using anonymous computer-mediated communication (Myers, 1987). When ordinary social cues are filtered out, 'the computer creates anonymity, which leads to a decrease in social inhibition and an increase in 'flaming' [the use of personal comments of a negative, insulting or invective nature]' (Baym, 1995: 141).

[. . .]

I had monitored the exchanges on the Chat Room live since July 1997 and via the archives since its beginning in October 1996. The first negative exchange that I witnessed began with a complaint about John Prine on 4 February 1998:

> my meeting [john prine] turned me off greatly. I had previously e-mailed his office on numerous occasions and I was under the impression from his webmaster that he loved receiving e-mail. however, when I mentioned [my nickname] (a name given to me in vietnam) he looked like he didn't know what I was talking about and he looked at me like he couldn't give a flying fuck – so much for the downhome image.
>
> (Chat room 'vet2', 11:16)

> Sorry you are of such self-importance that you think after a performance you would think JP should remember 1 fan out of the thousands – man you got a problem. Sorry you didn't just enjoy the music.
>
> ('Regular', 12:34)

> I am listening to JP as I type this out as not to offend these crybabies who talk JP 24 hours a day.
>
> ('Vet1', 13:27)

> Hey 'Regular' why don't you wake up before you start flapping your jaws! If you read my message carefully, you would have read 'We experi-

enced a great show' – so don't tell me I didn't enjoy the music. Yes I
have a problem – assholes like you that pre-judge me half-cocked!

('Vet2', 13:31)

[. . .]

The nature of the particular software imposes its own dynamic on the communicative process. If two or more chatters are logged on at the same time, the exchange
happens in more or less real time. However, a chatter can respond to a message
left hours earlier and the response will perhaps never be seen by the addressee.
Chatters must complete 'name' and 'email address' fields before their message will
be accepted, but there is no check that an actual email address has been entered,
and, in fact, the program will recognise a tap on the space bar as completing the
required field. Once an attack on those who were seen to have hijacked the Chat
Room had been legitimated by example, the anonymity provided by the program
allowed the exchange of invectives to escalate rapidly. It is highly probable that the
various 'no name' messages were left by more than one person. For example, the
following insults seem substantially different semantically and linguistically.

How much does you mother charge these days? I bet your are a registed
child molester I heard thru the grapevine u wear womens clothes.

('No Name', 13 April 1998)

Let me guess: You have a Liberal Arts degree and are now working a
low-wage job in the service sector. Close? This would explain your ennui
and the enormous amount of time you seem to have on your hands.

('No Name', 30 March 1998)

The very characteristic that facilitated the exchange made it impossible for a
researcher to categorically establish the parameter of the exchange. Abusive and
derogatory messages directed primarily at Vet1 and Vet2 were left during periods
when no one else was logged on, by a person or persons who did not give a name
or email address, or gave an unrecognised name and a false email address. Obscene
and/or offensive replies were posted by Vet1 and Vet2, or people purporting to
be them, and by posters with unknown names who were suspected to be either
Vet1 or Vet2. The postings identified as belonging to Vet1 and Vet2 became increasingly critical of John Prine:

'Hello Mr. Prine. I am one of the losers here on the chatline. I am one
of the losers who buy tickets to your shows. I am one of the losers who
have over the years bought your albums and cds . . . I am one of the
losers shot in the conflict overseas. I am one of the losers who is on
disability at the expense of your tax dollars . . . on the James Taylor
chat line the webmaster monitors their chat page closely and boots off
people like no name . . . You are a over the hill washed up can't get air
play mf . . . you are no better than they are.

(Chat Room 'Vet1' 18 March 1998)

Oh Boy Records closed the Chat Page. It was re-opened with a disclaimer that the page was unmonitored and did not reflect the view or opinions of Oh Boy or John Prine. However, when the negative exchanges continued, the page was briefly replaced by a filtered message board and was then discontinued altogether.

Conclusion

[. . .]

The Chat Page enabled the formation of a community around Oh Boy Records and included fans, performers and record company. Through the Chat Page, Oh Boy established a 'local' presence, in that their Chat Page was a specific place available as a meeting place for a particular audience and a site for the emergence of a sense of identity that was grounded in a concept of community.

The benefit for the fans was the tangible link to each other and to John Prine. While connections between fans and musicians are usually more a belief than a reality, the Chat Page strengthened this belief in a tangible way by providing a delineated place for social contact. In connecting dispersed fans and providing them with a link to John's record company, the Chat Page enabled the possibility of a direct connection with Prine. The location of the Chat Page on Oh Boy's website encouraged the notion that Prine was part of the community, and the anonymity of the forum enabled this belief. Since the Oh Boy chat forum was discontinued, a number of other message and chat forums have been established by those who participated in it, but the absence of the direct connection to John Prine is apparent. The links between fans remain, and the sharing of information continues to an extent, but the aura of a concrete link to John Prine is more difficult to sustain in the absence of a meeting place that is Prine's own.

The combination of a small company owned by the performer and a forum where fans could communicate with each other and with the company (and possibly the performer) went a long way towards dispelling the alienation that followed the industrialisation of pop music; highlighting the consumption of music as an active, incorporative practice; and solidifying the often illusory bonds between performer and consumers. The record company's Home Page became 'home' for the chatters, a virtual place that facilitated the belief in a local music community that included both fans and performer. The demise of the Chat Page underlined the essential problem that with anonymous communication 'anonymity dissolves community' (Rheingold, 1997: 1). However, its eighteen-month success showed how the Internet can provide a place in which new music communities can be formed.

Popular music media

Introduction to Part Eight

■ Andy Bennett

CRUCIAL TO THE DISSEMINATION OF POPULAR MUSIC, and ultimately therefore to its everyday significance as a primary form of contemporary leisure, is the role played by the various forms of entertainment media. Radio, television and film, together with various forms of print media, each play an important part in the public dissemination of popular music. While radio remains the most common medium for popular music, television is also an important medium through which popular music is broadcast and consumed. With the development of video in the late 1970s, the role of television as a popular music medium was boosted considerably. During the 1980s, video became an increasingly important promotional device for popular music artists, giving rise to television channels dedicated primarily to the showing of music videos. Beginning with the launch of the US-based MTV in 1981, the next fifteen years saw a rapid growth in the number of popular music television channels throughout the world, including several local variations of the MTV format. In more recent years, cinema films have also become an important platform for the promotion and consumption of popular music. Indeed, a number of songs have become hits on the strength of their inclusion in films. Not only do popular music songs increasingly form part of film narratives, but also constitute an additional commercial incentive in the film-making process, many new films being accompanied by a simultaneously released soundtrack. The period since the early 1980s has also seen a parallel growth in the number of print media publications dedicated to popular music, including genre specific publications, such as the heavy metal magazine *Kerrang*, and retro magazines, notably *Classic Rock*. As well as featuring and articles on established and up-and-coming popular music artists, print media publications provide reviews of new CD and DVD releases, tour dates, advertisements for fan memorabilia, and so on.

The chapters featured in this part demonstrate the importance of the entertainment media in the promotion of popular music. Rothenbuhler and McCourt's chapter considers the factors influencing music selection and programming by commercial radio stations. As Rothenbuhler and McCourt observe, commercial radio exerts a great deal of influence over popular music in several key ways. To begin with, the relative success of a song in terms of sales and, consequently, chart position is directly related to the amount of airplay it is given on release. Thus, the chances of a song becoming a hit are substantially determined by the decisions made by radio programmers. This, in turn, has a predictable effect on the choices made by record companies about which new artists to sign, and which existing artists to promote. Thus, as Rothenbuhler and McCourt illustrate, record companies choose artists whose music is deemed to be radio friendly and thus likely to secure maximum radio airplay. Ultimately, then, radio has a highly significant part to play in determining public taste cultures with regard to popular music. The sounds and styles that are most heavily purchased, and thus become mainstream, are those that are given priority for radio airplay.

In more recent years, popular music theorists have become increasingly interested in the relationship between the local and the global, as this relates to the production and consumption of popular music. While the global popular music industry continues to be dominated by Anglo-American product, the balance is slowly beginning to shift with the introduction of increasing amounts of non-Anglo-American popular music into the global flow. This reflects a growing demand at the local level for local artists, their work being recognised as an important dimension of local culture and cultural identity. This, in turn, has had an impact on the ways in which popular music is packaged and presented by the music media in different parts of the world. Hanke's chapter on MTV Latino, the MTV variation broadcast in Latin and South America, provides an important insight into how the increasing importance of local artists and music informed the global development of MTV during the early 1990s. As Hanke's work demonstrates, the introduction of MTV into Latin and South America involved recasting it in ways designed to appeal to local youth audiences. At the most fundamental level, this involved mixing dominant Anglo-American pop and rock videos with those produced by local performers and the use of local Spanish-speaking presenters. Thus, as Hanke observes, while on the one hand music television represents a dominant form of global popular culture, its expansion on the global stage has been tempered by processes of transculturation and hybridisation. MTV Latino, as with other local MTV variations, is a medium in which commercial success has necessitated the incorporation of local elements specifically designed to appeal to local audiences.

Film is also becoming an increasingly important medium for popular music. Indeed, popular music is used in variety of ways by film-makers. Thus, while songs are sometimes used either to introduce a film's topic, as for example with the Bruce Springsteen's 'Philadephia', or alternatively featured at the end of a film to accompany the credits, they are also often used as background or incidental music that play on or highlight particular aspects of a film's narrative. Smith's article considers a number of ways in which popular music songs are used to such effect. As Smith observes, a popular way in which songs are incorporated in to film narratives is in the creation of puns. A common instance of this is when an alternative way of interpreting a song's title, or the meaning of its lyrics, is presented to the film audience through the positioning of the song in a particular scene or sequence of actions. Using an elaborate series of examples from contemporary cinema film, Smith demonstrates the apparently infinite number of ways in which songs can be used to this effect. As Smith shows, the meaning of a song can be radically altered – for example, a sexual innuendo created where none existed in the original text, or an original theme of heterosexual love being rearticulated to suit a context of homosexual love.

The final piece in this section is a specially commissioned essay on popular music journalism written by Dave Laing. Although an established medium for popular music, until quite recently very little attention has been paid to popular music journalism by academic researchers. Laing's account is thus important both in terms of its historicisation of popular music journalism and its detailing of some of key specificities associated with the art of writing about music. Although Laing's focus throughout the essay is on Anglo-American examples, much of the ground he covers can be easily applied to other national contexts with a developed or burgeoning popular music press. As Laing observes, the music journalist functions as a cultural intermediary between producers and consumers of music. Through reviewing new CD releases and live performances, journalists inform patterns of public taste. Indeed, notes Laing, in a number of cases, music journalists have been largely responsible for the creation of music scenes/genres, a recent well-known example being Britpop. In addition to writing about established genres, Laing considers how music journalists can also be responsible for informing potential audiences about emergent musical styles, particularly where these do not attract radio and television airplay. As Laing notes, this has particularly been the case in the UK where styles such as punk and new wave were initially brought to public attention through reports in UK music press publications such as *Melody Maker*.

Chapter 35

Eric W. Rothenbuhler and Tom McCourt

COMMERCIAL RADIO AND POPULAR MUSIC
Processes of selection and factors of influence

P OPULAR MUSIC EVOLVES WITHIN TRADITIONS, reflects subcultural
influences, and registers the creativity of individuals and social movements, yet
'stylistic trends in popular sound recordings cannot be separated from the social
organizations that produce them' (Anderson, Hesbacher, Etzkorn, and Denisoff,
1980: 42). Commercial radio stations in the US are among these 'social organizations' that exert tremendous influence on contemporary popular music. Although
the radio industry certainly is not solely responsible for the content and style of
today's music, radio exposure largely determines which recordings become popular
and which remain obscure. Furthermore, because the recording industry measures
the value of particular songs in terms of how much airplay they receive – and the
sales that airplay helps stimulate – popular music is, for the most part, designed to
meet the needs of the radio industry rather than individual consumers or the culture
at large.

Radio as the popularizer of music

Most radio programmers base their decisions about what artists and songs to play
on industry indicators of popularity. In fact, radio airplay is determined in part by
radio airplay. Radio stations frequently add a song to their playlists simply because
it is being played by a competitor or by an influential station in another market.
McPhee (1977) finds that this multiplicative process leads to 'runaways' and 'abor-
tions.' Songs that receive sufficient initial attention will eventually gain maximum
popularity through accelerated exposure, while songs receiving less initial attention
recede quickly from public exposure and awareness.

Furthermore, the radio industry measurably affects the audience's attitudes and
behavior. Early studies by Erdelyi (1940), Jakobovits (1966), and Wiebe (1940),

for instance, all found that an inverse-U relationship exists between radio airplay/ music sales and public popularity. At first, exposure increases a record's popularity and sales while indicators of popularity rise and eventually peak. But further exposure negatively affects a record's popularity and sales. Still, the impact of radio cannot be overestimated. Fathi and Heath (1974) found that 'mass culture listeners' (as opposed to 'high culture listeners') frequently became interested in a specific song as a result of radio airplay. In their pre-MTV study of exposure to new music, Lull and Miller (1982) found that 59 percent of their respondents mention radio as the principal source for new music, followed by 35 percent for records and tapes, 3 percent for clubs, 2 percent for concerts, and 2 percent for television. Similarly, a study sponsored by the United States' Congressional Office of Technology Assessment (1989) reports that 79 per cent of recorded music purchases were selections that respondents had heard before on radio or television. Evidently, most music buyers do not rely on music stores as sources of information about music. Instead, buyers learn about the CDs, tapes, and records they plan to purchase mainly from radio and music video channels. Radio remains the principal popularizer of music.

The system

Radio functions within what MacDougald (1941) had already characterized as the popular music industry system. The players within this system include musicians, record producers, record company policy-makers, promoters, radio programmers, and the record-buying and radio-listening public (Hirsch, 1969; Ryan and Peterson, 1982). The roles they carry out in the system are linked to what Paul Hirsch calls a process of preselection – a means of anticipating and making choices for the public.

Preselection involves a sequential, staged filtering of over-abundant products in anticipation of an uncertain demand. Recorded music moves through the system linearly and is filtered (rejected or continued) at each stage. Decision-makers try to anticipate what will be successful at later points in the system by using feedback on recent successes (Davis and Willwerth, 1974; Hirsch, 1969; Peterson and Berger, 1971, 1975). As products move through the system, the decision-maker at each stage acts as a surrogate consumer for the next role (Hirsch, 1972). Songwriters, for example, may strive to write a hit, but must first write something that a producer and performer will select to record. Record producers may want to produce hits, but the recording session first must produce material acceptable to the executives in charge of recording budgets, artists' contracts, and release schedules. Songs that aren't recorded, recordings that aren't released, releases that aren't promoted aggressively, and records that don't get airplay cannot become hits.

The time and resources invested in a song and its potential for financial return increase as it passes through each stage. The foremost objective, however, remains radio airplay. This means two things: first, those who occupy decision-making positions in the radio industry are indeed very powerful. Second, as we have seen, many of the decisions that are made by songwriters, artists, producers, record company executives, and promoters are heavily influenced by anticipation of what the radio industry wants.

Making money

Although people often want to work in radio because they love music, radio stations are owned and operated to make money. This priority can be made clear by examining three key programming elements of commercial radio: songs, talk, and advertisements. If a song is inadvertently omitted from airplay because of an error made by the DJ, or if a DJ fails to read a public service announcement, no on-air apology will be made. The playlist will not be adjusted to ensure that the song receives its allotted airtime. The public service announcement will not be rescheduled. But if an advertisement is not played, or is interrupted, or is placed next to a competitor's commercial, repair work must be done. In most stations the DJ on the air at the time must make a note on the station program log and fill out a form. Later, what is called a 'make good' will be run on the air. This is a free repetition of the advertisement during equally valuable airtime – a procedure that reveals with perfect clarity that advertisements are the most important portion of broadcast programming.

Radio stations try to operate efficiently in order to produce maximum revenues. The preoccupation with efficiency limits the variety of music that is transmitted to the public because commercial radio stations believe that they benefit economically by making predictable choices about what music to play. The incorporation of computers into radio station operations, for instance, has diminished the autonomy of DJs to play their favorites and has increased the speed with which an 'aberrant' song can be eliminated from the playlist, which in turn contributes to the standardization of music that is played. Predictability, this increases the efficiency of the station's operation because an audience that is attracted by one song will remain tuned in for the next one, *if it is familiar*. As a result, radio concentrates on airing familiar and 'least objectionable' material in hopes of avoiding audience 'tuneout.'

Predictability also attracts advertisers searching for a specific audience. Commercial radio stations actually strive to attract advertisers rather than reach the largest audience or target marginal audiences (Glasser, 1984). As Meehan (1984) notes, broadcasters earn their revenues not by producing messages or audiences, but by selling ratings points to advertisers. Advertisers buy time slots that represent a certain number of ratings points, or shares of listeners, for specific audiences. The stations play music that is designed to lead the target audience to the commercials that are sold. But radio ratings are extremely unreliable. Differences in sampling techniques between competing ratings companies can produce wildly discrepant ratings reports. Some audiences, such as young males, are uncooperative with the ratings companies. Ratings, flawed as they are, nonetheless influence the range of acceptable music. Furthermore, some demographic categories are more attractive to advertisers than others. A heavy metal station in Chicago discarded its highly rated format in the mid-1980s, for example, because its young male audience, though big enough, was not considered marketable to advertisers.

The format

Regardless of whether they are used to avoid competition, maximize audience size, or increase profits, radio formats are mechanisms for managing the audience and selling airtime to advertisers. Formats are selected for their estimated ability to accumulate profit, rather than present music. At the same time, however, formats have greatly influenced the development of popular music. Because songs become popular through radio exposure, record companies try to anticipate what musical qualities will attract radio programmers – what songs will 'fit' into their formats. Music that falls between or overlaps formats may receive little or no radio airplay. Without airplay, of course, the chance for a record to become a hit and make money is virtually nonexistent.

The process of decision-making

One way to study media organizations is to examine occupational roles, including the recruitment, socialization, and career paths of people employed in any particular industry (see, for example, Elliott, 1979). Such information can help us analyze music's place in relation to the roles of those who influence and control popular music radio – consultants, trade sheet editors, program directors, music directors, record promoters and so on. One source of such information for radio is the *Program Director's Handbook* (Paiva, 1983). Here, in the description of the radio programmer's duties, music is certainly not given a high priority. Only 12 of the book's 160 pages are devoted to music, and this brief discussion depicts music as little more than a tool for commercial radio stations. Employees must understand and accept a 'business perspective' on the role of music. DJs in medium and large markets, for example, generally are powerless to decide what songs to play.

The 'taken-for-granted': decisions on airplay

Just as any other form of work, vocational routines in radio are institutionalized unreflectively and are performed as if they are the only way of getting things done. This form of 'taken-for-granted' knowledge is very resistant to change (see Schutz, 1970). Among these routines is a peculiar pattern we have observed – that radio personnel tend to treat albums as if they were already sorted into nearly permanent categories. Records are considered to be either current or not current (having to do not only with how recently they were released, but with their popularity at the time). Records are also considered in terms of whether or not they are presently receiving airplay. New releases from the music industry are classified upon a first impression and tend to remain in that category. The categorization scheme is typically directed toward artists rather than individual songs. Certain performers will never be considered for airplay because they are immediately categorized outside the format. Such perceptions are usually based on an artist's 'sound' or the way that previous releases were categorized, but can also be based on the race of the performer or the style of clothing that is worn on the album cover.

Sometimes the taken-for-granted judgments involve the radio station's competition. When MTV Music Television began cablecasting, for instance, it presented a vast amount of music that was being ignored by radio. The music director and program director at a successful Album Oriented Rock (AOR) station at the time told us that their station 'doesn't compete with MTV' and that the artists and groups who were becoming popular on MTV (mainly 'new wave' artists at the time) were 'too bizarre' for the station's midwest audience (Rothenbuhler, 1982). These inferences were logically based on previous experience and were confidently assumed. The station was the most popular rock station in the market, greatly influencing the area's music scene. Six months later, however, the Stray Cats – one of the new bands featured then on MTV – sold out a concert in town without ever receiving a minute of radio airplay! This development radically violated the programmer's assumed knowledge and, for the first time, called old work routines into question. A few weeks later, the program director and music director were paying close attention to MTV when making decisions about what songs to play.

Song selection in rock radio: the division of labor

Dimmick (1974) has found that two fundamental decision-making stages, or processes, exist in gatekeeping systems such as the decision-making at newspapers and radio stations. In the sensing process, decision-makers sift through the universe of records available for airplay and select those with the greatest promise for their stations. In the *valuation* process, records are judged against the availability and size of 'space' on the playlist, and the availability and 'hitworthiness' of other records deemed appropriate to the station format. The music director is the gatekeeper who usually is primarily responsible in the sensing process. He or she also gathers the necessary information for the valuation process. At the midwestern AOR station mentioned above, for example, the music director compiled an annotated list every week of albums to be considered for airplay. He also noted what songs the station was currently playing, how long the songs had been in rotation, how often their competitors were playing the songs, listener requests, record sales figures, and whether or not the DJs were tired of them. These data set the agenda in the sensing and information-gathering stages. The number of records discarded at this point is remarkable. Of the 467 albums that were available during a ten-week period, for example, only 81 (17 percent) were seriously considered for addition to the playlist. Of these 81 albums, 35 (43 percent) actually received airplay. The music director's 'sensing' had reduced the selection of music by a factor of six and the valuation process reduced it by a factor of slightly more than two. Overall, then, only 7 percent of the albums received by the station in those ten weeks got any airplay whatsoever.

The routine

Programming tasks fall into a weekly routine (Rothenbuhler, 1982, 1985). The music decision-making schedule is designed around the publication of weekly trade journals such as *Radio and Records*, *Billboard*, and the *Hard Report*. Trade journals are published late in the week and usually arrive at individual radio stations over the weekend or on Monday. These trade journals are major sources of information about music. They provide industry news, reports of national aggregate airplay, and record sales. Editors, radio programmers, music directors, and record promoters publish their evaluations of new records in the trades, and they consume news about songs, artists, and industry trends by reading these publications every week.

The midwestern AOR station we have been discussing here gathered information on the local market in a way to fit in with the standardized national decision-making schedule. On Monday afternoon an employee tabulated local record sales and song requests that had been logged during the previous week. Record promoters usually visited the station on Monday or Tuesday. They brought records to pitch, sales and airplay data, promotional materials, and information about what other radio stations had decided yesterday or that morning. Playlist decisions were made on Tuesday or early Wednesday morning, shortly after a conference with the station consultant – a practice that is becoming more and more common in markets everywhere. Record rotation cards, or whatever system is used, are updated after the decisions are made so that the DJs know what to play when. A version of the playlist that indicates what songs are to be placed in 'heavy,' 'medium,' and 'light' rotation is typed up for public release. The music director or program director then reports the decisions to the trade journals, information that will be published in that week's issues. Promoters from the various record companies frequently telephone the stations after all this is done to see how their releases fared that week.

Sources of information

Information sharing holds the music and radio industries together. Consultants are a primary link in the information network. Trade sheets organize and distribute information. Long-distance telephone calls are far more common than letters or written memos. Program directors rely extensively on friendships with other program directors to test their hunches. But it is the promoters from the music industry who play a preeminent role in the decisions that stations make about music. Their comments about an album may be received guardedly by program and music directors, but they are seldom dismissed outright. Although promoters push several albums every week, individual albums are pitched to the stations with an implicit rank ordering. Each is accorded a different amount of selling time in the discussions between promoters and music directors. Some LPs are accompanied by promotional items and advertising buys.

Programmers get relatively little information from or about their actual audiences. In an earlier study (Rothenbuhler, 1982), we found that programmers had 35 different types of contact with the local community. Of those 35, however, only 8 could be considered as sources of information about audiences. In the same study, 42 factors influenced programming. But of those 42, only 4 involved the station's audience. The audience figures only peripherally in the decision-making process, in part, certainly, because programmers lack accurate sources about the local listeners. Institutional sources that they do have, such as ratings, tell them little specifically about music.

Despite the standardization described in the previous section, some decisions that are made about music are in fact quite mystifying. Although many programmers and music directors claim to be able to recognize the hit potential of a song upon first hearing, their roles require a certainty of information that simply doesn't exist. Given this fact, they grasp at almost anything. In one of our studies, a song was boosted into higher rotation because the program director had heard his sister turn up the volume on her radio when the song came on. A second song from an album was added to the playlist at the same station after the music director noticed a young woman sing along word for word with the first song off the LP as she cleaned a barbershop. These examples typify the decision-making atmosphere at many popular music radio stations.

Record sales figures are also frequently said to be unreliable indicators for programming purposes. But nearly all stations collect sales data and report it to the trades who display this data prominently. Most important, sales data are often used in arguments for or against albums that receive airplay. If a record is deemed unplayable because it falls outside the format, for example, evidence of its popularity is ignored. The music director of an AOR station rationalized dismissal of a popular rock group by saying, 'New wave fans are not our audience . . . just look at the way they dress. We're a rock and roll station!'

Radio audience research has become somewhat more sophisticated since the introduction of techniques borrowed from the advertising industry. Two frequent methods of testing songs are 'focus groups' and 'callouts.' Although these methods ostensibly provide listener input into the decision-making process, they are designed to elicit passive, rather than active, participation from audiences. In the first method, a radio station hires an outside consultant to assemble a group of five to ten people sampled from the station's target demographics. Selected songs are played and group members respond verbally to them. Focus group participants are seldom, if ever, asked to recommend records for evaluation. A more frequent method is the callout, in which people are telephoned at random and played brief excerpts from new songs. Respondents are asked to answer some brief questions about the songs – whether the song is 'catchy', whether the person would want to listen to it on the radio. Answers are coded into yes–no categories. Not surprisingly, familiar-sounding records elicit more favorable responses than do more innovative songs. The primary motive for adding certain songs to the playlist, and not others, is that stations don't want to appear 'out of step.' In the process, the audience is expected to respond to, not determine, what is played. Programmers look instead to their colleagues in the radio and record business for advice about what to play.

The consensus cut

The 'consensus cut' phenomenon exemplifies the conservative way that songs are selected for airplay and the insular nature of the radio industry generally. Because audience requirements are uncertain, program and music directors find out what other stations are playing by reading the trade sheets. As a result, albums that are not recognized in the trades are virtually excluded from airplay. Even if an album receives considerable attention, but that attention is divided among different cuts, the album is unlikely to attain hit status (unless it is a superstar's release). Cautious stations often withhold airplay, or limit airplay to light rotation, until the national indicators of what songs to play are clear. This is the moment when consensus emerges. The result is that a song will not likely be played unless everyone plays it.

Conclusion

Commercial radio profoundly affects the style and content of popular music. This is due to the huge audience created by broadcast technology, radio's role in patterns of music sales, and the repeated exposure of 'typical' or 'non-objectionable' songs. The industry's reliance on formats, trade journals, music industry promoters, and consultants tends to reproduce the choices at station after station. In conjunction with the industry's obsession with profits and work routinization in the guise of efficiency, this means that, as a rule, contemporary commercial radio actively discourages significant stylistic innovation in popular music and the communicative potential that such creative endeavors would produce.

Chapter 36

Bob Hanke

'YO QUIERO MI MTV!'
Making music television for Latin America

THIS STUDY CONSIDERS THE TRANSNATIONALIZATION of music television, focusing on the introduction of MTV: Music Television in Latin America. As part of a new transnational media order in Latin America, MTV Latino raises old questions about the political economy of music television and its impact on Latin American popular music as well as the cultural identity of Latin American youth. However, it is also important to consider new communication technologies and emerging transnational networks within the context of globalization (Morley and Robins, 1995) and to theorize music television in relation to the process of transculturalization and hybridization (Lull, 1995). Only with such a dual focus can we begin to address what implications the diffusion of what Columbian-born MTV Latino producer Raul Estupinan calls 'a new language, an MTV language' may have for Latin American popular music and everyday life (quoted in Lorente, 1994).

Yo Quiero Mi MTV!

MTV Latino, a 24-hour, Spanish-language network, was launched on October 1, 1993. The cable service is owned by MTV Networks, a division of the entertainment conglomerate Viacom International Inc. The network's programming is produced by Post Edge, a production and satellite-signal distribution company. When it was launched, MTV Latino was MTV Networks' fourth global affiliate, joining MTV Europe (launched 1987), MTV Brazil (1990), MTV Asia (1991; relaunched 1995), and MTV Japan (1992). More recently, MTV Networks has launched MTV Mandarin (1995) and MTV India (1996). The worldwide audience for MTV Networks is currently estimated to be about 265.8 million households in 75 territories on five continents. At its launch, MTV Latinos estimated audience was 2.3 million households in 21 'territories'; by June 1996, the network claimed to reach

6.9 million households. Such estimates, provided by MTV Latino, do not merely reflect the size of the actual audience; they are part of the production of the audience commodity that is sold to advertisers of global brands. The estimated audience for MTV Latino is very small compared to MTV US, which is available in over 62.6 million households, and MTV Europe, which is available in 53.6 million households. Nonetheless, MTV Latino quickly established itself. By October 1994, MTV Latino was reported to be the number one cable network in South America (Faiola, 1994).

Putting the 'Pan-Latin' concept into practice

MTV Latino is building on the 'pan-European' concept developed for MTV Europe. In the case of MTV Europe, where the relationship between music television and transnational advertising was first developed, one major problem was 'that European youth is not a homogeneous entity, and [MTV's] aim must therefore be to combine global marketing with targeting regional consumers' (Sturmer, 1993: 52). The largest pan-European advertisers (Coca-Cola, Lévi-Strauss, etc.) turned to rock 'n' roll as an 'international language' in order to overcome linguistic and cultural 'barriers.' In this way, advertisers began to pursue the European youth audience, and to use music television to constitute pop audiences as a social group whose 'lifestyle' was expressed through rock sounds, stars, and styles (Frith, 1993).

In the European testing ground for MTV-as-world network, MTV executives were concerned about possible accusations of 'cultural imperialism'; thus, MTV's international operating maxim became 'Think globally, act locally.' According to William Roedy, London-based president of MTV Networks' international operations, MTV Europe was 80 percent American or British music when it began; but by 1995, when the network began to turn a profit, Roedy would claim the programming was 80 percent 'local European.' As Roedy sums up the operating logic: 'it's not like McDonald's or one-size-fits all. Really, its the antithesis of homogeneity' (quoted in Whitefield, 1995). MTV Latino represents an extension of this global strategy into the Latin American context.

MTV Latino, like its other global affiliates, aims to appeal to viewers from 12 to 34. The network clearly seeks to address and construct its young Latin American viewers as consumers. As Friend (1994) elaborates: 'they want Levis jeans and they want Reebok sneakers. They want the global brands that are big and it sort of gives the teen culture its own identity. But teens tend to look to America to set the trends, and we are sort of the voice of the MTV generation, of the teen generation.' In this statement, the locus of cultural identity appears to be completely circumscribed by global marketing interests. Whatever sociocultural or historical differences there may be between geographically dispersed Latin youth, 'there are things the audience shares in terms of their concerns and feelings that link them to a generation' (Levinson quoted in Silver, 1993). MTV Networks' search for Latin youth, as a transnational segment, thus involves the effort to define the sociocultural mentality of this 'generation', to give them a 'voice', and to help define their desires and sense of well-being or satisfaction through an international discourse through and about musical and nonmusical consumer goods (Leiss, Kline, and Jhally, 1990).

Programming a transnational music television network to fulfill these commercial ambitions entails a strategy of 'localization.' As Tom Hunter explains:

> While we have a huge advantage of a common language, the diversity within the territories we're talking about – I mean, just in South America, there are so many differences, and then you throw in Central American countries and the Caribbean countries, and the US Hispanic market, and you have a huge, wide range of experiences and tastes and appeals. Putting all that together is one of our greatest challenges, but its not a matter of finding the lowest common denominator. If you're gonna do that, then you really could do only one MTV for the whole world. We think that localization is everything.
>
> (quoted in Rodriguez, 1993)

How, then, does MTV Latino try to establish a presence in, and be a part of, local Latin American culture? We can begin to address this question by examining how the network reaches into the local through its production and programming practices. These include segments shot on location from South Beach, Miami; a daily viewer request program (*ConeXion MTV*), during which excerpts from viewers' letters are read, specials taped in Argentina, Chile, Colombia, Ecuador, Mexico, Peru, Venezuela, and Uruguay; or programs devoted exclusively to videos by lesser known acts that are popular in a particular country. In music programming, the playlists of local rock radio stations in Latin America are continually reviewed. In music videos, a local sense may be expressed by iconographic elements that signify particular cities or landscapes. In nonmusic programming, *Aufera* (Outside) and *Semana Rock* (Rock Week) highlight Latin American places or newsworthy events. *Playa MTV* – a series being developed to present the best beaches in Latin America – presents these places in Latin America as sites of international tourism and leisure. As the network 'regionalizes' its programming, there are plans to develop more programming devoted to local contests, events, and specials (e.g. *Ski MTV*).

At the same time, the meaning of 'local' is not without boundaries that limit MTV Latino's menu of music videos. Since the majority of the network's current viewers are in Mexico and Argentina, more attention is paid to local music tastes and markets in these countries. As far as local popular music in Miami is concerned, the most common complaint is that MTV Latino's selection of Latin music video clips excludes one of the most popular, and local musics of all – salsa – even though salsa music videos are available.

Programming the 'Latin American' feel

One of the obvious ways in which MTV Latino constructs an imaginary 'Latin America' is by employing Spanish-speaking VJs. The original VJs were 25-year-old Alfredo Lewin, from Santiago, Chile, 24-year-old Ruth Infarmato, from Buenos Aires, Argentina, and 27-year-old Conzalo Morales, from Mexico. Cuban American Daisy Fuentes hosts *Top 20 MTV,* as well as cohosting MTV US programs such as *Beach MTV* and *Rock N' Jock,* making her the only VJ who appears on both networks.

A sign on one of the MTV Latino sets reads: 'Spanish Spoken Here. Se Habla Espanõl'. MTV Latino VJs are not required to change the inflection of their native dialects, although there is an effort to avoid idioms that could be confusing or obscene in other parts of Latin America. The VJs use Spanish to introduce videos; however, when speaking to Anglo guests, they use English, and Spanish subtitles are added, since a large percentage of MTV Latino's viewers are assumed to speak English.

While Latin music videos are interspersed throughout the music programming schedule, the network's Latin music feel is most strongly expressed in shows such as *In Situ,* a one-hour program of 'all the Latin music that you can ask for,' and *Raisonica,* a twice-weekly half-hour program devoted to rock en español. The promotional spot for *In Situ* announces that this particular program is MTV Latino's answer to the dilemma of traditional and modern sounds of Latin music. During *In Situ,* Latin music that may not go into 'heavy rotation' will appear, including the occasional salsa or merengue music video.

MTV Latino's playlist would be familiar to North American viewers of MTV US, but it is not a replication of the MTV US playlist. Gabriel Baptiste, Director of Music Programming, reports that 45–50 percent of the playlist is influenced by US charts, 25 percent is influenced by European charts, and 25 percent is influenced by releases in Latin American markets (Baptiste, 1994). The network's musical emphasis is on rock, Anglo-American and Western European performers, 'superstars' such as Bon Jovi, Madonna, and Aerosmith, or international stars such as Green Day, Red Hot Chili Peppers, or Ace of Base. As for the predominance of Anglo performers, Baptiste (1994) explains:

> I think the one thing that there's perhaps a misconception about is that it would be a lot more Spanish than it is, but the problem that we have is that the international stuff – the Guns N'Roses, Nirvana – is the glue that holds the whole region together. There's a common denominator there in terms of rock radio. They're playing those artists. The thing that has not spread from one place to another are the artists from any one particular country. Like Argentina, the artists have traditionally not gotten a lot of play in Mexico, and vice versa.

Salsa and merengue, while immensely popular forms of Latin music, are regarded as incompatible with MTV Latino's core sound. As Baptiste (1994) explains:

> The problem is that it clashes with what tends to be the unifying factor there, which is Nirvana and Guns N' Roses and Ace of Base . . . Aerosmith, for example. I mean . . . you can't go from an Aerosmith, which is really the center of the channel, to merengue or salsa, and expect not to have a train wreck.

Similarly, there is very little Afro-Caribbean presence in the music programming, even though music videos by UB40 and Big Mountain are presented, as well as Bob or Ziggy Marley. According to Baptiste, MTV Latino would program more reggae 'but the videos are so atrocious' and 'they're not the center of attention of powerful, top-rated radio stations' (1994).

In light of these exclusions, it appears that particular Latin musicians and singers are getting heavy rotation and beginning to typify MTV Latino's vision of pan-Latin popular music. These are groups like Mano Negra (which first gained international exposure through MTV Europe), Los Fabulosos Cadillacs, Los Pericos, and Soda Stereo from Argentina; La Les, Los Tres, and Lucybell from Chile; Los Caifanes, Café Tacuba, and Maná from Mexico; Los Aterciopelados from Colombia, or Héroes del Silencio and Marta Sanchéz from Spain. Most of these groups and performers are on major record labels. Baptiste also observes that bands like Paralamas from Brazil are very big in Argentina so that 'if you take somebody from outside the region, you have a better chance of making them work across borders than somebody who's inside the region' (Baptiste, 1994). So while MTV Latino may give US, UK, or western European-based performers the ability to penetrate Latin American music markets, it also offers Latin performers some capacity to penetrate into the everyday life of young Latin Americans.

It is not possible for me to offer textual or ethnomusicological analysis of Latin music video clips here, but based upon my viewing of programming from June 1994 to April 1996, I can offer a few observations. The vast majority of Latin music videos feature male performers and all-male bands. Videos featuring female performers and singers (e.g. Alajandra Cuzman, Cecilia Toussant, Claudia Puyot, Marta Sanchéz, Soraya) are directed by men. As one might expect, love and male–female relationships are a standard theme; it is also evident that some music videos employ the codes and conventions for representing women as part of an adolescent male 'dreamworld' (see Jhally, 1995). There is a range of moods, themes, and styles, but there is a tendency towards performance-centered choreography, intercut with a pastiche of images that emphasize the central performer. The visual style may range from social realism to romanticism to surrealism or parody. While many Latin videos feature urban settings, some have featured performers in nature settings, intercutting shots of performers with panoramic shots of the landscape.

A more detailed analysis of the Latin music video texts remains to be done; it does appear, however, that some directors who have adopted the visual aesthetic of MTV have not had their creativity stultified. Nor does it mean that music videos featuring Latin rock stars cannot serve as a vehicle for popular memory, an expression of social consciousness, or as a means of organizing popular pleasures and/or desires. Indeed, the rapid editing rhythm may inhibit any preferred decoding of the stream of visual images, thereby privileging music, noise, and co-motion over linear narrativization and closure. As Walter Benjamin, reflecting on the Dadaist quality of motion pictures, wrote: 'The spectator's process of association in view of these images is indeed interrupted by their constant, sudden change (Benjamin, 1969: 238). Latin rhythms and styles thus provide a sonorous counterpoint to, and foundation for, this fragmented flow of images.

Beyond the refrain

For all of the ambiguities and contradictions that appear in implementing a strategy of 'localization,' it appears that MTV Latino serves mainly as a vehicle for promoting US, UK, and western European international rock music, and as a one-way vector of transnational advertising campaigns. From the perspective of US political economy, it has been argued that MTV Networks' near-monopoly on music television and its programming emphasis may 'intensify the one way flow of music and popular culture from these Western nations to other countries, eclipsing and marginalizing indigenous music' (Banks, 1995: 43). Banks concludes that 'MTV's programming is permeated by a relentless commercialism that attempts to nurture international youth culture based on ideals of consumerism . . . contributing to an erosion of indigenous culture, values, traditions' (ibid.: 49). In this refrain, MTV Latino does not appear to articulate with anything other than consumer culture and consciousness. The new language of MTV, even if it speaks or sings in the native tongue, is regarded as the same old imperializing one, producing a convergence of international musical taste that marginalizes Latin music, or standardizes rock *en español* as a segment within a homogeneous international style of popular music.

One could easily extend this general argument by drawing upon Attali's (1992) historical analysis of the production of Western music, and contend that MTV is an extension of the recording technologies that made the mass production and consumption of musical commodities possible. In the 'age of repetition', MTV operates as a televisual model for replication – 'the mold within which reproduction and repetition take shape' (Attali, 1985: 118). As a form of musical reproduction and repetition, MTV Latino functions as a mode of accommodating Latin popular music to the control of Warner, Sony, MCA, BMC, EMI, and Polygram (see Burnett, 1996). In this general argument, the molding of music and musicians according to the logic of commodification and ideological normalization results in a homogenized, Euro-Americanized popular music culture, even though the profits from these performers now flow to the US, Japanese, West German, Dutch, or British stockholders. Along with the loss of musical variety, the commodification of musical desires and pleasure results in silence, for people only 'hear the noises of commodities into which their imaginary is collectively channeled, where their dreams of sociality and transcendence dwell' (Attali, 1985: 122).

It is undeniable that MTV Latino represents and reproduces a popular music culture that no longer means what *cultura popular* means in Spanish or Portuguese, which is the 'culture of the people' (Lull, 1995: 72). At the same time, the inadequacies of the cultural imperialism thesis (see Tomlinson, 1991) with reference to popular music (see Laing, 1986; Goodwin and Gore, 1990; Robinson, Buck, and Cuthbert, 1991) have become apparent. It seems to me, therefore, that the question of MTV Latino's cultural effectivity must move beyond the cultural imperialism refrain, with its tendency towards reductionism, ethnocentrism, and fatalism. For in this refrain, all cultural flow between the transnational corporation and the national are one-way and any history of cultural mixing is either disregarded or only regarded as a form of desecration or deformation of some authentic, indigenous musical form. Recent work on world music reveals just how problematic such a standpoint on authenticity has become (see Davies, 1993; Barrett; 1996; Erimann, 1996); in the de- and reterritorialization of musical styles and genres composing popular music today, there is no singular moment of authenticity in terms of sound, instrumentation, or lyrics (Davies, 1993).

In the Latin American context, the cultural imperialism refrain ignores the historical specificity of the constitution of the 'popular' and the complex, and ambiguous relationship between popular classes and mass culture. To use Martin-Barbero's words: 'Mass culture does not occupy a single position in a system of social classes, but simultaneously embraces heterogeneous practices and products' (1993a: 19). Historically, popular cultures in Latin America have had an 'inter-penetrative relationship' with mass culture, so the space of the popular is one of dispersed sites, rather than a homogenous space of European, bourgeois hegemony, or US capitalist hegemony. As Rowe and Schelling also observe: 'Almost all cultures in Latin America are now mediated to some extent by the city, both in the sense of the massification of social phenomenon and of the communication technologies which make it possible' (1991: 97). So within an internationalizing, neoliberal Latin American political context, the Latin urban popular is a complex site of hybridiza-tion and deterritorialization in which cultural forms can be 'separated from existing practices,' and recombined 'with new forms in new practices,' and can be trans-lated (i.e. travel) from one location to another. So while MTV Networks' expansion beyond the US has been read as a 'symptom of an expanding American media world order' (Goodwin, 1992: 179), from the perspective of the continuous history of transculturization, it becomes problematic to describe the cultural impact of MTV Latino only in terms of a national discourse of imposition and assumed accultura-tion to US consumer culture. This disregards the process of 'massification' as well as Latin forms of social modernity. Notwithstanding the economic facts of the Latin American geoeconomy, it becomes problematic to see the effects of one-way flow of Anglo-Euro-American popular music as a displacement or degradation of indige-nous Latin music when rock *en español,* a tradition invented in the 1960s in response to imported American rock 'n' roll, is an indigenized form of popular music.

The cultural effectivity of MTV Latino will remain an open question until the dynamics of MTV Latino's uses and interpretations are investigated. Beyond the mediacentric framework of reception analysis, Martin-Barbero calls our attention to the places of 'mediation,' such as everyday family life, 'where the social mate-rialization and the cultural expression of television are delimited and configured' (Martin-Barbero, 1993b: 215). In this approach, the daily life of the family is seen as a primary place of transactions with television and a space of negotiations with, and resignifications of, Latin televisual genres. So in contrast to the *telenouda* and its melodramatic emphasis upon kinship identity, we may assume that MTV Latino will draw its young viewers into the international world of rock music and its less familial, youth-cultural repertoire of objects, practices, and messages.

Indications are that MTV Latino programming appears to extend the movement of homogenization that already exists within the Latin American radio and recording industry, a movement that began over three decades ago (Rowe and Schelling, 1991). Today, each Latin American country's popular music charts may be read as featuring the 'same, top 20 artists,' and thus, a 'common musical ground' (Saralegui, 1994). But this does not mean that MTV Latino's selection of Latin popular music is uniform in musical motifs, styles, rhythms, and preferred genres. To the contrary, as Martin-Barbero writes, the 'standardization of products and the uniformatization of gestures require a constant struggle against entropy and a periodic renovation of patterns of differentiation' (1993a: 19).

Rock *en español* is clearly an evolving hybrid cultural form of expression. As Gonzalez (1994) notes, a new generation of musicians, responding to Anglo-

American rock and inspired by such international superstars as Bob Marley, have been re-creating the sound of Latin popular music. Fashioned in their own image, this new music is 'worldly but rooted in local tradition. It takes its attitude from rock 'n' roll but its sound from a neighborhood party. It comes MTV-friendly but speaks the language of home. And it is finding a surprisingly large, avid audience' (Gonzalez, 1994). As part of Latin American 'mass' culture, rock *en español* is a remix of the foreign and the national, made by young musicians who are not only bilingual but bicultural (Gonzalez, 1996).

Latin American musicians have been working on this remix for some time, however. 'For 30 years, two generations of musicians and audiences in Latin America have been reinventing rock, mixing Delta blues and Chuck Berry with corridos and zambas, mimicking high-tech means with low-tech imagination, inventing their own races out of old family photos, Hollywood movies and MTV clips' (Gonzalez, 1996). Rising, and sometimes falling, local rock *en español* scenes also have their own geohistorical specificity. For example, in response to the sounds of imported Anglo-US and UK-based rock, two types of new rock appeared in Chile. Imitations of Anglo rock were sung in English for middle-class consumption, while rock national or rock *subterráneo* was sung in Spanish and produced in the urban periphery (Rowe and Schelling, 1991: 121).

From the perspective of Latin musicians, it is important to note, as Robinson, Buck, and Cuthbert (1991) have pointed out, that imitation is only the first stage of reaction to the dominance of Anglo-American rock (e.g. English covers of Chuck Berry and Little Richard, or Spanish remakes of Elvis Presley songs). Their research shows that a variety of factors lead musicians to pass from the stage of imitation to the stage to indigenization, writing and recording original material in Spanish in a way that preserves traditional musical styles. During this stage, imported music is not just a format for repetition; rather, 'sound and textual motifs are resemanticized in terms of the local' (Rowe and Schelling, 1991: 121). This new form of popular music first emerged in the 1970s in Argentina with figures such as Charly Garcia, and in Mexico in the 1980s with bands such as Los Caifanes, Maldita Vecindad, and Café Tacuba. In Argentina, there was a greater receptivity to native rock following the Falklands War with Britain in 1981 that allowed bands such as Los Dividodos and Los Fabulosos Cadillacs to become established (Moore, 1994).

Transculturalization, writes Lull, 'produces cultural hybrids – the fusing of cultural forms' that are 'popular almost by definition' (1995: 155). For example, the Mexican band Los Caifanes released its first album in 1981; their hit single 'La Negra Tomasa' was an update of Cuban *cumbia* music. Today, they blend ska, rock 'n' roll, and Mexican folk rhythms. Another band, Café Tacuba, mixes influences as diverse as classic Mexican boleros, *norteño*, ska, punk, and others. So the term rock *en español* refers to many sounds; it fails to characterize and to classify the vastly heterogenous popular music of Latin American recording artists. For example, contrast Dominican singer-songwriter Juan Luis Cuerra, who has reinvented merengue and *bachata* by using jazz harmonies and borrowings from South African choral singing, with Fito Paez, a band that could only be from Buenos Aires with their allusions to the Beatles and nuevo-tango. Rock *en español*, like American rock 'n' roll seen from a multicultural perspective, is a hybrid form of music that may be more dialogic than derivative (see Lipsitz, 1994).

While much of this music may never enter MTV Latino's playlist, the network does open up a new and important space for those who are successful in getting 'heavy rotation.' As musicians continue to work on the Latin mix and extend their praxis to the making of music videos, they gain access to an important means of representing the 'rock and roll apparatus' (Grossberg, 1984) and are able to achieve a kind of affectivity they could not otherwise have. The practice of making music videos is an aesthetic, expressive practice of translating the infinite possibilities of mutating, hybrid sounds into images that travel across time and space. Los Fabulosos Cadillacs, Los Caifanes, Charly Garcia, El Tri, Los Tres, Café Tacuba, Soda Stereo, and Illya Kuryaki y los Valderramas exemplify the mix of transcultural sounds and visions that are crossing ethnic, cultural, and national boundaries to create a new cartography of Latin popular taste.

Chapter 37

Jeff Smith

POPULAR SONGS AND COMIC ALLUSION IN CONTEMPORARY CINEMA

CONSIDER THE FOLLOWING SCENE FROM *CON AIR* (1997). The plot of this Jerry Bruckheimer action film concerns the escape attempt of several barbarous inmates who stage a daring skyjack during a simple prison-transfer operation. When Cyrus 'The Virus' Grissom (John Malkovich) and his cohorts succeed in gaining control of the plane, they celebrate by singing and dancing to the Lynyrd Skynyrd classic 'Sweet Home Alabama.' The film's reluctant hero, Cameron Poe (Nicolas Cage), looks on and wonders whether he will ever return to his home. A former special forces officer, Poe had hoped to serve the brief remainder of his sentence and return to his wife and child in Alabama. At the same time, however, the film's most vicious murderer, a cannibalistic serial killer named Garland 'the Marietta Mangier' (Steve Buscemi), points out a second irony in the use of 'Sweet Home Alabama.' Watching the inmates' celebration, Garland observes: 'Define irony. A bunch of idiots dancing on a plane to a song made famous by a band that died in a plane crash.'

While this example from *Con Air* is characteristic of the ways pop songs frequently function in films, it is somewhat unusual to the extent that it 'bares the device' of such musical allusion. Garland serves as a kind of diegetic auditor in the film, reminding spectators of the ironic function of the Skynyrd tune. In this sense, the character also serves as a surrogate for the film's narration. By explaining the reference for us, Garland invites us to admire the cleverness of the allusion as well as its self-consciousness. As this example implies, the use of songs as ironic commentary may be viewed as a particular configuration of postmodern culture, where a very self-conscious mode of textual address is situated within a larger network of intertextual references. But what does it mean to describe a song as a pun? What specific textual operations are necessary for a pop song to function as a form of ironic commentary? What features of the film text does the music comment on?

Musical puns and theories of film comedy

At first glance, it would seem that the notion of songs as puns poses several problems when weighed against current theories of film comedy. Even a cursory comparison shows that there are many differences between musical puns and the more conventional comic devices associated with cinema, such as verbal jokes and sight gags. The relation between musical puns and comedy can be assessed according to three criteria – namely, the musical pun's perceptual saliency, its narrative function, and its bisociative qualities.

As one might expect, music in the cinema usually occupies a different perceptual register than do jokes or sight gags. In order to preserve the intelligibility of dialogue, music and ambient sound tend to be mixed much lower than speech, and thus they often are comprehended by spectators only as part of an overall sound design. In contrast, the same sound-mixing conventions that subordinate music and ambient sound serve to foreground verbal jokes. In *Tomorrow Never Dies,* for example, James Bond (Pierce Brosnan) offers up one of his trademark double entendres in a verbal exchange with M (Dame Judi Dench). When Bond says that he is in the midst of taking language lessons to learn something of the 'Danish tongue', M trumps his double entendre by remarking that she always knew James was a 'cunning linguist.' Spectators might say that they do not 'get the joke' but this is a far cry from not having heard it. Similarly, framing and editing usually foreground sight gags, such that they can hardly go unnoticed by spectators. In this respect, musical puns are probably closer in their perceptual difficulty to some of the sight gags that appear in Jacques Tati's films. As Kristin Thompson points out in her analysis of *Play Time* (1967), Tati does not always foreground or center his sight gags, and sometimes stages several gags simultaneously, making it 'literally impossible to see all of them in one viewing.'

Despite this perceptual difficulty, though, musical puns, verbal jokes, and sight gags all share something in terms of their narrativity. One of the most hotly debated issues in theories of film comedy is the question of the extent to which gags and jokes are narrativized, and much of this debate has been framed in terms of whether or not gags function as moments of pure spectacle. My contention here is that musical puns, like gags and verbal jokes, can function as 'throwaways' in the sense that they engage a brief affective response but may be forgotten as soon as they are heard.

This is not to say, however, that musical puns have no bearing on a film's narrative. Rather, because they are frequently motivated as source music, musical puns may serve a concomitant function by contributing to a film's diegetic effect. Because of its close connection to its historical and social context, popular music is an especially effective means of denoting particular time periods or suggesting a particular sociocultural milieu. As such, it can serve as a kind of cultural shorthand for establishing setting or reinforcing the traits of a character.

Such narrative functions, however, are related more to the overall style of the music than they are to specific titles or lyrical content. More often than not, the humor derived from the use of musical allusion comes from the ironic juxtaposition of the lyrics or title of a particular song and the situation depicted in the narrative. As a resource for humor, the linguistic element of popular songs neither advances the film's narrative nor contributes much to our understanding of the diegesis. It is within this more limited sense that musical puns may exhibit a tension with cinematic narrative that is more generally characteristic of verbal jokes and sight gags.

A more significant similarity between sight gags, verbal jokes, and musical puns is that they are all bisociative. Koestler (1966) defines bisociation as the movement between two associative chains of logic, each of which represents a distinct interpretive frame. According to Koestler, humor arises from the juxtaposition of these two associative chains to create two incongruous ways of seeing something, such as a person, sentence, or situation. Bisociation thus requires that within the realm of humor its object must be both A and Non-A at the same time. Similarly, Mulkay (1988) notes that jokes are designed to display both congruity and incongruity simultaneously. Jokes may evoke two incongruous chains of associative logic, but they must do so in a manner in which the connection between these different frames of reference remains perfectly understandable.

Musical puns are also bisociative, albeit in ways that are subtly different from linguistic puns and sight gags. While some musical puns in films involve the play of aural similarities characteristic of a linguistic pun, they more commonly juxtapose two different ways of interpreting the song's title: that of the original scenario described or implied in the lyrics of the song and the more immediate situation represented in the cinematic text. These two frames of reference must be sufficiently different to create the incongruity upon which the pun is based; if the narrative frames of reference mirror one another, then the juxtaposition lacks the incongruity necessary to the bisociative process. Yet, while different, each frame of reference must also be associatively elicited by some linguistic element of the title. This is important since the spectator must recognize the title's relevance to the narrative situation depicted in the film to activate the two interpretive possibilities presupposed by the pun's play of meaning.

Musical puns in film require a certain detachment of a song's title from its original context and a concomitant recontextualization of the title in terms of the film's narrative. Consider the opening *of The Big Chill* (1983) which uses Marvin Gaye's classic recording of 'I Heard It Through the Grapevine' in a bisociative manner. For those viewers familiar with the song, the first frame of reference evoked by the title relates to the scenario of infidelity described in the song's lyrics. Told in the first person, the lyrics represent the perspective of the cuckolded lover and express the emotional anguish caused by his partner's romantic betrayal. As such, the title refers to the network of gossip that has informed the narrator of his lover's perfidy, the 'grapevine' that informally circulates information about the affair. The second frame of reference is provided by the narrative situation depicted in the film. The film's opening sequence also refers to the 'grapevine' as an informal information system, but in this instance the news that travels from person to person is that of a friend's suicide rather than a lover's infidelity. Thus, while both frames of reference draw upon the colloquial notion of a 'grapevine,' they also rely on the pronomial ambiguity of the 'it' of the song's title to evoke two incongruent narrative scenarios.

I do not mean to suggest here that audiences actively listen and comprehend song lyrics during the course of a film. Indeed, a spectator's attention is mostly directed toward the film's narrative and not toward the decipherment of often unintelligible rock lyrics. However, if the song is already well-known, then the matter of song lyrics becomes more a question of recognition rather than cognition. Instead of deciphering lyrics, viewers simply apply what they already know – a title or chorus – to the specific dramatic context that is depicted in the film. Thus, one need not have a thorough understanding of the song's lyrics, but simply the minimal information supplied by the song's title. Musical puns that are motivated as source music are bisociative in another way. When the allusion functions as part of the diegesis, the pun associated with the song's title generates two seemingly incongruous forms of textual motivation. On the one hand, the use of a song as source music enables the audience to motivate it realistically. In films, songs are commonly heard coming from boom boxes, jukeboxes, radios, and stereos, and the placement of the musical allusion within the diegesis allows the pun to arise 'naturally' out of the action the song accompanies. At the same time, however, insofar as the song can function as an expressive device, it can also be motivated as a form of authorial commentary. Since each of these categories of motivation maintains its own logic, the resulting tension between them produces a certain incongruity with respect to our understanding of its textual function. Here again, a certain frisson of pleasure may be produced by the fact that the song simply happens to be playing in the background of the scene, but is also a perfectly apt or ironic comment on the action depicted within the film. In such instances, some of the humor of the musical pun derives from the improbable coincidence implied by the juxtaposition of these two kinds of textual motivation.

Musical puns in contemporary cinema: examples and analysis

Having sketched out the theoretical context for the use of pop songs as musical puns in films, I now turn to some examples culled from contemporary mainstream films. At the outset, I should point out an axiom common to all of the examples I will discuss – namely, lexical ambiguity. Although the musical pun derives its humor from incongruity, this incongruity itself is made possible by a semiotic ambiguity evident in the phrasing of a song title or lyric. This ambiguity may take on several forms, but its play of meaning commonly falls into one of four categories: pronomial ambiguity, syntactic ambiguity, semantic ambiguity, or the juxtaposition of the literal and figurative.

The aforementioned example from *The Big Chill* offers a good example of the first category. The lack of a clear referent for the word 'it' in the title 'I Heard It Through the Grapevine' renders it a somewhat empty signifier. Virtually any scenario can provide the 'it' heard by the subject of the title. Song titles that contain this type of pronomial ambiguity offer certain advantages to directors and music supervisors in that they are often applicable to several dramatic contexts. Not surprisingly, films that deal with gender issues sometimes make use of this type of pun as a means of extending the text's thematic implications. In *The Long Kiss Goodnight* (1996), for example, the film's soundtrack periodically comments on the heroine's transformation from femme to femme fatale. This is most evident during the moment when Sam (Geena Davis) finally makes herself over as Charlie, a change signified by a montage of Sam cutting her hair and dyeing it blonde. The sound-track ironically underlines this transformation through the choice of Santana's cover of 'She's Not There.' Playing on the ambiguity of the pronoun 'she,' the song's double meaning comments on both the narrative and thematic implications of Sam's metamorphosis. On the one hand, the 'she' of the song title refers to Samantha herself and Charlie's rejection of her previous incarnation as wife, mother, and PTA member. On the other hand, the 'she' of the title refers more broadly to the absence of femininity in Charlie and her emergence as a phallic heroine more generally associated with the action film.

The film *Bound* (1996) offers a good instance of the second category: syntactic ambiguity. In an early scene set in a Chicago bar, two women approach and proposition one of the film's protagonists, a tough ex-con named Corky (Gina Gershon). The sexual orientation of the characters in this scene is ironically underlined by a song playing on the bar jukebox – namely, Aretha Franklin's recording of '(I Never Loved a Man) The Way I Love You.' In this case, the shift between lyrics and film as frames of reference simply recontextualizes the implied meaning of the title. The scenario of normative heterosexual romance implied in the song's lyrics suggest that the title of Aretha Franklin's recording might be more properly phrased 'I Never Loved a(ny other) Man (The Way I Love You).' In the film, however, the setting of the lesbian bar recontextualizes the title such that it might be rephrased as 'I Never Loved a(ny) Man (The Way I Love You).' This recontextualization not only effects a shift from the particular to the general (i.e. one hypothetical man becomes all men), but it also effects a shift in the gender of the unspecified pronoun 'you.' Where the lyrics imply a male object in the title, the film suggests one that is female.

A good example of the third category, semantic ambiguity, when the song title is unmoored from its original lyrical context, comes from *A Very Brady Sequel* (1995). In several scenes where Marcia and Greg amorously ogle one another, Luther Vandross's recording of 'If Loving You Is Wrong' plays nondiegetically on the soundtrack. Although the unspecified 'you' seems to hint at a pronominal ambiguity, the key term of the song's title is the word 'wrong' that ambiguously suggests some unnamed taboo. Here again, the cinematic signifier serves to recontextualize the meaning of the original lyrics by suggesting a taboo different from the one described there. Where the original lyrics describe the narrator's desire for a married woman, the scene the song accompanies in *A Very Brady Sequel* broadly hints at desires of a more incestuous nature. In doing so, the song literalizes a subtext that was only hinted at in the television series upon which the film was based.

This example also points up the importance of audience foreknowledge. Early on, the song is excerpted such that the cues accompanying Greg and Marcia's first stirrings of desire work as an instrumental theme. Without lyrics, the song functions largely as background music. Later, we will hear a slightly longer, vocalized excerpt of the song that makes the connection between song and scene more explicit. What makes this progression interesting is the extent to which it foregrounds the importance of the song's familiarity. Those who know the song get the joke on the first hearing. Others will get it later when the song's lyrics make the joke more obvious.

The fourth type of musical pun involves the juxtaposition of figurative and literal meanings of a term. In such instances, playing the song in a dramatic context may literalize some aspect of the song's title or vice versa. A brief sequence from *Romy and Michele's High School Reunion* (1997) offers a paradigmatic example of this kind of comic allusion. As the titular characters page through their high school yearbook, the pictures they view motivate a series of brief flashbacks. The last of these flashbacks depicts those on the lowest rung of the class's social ladder, the geeks who take part in the school's science fair. Accompanied by Thomas Dolby's 'She Blinded Me with Science,' the sequence shows Toby photographing Heather (Janeane Garafolo) and Sandy (Alan Gumming) for the school's yearbook. Not only does the sequence play off the song's reference to science, but the flash of Toby's camera momentarily whites out the screen, literalizing the metaphorical 'blind'-ness of the song's title.

A rather more complex example of this type of allusion occurs in Wes Craven's *Scream* (1996). After the gruesome prologue in which Casey (Drew Barrymore) is savagely stabbed by an assailant garbed in a 'Grim Reaper' costume, the scene shifts to the bedroom of Sidney (Neve Campbell), the film's virginal heroine. As Sidney works at her computer, her boyfriend Billy (Skeet Ulrich) sneaks into her room through the window. During a conversation about their relationship, an acoustic cover of 'Don't Fear the Reaper' plays softly in the background, an ironic comment on the brutality of the film's opening sequence. More importantly, however, the allusion to the Blue Oyster Cult classic recasts the song's title by literalizing its meaning. While the title itself invokes the Reaper as a popular symbol of death, the film presents us with an actual person who not only dresses as the Grim Reaper but also unleashes homicidal vengeance on the other characters of the film. The irony here, of course, is that Billy himself proves to be one of the film's dual slashers and is, in fact, the 'Reaper' to be feared.

The juxtaposition of literal and figurative meanings is also evident in a brief sequence from *The Big Lebowski* (1998), but in this case the film inverts the relationship seen in the previous two examples. Rather than literalize the figurative, this sequence recasts the literal as metaphor. The sequence in question is one in which Dude (Jeff Bridges) is sent to a doctor by Maude Lebowski (Julianne Moore), a zany performance artist seeking to conceive a child. Although the exam is ostensibly for a punch in the jaw, Dude later learns that he was surreptitiously being checked as a prospective sperm donor. The brief sequence concludes with the doctor asking Dude to remove his undergarments, presumably for a prostate check. As Dude hitches down his shorts, the familiar skiffle-style intro of Creedence Clearwater Revival's 'Lookin' out My Back Door' sneaks into the soundtrack and provides a sound bridge to the next sequence in which Dude sings along to the song on his car radio. Of course, the sequence offers an elaborate pun on the more scatological implications of the term 'back door' – namely, the orifice probed in the elided prostate exam. More to the point, however, the sequence inverts the relationship seen in earlier examples. In John Fogerty's song, the 'back door' of the title is the door to the narrator's back porch. *The Big Lebowski* thus recontextualizes the meanings of the original lyric by encouraging us to focus on the possibly prurient connotations of the song's title.

In sum, while musical puns often function in films as a resource for humor, they also serve or reinforce other narrative functions more generally associated with film music. As the examples above indicate, musical puns sometimes reinforce thematic implications, comment on characters or situations, cover ellipses between sequences, or foreshadow later narrative developments. Yet as the examples also indicate, the use of musical puns in films is usually done in a rather piecemeal fashion. While most of these films contain several popular recordings, only a few in each film actually function as musical puns.

Conclusion

As the use of popular music in film grows, so does the use of popular songs in the form of musical puns. The use of popular songs in specific dramatic situations enables a shift in the title's meaning away from the context provided by the song's lyrics and toward the context provided by the film's strategies of representation. These two contexts provide two incongruous frames of reference for interpreting the film's title, and the humor of the pun derives from the juxtaposition of these seemingly incompatible but nonetheless understandable hermeneutic potentialities. As *The Hollywood Reporter* points out:

> A film's composer handles the score, but supervisors are responsible for every other bit of music that turns up in a film – from a snatch of something on a car radio to the tune behind an MTV-ready montage sequence to an original hit-in-waiting over end credits.

The use of popular songs as musical allusions remains an important weapon in the supervisor's arsenal. At their best, musical allusions not only serve conventional dramatic functions, but also provide viewers with moments of postmodern pleasure.

Chapter 38

Dave Laing

ANGLO-AMERICAN MUSIC JOURNALISM
Texts and contexts

P OPULAR MUSIC IS NEVER ENTIRELY 'ITSELF'. Almost every context of performance or listening is framed by language. This language may prepare an audience for the musical experience, provide background information or seek to persuade listeners to become consumers through the purchase of a CD or a concert ticket. The framing language may derive from various places within the music industry or beyond it, and it is a major component of what Timothy Taylor has called the 'metatext' (Taylor, 1995). One of the most important contributors to the metatext is the practice of music journalism.

This chapter is concerned with both the context and institutions of popular music journalism and also the texts of music journalism – what is written and how it is written and by whom. The contexts of music journalism include its relationship with music audiences, with musicians and with the music industry. The institutions of music journalism are the publications in which it appears, and also other music media such as radio and television. The principal texts or forms of music journalism are the review and the interview.

The sites of music journalism are the different categories of magazines and newspapers in which reviews and interviews appear. There are four principal categories: the general press (daily and weekly newspapers and magazines), trade publications aimed at those working in the music industry, fanzines (now including weblogs or blogs) and the specialist music press.

Music journalism has appeared in general newspapers and journals for more than three hundred years: according to the editor of a collection of writings on Western classical music, 'journalistic criticism was largely the creation of the eighteenth century' (Haskell, 1995: xiii). By the middle of the twentieth century, some jazz reviews were appearing in daily newspapers and in the 1960s this began to be extended to contemporary popular music by writers such as Robert Shelton of the *New York Times* who gave Bob Dylan his first review in 1961 and William Mann, chief classical music critic of *The Times* of London, who praised the songs of John Lennon and Paul McCartney in 1963. Subsequently, a few general press critics (notably, John Rockwell of the *New York Times*) have written about both classical and popular music, but it is more frequently the case that daily and weekly publications have specialist critics who deal with only one area of music, although the 'pop' or 'rock' reviewer is expected to show expertise in every genre that is not either classical or jazz.

In 2004 the US trade publication *Billboard* profiled the popular music journalists of the leading 20 newspapers whose combined circulation was almost 16 million copies (Hay, 2004). Only three of these reviewers were female. Such journalists are faced with the fact that most of their potential readers will be unfamiliar with most of the work they are reviewing and consequently a large proportion of most reviews of concerts or CDs is taken up with an introduction to the artist under review.

Billboard and other trade publications, such as *Music Week* in Britain, treat music as an industry and have as much in common with the trade publications of other retail, manufacturing and media industries as with music magazines aimed at consumers. Their reviews of CDs and concerts reviews are intended for music retailers and industry professions, and are orientated to the commercial potential of the songs and artists. A variant of the trade publication is the 'tipsheet' which predicts which new records will be hits and attempts to influence radio station programmers in particular.

The term 'fanzine' was first used to describe amateur publications produced by enthusiastic readers of science fiction to express their enthusiasm and to publish esoteric details about stories and writers of interest only to other fans. One history of the fanzine defines it as 'non commercial, non professional, small-circulation magazines which their creators produce, publish and distribute by themselves' (Duncombe, 1997: 6). Popular music fanzines are devoted to either a single artist or single genre, such as punk in the 1970s (Laing, 1985).

Fanzines are one source from which the journalistic personnel of specialist music publications have been recruited. However, the specialist publications cover a much wider range of music and are operated on a commercial basis. Increasingly, these publications are owned and controlled by large publishing corporations that own numerous other magazines devoted to all types of leisure pursuit. In the case of the UK, Eamonn Forde has argued that the oligopolistic pattern of ownership of popular music periodicals involved 'complex shifts in working and employment conditions in the major magazine publishing corporations' that led to a growing conformism of journalistic style in the 1990s (Forde, 2001a: 23–4).

The first specialist magazines devoted to jazz and popular music in the US and Britain appeared in the 1920s and 1930s. *Melody Maker* was founded in London in 1926 as a monthly publication for dance band and jazz musicians, followed by *Down Beat* in the US (1934) and *Le Jazz Hot* in France (1935). After the Second World War, *Melody Maker* mutated into a general popular music weekly read by consumers as well as musicians. Its principal rival, *New Musical Express* (*NME*), appeared in 1952. Subsequently, new magazines appeared in response to each major phase in the evolution of rock and pop. The rock 'n' roll explosion of the mid-1950s inspired the launch of numerous youth-oriented magazines in the US, while *Rolling Stone* was founded in San Francisco in 1967 at the height of the psychedelic rock era. In the 1980s and 1990s, the popularity of dance music and hip-hop led to the foundation of such US publications as *Vibe* and *The Source* and *Mixmag* and *Muzik* in Britain.

Fluctuations in the sales and profitability of specialist publications are not primarily due to the quality of their journalism but are caused by several external forces. The most important of these is the changing taste of the popular music audience. *Melody Maker* reached a sales peak of over 160,000 copies in 1966 in the beat group age, but it chose to ignore the popularity of dance music in the 1980s and 1990s and was selling only 40,000 when it ceased publication in 2001. As rap and hip-hop gained in popularity in the US in the 1980s and 1990s, magazines such as *The Source* and *Vibe* thrived at the expense of the former market leader *Rolling Stone*.

The importance of specialist magazines in the metatext of popular music is also closely linked to the extent to which radio and television disseminate various types of music. Until the 1980s, Britain had up to five competing weeklies at a time when only a limited amount of new music could be heard on radio and the country's few television channels. In this era the specialist music press played a key role in the development of music and audiences. The US was much better served by local radio and had a less influential magazine sector comprised of fortnightly and monthly titles.

Gatekeeper or intermediary?

The music journalist as reviewer or interviewer is a 'relay' between producer (musician and/or music industry) and consumer (the audience for popular music). Radio programmers, disc-jockeys and music journalists have sometimes been defined in scholarly writing as 'gatekeepers' or 'cultural intermediaries'.

The concept of the journalist as gatekeeper with the power to include or exclude news items originated in a study of newspaper newsrooms (White, 1950). In the context of popular music, a gatekeeper may prevent knowledge of certain products from reaching an audience, as when a radio station programmer selects a playlist or a magazine editor decides which albums will be reviewed and which will be ignored. However, this binary model (exclusion/inclusion) is less appropriate for most music journalism, not least because the critical function of such writing demands the recognition of 'bad' music as well as 'good' music. The gatekeeper model is more relevant to the practices of record company press officers who have increasingly adopted the Hollywood publicists' approach of denying or closely monitoring the access of journalists to musicians (Forde, 2001b).

The concept of 'cultural intermediary' has been widely used in media studies. It was first used by Pierre Bourdieu in the late 1970s to define a subset of a 'new petite bourgeoisie' employed in the industries of 'presentation and representation' (Bourdieu, 1984: 359). The original study embedded the cultural intermediary within a densely described French milieu and it has been pointed out that attempts to transplant the idea to British contexts have sometimes conflated this subset with the larger class fraction of which it a part (Hesmondhalgh, 2002: 53–4). Nevertheless, it remains a useful term for the journalistic interpretation of cultural products to their potential audience. It is particularly apt for those mediating practices that collude with the culture industries' definition of listeners as consumers. A prime example is the structure of numerous music magazine reviews sections as 'consumer guides', awarding each album reviewed marks out of ten or stars out of five.

The music journalist as 'cultural intermediary' also contributes to the broader processes of historicizing popular music (Thornton, 1990) and its 'legitimization' and 'canonization' (Regev, 1994). Indeed, Gestur Gudmunsson *et al.* (2002), drawing on Bourdieu's field theory, argue that the construction of a semi-autonomous field of rock journalism has played a key role in such legitimation. These processes are generally slow-paced and marked by the repetition and accretion of statements and judgements although Bernard Gendron has highlighted the explicit conflict over legitimization in the jazz field in the 1940s when critics stridently debated the merits of the new (bebop) and the old (Dixieland) (Gendron, 2002).

Reflecting on his own practice in the rock era, the veteran *Village Voice* 'consumer guide' reviewer Robert Christgau, has written that in the early 1970s 'it felt essential in a reflexively hierarchical cultural environment to argue that rock 'n' roll was 'art' every bit as worthy as the English lit of my baccalaureate and the jazz, classical and folk to which it was invidiously compared'(1998: 2). In the same vein, Jason Toynbee has described how a certain style or tone of music journalism was used in Britain to form the taste of readers and 'discipline' that taste by rhetorical means (Toynbee, 1993). That taste has generally taken the form of what has been called 'rockism', a term that highlights the elevation of the particular characteristics of 1960s rock music to become universal critical values across the diverse fields of popular music (see Fenster, 2002; Laing, 1997).

Professional ideologies

Even though music journalism is a specialist profession, it is closely linked to the written and spoken media as a whole. It has become a stepping-stone into the broader media for numerous personality writers and film-makers. More than one British national newspaper editor was formerly a music journalist and more than one US music writer became a film director. The historian of *Rolling Stone* even made the claim that 'among the nation's liberal arts community [former *Stone* writers] . . . have ascended to the positions of greatest influence. They have become the Establishment' (Draper, 1990: 13). A much smaller number of journalists have become successful as musicians – the most notable examples being Lenny Kaye, Michael Nyman and Neil Tennant.

The so-called 'new journalism' of the 1960s has been defined as one where ' personal involvement and immersion were indispensable to an authentic, full-blooded account of experience' (Pauly, 1990: 114). This ethos made an indelible mark on rock journalism in both the US and Britain. Instead of regarding themselves as journalists, critics or reviewers, many individuals preferred the term 'writers', thereby aligning themselves with creators of fiction rather than the reporters of facts. The most celebrated example remains the late Lester Bangs, the only rock writer to be the subject of a biography (DeRogatis, 2000) and to be portrayed in a Hollywood film (*Almost Famous* (2000), directed by former rock writer Cameron Crowe).

In Britain, the new journalism colonised music journalism when the writers Charles Shaar Murray and Nick Kent were recruited to *NME* from the 'underground' press in the early 1970s. Interviewed in 2000, Murray said:

> My heroes were Hunter S. Thompson, Tom Wolfe and the whole New Journalism trip. I love Raymond Chandler and Norman Mailer's political journalism . . . I was reading a lot, writing an awful lot and doing terrifying amounts of speed, biker sulph, like snorting razor blades off a toilet floor.
>
> (Gorman, 2001: 177).

In the 1970s, the provocations of this first generation of British new journalism-influenced writers had a salutary shock value. True to their underground press roots, they were obsessed with excoriating the record industry that supported their magazines financially through advertising. Murray recalled that 'we despised the record industry, gave not even two hoots for the sensitivities of our publishers or the profits of their shareholders' (Gorman, 2001: 183).

So traumatic was this eruption of the values of new journalism and counter-cultural rebellion that the mainstream of popular music journalism (at least in Britain) has never recovered from it. In the early twenty-first century, reviewers and critics in the general and specialist press reprised the aggressive rhetoric of Murray and his contemporaries, but in a very different cultural and commercial environment.

Reviews and interviews

For more than half a century, the key forms of music journalism have been the review and the interview.

Music journalists regularly review recordings (albums, singles, DVDs) and performances (individual gigs and festivals). Some publications will also review broadcasts and books. The ethos of the reviewer ranges from traditional criticism to consumer advice. The first pole involves the disinterested judgement of an artefact or event against objective standards, the second a 'value for money' guide. Although it is sometimes assumed that the consumer guide is a relatively recent innovation, the *Gramophone* magazine introduced a rating system for popular music recordings in 1924: two stars for a first-class disc, one-star for an inferior one (Welburn, 1985: 123).

The characteristics of the typical contemporary popular music review are similar to those defined by Wyatt and Badger as 'evaluative journalism' where judgements are presented 'in a highly individualistic and self-conscious style' and readers form a relationship with such reviewers that 'may involve trust, or, in some cases, antipathy, after an audience member comes to know the tastes and prejudices of the critic' (Wyatt and Badger, 1990: 361).

With 'tastes and prejudices' derived from the New Journalism and 'rockist' ideologies of the 1970s, much current journalism condemns artists not for the quality of their music but because of the real or imagined fans they attract. Reviews published in the British national newspapers *The Guardian* and *Independent on Sunday* between 2002 and 2004 included such comments as 'middle-paced, middle-brow, middle-class, this is barely music' (on Dido's multi-million selling album *Life For Rent*) and (on Norah Jones) 'she makes the sort of music that middle managers from Basingstoke put on in the background when they think they're going to get their leg over'. Elsewhere, the response to rapper Ice T's praise for Phil Collins was that 'when hip-hop and R&B artists turn their attention to rock music, they appear to be seized by a madness that destroys their sense of good taste'. For another reviewer, Collins was 'rock's archetypal double-glazing salesman' and 'he never strains for the outlandish gesture. Instead he is Hounslow Man personified' (for the faux-bohemian rock 'n roll rebels that contributed these reviews, Basingstoke and Hounslow are metonyms for the despised suburbs).

It is not coincidental that a high proportion of artists dismissed automatically by these contemporary rock critics are female. Helen Davies and others have valuably catalogued the explicit sexism of much mainstream music journalism (Davies, 2001), while Kembrew McLeod has shown how the choice of adjectives to praise or condemn music is itself gendered (McLeod, 2002).

The interview is the second principal form taken by music journalism. While our knowledge of the history of jazz, blues and folk musics has been largely dependent on the oral testimony of musicians, with a few exceptions, the popular music press interview does not belong to this tradition. Instead, its roots lie in the print media associated with the film star culture generated by Hollywood movies in the 1930s and 1940s. This star culture operated with a dual notion of the actor as fictional screen character and 'real personality'. Since the realist or naturalistic mode of film-making called for the actor to simulate a psychologically 'real' individual on-screen, fan adulation included the desire to know what the star was like 'off-screen'. This led to a genre of articles purporting to reveal the habits and tastes of the 'real life' Ava Gardner or Clark Gable.

As popular music grew in importance, its specialist press adopted this already debased formula. With few exceptions (notably some *Rolling Stone* interviews of the 1960s and articles in the technical press concerning performance or composition techniques) subsequent generations of music journalism has focused on portraying musicians as personalities rather than artists. A music journalist from the *Washington Post* admitted that the popularity of the interview format is due to the fact 'it is easier to write about personalities than art' (Geoffrey Himes, quoted in Weinstein, 1999), something confirmed by the British writer Steve Sutherland in the introduction to an interview published in *Melody Maker* in 1985:

> Why am I squirming? Here's my problem: the Cocteau Twins can't talk
> about their music because there's nothing to say and I can't write about
> it because, as it's instrumental with vocal expressions, all I can produce
> is mind's eye gibberish.

In this context, Frank Zappa was once quoted as saying that 'rock journalism is people who can't write interviewing people who can't talk for people who can't read' (Botts, 1980: 74). And because many musicians wish to be known for their art rather than their personality, the interview often becomes the site of a power struggle where the journalist strives to uncover some hidden truth of a musician's 'personality'. In a parody of hard-boiled detective fiction, Charles Shaar Murray once unconsciously underlined this fact by writing up a 1974 interview with Elton John as if it were an interrogation: 'we tie Elt to his chair, shine bright lights into his eyes and start asking all them tough hard-hitting questions' (Murray, 1991: 53).

As early as 1965, Bob Dylan reacted against the personality interview in an exchange with the hapless Lawrie Henshaw of the British weekly magazine *Disc*. Asked, 'What would you say has been the greatest influence on your life?' Dylan replied with irony: 'You ! Your paper happens to influence me a lot.' Followed by a direct attack: 'I don't want to be interviewed by your paper. I don't need it. You don't need it either.' Dylan continued with some advice for *Disc* that was prescient in its description of the motivation of much of music press interview practice:

> You can build up your own star. Why don't you just get a lot of money and bring some kid out here from the North of England and say: 'we're gonna make you a star. You just comply with everything we do. Every time you want an interview, you can just sign a paper that means we can have an interview and write what you want to write. And you'll be a star and make money!
>
> (Mabey, 1969: 169)

Conclusion

In the period since the rise of rock 'n' roll, popular music journalism has played an important part in the production and circulation of meanings, judgements and inter-pretations of music. It has contributed in particular to the recognition of the new emergence of multi-channel satellite broadcasting and the availability of music on the Internet has already substantially lessened the influence of the music journalist as a cultural intermediary. The persistence of outdated critical ideologies has further isolated much music journalism from mainstream audiences and traditional print media music journalism faces an uncertain future in the twenty-first century.

Popular music, gender and sexuality

Introduction to Part Nine

■   Jason Toynbee

RESEARCH INTO GENDER AND SEXUALITY in popular music now ranges very wide indeed. The contributions in Part Nine deal with just part of the range, in effect mapping two broad positions on the politics of gender. In the first place, there is an argument that popular music represents patriarchal society in microcosm. Guitar-toting men hold the desirable high ground of authentic rock 'n' roll, and women are either excluded or have to fight their way through against all the odds. This critical feminist position can then be contrasted with what might be described as a redemptive approach. Here the emphasis is on showing how women may, paradoxically, be empowered within the existing structures of rock and pop.

This distinction in the literature is an important one, yet it would be wrong to put too much stress on it, for, as it turns out, the redemptive approach is critical too. Women may have gone a certain way towards establishing their own values and space in popular music, but invariably a qualification is made by writers who suggest this, to the effect that the struggle is far from over. By the same token, critical feminists usually mention the achievements made by women and point out how far they have already advanced over hostile terrain.

Mavis Bayton does this. Her chapter on the subject of constraints analyses the material factors that hold back girls and young women who want to make rock music. These include the difficulties of getting access to equipment and transport, but also the lack of private space in which to rehearse. Just as significant a constraint is women's limited ability to move through public space, in particular the after-dark urban landscape that provides the setting for rock culture and performance. Here, the threat of violence, both real and imagined, represents a significant deterrent to the involvement of women and girls. Another, intangible, yet in practice utterly material factor comes in here. The time of female musicians is much more tightly controlled than is the case with their male counterparts. Girls are pressed to stay in the house to a much greater extent, while boyfriends and husbands make consider-able demands on the time of partners, and tend to resent their participation in bands.

If the foresaid seems to paint a bleak picture, the testimony of the musicians who Bayton has interviewed suggests that, despite these problems, girls and young women *are* setting up bands and making music. 'Frock rock' (a phrase Bayton uses for the title of her book) actually exists.

The second piece is concerned with music-making too, but here the focus is on one particularly militant moment in women's music-making. Joanne Gottlieb and Gayle Wald give an account of the Riot Grrrl movement which emerged in the US during the late 1980s and early 1990s. How, they ask, have the music makers in this scene managed to produce a subculture and style using the uncongenial raw materials of rock. The answer, they suggest, is that these women subvert 'a tradi-tionally masculine rock performance position' by using a variety of tropes. One example is the scream. This is a sound that signifies righteous feminine anger, fear of rape yet also orgasmic delight. The ambiguity and emotional oscillation that result profoundly disturb rock's male order.

In one sense, Gottlieb and Wald are redemptive feminists. Riot Grrrl represents powerful women in the ascendant who, momentarily at least, find new ways of imag-ining themselves, new ways of signifying this identity. Yet at the same time the authors show rock's deeply macho structure of feeling, and the massive obstacles that women face in trying to work through it. If this is revolution, as their title suggests, then its outcome is by no means certain.

For Susan Fast, conversely, rock's structure of feeling as it already exists is relatively open, and susceptible to reworking by women. Using a bank of interviews she has conducted with female Led Zeppelin fans (and with some male subjects as well), Fast builds up a picture of an active, interpretive community. The women in it construct the band members and their music in a spiritual, tender, as well as sexual fashion. Not only do these women subject Led Zeppelin to a 'female gaze' – Fast is here switching around the important formulation of the 'male gaze' by film theorist Laura Mulvey – they also exert material power over the band: to an extent, Plant and co. dress and perform *for* them.

Fast's account is especially compelling because of the variety of methods she uses: an analysis of her own responses as a fan and in turn of her interview material, then musicological and visual analysis of Led Zeppelin performances. This multi-method research work enables a kind of 'triangulation', whereby the phenomenon being studied is investigated from different angles. The result is a much fuller under-standing than might be achieved using just one method, and suggests, by the way, just how far interdisciplinary approaches have progressed in popular music studies.

Gottlieb and Wald posit militant riot grrrls engaged in a symbolic guerrilla campaign. For Fast, women fans of Led Zeppelin are active interpreters and shapers able to create feminised meanings from the performances of this apparently macho man's band. However, Maria Pini's view of the politics of popular music and gender has another emphasis again. In her study of women and British rave culture, she argues that although some of the women she has interviewed experience this new dance scene as a 'text of danger', the predominant view from female participants is that rave is open and brings a strong ethos of collective identity. This can be contrasted with their perception of the conventional 'cattle market' disco which is organised around the pick-up and male sexual predation.

In fact, the kind of female empowerment at stake in Pini's analysis differs significantly from that characterised by the other women writing in Part Nine. Where Fast's Led Zeppelin fans appropriate images of men and male performance, rave, according to Pini, has no performers except the dancers. The latter are anyway oriented towards one another rather than an on-stage spectacle. Women ravers can also be differentiated from riot grrrls. If both groups are participants in social movements, these are of quite distinct complexions. As Gottlieb and Wald argue, riot grrrl is explicitly political, and the bands from that scene have what amounts to a programme for asserting riot grrrl values and subverting macho rock posturing. Rave, however, repudiates any notion of a political project. Dancing and losing yourself in submission to the beat is the only goal. As one of Pini's informants, Caroline, puts it, '[y]ou don't need *think*. You just *feel*. You have to just get into *feeling* the energy and all the things going on around you' (original emphasis). In rave, then, participants work towards a fusion of body and mind. Or better, Pini suggests – and adopting Donna Haraway's conception – this is a cyborgian body that is integrated in the technological apparatus of the dance club. Lights and beats and dancing bodies are all part of the same 'circuit'. Paradoxically, it seems that Pini's women ravers escape from the subordination of their gendered roles in everyday life through a *reduction* of agency and a temporary loss of individual subjectivity.

Our last piece, by Richard Smith, at first sight seems to be doing quite different things from the other chapters in Part Nine. Smith acutely describes an enduring pop tradition: the 'unmanly' male performer. Tracing the lineage of this back to Rudolph Valentino in the 1920s, Smith focuses on several key performers who are both strongly effeminate and adored by female, and often middle-aged, fans. Liberace, who appeared in the 1950s, is perhaps the most extraordinary example. Widely derided in the press, pianist and singer Liberace was flamboyantly and excessively camp, as well as being gay in real life. Yet he was adored by women fans, 'receiving over a dozen marriage proposals a week' at the height of his fame.

What lay behind this attraction? Smith proposes that it was ambivalence. On the one hand Liberace was seen as a mummy's boy, and a suitable subject of maternal care and affection. On the other hand, his very campness enabled him to become an object of female sexual desire. What is at stake here, Smith suggests, is not homosexuality as such, so much as 'homosexual-ness'. Indeed, several leading exponents of the 'unmanly man' tradition such as Barry Manilow are not gay at all.

One implication of this argument is that sexuality (having to do with bodily desire) and gender (deriving from social role) are much less clear-cut categories than has been previously assumed. Rather, they blur into one another, or else intersect in complex and paradoxical ways as in the case of pop's unmanly men. This suggests that Smith is actually quite close to the sort of politics of gender and sexuality espoused by the authors of the earlier pieces in Part Nine. In all of them, what is raised is the issue of the instability of apparently 'fixed' roles and hence too of gendered power in popular music. It is this that makes popular music such an important site of struggle.

Chapter 39

Mavis Bayton

WOMEN MAKING MUSIC
Some material constraints

SUBCULTURAL THEORISTS (HALL AND JEFFERSON, 1976) took for
granted young people's ability to choose what to do in their leisure time, and
thus merely addressed the question of how their choices should be interpreted. In
contrast, Frith (1981) argued that different leisure patterns are a reflection, not so
much of different values, as of the different degrees of opportunity, restriction, and
constraint that are afforded to different individuals and social groups. A particular
leisure pursuit may be made easy or difficult for an individual according to their
social structural position, gender (along with class, 'race', etc.) being one aspect of
such societal location. Frith [(1981) argues] that, for everyone, leisure, consumption, and style involve a relationship between choice and constraint. I wish to argue
that such constraints are crucial to the explanation of women's absence from rock.
I shall be considering the degree to which gender operates within the different social
classes. One thing which stands out, however, is the extent to which girls and young
women in all social classes and ethnic groups are restricted in their leisure pursuits
compared to boys/young men.

[. . .]

Money

Despite widespread myths, the gender gap in average earnings has stayed fairly constant in real terms since 1971. Because of the persisting sex segregation of occupations and 'deskilling', equal pay legislation has made little difference so that, in the
1990s, women in both manual and non-manual occupations earn, on average, about
half as much 'independent' gross income as men and in most heterosexual couples
the male partner earns more than the female (*Social Trends*, 26, 1996). [. . .] Moreover, market researchers Fisher and Holder (1981) found that in their large and

statistically representative sample, twice as many boys as girls had a part-time job and that, therefore, the boys were better off. Schoolgirls had to rely mainly on pocket money – to buy clothes, make-up, bus and train fares, club and disco entrance fees, and drinks – which left little for a set of strings, let alone a guitar. Playing in a rock band is a fairly expensive hobby. Costs include: the purchase of instruments and ancillary equipment, strings, drumheads, repair bills, transportation, hire of rehearsal space, etc., and the more you get into playing the more aspirations rise and the more costs escalate. My argument is that women are less able to afford these outgoings.

Equipment

> I always had ideas of being in a band, but I never had the opportunity of doing anything about it, really. In the back of my mind I'd always wanted to do something like that. But where would you get electric guitars from, and things like that?
>
> Aimee Stevens, from the band, Frances Belle

Young women typically lack access to rock equipment because parents and schools do not provide it and girls lack the money to purchase their own. Moreover, where equipment is, sometimes, provided (for example, at youth clubs) boys tend to take it over. The reason for this is that instruments are gender stereotyped. [. . .] Indeed, instruments have often been portrayed anthropomorphically as 'Felicity the flute', 'Tubby the tuba', and so on. Because they are classified as 'male', parents, teachers, and male peer groups deny girls access to rock instruments.

> That's another thing about parents. They think that you're going to be 'hard' as well. They want you to be girly. They think as soon as you say 'electric guitar', 'No, that's for boys'. They think you're going to change, as well . . . I think my mum would just prefer me to play the violin because it's feminine and she says, 'You've had all these classical chances, we've paid for you to do this, and now you go and play that noisy instrument.' Things like that.
>
> Terri Bonham (Frances Belle)

[. . .]

Transport

Because young women are less likely to own a car than are men, they will be dependent on someone else (often parents) for their physical mobility. This is particularly the case for girls living in rural areas: 'Parents. That's how we'd get around. [. . .] It was the only way we could, because there are no buses at nights' (Terri Bonham). Frances Belle were lucky. Adolescents rely greatly on their parents transporting them to and from their various leisure activities but parents are less likely to approve of their daughter's involvement in a rock band than in dancing classes or a swimming club. Lack of money and transport forces many women to rely on men, boyfriends being used for lifts and the loan of equipment, a dependency that gives considerable power to the men in such relationships. Here we have in microcosm the situation in the wider society: women's lack of material resources creates their lack of social power.

Space

In general, in our society, women (especially working-class ones) have less access to space than men. They take up a smaller physical area by the way they sit and use their bodies and there are fewer 'female' spaces.

Lack of private space

Schoolgirls, or young women living at home, are unlikely to have much space, yet they often cannot afford to move out. Louise Hartley (Kid Candy):

> When we do gigs I have to borrow amps, because I haven't got room in the house for any. At home I can't make a lot of noise. My parents like silence and I really don't have the space.

Working-class girls are allowed less space than their brothers within the home (Leonard, 1980), which makes parents' attitudes crucial. How far will they allow the living room to be taken over by the noise and clutter of rock? Once married, the husband may have a study or workshop, but the wife's space is often defined as 'public' – the kitchen, the bedroom – and invaded by husband and children. Women with pre-school children are mostly tied to the home. How would such women meet others with whom to organize a band? And if they did meet them, how would they be able to arrange their lives in order to be able to rehearse and do gigs?

Exclusion from public space

The provision and use of public spaces reflects the inequality of leisure between men and women. So-called 'public' space is actually dominated by men, as is first learnt at school, where the boisterous activities of boys monopolize the playground and force girls to the edges, in a similar way to which they marginalize girls within the classroom and claim the greater part of the teachers' time. [. . .] (Lucy Green's (1997) research shows that music teachers still typically perceive girls to be musically inferior to boys, a fact that must surely translate itself into expectations and create a self-fulfilling prophecy.) It is not that girls are generally less confident in their lives. For instance, girls are more confident about singing and dancing than are boys. Playing supposedly masculine instruments works to undermine their femininity and this is why they feel unsure of themselves. [. . .] Likewise, the space in which rock music is situated is male-dominated, music shops affording a particularly interesting example. Although some male musicians have told me that they feel anxious trying out equipment, the fact that both customers and assistants are overwhelmingly male means that music shops are their preserve, and, there-fore, boys are more at home than girls. In any of these shops you can observe the assertive way in which young males try out the equipment, playing the beginning of a few well-known songs time and again, loudly and confidently, even though this may be the sum total of their musical knowledge. [. . .] [Aimee Stevens of Frances Belle described her experience as follows:]

> I feel very intimidated. Especially going to ask – they're all stood behind the counter, these massive metal blokes. Well, that's what they look like, judging by their image. I go up and go, 'Can I have a top E string?' because I don't know the proper names or anything, so it's even worse. And they go, What gauge? What sort?' And I'm like, 'I don't know. So I don't like going in and looking at guitars or anything in music shops. . . . When you're trying they're just staring at you. If you don't know much as well – and then they pick it up and go [imitates complicated guitar playing] and you're going, 'Oh no. I'll just take that.'

Experienced players [such as Fran of Sub Rosa] related tales of condescension and patronization:

> You go in and all the blokes are sitting in one corner talking about some riff that they came up with last night, totally ignoring you. They are very patronizing. They see that you're a woman and they think, 'How did you dare come in our music shop?'

More than one interviewee told me that, if a woman guitarist goes into a shop with a man, the assistants tend to talk to the man not the woman, even if the man is not actually a guitarist. Delia (of Mambo Taxi) confessed that she adopts the strategy of pretending to know less than she does because then the assistants are more helpful.

Frith (1981) argued that leisure in general is perceived to be a male preserve, the 'private' realm of the home being a female domain. He argued that girls, especially in the working class, spend far more time inside the home than do boys, and that they are more closely integrated into family life, whereas boys, encour-aged to model themselves on their fathers, spend more time outside the home. This means that girls are less likely than boys to go to gigs, and even less likely to become members of rock bands.

However, the main way in which women's leisure is controlled by men is through the fear of violence. [. . .] Over 50 per cent of women feel unsafe when walking home at night compared to only 16 per cent of men, and rape is the crime that most worries women in their teens and twenties in England and Wales (British Crime Survey, 1994, reported in *Social Trends*, 26, 1996). Although, in reality, women are far more likely to be attacked in their home and by someone they know, research has shown that large numbers of women are afraid to go out alone at night. Indeed, concern about violence determines the leisure patterns of women, especially after dark and where transport is poor (Green *et al.*, 1990). [. . .] Avoidance procedures are learnt from early adolescence. As women also have to be careful what they wear (for fear of 'provocation'), many female musicians feel that they have to change clothes to get to and from the venue. Sixteen-year-old Charlotte Clark usually travels to and from the gig by bus in her stage clothes (a see-through lace dress) and this has been a very scary experience. Thus, women live under a partial curfew that men find very difficult to understand as, although they are more at risk from violence than women, men are rarely killed simply because they are men. The fact that some men sexually attack women means that public spaces become male terrain.

[. . .]

If the world of leisure poses threats for women, that is particularly true of pubs. This phenomenon has been most fully explored by Valerie Hey who states that public houses have never actually been public for women, but are 'male "playgrounds" to which women are "invited" on special terms' (Hey, 1986: 3). [. . .] The masculine tradition of drinking and making coarse jokes usually focuses on the 'dumb sex object', the 'nagging wife' or, more derogatively, 'horny dogs' and 'filthy whores'. Learning to be masculine invariably entails learning to be sexist: being a bit of a lad and being contemptuous of women just go 'naturally' together (Lees, 1993: 31).

In general, then, it can be argued that male domination of leisure space, coupled with the dual standard of sexual morality, operates to exclude women from the world of rock. In particular, male control of drinking places has particular relevance for young women and rock, for pubs are the most common venue for gigs.

[. . .]

The regulation of female play

Parental restrictions

Girls living at home are under pressure to conform to constraints imposed by parents. Staying in more than boys and getting home earlier at night, they are not allowed out just anywhere and with anyone: companions and destinations are vetted for reputation. Clearly, this higher level of social control is based on the real dangers already discussed. [. . .]

The sort of venues where local gigs are held would be considered unsuitable by many parents, especially middle-class ones who would perceive joining a band as a serious threat because the rock world is peopled mainly by men, associated with sex, drugs, and late hours. Apart from doing gigs, being in a band is inseparable from a shared social life with other band members. If a young woman cannot join in with all this she will not be treated as a full and equal member of the band and her commitment will be questioned.

These kinds of restrictions were mentioned by a number of my interviewees. 'Kassandra''s (upper-middle-class) parents used to lock her in the house to prevent her from going out to rock venues. Annette was a black working-class 20-year-old living at home, whose mother considered playing percussion to be degrading, whereas it was seen as all right for Annette's brother to be in a band. This gender-specific protective attitude is laid on top of a general concern which parents have for their children to get well-paid, secure jobs. This was true of my 1990s school students, as well as my 1980s interviewees.

[. . .]

I just think parents are more inclined to give sons freedom, because if you have a daughter she can't wander round on the streets at night. I mean, if it's still daring for boys to do that anyway, but it doesn't seem that way. I think parents are more protective over their little girl than their little boy.

Miriam Cohen, Kid Candy

However, as parental constraints are also to do with getting girls to conform to gender-appropriate behaviour, the range of activities and hobbies considered 'suitable' for girls is considerably narrower than for boys (Leonard, 1980). Since rock music-making is seen as a 'male' domain and rock musician a 'male' role, parents discourage their daughters from getting involved in it.

Boyfriends' and husbands' constraints

Boyfriends are much more significant in the lives of girls than vice versa and constitute an actual or potential constraint on young women's music-making. A young woman already in a band may acquire a new boyfriend who, while admiring her musicianship, may still encourage her to leave. I encountered women who had experienced this. Many young women are dissuaded by their boyfriends from band participation right from the start. Why is this? First, the boyfriend may think it inappropriate that his girlfriend should be seen as more important than himself in the eyes of others. Many males in this situation feel that they are only seen as so-and-so's boyfriend – the 'I'm with the band' syndrome. Men may resent the perceived 'femininity' of such a role. Second, many men feel that being able to cope with all the knocks and strains, both physical and mental, which it entails is 'masculine', whereas a 'real' woman needs a man to shield her from such situations. Third, men often think that they can or could do it better than women, which explains the phenomenon of men jumping up on stage at the beginning, middle, or end of gigs and trying to take over the equipment, mostly ones with negligible skills, their misplaced confidence coming merely from being male (and usually drunk). Fourth, a man may feel threatened sexually by his girlfriend's public exposure to other men's eyes. Marion Asch's first husband, tormented by jealousy and possessiveness, tried to prevent her going abroad on tour with the Mission Belles.

[. . .]

[Conversely, a] number of the married women I interviewed said that being in a band (and earning money from it) was the only way they were allowed to get out of the house, conjugal norms which may also be reinforced by the wider family and local community. [Terry Hunt of Jam Today explained:]

> 'Do you go on tour? Oh. How does your boyfriend feel about that?' I've never [heard] them ask that question of male musicians. It is accepted. But they find it really freaky, the idea of women going off and touring on their own.

[. . .]

Many other women musicians [such as 'Kassandra' of the 1980s new wave band] I interviewed made similar comments:

> Women who've got relations with men tend to wrap themselves around men, tend to live their lives around men, so that they've got less space to develop themselves. So, [to become a female musician] you either need a gay woman, or a woman who has come to the conclusion in her life that she's going to dedicate her energy to something, no matter what.

Exclusion by male musicians

Rock is associated with youth, and research shows that a major preoccupation of young men is establishing their 'masculinity', which exaggerates these so-called masculine traits (Fisher and Holder, 1981). Moreover, masculinity and femininity are relational, each only making sense in terms of its opposite. The very 'masculinity' of activities can only be maintained by the exclusion of girls: 'In order to develop a masculine identity a boy needs to dissociate himself from all that is feminine. He needs to denigrate girls in order to dominate them' (Lees, 1993: 301). It is in their younger teens that most male rock musicians start playing in bands so that it is hardly surprising that girls are excluded, since to have one on drums would undermine rock's latent function of conferring masculine identity on its participants. It is precisely because of the fragility of adolescent gender identity that so much 'work' is invested in patrolling the ideological boundaries (by name-calling, boasting, and so on). Girls fulfil the role of 'outsiders'.

If a young woman does acquire a rock instrument and express an interest in joining a band, she may find that no one wants to play with her, which is what happened to Alison Rayner (of Jam Today), who had wanted to play in a band since the age of 12 years:

> I couldn't think who I could play with. The boys at home . . . wouldn't play with me, because they wouldn't have a girl in their band. I was too young to approach older people about it. I had the electric guitar for about two or three years and didn't actually have anybody to play with.

All-women bands may be formed for a number of reasons, from feminist politics to an opportunist strategy for commercial success, but some women who started playing in their teens set up all-women bands simply because male bands would not accept them. For instance, Enid Williams (of Girlschool) started playing with other women when she was 14 years old, although not for ideological reasons:

> I've played in a lot of all-women bands. It was always an all-women band at that time. And that came about because the men we knew who played in bands weren't interested in playing with us.

[. . .]

Jackie Crew of Jam Today explained her experience as follows:

> Quite often the musicians you come into contact with when you first start are men. I've found it's very hard to get them to show you things. They're very reluctant to part with their bits of information and know-ledge. And they'll show you it all fast and say. That's how it goes'. And you say, 'Could you show me it a bit slower?' and they go, 'Oh!' As often as not they can't play it slower. They only know that little bit and that's how they do it. Then you try it a couple of times. And when you can't do it, they say, 'Oh, well. You can't do it yet.'

Conclusion

I have presented a whole range of factors which, I believe, explain the relative absence of women from bands. I have not attempted to prioritize them, because they are interrelated in subtle and complex ways and, typically, more than one is in operation at the same time in the life of an individual woman.

Chapter 40

Joanne Gottlieb and Gayle Wald

SMELLS LIKE TEEN SPIRIT
Riot grrrls, revolution, and women in independent rock

I**N THE METEORIC RISE OF QUINTESSENTIAL** Seattle grunge band Nirvana from indie obscurity to corporate rock fame, a rumor emerged among rock circles nationwide: that the cryptic title of their megahit 'Smells Like Teen Spirit' was the invention not of Nirvana lead singer Kurt Cobain, but of his neighbor Kathleen Hanna, who jokingly scrawled it on the wall of Cobain's house prior to his ascension to rock stardom [Arnold, 1992]. From this one gesture and its retelling ensue multiple ironies, dizzying in their cumulative effect. First, the anecdote hints at the creative invisibility of a woman behind what was to become a ubiquitous, industry-changing, Top 10 hit for a male rock group. The story additionally implies the male appropriation of Hanna's own ironic reference to a brand name deodorant marketed to teenage girls (Teen Spirit). While the pointedness of Hanna's reference gets lost in Nirvana's translation, she uses a brand name which itself conjures not of female teenage identity, group activity and group solidarity; in short, in an ambiguous use of 'teen' which actually refers specifically to female teens 'Teen Spirit' creates a marketable fantasy of female youth culture. Moreover, in contrast to her previous invisibility, Hanna now suddenly occupies a position of mass visibility as lead member of Bikini Kill, a band that has gained particular prominence, both within the independent music scene and in the corporate rock press, for its role in fostering the Riot Grrrl 'movement' of young feminist women in underground rock. Given these origins, Henna's slogan consolidates several themes that we propose to explore in this essay: namely, girl-specificity within commodity culture and youth subculture; the historical invisibility of women in rock; the newfound prominence of women bands; the relation between performance gender and sexuality; and the possible links between women's musical production, feminist politics and feminist aesthetics.

We will examine these themes in the context of the recent explosion onto the independent or underground rock scene of all-women bands or individual women artists making loud, confrontational music in the ongoing tradition of punk rock. The appearance of these bands and their widespread recognition in both the mainstream and alternative presses would seem to signal a heady change, one that situates the broadened access of girls and women to the transgressive potentialities of rock, and especially punk, subculture within the larger narrative of gains made by women in the wake of feminism. At best, this change promises to expand the possibilities for women's public self-expression, individual or collective gender identifications, and transgressive behaviors – at least within the bounds of white, middle-class culture in which this scene is primarily staged. The recent visibility of women in rock not only signals greater access for women to male-dominated realms of expression, but also specifically frames these expressions in terms of femininity and feminism. [. . .]

[. . .]

Our optimism is tempered, however, by two crucial observations: first, despite the advances of particular female performers, the ongoing tradition of rock is still deeply masculinist; and second, because of patriarchal restrictions, the youth cultures of girls historically have been defined by very different parameters from those of boys. As a result of this second circumstance, girls may have different access to the expression of, or different ways of expressing, nascent teenage sexuality and rebellion against parental (that is, patriarchal) control, two themes that predominate not only in rock music, but in the formation of Western teenage identity in general. The conjunction of these two terms intimates that the forms of resistance offered by rock culture are closely linked with the music's frank expressions of sexuality.

This means that rock 'n' roll is a potentially, though by no means an inherently, feminist form; indeed, among male punk and hardcore performers, there is a long tradition of this rebellion being acted out at the expense and over the bodies of women. [. . .]

Punk spawned a tradition of male bands semi-ironically naming themselves after exaggerated phallic symbols (Sex Pistols, Revolting Cocks, Dickies, Meat Puppets, Prong, Fishbone), as well as bands that identified themselves with distanced and objectified references to women, women's genitals, or women's sexuality (Mudhoney), from which they derive a certain self-conscious masculinity. Conversely, many of the new women's bands name themselves in response to a ubiquitous and negative vocabulary for the female body, calling themselves Hole, Burning Bush, Thrush, Queen Meanie Puss, Snatch, Pop Smear, Ovarian Trolley, and Dickless. Women bands have also employed names to communicate a succinct critique of masculinity, as in the names Pork, Thrust, Spitboy, and Weenie Roast. In one particularly interesting example, a band that used to call itself PMS later adopted the name Cockpit, combining references to both sexes. Self-naming here becomes a tactic not only of reclaiming and recirculating masculinist terms (and thereby depleting their potency), but also of outing or enabling women's uses of vocabularies otherwise forbidden to 'good' girls, who are never supposed to swear or speak to loudly in public, let alone refer explicitly to their genitals and what they do with them.

These bands find a precedent for their parodic self-naming in the example of the Slits, one of the greatest and earliest all-female punk bands of the late Seventies. This brings us to another aspect of the 'women in rock' phenomenon: despite its apparent novelty, its roots date back approximately fifteen years, with the emergence of women out of the 1970s punk movements in Britain and America. Women could participate in punk in part because the lack of musical experience – or even prejudicial beliefs about female musical incompetence – were relatively unimportant in punk, which rejected technical virtuosity and professionalism in favor of amateurishness, iconoclasm, and a do-it-yourself aesthetic. [. . .]

Before moving on to a specific consideration of the riot grrrl phenomenon, we want to explore the problematics of women in subculture, and specifically women in rock. To do so, we draw on two figures in British cultural studies: Simon Frith, who has written key texts on youth, music, and politics; and Angela McRobbie, who has worked on the culture of girls, and who has attempted a feminist rereading of male-authored theories of subculture. The study of the gendering of subculture helps in part to explain why girls historically have not participated as actively as boys in rock culture – both because of the patriarchal restrictions on girls, and because their pleasure and identity-formation, in response, tend to take a different form from those of boys. Social restrictions on girls, their limited access to the street, and their greater domestic role make the public spaces in which subcultures are acted out (clubs, the street, bars) prohibitive and exclusive for them. The street often poses a threat to girls and women, insofar as they are liable to male heckling, harassment or assault. Though women historically have participated in street culture as prostitutes, such access is nevertheless regulated by patriarchal ideologies that designate women sex-industry workers 'unfit' to occupy domestic roles. Therefore, while male youth culture is public, oriented around the street, girls' culture often takes forms that can be experienced within the home, such as dressing up, or engaging in the creative consumption of mainstream pop idols, including fan-oriented visual materials such as magazines, photographs and, most recently, videos.

The conclusions of Frith and McRobbie suggest that rock 'n' roll subculture is not the place to look for female participation, especially in terms of rock's production, and at first glance rock history seems to bear this out. In the past, when women have participated in rock culture, they have tended to do so as consumers and fans – their public roles limited to groupie, girlfriend, or backup singer, their primary function to bolster male performance. When women performed, Frith writes, it was 'almost always as singers, fronting a performance or record, their musical abilities confused with their visual images and style.' Frith accounts for the exclusion of women from rock production as part of an ideology of rock growing out of bohemian culture. Rock was a place for male friendship in a resistive unregulated life-style, where women represented unwelcome demands for 'routine living,' for the provision of money for food and rent [Frith, 1981: 85–7]. Moreover, rock culture, like other forms of oppositional culture that McRobbie describes, developed signifying systems that privileged masculinity, systems in which '[t]he meanings that have sedimented around other objects, like motorbikes or electronic musical equipment, have made them equally unavailable to women and girls' [McRobbie, 1991: 29].

[However,] [w]hen the traditional association of love and romance with popular music (as well as the association of sex with pleasure) came apart in punk, women's voices began to emerge, 'shrill, assertive, impure, individual voices, singer as subject not object [Frith, 1981: 243–4]. As punk performers, participating in a new way, these women 'brought with them new questions about sound and convention and image, about the sexuality of performance and the performance of sexuality . . . [P]unks opened the possibility that rock could be *against* sexism (Frith 1981, 244). What precisely are women punk rockers saying about the sexuality of performance and the performance of sexuality?

In order to answer this question, we need to look back to the what male rock performers have done – in other words, what male rock performance means. Women punk rockers emerged out of a decade of male rock experiments with gender, such as those of Gary Glitter or David Bowie. That is, the trajectory of (male) rock up through the late Seventies was marked by increasing androgyny and gender ambiguity. The male gender bending of Seventies glam-rock forms an important node in this history: breaking with the heterosexual romance paradigm of Elvis or the early Beatles, the glam-rocker elevated the erotica of performance to a high narcissism, alternately playing alien, outcast, deviant, prophet, high priest, and messiah. [. . .]

Glam-rock produced some freakish results in the form of heavy metal cock-rock, which attempted to recoup this performance tradition for masculinity. In this genre, glam's camp and sexual ambiguity became cockrock's baroque staging of a peculiar form of longhaired, becostumed hypermasculinity – a phenomenon easily parodied, for instance, in the documentary spoof film *This is Spinal Tap*. The progression from glam rock into cockrock (the masculinity of which is actually ambiguous and conflicted) suggests that within rock performance, there is a struggle with femininity that may stem from the feminine gendering of the performance position itself. [. . .]

[. . .]

Women performers [thus] go through complicated contortions as they both appropriate and repudiate a traditionally masculine rock performance position which is itself premised on the repression of femininity, while they simultaneously contend with a feminine performance position defined primarily as the erotic object-to-be-looked-at. These complexities are also played out historically. Although male experiments with gender did not translate into an equal flexibility for women, glam and disco helped to erode the necessary association of popular music with romance and heterosexuality, thereby preparing the way for female performance in punk rock. Introducing explicit homoerotics onto the rock stage, male glam-rockers – like their female punk successors – revealed the performativity of gender. Ironically, the same years which saw women emerge as punk artists also witnessed the establishment of a new cultural form – MTV. The advent of music video provided a space for women rockers based on traditional aspects of female musical performance – the visual and emotive connotations of the female vocalist [Lewis, 1990: 69]. A generation whose teenybop idols included for the first time women who displayed not only sexuality but also some degree of independence and sexual power, Riot Grrrl emerged from punk via Madonna.

If MTV provided multiple images of women rockers, including Madonna's street smarts and her easy assumption and rejection of various feminine roles, punk's staging of defiance and impropriety allowed female punk performers to negotiate the paradox of femininity on the rock stage by enacting transgressive forms of femininity, for instance, in frighteningly unconventional hair, clothing styles and stage activities. [. . .] In one of the most outrageous examples of the feminist appropriate and adaptation of male punk stage antics, one member of the band L7, in response to heckling from a male audience member at a concert in Boston in fall 1992, reportedly pulled down her pants, pulled out her tampon, and threw it at him. Aside from raising the question of what happens when women exercise their power in the form of an aggressive and confrontational expression of their sexuality, this act – a reverse rape? – takes the notion of a woman's being 'on the rag' and literally hurls it back at patriarchy.

[. . .]

In one response to the complexities and contradictions of their performance positions, women rockers, from Yoko Ono and Tina Turner and continuing up to Bikini Kill, have resorted to the strategic use of the scream, a radically polysemous nonverbal articulation that can simultaneously and ambiguously evoke rage, terror, pleasure, and/or primal self-assertion. In the examples of Ono and Turner, we link the female scream with two divergent musical traditions – the performance art tradition in which Ono was a germinal figure, and the R & B tradition embodied in Turner, especially in her role as a crossover artist. Gaar notes that 'shouting and screaming' figured highly in the R & B tradition from which Turner's musical style emerged (Gaar: 89). Screams work as linguistic signs, having no particular referent outside of the context in which they are uttered; the scream can be read as a kind of jouissance, a female body language that evades the necessity to signify within male-defined conventions and meanings. But far from being a fluid signifier, screams are also emotional ejaculations bearing specific associations with highly charged events – like rape, orgasm, or childbirth. Often associated with femininity at its most vulnerable, the scream in its punk context can effect a shocking juxtaposition of sex and rage, including the cultural terrors of the open expressions of female sexuality, or feminist rage at the sexual uses and abuses of women. If female screams are often associated with women's sexual violation and rape, then these examples seem to voice a collective outrage at such abuse. An attention-getting device, the scream publicizes private or internal experience. These girl screams, moreover, voice not only rage, but rage as pleasure, the scream as orgasm. Taken together, they seem to be suggesting something new – not just that women are angry, but that there's pleasure in their performances of anger, or even just pleasure in performance; the scream thereby replaces the pleasant, melodious and ultimately tame emotionalism traditionally associated with the female vocalist. Conversely, these screams can communicate a profound ambiguousness about consent and coercion, a fine line between orgasm and rape, as when Kat Bjelland of Babes in Toyland chillingly apposes the chanted phrases 'I'd love to/I had to' and punctuates them by a piercing 'Good God!' in the song 'Blood.' A form of expression both denied to women in public (screaming is unladylike) and devalued in private (women are so emotional), punk screams are a wordless protest against the overdetermined femininity that these female performers – performing *as* women – must occupy; the scream musters the energy of the whole body to burst these constrictions. Unruly and unexpected, these screams deploy punk values to violate the demand that women remain patient, uncomplaining, and quiet.

[. . .]

[In fact,] [i]nstead of tirelessly insisting on the right to be called 'women,' as mainstream feminism has long been advocating, riot grrrls foreground girl identity, in its simultaneous audacity and awkwardness – and not just girl, but a defiant 'grrrl' identity that roars back at the dominant culture. Indeed, reclaiming the word 'girl' and reinvesting it with new meaning within their own feminist punk vernacular has proved one of the most salient aspects of the riot grrrl revolution. Such a recuper-ation of patriarchal language in part reflects the subculture's celebration of preteen girlhood – indeed, precisely those years in girls' lives that Frith and McRobbie deem so crucial in understanding their ongoing relation to and participation within subculture, and the same years on which feminist theorists Carol Gilligan and Lyn Mikel Brown [1992] focus in terms of women's relation to society broadly defined. In their song 'Girl Germs,' for example, Bratmobile revel in the idea of their toxicity to boys/men; in the age of AIDS, they ironically relate germs to girls' self-protection and their ability to repel unwanted sexual advances. 'Germs' here also suggests 'germinal,' the potential girls have to develop into powerful women; alter-natively, it refers to girl-specific culture in its embryonic stages. While parody and wordplay are central to the riot grrrl redefinition of 'girl,' there is also, admittedly, a crucial element of fantasy in their self-construction – a nostalgia for the appar-ently close relationships between girls prior to the intrusion of heterosexual romance and its spin-offs, sexual competition, and sexual rivalry. (In Bikini Kill, for one, jealously is a favorite target of critique.) Bikini Kill's song 'Rebel Girl' asserts the importance of such girl solidarity as a response to the sexual commodification, cate-gorization and subsequent or resultant (self)-division of women: 'They say she's a slut,' they sing, 'but I know she is my best friend.' Most important in light of our earlier discussion of the journalistic labels that have come to define women in rock, the riot grrrls, in rewriting 'girl' as 'grrrl,' also incorporate anger, defiance, and rebellion into their own self-definition, construing female rage as essential and intrinsic to their collective punk identity.

Unlike some other women in the punk and postpunk alternative music scenes, riot grrrls draw upon their experiences of girlhood to emphasize female difference *in* concert *with* female equality. In other words, riot grrrls both assume women's equality and understand that it has not necessarily been efficacious in securing them recognition as 'legitimate' rock musicians.

[. . .]

The band Bikini Kill is in this regard both representative and exemplary. An essential part of their 'Revolution Girl Style' is their attempt to encourage young, predominantly white, middle-class girls to contest capitalist-patriarchal racism and sexism, precisely through acts of individual transgression against the implicit or explicit norms of 'ladylike' or 'girlish' behavior. The band links these individual challenges to private (that is, domestic, local, or familial) patriarchal authority to collective feminist resistance and struggle. McRobbie supports this notion in her suggestion that many middle-class girls' first political experiences involve escape 'from the family and its pressures to act like a "nice" girl' (32–3). Bikini Kill makes this connection between personal transgression and progressive feminist politics explicit in a song such as 'Double Dare Ya,' in which singer Hanna screams:

You're a big girl now
you've got no reason
not to fight
You've got to know
what they are
Fore you can stand up
for your rights
Rights rights Rights?
you have them, you know

[. . .]

[. . .] In concert, Hanna sometimes parodies Madonna, appearing on stage in a
black bra and biker shorts, the word 'SLUT' penned in across her abdomen. The
ways in which riot grrrls perform on and through their bodies reaffirms the very
themes articulated in their songs. The abuses of girls' and women's bodies are
constantly represented by riot grrrls, both in their music and zines; since such abuses
are generally associated with women's alienation from their bodies, the ability to
be embodied – the deployment of the body in performance – provides an antidote
to its previous violations. Not only do girls wield their bodies in performance, but
they do so in such a way as to make their bodies highly visible: this visibility coun-
teracts the (feelings of) erasure and invisibility produced by persistent degradation
in a sexist society. Such performance recuperates to-be-looked-at-ness as something
that constitutes, rather than erodes or impedes, female subjectivity.

In this respect riot grrrl performances build upon (and surpass?) the challenge
to the male gaze that Hebdige describes when he writes that female punks of an
earlier generation 'turned being looked at into an aggressive act.' [1983: 85]. The
current generation of riot grrrls derive their strategies from the first women punks,
who put on

> the conventional iconography of fallen womanhood – the vamp, the
> prostitute, the slut, the waif, the stray, the sadistic mistress, the victim-
> in-bondage. Punk girls interrupt[ed] the flow of images, in a spirit of
> irony invert[ed] consensual definitions of attractiveness and desirability,
> playing back images of women as icons, women as the furies of classical
> mythology.
>
> [ibid. 1983: 83]

The current generation work changes on the iconoclastic methods of early
female punks, replacing punk's angry masochism with a deep sense of abuse and a
stronger critique of patriarchy, and relating it ultimately to what happens, not only
in the street, but also in the home. Rather than reducing the political to issues of
self-esteem, riot grrrls make self-esteem political. Using performance as a political
forum to interrogate issues of gender, sexuality, and patriarchal violence, riot grrrl
performance creates a feminist praxis based on the transformation of the private
into the public, consumption into production – or, rather than privileging the traditionally male side of these binaries, they create a new synthesis of both.

Chapter 41

Susan Fast

RETHINKING ISSUES OF GENDER AND SEXUALITY IN LED ZEPPELIN

A woman's view of pleasure and power in hard rock

[. . .]

WHEN I FIRST BECAME ATTACHED TO 'IMMIGRANT SONG' at the age of fourteen, it had nothing to do with the band members (I didn't know who they were, let alone what they looked like; in fact, I recall that the lack of information about the band on album covers intimidated me somewhat), but rather the sound of the music. My parents and siblings were substantially older and so I felt a certain isolation from the rest of the family. I was a bit of a loner outside the home as well, the only social/academic circles I belonged to involved theater and music, and those of us interested in 'artsy' things were marked as other by those who fit more happily into the mainstream. My retreat from all of this was often the rec room in our basement: the home of the stereo and my burgeoning record collection. Listening to the energy and strength of 'Immigrant Song' was an incredibly empowering experience. I had no idea what the lyrics were – I could understand only snatches of them – but that riff, with its crisp octave snap that repeated at about the same rhythm as an energized heartbeat, its timbre so insistent and confident, the bass guitar pounding that rhythm into every part of my body, and Plant's majestic if incomprehensible proclamations: that song was where I wanted to live. Later, I began collecting all of Zeppelin's albums, books on them, and bootleg recordings. I came to identify with Robert Plant partly because I was in awe of his abilities as a singer (as an aspiring singer myself), but partly because I was sexually attracted to him. I am not sure that the two can be separated.

When I fantasized about knowing Plant and the rest of the band, two elements were always inextricably bound together: I was a musician of equal stature to them – as talented and commercially successful – and I was also beautiful and sexy and loved by them for that reason as well. In other words, my fantasy involved being powerful and attractive, and respected for both characteristics. I did not quite want to be Robert Plant, rather I wanted to be just like him in terms of his ability to sing and his success in practicing his art. This is similar to those responses Ehrenreich *et al.* reported from women fans of the Beatles in the mid-Sixties: appropriating the power of those performers for oneself was as important for some as was the sexual freedom they suggested (although the two are not inextricably linked in that study) (ibid. 1986: 36). And for some reason I thought that this was in the realm of possibilities, certainly not that it would be impossible because I was a woman. Perhaps this is because there were at least a few women who had already occupied such positions – Janis Joplin, Grace Slick, a little later Ann and Nancy Wilson of Heart and Stevie Nicks, for example – although I did not gravitate toward these women performers myself. For about six years I absorbed every drop of information I could about the band and listened to their music with pathological exclusivity because it was such a powerful, liberating, intellectual, sexual, and spiritual experience for me.

Of the 323 completed fan surveys I received [for the study discussed here], 248 were from males, 76 from females; they range in age from ten through fifty-nine and are in occupations that include professionals (doctors, dentists, lawyers, professors), business owners, artists, managers, laborers, retail sales clerks, computer programmers and consultants, and students. Most of the fans – male and female – who answered the questions on my survey relate similarly powerful experiences with the music. [. . .] Answers to several questions related to gender and sexuality reflect the complexity and depth of experience most avid fans have with the music and visual iconography. Responses generally reflect fans' knowledge of the entire repertory, not just a few songs (this is one of the problems with so many journalists and academics who write about the band), a variety of visual images of the band members, and what is known of the band's biography. While the majority of women acknowledge that they are sexually attracted to band members and find the music sexy, they tend to want to point out that there is more to their attachment than this, or that questions of gender and sexuality cannot be separated from the rest of the experience of the band, from the 'power' and 'emotion' of the music (which is in some cases equated with something they describe as elemental or 'primal' that operates at a 'deeper' level than the sexual), from the energy it gives to them and how they can experience the songs on various levels (and from my own experience, I would say that these can be experienced simultaneously). These women wrote:

> I'm not sure if I relate to it differently [because of gender]. The band as a whole is so powerful, the music so potent.

> I don't think I do. I'm a die-hard music fan and that is how I listen to all music. I'm very critical and I listen very carefully.

> Yes, as a woman I found them and their music quite sexy; however, the songs had interesting content, unlike some heavy metal/hard rock groups, whose songs were only about sex and pretty misogynistic sex, at that!

> Part of it is sexual . . . the band I mean . . . Robert Plant makes me have involuntary – non chemically induced – dreams of every fantasy I have ever had in my life . . . from sexual to religious. BUT – the music itself . . . I don't know how to describe it . . . the music makes the knots in my back muscles disappear. Moby Dick at full blast – or [the 1998

Page/Plant single] MOST HIGH!! — or No Quarter with or without John Paul Jones and/or Egyptians, at full volume on my car CD on the way home from work gives me strength to face the 'second shift' of washing, cooking and cleaning. And I am not Zombieing through being the 'Mom' and Hausfrau, daydreaming of 'Going to California . . .' Zeppelin is a better mood-altering drug than any chemical! . . . To steal a line from a preeminent baby boomer politician, ('It's the economy, stupid . . .') IT'S THE MUSIC, STUPID!!!!!! (. . . not meant to be ugly . . . just emphatic) . . . the difference between Zep and all the others is the RAW EMOTION in their music.

[. . .]

[. . .] Many comments concerning sexuality were made in response to questions other than the one asking about gender/sexuality specifically. For example, in response to my query, 'Your comments on Page's guitar solos,' several women remarked:

Better than sex.

He's having sex with his guitar and the audience.

Electric prolonged orgasms.

But these responses need to be balanced by the many that talked about the soulful or emotional quality of Page's solos:

Page's solos are definitely from the heart. Can be sloppy if he's not up to it, but when he's hot he's on fire! So emotional — baring his soul.

A part of his soul.

Very soulful.

LIVE, IF HE'S ON, UNEARTHLY, MAJICKAL, SOUL STEALING.

[. . .]

In answer to the question 'Which band member(s) do you identify with most closely and why?' 30 women said they identify most closely with Plant, 24 with Page, and 15 said they do not identify with any band member. The near-even split between women who identify with Plant and Page is interesting: one might have thought that the singer — the front man — would have been the overwhelming draw for women, but this is not the case (it might possibly have been different in the 1970s). Comments concerning why women fans identify with a certain band member are also revealing. In the case of Plant, only a handful of women mentioned his looks or sexiness as the reason for their identification; many, however, pointed to a range of other traits: his sensitivity, energy, charisma, aura, mysticism, his search for the unattainable, and the difficulties in his personal life (the loss of his five-year-old son, his near-fatal car accident), knowledge of which not only makes him more human, but gives him 'depth' and suggests a vulnerable man who might need gentle nurturing.

> I love Robert Plant the best. Because he is a really awesome singer and
> he seems so cool and a really cool, nice person to be around.

> Robert Plant. Because, like me, he always had a lot of responsibility.
> He was the leader, the decision maker, yet his life was so tragic.

Those who identified most closely with Page cited his interest in the occult or
mysticism, his outstanding musicianship (several of these women are guitar players
themselves – again, this was probably not the case when the band was together), or
his leadership in the band; several combined comments about his musicianship with
those that spoke about his sexiness, or the fact that they had a 'crush' on him.

[. . .]

Fan responses make it clear that normative gender identities with respect to Led
Zeppelin's music – gender identities that have become accepted as 'natural' – need
to be reevaluated. Under the paradigm heretofore constructed, there is no way to
account for these responses: for women who enjoy the machismo images of Plant,
who know the repertory as well as their male counterparts, who prefer the 'heavy'
songs over the more acoustically based ones, men whose concept of sexuality in the
music encompasses tenderness as well as the crude and 'heavy' side, and the messy
way in which issues of sexuality and gender are entangled with ideas concerning
spirituality, soul, and so on. One way of getting beyond rigid definitions of gender
is to invoke Judith Butler's concept of gender performativity. Butler writes that
'[the gendered body] has no ontological status apart from the various acts which
constitute its reality.' (1990: 116) In other words, we do not operate from a fixed
identity with respect to gender (or, I would add, anything else), but rather we
perform gender through our actions, actions that may appear contradictory and that
may cause us continually to rethink our understanding of what behaviors constitute
masculinity and femininity. I wish to explore this idea with respect to Led Zeppelin
further – to try to account for fan responses, including my own – by examining in
some detail both the visual iconography and the musical sounds of the band.

Visual iconography

[. . .]

[T]here is no question that on one level [visual] images [of the band] can be interpreted as representations of machismo and that men might identify with the display
of power; but female fan responses to these images, including my own, reveal
that they are also a source of erotic pleasure for women. I received no indication at
all from those who responded to the survey that this kind of iconography was ever
off-putting or frightening to women, even in the 1970s, as Frith and McRobbie
claimed, only that it was/is a source of pleasure for them. Women's erotic pleasure
at such imagery has not been much discussed; better than ten years ago Suzanne
Moore wrote that 'to suggest that women actually look at men's bodies is apparently
to stumble into a theoretical minefield which holds sacred the idea that in the
dominant media the look is always already structured as male' (Moore, 1988: 45).

At least in writing about rock music not much has changed. It seems [. . .] the idea that women do not generally enjoy sex, or that, even if they do, it is not very polite to acknowledge it, is still entrenched in our culture, enforced in the discourse on hard rock, perhaps, by men – or women – who are made uncomfortable by the notion of a woman confident and curious in her sexuality. I wonder how many of those reading the unabashed responses from female fans above stereotyped these women as 'loose,' or 'slutty'; or is it finally possible to understand their answers in the context of their lives as professionals, mothers, wives, and a whole host of other identities of which their erotic engagement with Led Zeppelin's music and imagery is one integral part?

In fact, the spectacle of male hard rock and metal performance is a powerful reversal of Laura Mulvey's theory of the male gaze (1989: 14–26). Mulvey argues that in mainstream film the woman is put on display for the visual pleasure of the male viewer; protagonists (heroes) are generally men, with whom male viewers also identify. One critique of Mulvey's now canonic theory was undertaken in *The Female Gaze*, a collection of essays that discusses various ways in which the woman viewer is catered to in popular culture (Gamman and Marshment, 1988). Regrettably, popular music is not discussed in any of the essays, but certainly in performances of so much rock music it is the male body that is displayed – as a symbol of masculine strength and power to male and female spectators, and as an object of erotic desire for female (and perhaps also male) spectators. [. . .] As [Judith] Butler theorizes, just because Page has a body that is 'culturally intelligible' as male does not mean that we must always understand the actions he performs as 'male'. Actions that are perceived as belonging to a feminine identity, or actions that cannot so unproblematically be assigned to male or female identities, can be written onto this 'male' body (Butler, 1990: 123). In a concert situation, these visual images may act to momentarily 'freeze the flow of action in moments of erotic contemplation' for both women and men, as Mulvey suggests that the image of a woman might in a film (1989: 19). [. . .] And, just as Mulvey argues that the act of males gazing at female screen stars as erotic objects is empowering, so I would argue that it is empowering for female fans to gaze at male rock stars – that, in fact, they know they exercise control over the way in which rock stars dress and act in order for them to attract women, and also that their gaze on these men offers them an opportunity to explore and express something important about their sexuality.

[. . .]

Erotic pleasure is, however, only one way in which these images of Page and Plant can be received, and again, it is unlikely that eroticism can be neatly separated out from various other responses. [. . .] [F]or me, Page's machismo poses are always uneasily negotiated through his slender, lanky frame, the delicacy of his features, the way in which he so often bends his body inward in collapse as he plays, materializing the general 'frailty' that journalistic writers have commented on, and, especially in early days, but even still to some extent, the child-like qualities of his face. Quite aside from the sometimes frilly or glittery clothes that he wore, or his curling-ironed long hair, his body, face, and elfin gestures (journalist Chris Welch once called them 'feline') (1977: 30) have an androgynous quality that is difficult to ignore. This is another reason why it is so important to examine individual artists

– in what but the most superficial way can Page's visual iconography compare to, say, that of Guns N' Roses guitarist Slash, to take an extremely contrasting example? Or how can the performance of gender by Elvis, Mick Jagger, Roger Daltrey, and Plant – the four performers that Frith and McRobbie (1990) lump together – be taken as the same in anything but the most superficial of ways? These alternative readings of Page's and Plant's visual iconography offer instances of various gendered identities being written onto the male body (what Butler calls 'figure to ground'), creating 'highly complex and structured production[s] of desire' (1990: 123).

[. . .]

Music

> My vocal style I haven't tried to copy from anyone. It just developed,
> until it became the girlish whine that it is today.
> Robert Plant (Young 1990: 47)

One of the most sexually explicit Led Zeppelin songs, in terms of both lyrics and music, is 'Whole Lotta Love.' Lyrically, the song is a cover of Willie Dixon's 'You Need Love,' which Plant, at least, knew from Muddy Waters's 1963 recording; musically, the two versions share a similar melodic line, but other than this, Zeppelin's version departs significantly from Waters's. [. . .] [Plant] sings the verses in a high range and even though he does not use falsetto (he almost never does), the sound he produces comes mostly from his throat: it is strained and he uses plenty of distortion. John Shepherd has suggested that the production of sound in the throat as opposed to 'deeper' within the body, and the strained sound of this kind of singing belie 'the tension and experiential repression encountered as males engage with the public world,' and that because the sound is produced in the throat, there is little of the body behind it: '"Macho" vocal sounds are, in a manner of speaking, "all mouth", all projection into the public world with little behind them.' (Shepherd, 1991: 170) [. . .] This way of viewing hardrock singing may also provide an answer to Simon Frith, who has wondered why intensity and sincerity in male rock singing has become equated with singing in a higher, strained register. Perhaps drawing on Shepherd, Frith concludes that this higher male voice does not have much of the body in it: 'It's as if in rock convention . . . the sexiest male voice is the least bodily' (1996: 195). But it is precisely this straining and the use of distortion that puts the body into the music, it is this through which we hear the body as container, spilling over its boundaries – or about to. Furthermore, this high male voice opens another interesting space for the consideration of gender performance. Robert Plant may joke about his voice becoming a 'girlish whine' in the quote above, but male fans have commented on this as a desirable attribute of his voice. One man wrote concerning Plant's voice 'Feminine. Sometimes. Gorgeous. Powerful. Perfect.' When I was a member of the Led Zeppelin Internet discussion list a few years ago, I was struck by a similar comment made by a male fan, in which he said that he liked Plant's voice best in 1969 because that was when he sounded most like a woman. And another male fan in a response on the questionnaire, said, '[His voice is] so raunchy, torrid and dramatic. No wonder women wanted to fuck him! And I'm a straight male writing these things!' [. . .] In fact, the moaning, screaming, and 'overflowing of channels' characteristic of hard-rock singing points very strongly to an emotional landscape that has traditionally (and also essentially) been associated with femininity.

[. . .]

While Shepherd's location of gender and sexuality in singing styles is a way into understanding the phenomenon – a beginning – it is nonetheless problematical. Isolating the voice – and further only one aspect of it, such as vocal timbre (and even then, generalizing that there are a handful of available timbres when, as I have tried to point out with respect to Plant's voice, there are in fact many different ones) – from melodic range, harmonic motion, instrumental parts and various other aspects of the music is of limited use in trying to get at the cultural meanings in a song because we do not hear an element such as timbre on its own. [. . .] Perhaps the most defining musical gesture [in 'Whole Lotta Love'] is Page's riff, which in terms of pitch and rhythm is also mostly static, adding to the insistence implied by the restricted harmonic motion. The riff consists of a pickup to the tonic, the implied harmony of which is the flat VII chord (the pitches are B and D natural), which comes to rest on the downbeat on the tonic E – doubling the tonic an octave lower, so that the sense of release that comes with the tonic is magnified by the downward motion of the octave drop. This tonic chord is repeated for nearly two full measures during the introduction (before Plant enters) prior to the pickup being repeated, using a rhythm that emphasizes the beat (beats 1, 2, and 3) and consists of regular eighth notes. (The riff is contracted when Plant enters, one measure of these repeated eighth notes being dropped.) The pickup notes are set in rhythmic and harmonic relief to this regularity. The pickup comes on the second half of beat 3 – a sixteenth note that immediately moves to an eighth note on the last sixteenth note of beat 3, creating syncopation. The sound of Page's guitar playing the riff for the first time is also important to consider here. Not only is there a raw timbre created through the use of distortion, but the notes sound slightly 'out of tune,' the pitches bent out of shape, perched precariously on the edge of where they should be, pulling the body with them, coaxing it to come along, to conspire with the transgression. The timbre is further distorted and amplified through the use of backwards echo on the guitar. The riff is also played in a low register on the guitar – magnified by the lowness of the bass when it comes in – and I always map the image of Page's low-slung guitar onto the low sound of this riff when I hear it, much as I do when I hear the riffs to 'Heartbreaker' and 'Moby Dick,' which are similarly low in range.

The effect of the pickup – syncopation, its metric placement just before the downbeat, the harmonic change and the raw timbre – is physical in a very specific way: we experience the pickup as an intense force acting on the body, which is released when the timbre, rhythm, melody and harmony change to the tonic. The riff might be experienced metaphorically as the body being jolted back during the pickup and released at the tonic. Because the riff is so short and because it repeats throughout the verses and choruses of the song, the body is continually – relentlessly – hit by the intensity of the pickup. In effect, the body is kept in a fairly constant state of intensification or arousal by this riff.

[. . .]

Despite the insistence of the riff, with its intense physicality, there are three moments in Zeppelin's version of this song when it is not heard, during which the rhythmic/metric structure of the song collapses into something entirely different: the electronic middle section, the stop-time guitar solo and Plant's a cappella singing (punctuated – a bit like recitative – by chords from the band) near the end of the tune. Two of these moments are not dominated by Plant at all – the electronic middle section, as I have described above, and Page's guitar solo, the latter of which is like a third party coming into the narrative (we haven't heard Page's solo guitar at all up to this point). The different 'speakers' or 'players' in this song, with the varied musical languages that they speak, offer a narratively open text, one that encompasses multiple possibilities for a semiotic reading of gender identity and sexual experience.

[. . .]

Conclusion

[. . .] [W]hy has rock music been so unproblematically interpreted as phallic? [. . .] [Sue] Wise (1990) supplies the answer . . . , the same one that I would offer here: that interpretations are based on a selective understanding of an artist's career, that it is mostly men doing the interpreting, and, perhaps most important, that it is undoubtedly a prospect threatening to men and many women that male rock stars' power and sexuality could be understood, appropriated, or even controlled by women (as a woman wrote to me concerning my work on this project: 'a woman . . . taking the "phallic" power for herself . . . . I think that this is what scares the beejesus out of many people'). It is much easier always to begin from the premise that the music and images are sexist and macho because not only is it a comforting notion that this kind of semiotic stability might exist, but it simultaneously locks out the dangerous possibility of woman as sexual and powerful. As Wise puts it, 'this is something that we, as feminists, must recognize: that is, we must never take anything on trust, we must ask our own questions, seek out our own knowledge, and always look gift horses, in the form of other people's knowledge, firmly in the mouth' (1990: 397).

[. . .]

It was my profound involvement with Led Zeppelin that made me want to study the band academically – in order to try to understand my experience more fully; it was the disjuncture that I observed between my experience of the music and the way journalists and academics were writing about it that prompted me to write a book about Led Zeppelin. One of my hopes is that it will suggest to the latter, those generally on the outside of a music culture, to handle more delicately and with greater subtlety the experiences of those who love a particular music, to admit to the possibility that an interpretation based on the surface noise of a song or image might need to be probed more deeply and to examine their own reasons for taking a particular critical stance toward certain musics. Increasingly, those inside the culture should be given louder voices [. . .] We should also make sure to check a discourse that slips unproblematically into a particular point of view, examining the ideologies that lie behind such entrenched positions.

Chapter 42

Maria Pini

WOMEN AND THE EARLY
BRITISH RAVE SCENE

[. . .]

FOR WELL OVER A DECADE NOW, feminists involved in researching youth culture have sought to contest the familiar association of 'youth' with masculinity. This has involved highlighting the extent to which the category of youth is structured (within academia as much as within pop journalism) around a particular (and often romantic) concern with questions of 'deviance' and 'resistance', and a prioritisation of musical production and stylistic 'innovation' (McRobbie, 1991). Despite this feminist attempt to shift focus away from the 'street' and the 'gang', and to move beyond an exclusive concern with questions of cultural *production,* there is still a considerable absence of work on girls' and young women's lived locations within, and experiences of, youth cultural practices. The almost complete lack of academic interest in social dance, for instance, clearly illustrates the extent to which women's activities and experiences are largely 'written out' of youth-cultural histories (McRobbie, 1984; Ward, 1993).

[. . .]

In what follows, I will draw upon material collected in a series of in-depth interviews with (mainly) women involved in the early London rave scene. [. . . F]or many women, rave represents an undoing of the traditional cultural associations between dancing, drugged, 'dressed-up' woman and sexual invitation, and as such opens up a new space for the exploration of new forms of identity and pleasure. In short, if, as Rumsey and Little (1989) argue, women have traditionally been denied the kinds of 'unsupervised adventures' celebrated within previous youth-cultural scenes, then I am suggesting that rave allows for such adventure. Further, within rave, producing the 'self out of a relentless drive for the maximisation of pleasure is central. Being 'ecstatic' has in many ways replaced previous youth-cultural 'styles of being': being 'political', being 'angry', being 'hard' and even (certainly at the very beginning of rave in London) being 'fashionable'. Physical and mental enjoy-ment becomes a central point of involvement. In many ways, open displays of 'happiness', auto-erotic pleasure, 'friendliness' and enjoyment of dance are tradi-tionally more closely associated with femininity, and gay male culture (Dyer, 1990). In this sense, rave can be read as a challenge to heterosexual masculinity's tradi-tional centrality, and for this reason alone is worthy of attention.

Researching rave: identity and textuality

To explore these issues I have embarked upon a kind of 'identity ethnography' (McRobbie, 1992) which involves an exploration of the personal meanings an involvement with the practices of rave has for the women interviewed, and the particular 'subjectivities' encouraged within this scene. In drawing upon personal accounts, I am not claiming to have gained privileged access to the essential 'truth' about rave. Rather, I am giving a reading of accounts which are themselves partial, provisional and located readings and reports. My focus is upon how particular under-standings and experiences are produced, generated and reinforced within this scene. The notion of 'textuality' is used to suggest that far from being basic to the activ-ities involved, certain emotions and experiences are actually 'bound up' with cultural narratives and organisational practices, which make up the background of, and give meaning to these practices (Curt, 1994). In this sense, 'experience' is lived, nego-tiated and understood through a variety of 'storying practices' and it is through such processes that identities are produced.

[. . .]

This emphasis on 'texts' within rave is partly influenced by the work of Maria Milagres Lopes (1991), who in a study in Puerto Rico uses the concept of a 'text of fear' to illustrate the interrelationship between the discourses of authorities and the press, and the personal fear experiences of the public. Centrally, Lopes is concerned with how even the subjective understandings of actually being assaulted are not inherent to the act but prescribed and retold in context-specific ways. 'Each story', she argues, 'is part of a larger one that reproduces itself in each individual storytelling.' In the same way, personal experiences and accounts of rave can be thought of as 'textualised'. [. . .]

Rave's 'text of excitement'

For those directly involved, and even for many looking on from the sidelines, the early rave scene was surrounded by an air of thrill, illegality and mystery. Aside from the panic generated by the early press around the use of drugs, the occupation of unsafe, abandoned warehouses and the motorway convoys, there were the excited accounts of participants who adopted new 'raver' identities and talked repeatedly about how nothing could ever be as good as dancing on 'E'. Indeed, as Miriam suggests, there was a general feeling that what had developed was a kind of 'cult' of devotees prepared to go to great lengths and expense to rave. As Sonia remarks: 'I can't believe how far we would travel. And *then,* you didn't even know for sure whether it would even be on when you got there.' [. . .] Mary says, 'I drove for miles – but I didn't mind. It was exciting 'cause you kept imagining what it would be like.' The senses of mystery and excitement were heightened by the variety of pirate radio stations that called out to 'children of London' announcing phone numbers, code names and meeting points from which various 'magical mystery tours' would begin on their 'Orbital convoys'.

The generation of this panicked excitement was also reinforced by the actual set-up of events. Dark, badly ventilated and often overcrowded rooms, dripping with condensation were usual venues. As interviewees suggest, success of an actual event was often understood in terms of numbers, where the more the better, and the more crowded the venue the more intense the experience. Added to this general 'intensity' and taking the crowd even 'higher' were DJs screaming for everyone to 'Go fucking Mental'. Hillegonda Reitveld accurately describes early 'Acid House' music as having 'a rather schizophrenic feel to it; the texture of the baseline continually changes and voices and other fragments of stolen sound make a 'disembodied' appearance' (1994: 23). The use of strobes and 'dry ice' can also be seen as serving to create a general scene of 'disembodiedness', slowing down, and fragmenting the movements of dancers, giving the whole crowd the appearance of a complicated mechanical circuit.

Obviously central to the production of 'excitement' was the heavy use of 'Ecstasy', and the bodily 'rushes' associated with it. All of the women interviewed here had used the drug at the start of their involvement in rave, but many had stopped using it after about a year. Almost all of them, however, claimed that taking 'E' at least once was necessary in order to fully experience the pleasures involved in raving.

[. . .]

This 'text of excitement' can be supplemented with that of a mutually dependent 'text of fear', because in many ways the set-up of events appeared to actively play on and heighten senses of panic and anxiety. This was obvious in a range of practices, from the ways in which 'bouncer outfits' seemed to exaggerate the potential for danger, to the ways in which DJ chants often played on the possibilities of someone having a 'bad trip'. [. . .]

Elaine indicates the way in which particular fears are actively played on by DJs:

> That was the time when the DJ kept screaming on about going mad and he kept saying 'do you know what you've taken?' . . . I was getting really freaked out and it was nearly impossible to get away from it all. And he just kept shouting down the mike that you were going mad and that.

> All of this took place within the context of the dark, crowded space where often people had bought 'pills' from strangers and spent at least some time anticipating the effects. 'Coping' with the obvious anxieties and keeping these at bay became a theme. [. . .]

Similarly, the uses and understandings of technology within the scene also worked towards a heightening of excitement and fear. The body abandoned to machinery was central and clearly suggested by the computerised and mechanical music, which was seen as taking over the body. The early 'Trance Dance' illustrates this ideal of an absolute absorption in music. Fliers also sold events on the power of their machinery. Themes of space exploration and technological progress feature strongly in these. Many outdoor events often included funfairs, and here machinery could take over the heightening of bodily pleasures and intensify these further.

In the sense outlined above, rave can partly be seen in terms of a celebration of excitement and pleasure. I have elucidated these themes in terms of a 'text of excitement' to show how rave can be seen as threaded through with a particular set of narratives that operate as much on the organisation level as they do at the level of personal experience. This is certainly not to suggest that this is the *only* way of experiencing this scene, or that *everybody* would experience a sense of excitement in this same way. On the contrary, pointing to the 'textuality' of rave enables us to see how a particular manner of textual engagement is required for a full 'appreciation' of the scene.

Rave's emphasis on excitement and thrill is common to many youth cultures. My argument, however, is that unlike many previous scenes, women within rave draw upon a 'text of excitement' as much as the boys and young men involved. It is difficult to overstate the extent to which interviewees insist upon rave's 'progressive' sexual politics, and the degree to which they view rave as providing a new space in terms of sexual relations. To offer simply a few examples of responses to the question of how rave was different to other club scenes interviewees had been involved in:

> It was *totally* different to other scenes . . . because . . . well, the only thing that I thought was similar was the fact that there was music. I saw clubs very much pick-up joints where you got men just staring at you, or coming up to chat you up.
>
> Miriam

> It was strikingly different to other club scenes. There was no alcohol around, so little aggression and little emphasis on chatting people up and the 'cattle-market' element of, say, disco, didn't seem to be around.
>
> Ann

[. . .]

The erosion of difference and the constitution of particular mind/body/spirit relations

In order to briefly explore the discursive construction of these seemingly different gender relations, and to suggest what seem to be new forms of gendered subjectivity, I want to elucidate the two interwoven themes mentioned above.

First, rave can be seen to be partly organised around a 'text of sameness': a phrase that I am using to get at the assemblage of themes which stress rave's non-oppositionality, its accessibility to everyone and its potential to break down social boundaries. The following interviewee statements clearly illustrate this text:

Rave attracts all sorts of people: black and white, women and men –
from all classes.

Ann

Rave tended to bring everyone together.

Helen

Everyone was in it together and there was an instant sort of bond.

Miriam

[. . .]

'Unisex' clothes and the whole 'dress-to-sweat' emphasis of the scene are important
factors in the perceived erosion of sexual differences. Nearly all of the interviewees
mentioned this aspect as central to their understandings of rave as progressive in
terms of sexual politics. Although this perceived erosion of social differences is
related to the empathetic effects of 'E', many enjoy 'raving' without this. For this
reason it becomes implausible to attribute the emergence of this theme solely to
the drug – the drug is just one part of the ensemble.

The breaking down of boundaries applies not only to social differences, but is
also related to ideas of breaking down individual boundaries, so that the raver
can describe losing her sense of 'self and becoming part of something 'bigger'.
Catherine describes this as an 'ideal state' to be worked towards: 'It's a very strange
sensation really – an ideal state is where you're not centred on yourself. You're
part of the whole crowd of people – like your identity is a much broader one.'
[. . .] The rave experience, then, can be viewed as being bound up with a range
of self techniques (such as working towards a blissful absorption of the self into
the dancing crowd) which encourage a certain manner of textual engagement.
Location within this text is not something that comes 'naturally'. Rather, reaching
the desired state is, as many song lyrics and DJ chants will tell you, something you
have to 'work for'.

A key aspect of this 'governing' or 'managing' of experience is brought out, I
would argue, in a theme of 'positivity', that is simultaneously a 'policing' of 'negativity'. This 'ethics of pleasure' is highlighted in a number of interviewee accounts
that stress the importance of the right attitude, which includes avoiding the power
of 'negative vibes' to 'bring you down' (and which seems, at times, to mean refusing
to acknowledge 'difference' or tensions). In many ways, Jazzie B's lyric, 'Enrich
your positivity – no time for negativity', sums up this aspect of the early scene. As
the statement below suggest[s], this 'positivity' wears thin when confronted with
tensions, or resistance:

> No one wanted to hear I was having a bad time. They'd all been really
> nice up until then. I felt really bad and no one would listen – they all
> just kept dancing and avoiding me.
>
> Elaine

[. . .]

This 'positivity' aspect, along with ideas that stress the power of rave to break
down social and individual boundaries, relates to rave's intertextuality with certain

'New Age' discourses (I am using the term 'New Age' broadly to refer to what Andrew Ross describes as a set of ideas claiming an 'alternative world-view, distinct from orthodox rationalism', 1992). Specifically, certain understandings of the self within rave resonate with particularly 'New Age' discourses on mind/body relations. I argued that the 'text of sameness' involves ideas about the erosion of differences, and a construction of the individual body as part of 'something bigger'. These ideas correlate with 'New Age' stress on the interrelation of mind/body/ spirit. The body in rave is commonly conceived of in terms of a holistic mind/ body, and participants stressed the absence of any clear separation and the connectedness between themselves and others. Just as the 'text of sameness' strives to challenge external and interpersonal boundaries between selves, in this configuration, internal and intra-personal boundaries are challenged. Any prioritisation of mind over body, or 'rational thought' over pleasure, is seen as an 'imbalance'. As Catherine states, 'You don't need to *think*. You just *feel*. You have to just get into *feeling* the energy and all the things going on around you.' [. . .]

Rave then, can be seen as a 'body' culture, but this 'body' is no longer separate from mind and spirit. Rather, emphasis is on being 'in touch' with all of these at once. Hence, the rave event is seen as breaking down standard mind/body dualisms. 'Thought' and 'rationality' within such configurations are seen as potentially obstructive to the achievement of full pleasure, and indeed any prioritisation of these is seen as signalling a conspicuous imbalance of mind/body relations. In speaking of the pleasures of dance, Miriam contrasts this to reading and writing: 'When you read or write, you don't use your body – you don't move it'. Hence, the body/mind in rave becomes sensitive or 'open' to 'vibes', 'spirituality', non-verbal communication and so on. The outer boundaries of the mind/body are thus extended – or 'stretched' as Jane put it earlier – and made permeable. This body thus becomes a rather more 'cyborgian' one, not separate from its environment, but an integrated part of this circuit (Haraway, 1991). As Miriam puts it: 'You're not separate from the music – the music *is* you. You are part of the music and . . . there's no relationship even 'cause you're one'. As with the Vibrasound machine, technology – in the form of music and 'visuals' – is seen as 'working through' the body. [. . .]

To draw towards a close, I want to mention a final (clearly related) theme: that of the constitution within rave of a particular, 'ecstatic' mind/body/spirit/ technology assemblage. [. . .] The self is no longer a neatly 'bounded', individual self. Rather, involvement and pleasure are experienced in terms of connections between self and others, and between mind, body and machine. Individuality or 'self-consciousness' are seen as actually getting in the way of full enjoyment, and as suggested above, a certain 'positivity' seems to operate to maintain the notions of 'sameness' and unity which prop up this understanding of self.

[. . .]

Women and rave: some conclusions

In this chapter, I have tried moving away from the more traditional foci of youth-cultural studies and attempted to direct attention towards issues of subjectivity and experience. Taking women's own personal accounts as my starting points, my aim was to illustrate the kind of 'selves' encouraged within rave, and to outline the practices and 'texts' which can be seen to make for an understanding of rave as sexually progressive. In general, I would argue that rave's appeal to women is tied with its opening up of new modes of 'looking', its set-up of particular interpersonal relations and its encouragement of new understandings of 'self'. Women within this context feel freed from traditional associations of dancing with sexual invite, and in this sense rave seems to represent an 'alternative' space.

[. . .]

The rave dance-floor, I would argue, is one of the few spaces that afford – and indeed, encourage – open displays of physical pleasure and affection. Explicit displays of 'ecstatic' happiness, and the relentless drive to achieve this, have never been so central to a youth culture's meaning. Arguably rave represents the emergence of a particular form of 'jouissance', one that is more centred on the achievement of physical and mental transformation and one that is possibly best understood as a non-phallic form of pleasure. Many of the interviewees *did* speak of rave pleasures as being 'sexual', but many had difficulty in clearly 'languaging' what this 'sexual' was. I would suggest that this is because these pleasures do not clearly 'fit' standard, patriarchal definitions of sexuality, and eroticism. To illustrate this difficulty:

> I kind of see it as a place where I can feel sexually about other people, but it doesn't actually go anywhere . . . It doesn't *have* to go anywhere 'cause that's it really.
>
> Catherine

> It's not sexual, but orgasmic . . . I wouldn't say it was sexual. It's different from being sexual. It's orgasmic in the sense of being very intense and reaching a peak.
>
> Miriam

> Well it's sexual kind of . . . no, it's *not* sexual – it's different.
>
> Helen

[. . .]

Hence, what seems to emerge within rave is a space for new modes of femininity and physical pleasures. In terms of how this space fits within a wider life-context, many interviewees described the rave scene as providing a space for the expression of 'other sides' of themselves. As Jane puts it:

> It's about letting go of being conformist, and being professional and proper and . . . 'together'. It's 'other' to presenting that face of you. It's not necessarily the dark side of you – but it's the messy side of you . . . It's about something you do which isn't about working. It's about the time you spend doing things which are about freedom.

To close then, despite women's relative absence at the levels of rave production and organisation, at other levels rave can be seen as indicating an important shift in sexual relations, and indeed might suggest (with its emphasis on dance, physicality, affection and unity) a general 'femi-nisation' of 'youth'.

Chapter 43

Richard Smith

HOUSEWIVES' CHOICE
Female fans and unmanly men

IT IS 1926, AND VALENTINO, the age of mass media's first great heart throb is dead. At his funeral there's a surging mob of women over one hundred thousand strong. But while the women were going mad for him, the men just couldn't see it. There was something about Valentino that wasn't quite right. He was a little too delicate, over concerned with his appearance – you understand?

Fearful heterosexual men had whispered in consternation: a few more chaps like Valentino could signal the collapse of Western civilization. These whispers first went public with an editorial in the *Chicago Tribune*. Beneath the provocative headline 'Pink powder puffs', the writer expressed his outrage at finding 'A powder vending machine! In the men's room!' and went on to squeal in an orgy of exclamation marks 'Homo Americanus! Why didn't someone quietly drown Rudolph Guglieme, alias Valentino, years ago? Do women like that type of 'man' who puts pink powder on his face in a public washroom and arranges his hair in a public elevator?' Readers didn't have to be too intellectually spectacular to figure out just what kind of a 'man' he thought Valentino was. Putting on make-up! In public! And worst of all, oh horror of horrors, women clearly *did* like that kind of 'man'.

Valentino started off the great tradition of male stars who didn't seem overly concerned with appearing butch, and who built up a huge and fanatical female following while the rest of the world was united in the suspicion that he was, well . . . not as other men. It's one of life's great mysteries: what did nice, middle-aged women see in men who, to the rest of us, just didn't seem like the marrying kind?

Take Liberace. In 1956 he successfully sued *The Daily Mirror* for printing an article that he claimed 'implied I was an unmanly man'. For someone who seemed to have dedicated his whole career to implying that he was an unmanly man, that seems rather an odd thing to do. Nevertheless, when the *Mirror* dismissed him as 'the biggest sentimental vomit of all time . . . a deadly, winking, scent impregnated luminous, quivering, giggling, fruit flavoured, mincing ice covered heap of mother love' they also had to concede he had an uncanny hold over 'teenagers longing for sex and middle aged matrons fed up with sex'.

Sex isn't the first word that comes to mind when one thinks of Liberace – with Valentino, heavy-lidded, perfumed and pouting, cute romantic little Latin fool that he was, yes – but *Liberace*? The latter was, if anything, sexless, playing up an image that exuded safety and homeliness. Here was a guy who dyed the hair at his temples grey to make him look more mature, a professional mummy's boy whose television show had just three props: a piano, a nice candelabra and his dear old mom, who'd stand there with the patience of a saint as he assaulted her with a constant barrage of dedications, naughty winks and flashes of that most cheesy of grins. But to the millions of women who watched and made his show the only real rival to *I Love Lucy* in the Fifties, was he more than just a nice boy who was kind to his mom? Did they reach the same conclusions about him as the gangs of teds who picketed venues on his first British tour brandishing placards proclaiming 'Queer go home'? If all those women thought the same about him as *The Daily Mirror*, then why was he receiving over a dozen marriage proposals a week?

Sure, they knew he was unmanly but that didn't mean he was 'you know' – and besides, they liked him that way. They even thought it best that he didn't marry (according to one fan magazine's readers' poll), because that meant 'he can love his mom better'.

Liberace soon changed, proving perhaps that deep inside of every mummy's boy there's a screaming queen trying to claw her way out. By the Sixties, he had lapsed into complete self-parody ('Pardon me while I slip into something more spectacular') and began coming on like a man in real need of a taste transfusion. It was a sort of strategy. 'I began to disarm my audience and say what people were thinking before they had a chance to say it. I heckled myself'. Thus he slipped out of one great show-business tradition and into another: the queen as a figure of fun, indulging in wild, over the top campery that is forgivable because it's all but act and affectation.

His fame waned until the Eighties – when he found himself selling out bigger venues than ever before, leading him to comment wryly that in the age of Boy George he'd become safe once more. This second wave of success survived his celebrated 'palimony' case and lasted right up until his death from AIDS in 1987.

Both Johnny Mathis and Johnnie Ray found that fans can stay steadfast, loyal and true even after their homosexuality is made public knowledge. Mathis told *US* magazine in the early Eighties that he had two male lovers, and yet his fans still turn out in their droves to hear him warble his way through 'The Twelfth Of Never'. And Johnnie Ray's British fans stuck with him right up until his death [in 1990] in spite of not one, not two, but a mighty three arrests for cottaging. Could it be that such artists' homosexuality, suspected or real, is a major factor in their appeal and that this phenomenon – The Liberace Syndrome – is no more than fag-haggery on a mass scale?

Poor old Johnnie Ray was certainly one 'unmanly man'. His whole act, indeed, his whole fame, rested on his breaking a great taboo: he showed that big boys *do* cry. Actually, all that Johnnie did was cry. He'd walk on stage, the girls would start screaming, he'd put his hand over his hearing aid as if it had started howling feedback, then he'd let rip with that huge tidal wave of a voice – but before he'd reached even the end of the first verse something in Johnnie would click and he'd remember what a rotten old life it was and begin to blub away, banging his pretty little head against the piano in unconsolable grief.

Johnnie was important for lots of reasons. He was just a teensy bit too early for rock 'n' roll, but was one of the people who dictated its shape and eased its passage. He was a heart-throb who showed that it was OK for a man to be vulnerable and sensitive and hurt. He also showed that a lot of women like a man like that.

You can still hear the echoes of his sobs in the charts to this day. But he also influenced those who operate more or less outside of pop. The housewives' choices who trade on their personalities, on the singer not the song. Barry Manilow is the prime contemporary example. He's got the largest and the most fanatical following. He stressed that he's not pop, he's *more* than pop. He's showbusiness, a professional. He's charismatic. A little bit naughty, but basically nice boyish and self-mocking, he's sincere and humble. And his fans? They like Barry's bum.

Manilow started out in 1972 playing piano for Bette Midler while she sang to a crowd of men wearing nothing but moustache and towels at New York's Continental Baths. His act borrows heavily from hers. It's a lot less brassy and a little less camp, but it's basically cabaret: big ballads with death-defying key changes and, most important, lots and lots of on-stage chat. 'I try stopping myself,' he said unconvincingly to one interviewer, 'but when I'm out there it's like I'm sittin' in my living room talkin' to my friends.' Like Liberace, Manilow excels at creating the illusion of intimacy – at making Mrs Average feel special, as if he's performing just for her.

It would be too easy to reduce all this down to 'nice personalities'. Because the men seem to be 'nice boys' (nudge, nudge) and 'mummy's boys' (wink, wink) it becomes difficult for many to see them as possibly representing anything other than a surrogate son to these women. Thus, any sexual component to the relationship is conveniently negated. A similar reluctance to consider any kind of autonomous female sexuality – especially in middle-aged women has led to the myth of maternalism, a belief that the only thing such women could possibly want to do with these men is mother them. But with Barry's fans, if these are maternal feelings, then they're of deeply oedipal hue. You don't scream at and chase after and molest someone you want to mother. You certainly don't swap and collect 'bum shots' of them with your friends. You knit them sweaters and take spit-sodden kleenexes to the chocolate smears on their face. What we are talking about with Barry is lust, pure and simple.

A singing crotch like Tom Jones holds little appeal for most women – with the only attraction being the thrill or the giggle of the girl's night out. Like the current vogue for those troupes of American beefcake strippers such as The Chippendales, what they provide is a 'girls' together' environment, a space where heterosexual women are allowed (or, rather, allow themselves) to behave in ways that they usually can't. The act is not the focus of attention – they are merely providing the women with an excuse for being there, for congregating with other women. What is true for the macho performers also holds true for today's more nelly entertainers.

We can even trace some kind of progression from Valentino (cinema and theatre matinee performances were tailored towards and attended almost exclusively by women while their husbands were away at work) through Liberace (beamed into the home in the early evening or a concert attraction to which women would drag their reluctant husbands as chaperons) to today, when it's no longer taboo for women to attend, say, a Cliff Richard concert with their female friends rather than their husbands. This progression has been a search for space, an escape from the home – somewhere that for most women is still a place of work rather than rest.

There's also been a marked progression in the way women behave in the concert hall. Fans of Liberace exercised decorum and restraint. Johnnie Ray's concerts marked a watershed – women let themselves go. [In 1991] a Barry Manilow concert is a scene of near debauchery. The sexual component in the fans' adoration is made resoundingly clear – although how much of it is for real and how much of it is simply play is vague. As is the more interesting question of how much of it is really directed at him. Here's Manilow on why he persists with his 'sexy' stage antics even though he looks so uncomfortable when he's doing them:

> I do it because they want it . . . wiggling my ass – that's the bit I really don't like. I've never enjoyed that part of it . . . the only way I can think to get round the problem is by camping it up and fooling around. That Liverpool gig was uncomfortable for me. They wouldn't allow me to do the job. They wanted me to be cute and wiggle my ass and tell dirty stories. I was disappointed because I take the work I do seriously and now and again I fall into the trap of pandering to them.

Compare that sorry tale of woe with a fan's experience of a concert:

> It's a real sexual thing . . . but it isn't only that, because I've been to lots and lots of concerts but I've never felt that kind of atmosphere and that kind of closeness. Complete strangers catch hold of your hand and you are united as one. When they start singing 'We'll Meet Again' and all join hands you can almost feel the love. Something runs between us like an electric shock. It's just wonderful.

Perhaps it's this collision between the sense of female solidarity and the eroticism that Barry acts as a catalyst for, that creates the fabled 'Manilow magic'.

What becomes clear is that there are widely disparate reasons for why women adore Valentino or Liberace or Johnnie Ray or Barry Manilow or whoever. It would be foolish to try to seek out one unified reason. They are, however, a variety of responses to just one type of man, an 'unmanly' one. The attraction is rarely a presumed homosexuality – for we know that people have a quite remarkable capacity for self-deception (and many of these fans are more than likely rotten old homophobes) – it's more perhaps an attraction towards these men's 'homosexual-ness'. Many of the artists may be straight, but their popularity rests on them being 'gay-acting, gay-looking'. It should be borne in mind that not everyone automatically equates 'unmanly men' with homosexuality and that one man's camp is another's good taste. Some see a gay man up there, others a gentle straight man. Some see a silly queen, others the perfect son. Some see an ideal lover, others a bumpy stud. They can represent danger just as easily as they can safety.

All this belies a certain lack of compatibility between straight men and straight women. Between how 'men' are and what women want. A shortfall betwixt ideal and reality. A Liberace or Manilow is derided for homophobic reasons. Their fans for misogynistic ones. In so doing their critics are seeking to avoid facing the fact that, like it or not, some women like their men unmanly, perhaps even somewhat androgynous. There's a need to dismiss these women's opinions because what they are saying is something deeply threatening: real men are crap.

References

Abrams, M. (1959) *The Teenage Consumer*, Press Exchange: London.

Ackerley, C. (1978) 'Women and guitar', in J. Ferguson (ed.) *The Guitar Player Book*, New York: Grove Press.

Adorno, T. W. (1990 [1941]) 'On popular music', in S. Frith and A. Goodwin (eds), *On Record: Rock, Pop and the Written Word*, New York: Pantheon.

American Music Conference [AMC] (1988) *Music Software Consumer Survey*, Chicago.

Ampigny, M-L. (1987) 'Kassav: l'année de tous les success . . .' *France Antilles*, 17, May.

Anderson, B., Hesbacher, P., Etzkorn, K. P. and Denisoff, R. S. (1980) 'Hit Record Trends, 1940–1977', *Journal of Communication*, 30: 31–40.

Anon. (1988) "1er symposiu, sur le zouk." Press release, n.p.

Arnold, G. (1992) 'Bikini Kill: "revolution girl-style"', *Option* 44, May–June, 46.

Atkins, L. [former staff musician] (1988) Interview with James P. Kraft, Los Angeles, 7 September.

Attali, J. (1985) *Noise: The Political Economy of Music*. Minneapolis, MN: University of Minnesota Press.

Awan, S. (1994) 'Bhangra Bandwagon', in K. Burton (ed.) *Rough Guide to World Music*, London: Penguin.

Banerji, S. and Baumann, G. (1990) 'Bhangra 1984–8: fusion and professionalization in a genre of South Asian dance music', in P. Oliver (ed.) *Black Music in Britain: Essays on the Afro-Asian Contribution to Popular Music*, Milton Keynes: Open University Press.

Banks, J. (1995) 'MTV and the globalization of popular culture', paper presented at the Intercultural/International Communication Conference, Miami, FL, February.

Baptiste, G. (1994) Personal interview, 5 August.

Barrett, J. (1996) 'World music, nation and postcolonialism', *Cultural Studies*, 10: 237–47.

Barthes, R. (1976) 'The death of the author', in *Image-Music-Text*, London: Fontana.

—— (1977) 'The Grain of the Voice', in *Image-Music-Text*, trans. Stephen Heath, New York: Noonday.

—— *Image-Music-Text*, trans. Stephen Heath, London: Fontana.

Baudrillard, Jean (1981) *For a Critique of the Political Economy of the Sign*, trans. Charles Levin, St Louis, MO: Telos Press.

—— (1983) *Simulations*, trans. P. Forr, P. Patton and P. Beitchman, New York: Semiotext(e).

Bauman, Z. (1993) *Postmodern Ethics*, Oxford: Blackwell.

Baumann, G. (1990) 'The reinvention of Bhangra: social change and aesthetic shifts in a Punjabi music in Britain', *World of Music*, 32 (2): 81–95.

—— (1997) 'Dominant and demotic discourses of culture: their relevance to multi-ethnic alliances', in P. Werbner and T. Modood (eds) *Debating Cultural Hybridity: Multi-Cultural Identities and the Politics of Anti-Racism*, London: Zed Books.

Baym, N. (1995) 'The emergence of community in computer mediated communication', in S. G. Jones (ed.) *Cybersociety: Computer Mediated Communication and Community*, Thousand Oaks: Sage.

Bayton, M. (1990) 'How women become musicians', in S. Frith and A. Goodwin (eds) *On Record: Rock, Pop and the Written Word*, New York: Pantheon.

Beck, U., Giddens, A. and Lash, S. (eds) *Reflexive Modernisation*, Cambridge: Polity Press.

Becker, H. (1982) *Art Worlds*, Berkeley, CA: University of California Press.

Benjamin, W. (1969) 'The work of art in the age of mechanical reproduction', in H. Arendt (ed.) *Illuminations*, trans. H. Zohn, New York: Schocken Books.

Bennett, A. (2000) *Popular Music and Youth Culture: Music, Identity and Place*, London: Macmillan.

Bennett, H. (1983) 'Notation and identity in contemporary popular music', *Popular Music*, 3: 215–34.

Bennett, T., Frith, S., Grossberg, L., Shepherd, J. and Turner, C. (eds) *Rock and Popular Music: Politics, Policies, Institutions*, London: Routledge.

Benson, J. (1994) *The Rise of Consumer Society in Britain, 1880–1980*, London: Longman.

Bernabe, J. (1986) 'Chroniques d'une fin de vacances: Pt. 1, Zouk et zouk', *Antilla*, 209: 15–16.

Bocock, R. (1993) *Consumption*, London: Routledge.

Bordwell, D., Staiger, J. and Thompson, K. (1985) *The Classical Hollywood Cinema: Film Style and Mode of Production to 1960*, New York: Columbia University Press.

Botts, L. (1980) *Loose Talk*, New York: Rolling Stone Press.

Bourdieu, P. (1984) *Distinction: A Social Critique of the Judgement of Taste*, trans. R. Nice, Havard University Press: Cambridge, MA.

—— (1989) *Outline of a Theory of Practice*, Cambridge: Cambridge University Press.

—— (1990a) *In Other Words: Essays Towards a Reflexive Sociology*, Cambridge: Polity.

—— (1990b) *The Logic of Practice*, Stanford: Stanford University Press.

—— (1993) *The Field of Cultural Production*, Oxford: Polity Press.

Burnett, R. (1996) *The Global Jukebox: The International Music Industry*, London: Routledge.

Burton, K. (ed.) *Rough Guide to World Music*, London: Penguin.

Butler, J. (1990) *Gender Trouble: Feminism and the Subversion of Identity*, London: Routledge.

Cagle, V. M. (1995) *Reconstructing Pop Subculture: Art, Rock and Andy Warhol*, London: Sage.

Cale, J. and Bockris, V. (1999) *What's Welsh for Zen? The Autobiography of John Cale*, New York: Bloomsday Books.

Central Statistical Office (1972–86) *The General Household Survey*, London: Her Majesty's Stationery Office.

Cerulli, D., Korall, B. and Nasatir, M. (eds) *The Jazz Word*, New York: Da Capo.

Chambers, I. (1985) *Urban Rhythms: Pop Music and Popular Culture*, London: Macmillan.
——— (1994) *Migrancy, Culture, Identity*, London: Routledge.
Chang, K. and Chen, W. (1998) *Reggae Routes: The Story of Jamaican Music*. Philadelphia: Temple University Press.
Christenson, P. and Peterson, J. B. (1988) 'Genre and gender in the structure of music preferences', *Communication Research*, 15(3), June.
Christgau, R. (1998) *Grown Up All Wrong: Great Rock and Pop Artists from Vaudeville to Techno*, Cambridge, MA and London: Harvard University Press.
Clarke, G. (1981) 'Defending ski-jumpers: a critique of theories of youth subcultures', in S. Frith and A. Goodwin (eds) *On Record: Rock, Pop and the Written Word*, London: Routledge.
Clarke, J. (1976) 'The skinheads and the magical recovery of community', in S. Hall and T. Jefferson (eds) *Resistance Through Rituals: Youth Subcultures in Post-War Britain*, London: Hutchinson.
Cohen, P. (1972) 'Subcultural conflict and working class community', *Papers in Cultural Studies 2*, University of Birmingham.
Cohen, S. (1994) 'Identity, place and the Liverpool sound' in M. Stokes (ed.) *Ethnicity, Identity and Music: The Musical Construction of Place*, Oxford: Oxford University Press, pp. 117–34.
Congressional Office of Technology Assessment (1989) *Copyright and Home Copying: Technology Challenges the Law* (OTA-CIT-442), Washington, DC: Government Printing Office.
Copeland, Roger (1990) 'The presence of mediation', *Tulane Drama Review*, 34(4): 28–44.
Cowie, C. and Lees, S. (1981) 'Slags or Drags', *Feminist Review*, 9.
Crane, J. (1986) 'Mainstream music and the masses', *Journal of Communication Inquiry*, 10(3).
Curt, B. (1994) *Textuality and Tectonics*, Buckinghamshire: Open University Press.
Dalton, D. (1991) *Piece of My Heart: A Portrait of Janis Joplin*, New York: Da Capo.
Davies, C. (1993) 'Aboriginal rock music', in T. Bennett, S. Frith, L. Grossberg, J. Shepherd and C. Turner (eds) *Rock and Popular Music: Politics, Policies, Institutions*, London: Routledge.
——— and Willwerth, J. (1974) *Clive: Inside the Record Business*, New York: William Morrow.
Davies, H. (2001) 'All rock and roll is homosocial: the representation of women in the British music press', *Popular Music*, 20(3): 301–19.
Davis, M., Pfeil, F. and Sprinker, M.(eds) *The Year Left 2: An American Socialist Yearbook*, London: Verso Books.
Dawson, P. (1976) WNEW-FM Radio, *Prime-Prine* liner notes.
Dennett, D. (1995) *Darwin's Dangerous Idea: Evolution and the Meanings of Life*, New York: Simon & Schuster.
DeNora, T. (1995) 'The musical composition of reality? Music, action and reflexivity', *Sociological Review*, 43: 295–315.
Denselow, R. (1989) *When the Music's Over*, London: Faber & Faber.
DeRogatis, J. (2000) *Let It Blurt. The Life and Times of Lester Bangs*, London: Bloomsbury.
Dimmick, J. (1974) 'The gate-keeper: an uncertainty theory', *Journalism Monographs*, 37.
Dorr-Doryneck, D. (1987) 'Mingus', in D. Cerulli, B. Korall and M. Nasatir (eds) *The Jazz Word*, New York: Da Capo.
Draper, R. (1990) *The Rolling Stone Story: The Uncensored History*, Edinburgh, Mainstream Publishing.

Duncombe, S. (1997) *Notes From Underground: Zines and the Politics of Alternative Culture*, London: Verso.

Dunsby, J. and Whittall, A. (1988) *Music Analysis in Theory and Practice*, Boston, MA: Faber.

Dyer, R. (1990) 'In defence of disco', in S. Frith and A. Goodwin (eds) *On Record*, London: Pantheon.

Eberly, P. (1982) *Music in the Air: America's Changing Taste in Popular Music, 1920–1980*, New York: Hastings House.

Ehrenreich, B., Hess, E. and Jacobs, G. (1986) *Re-making Love: The Feminization of Sex*, New York: Anchor Press/Doubleday.

Elliott, P. (1979) 'Media organisations and occupations: an overview', in J. Curran, M. Gurevitch and J. Woollacott (eds) *Mass Communications and Society*, Beverly Hills, CA: Sage.

Erdelyi, M. (1940) 'The relation between "radio plugs" and sheet sales of popular music', *Journal of Applied Psychology*, 24: 696–702.

Erimann, V. (1996) 'The aesthetics of the global imagination: reflections on world music in the 1990s', *Public Culture*, 8: 467–87.

Euromonitor (1989) *The Music Video and Buyers Survey: Tabular Report and Appendices*, November.

Evans, L. (1995) *Women, Sex and Rock 'n' Roll: In their Own Words*, London: Pandora.

Faiola, A. (1994) 'Now youngsters are demanding Yo Quiero Mi MTV', *Miami Herald*, 9 October, 1 K.

Fanon, F. (1967) *Black Skin, White Masks*, New York: Grove Press.

Fathi, A. and Heath, C. L. (1974) 'Group influence, mass media and musical taste among Canadian students', *Journalism Quarterly*, 51: 705–9.

Faulkner, R. (1971) *Hollywood Studio Musicians: Their Work and Careers in the Recording Industry*, Chicago: Aldine Atherton.

Featherstone, M. (1990) (ed.) *Global Culture: Nationalism, Globalisation and Modernity*, London: Sage.

Feld, S. (1994) 'Notes on "world beat"', in C. Keil and S. Feld (eds) *Music Grooves: Essays and Dialogues*, Chicago: University of Chicago Press.

Fenster, M. (1995) 'Two stories; where exactly is the local?' in W. Straw, S. Johnson, R. Sullivan and P. Friedlander (eds) *Popular Music: Style and Identity*, Montreal: The Centre for Research on Canadian Cultural Industries and Institutions/International Association for the Study of Popular Music.

—— (2002) 'Consumers' guides. The political economy of the music press and the democracy of political discourses' in S. Jones (ed.) *Pop Music and the Press*, Philadelphia, PA: Temple University Press.

Fine, G. A. and Kleinman, S. (1979) 'Rethinking subculture: an interactionist analysis', *American Journal of Sociology*, 85: 1–20.

Fisher, S. and Holder, S. (1981) *Too Much Too Young*, London: Pan.

Forde, E. (2001a) 'From polyglottism to branding. On the decline of personality journalism in the British music press', *Journalism*, 2(1): 23–43.

—— (2001b) 'Music journalists, music press officers and the consumer music press in the UK', unpublished Ph.D. thesis, University of Westminster.

Forss, K. (2001) *The Export of the Swedish Music Industry: An Update for the Year 2000*, Stockholm: Export Music Sweden.

Foucault, M. (1979) *Discipline and Punish*, London: Penguin Books.

Friedman, M. (1992) *Buried Alive: The Biography of Janis Joplin*, New York: Harmony.

Friend, B. (1994) Personal interview, June 23.

Frith, S. (1978) *The Sociology of Pop*, London: Constable.

—— (1981) *Sound Effects: Youth, Leisure and the Politics of Rock 'n' Roll*, New York: Pantheon.

—— (1983) 'Popular music 1950–1980', in G. Martin (ed.) *Making Music*, London: Muller.

—— (1986) 'Art vs technology', *Media, Culture and Society*, 8: 263–79.

—— (1990) 'Video pop: picking up the pieces', in S. Frith (ed.) *Facing the Music: Essays on Pop, Rock and Culture*, London: Mandarin.

—— (1993) 'Youth/Music/Television', in S. Frith, A. Goodwin and L. Grossberg (eds) *Sound & Vision: The Music Video Reader*, London: Routledge.

—— (1996) *Performing Rites: On the Value of Popular Music*. Cambridge, MA.: Harvard University Press.

Frith, S. and Goodwin, A. (eds) (1990) *On Record: Rock, Pop and The Written Word*, New York: Pantheon.

Frith, S. and McRobbie, A. (1990) 'Rock and sexuality', in S. Frith and A. Goodwin (eds) *On Record: Rock, Pop and the Written Word*, New York: Routledge.

Frow, J. (1987) 'Accounting for tastes: some problems on Bourdieu's sociology of culture', *Cultural Studies*, 1(1), January.

Gaar, G. (1992) *She's a Rebel*, Seattle: Seal Press.

Gabali, J. (n.d.) *Daidyee, gwoka*, n.p.

Gamman, L. and Marshment, M. (eds) (1988) *The Female Gaze: Women as Viewers of Popular Culture*, London: The Women's Press.

Garfinkel, H. (1967) *Studies in Ethnomethodology*, Cambridge: Polity.

Garnham, N. (1993) 'Bourdieu, the cultural arbitrary and television', in C. Calhoun, E. LiPuma and M. Postone (eds) *Bourdieu: Cultural Perspectives*, Cambridge: Polity.

Garnham, N. and Williams, R. (1986) 'Pierre Bourdieu and the sociology of culture', in R. Collins *et al.* (eds) *Media Culture and Society: A Critical Reader*, London: Sage.

Gay, L. C. (1995) 'Rockin' the imagined local: New York rock in a reterritorialized world', in W. Straw, S. Johnson, R. Sullivan and P. Friedlander (eds), *Popular Music: Style and Identity*, Montreal: The Centre for Research on Canadian Cultural Industries and Institutions/International Association for the Study of Popular Music.

Gellatt, R. (1977) *The Fabulous Phonograph 1877–1977*, London: Cassell.

Gendron, B. (2002) *Between Montmartre and the Mudd Club: Popular Music and the Avant Garde*, Chicago: The University of Chicago Press.

George, N. (1988) *The Death of Rhythm and Blues*, New York: Plume.

Giddens, A. (1991) *Modernity and Self Identity: Self and Society in the Late Modern Age*, Cambridge: Polity.

Gilligan, C. and Brown, L. (1992) *Meeting at the Crossroads: Women's Psychology and Girls' Development*, Cambridge, MA.: Harvard University Press.

Gilroy, P. (1987) *There Ain't No Black in the Union Jack*, Chicago: University of Chicago Press.

—— (1988) 'Cruciality and the frog's perspective: an agenda of difficulties for the black arts movement in Britain', *Third Text*, 5: 33–44.

—— (1993) *The Black Atlantic: Modernity and Double Consciousness*, Cambridge, MA: Harvard University Press.

Glasser, T. L. (1984) 'Competition and diversity among radio formats: legal and structural issues', *Journal of Broadcasting*, 28: 122–42.

Glissant, E. (1989) *Caribbean Discourse*, trans. J. M. Dash, Charlottesville, VA: University of Virginia Press.

Goldberg, R. (1988) *Performance Art: From Futurism to the Present*, New York: Harry Abrams.

Gonzalez, F. (1994) 'Out of Colombia hillbilly goes pop', *Miami Herald*, 19 June, 11.

—— (1996) 'Rock en Espanol', *Miami Herald*, 8 March, 20C-21G, 22C.

Gonzalez, L. M. (1993) 'A gusto con la quebradita', *La Opinion*, 18 August.

Goodwin, A. (1990) 'Sample and hold: pop music in the digital age of reproduction', in S. Frith and A. Goodwin (eds) *On Record: Rock, Pop and the Written Word*, New York: Pantheon.

—— (1992) *Dancing in the Distraction Factory: Music Television and Popular Culture*, Minneapolis, MN: University of Minnesota Press.

—— and Core, J. (1990) 'Worldbeat and the cultural imperialism debate', *Socialist Review*, 20: 63–80.

Gorman, P. (2001) *In Their Own Write: Adventures in the Music Press*, London: Sanctuary.

Gravenites, N. (1968) 'Stop this shuck, Ralph Gleason', *Rolling Stone*, 25 May: 17.

Gracyk, T. (1996) *Rhythm and Noise: An Aesthetics of Rock*, London: I.B. Tauras.

Green, E., Hebron, S. and Woodward, D. (1990) *Women's Leisure, What Leisure? A Feminist Analysis*, London: Macmillan.

Green, L. (1997) *Music, Gender, Education*, Cambridge: Cambridge University Press.

Gronow, P. and Saunio, I. (1998) *An International History of the Recording Industry*, London: Cassell.

Gross, J., McMurray, D. and Swedenburt, T. (1994) 'Rai, rap and Ramadan nights: Franco-Maghribi cultural identities', *Diaspora*, 3(1): 3–39.

Grossberg, L. (1984) 'Another boring day in paradise: rock and roll and the empowerment of everyday life', *Popular Music*, 4: 225–58.

——, Nelson, C. and Treichler, P. (eds) (1992) *Cultural Studies*, London: Routledge.

Gudmundsson, G., Lindberg, U., Michelson, M. and Weisethaunet, H. (2002) 'Brit crit: turning points in British rock criticism 1960–90', in S. Jones (ed.) *Pop Music and the Press*, Philadelphia, PA: Temple University Press.

Guevara, N. (1987) 'Women writin' rappin' breakin''', in M. Davis, M. Marable, F. Pfeil and M. Sprinker (eds) *The Year Left 2: An American Socialist Yearbook*, London: Verso Books.

Guilbault, J. (1990) 'On interpreting popular music: zouk in the West Indies', in J. Lent (ed.) *Caribbean Popular Culture*, Bowling Green, OH: Bowling Green University Press, pp. 79–97.

—— (1993) *Zouk: World Music in the West Indies*, Chicago: University of Chicago Press.

Gupta, A. and Ferguson, J. (1992) 'Beyond culture: space, identity, and the politics of difference', *Cultural Anthropology*, 7: 6–23.

Guralnick, P. (1986) *Sweet Soul Music: Rhythm and Blues and the Southern Dream of Freedom*, New York: Harper & Row.

Hall, S. and Jefferson, T. (eds) (1976) *Resistance Through Rituals: Youth Sub-Cultures in Post-War Britain*, London: Hutchinson.

Haraway, D. (1985) 'A manifesto for cyborgs: science, technology and socialist feminism in the 1980s', *Socialist Review*, 80: 65–107.

—— (1991) *Simians, Cyborgs and Women*, London: Free Association Books.

Haskell, H. (1995) *The Attentive Listener: Three Centuries of Music Criticism*, London: Faber.

Hay, C. (2004) 'Meet the critics', *Billboard*, 20 March, 1: 88.

Hebdige, D. (1976) 'The Meaning of Mod', in S. Hall and T. Jefferson (eds) *Resistance Through Rituals: Youth Subcultures in Post-War Britain*, London: Hutchinson.

—— (1979) *Subculture: The Meaning of Style*, London: Routledge.

Hesmondhalgh, D. (1996) 'Flexibility, post-Fordism and the music industries', *Media, Culture and Society*, 18: 469–88.

—— (1997) 'The cultural politics of dance music', in *Soundings*, 5: 167–78.

—— (2002) *The Cultural Industries*, London and Thousand Oaks, CA: Sage.

Hetherington, K. (1992) 'Stonehenge and its festival: spaces of consumption', in R. Shields (ed.) *Lifestyle Shopping: The Subject of Consumption*, London: Routledge.

Hey, V. (1986) *Patriarchy and Pub Culture*, London: Tavistock.

Hirsch, P. (1969) *The Structure of the Popular Music Industry*, Ann Arbor, MI: Institute for Social Research.

—— (1972) 'Processing fads and fashions: an organization-set analysis of cultural industry systems', *American Journal of Sociology*, 77: 639–9.

Hobsbawm, E. (aka Francis Newton) (1989) *The Jazz Scene*, London: Weidenfeld & Nicolson.

Hoetink, H. (1983) *The Dominican People 1850–1900, Notes Toward a Historical Sociology*, trans. Stephen K. Ault, Baltimore, MD: Johns Hopkins University Press.

Holloway, J. E. (ed.) *Africanisms in American Culture*, Bloomington, IN: Indiana University Press.

Hosokawa, S. (1984) 'The walkman effect', *Popular Music*, 4: 165–80.

Huyssen, A. (1986) *After the Great Divide: Modernism, Mass Culture, Postmodernism*, Bloomington, IN: Indiana University Press.

IFPI (2000) *World Sales 1999*, London: International Federation of the Phonographic Industries.

IFPI (2001) *The Recording Industry in Numbers 2001*, London: International Federation of the Phonographic Industries.

Jakobovits, L. A. (1966) 'Studies of fads: I. The hit parade', *Psychological Reports*, 18: 443–50.

Jefferson, T. (1976) 'Cultural responses of the Teds: the defence of space and status', in S. Hall and T. Jefferson (eds) *Resistance Through Rituals: Youth Subcultures in Post-War Britain*, London: Hutchinson.

Jhally, S. (1995) 'Dreamworlds 2: desire, sex, and power in rock video', Northampton, MA: University of Massachusetts.

Jones, A. (1988) 'Kassav are Ambassadors of Zouk', *Montreal Gazette*, 26 May: C13.

Jones, L. (1963) *Blues People*, New York: Morrow Quill.

Joplin, L. (1992) *Love, Janis*, New York: Villard Books.

Kaplan, A. and Pease, D. (1994) (eds) *Cultures of United States Imperialism*, Durham, NC: Duke University Press, pp. 474–95.

Kealy, E. (1990 [1979]) 'From craft to art: the case of sound mixers and popular music', in S. Frith and A. Goodwin (eds) *On Record: Rock, Pop and the Written Word*, New York: Pantheon.

Keck, G. R. and Martin. S. V. (1989) (eds) *Feel the Spirit: Studies in Nineteenth-Century Afro-American Music*, Westport, CT: Greenwood Press.

Keil, C. and Keil, A. V. (1992) *Polka Happiness*, Philadelphia, PA: Temple University Press.

Kerman, J. (1985) *Musicology*, London: Fontana.

Knight, C. (1974) *Jimi: An Intimate Biography of Jimi Hendrix*, New York: Praeger.

Koestler, A. (1966) *The Act of Creation*, London: Pan Books.

Kozul-Wright, Z. and Stanbury, L. (1998) *Becoming a Globally Competitive Player: The Case of the Music Industry in Jamaica*, UNCTAD/OSG Discussion Paper No. 138, Geneva: United Nations Conference on Tradition and Development.

Kraft, J. (1994) 'The "pit" musicians: mechanization in the movie theatres, 1926–1934', *Labor History*, 35: 66–92.

Lafontaine, M. C. (1982) 'Musique et societié aux Antilles: "Balakadri" ou le bal de quadrille au commandement de la Guadeloupe', *Presence africaine*, 121/122: 72–108.

—— (1983) 'Le carnivale de l'autre: à propos d'authenticite en matière de musique guadeloupéene, theories et realities', *Les temps modernes*, May: 2126–73.

Laing, D. (1985) *One Chord Wonders: Power and Meaning in Punk Rock*, Milton Keynes: Open University Press.

—— (1986) 'The music industry and the cultural imperialism thesis', *Media, Culture and Society* 8: 331–41.

—— (1997) 'Rock anxieties and new music networks', in A. McRobbie (ed.) *Back To Reality? Social Experience and Cultural Studies*, Manchester: Manchester University Press.

Lancreot, F. (1988) 'Quadrille et gro-ka: deux aspects de la culture guadeloupéene', n.p.

Lash, S. (1994) 'Reflexivity and its doubles: structures, aesthetics, community', in U. Beck, A. Giddens and S. Lash (eds) *Reflexive Modernisation*, Cambridge: Polity Press.

—— and Urry, J. (1994) *Economies of Signs and Space*, London: Sage.

Lees, S. (1993) *Sugar and Spice: Sexuality and Adolescent Girls*, London: Penguin.

Leiss, W., Kline, S. and Jhally, S. (1990) *Social Communication in Advertising: Persons, Products, and Images of Well-Being*, New York: Routledge, Chapman & Hall.

Leonard, D. (1980) *Sex and Generation*, London: Tavistock.

Lewis, E. (1956) *No C.I.C*, London: Decca.

Lewis, L. (1990) *Gender Politics and MTV: Voicing the Difference*, Philadelphia, PA: Temple University Press.

Lipsitz, G. (1994) *Dangerous Crossroads: Popular Music, Postmodernism, and the Poetics of Place*, New York: Verso.

Loesser, A. (1954) *Men, Women and Pianos*, New York: Simon & Schuster.

Longhurst, B. (1995) *Popular Music and Society*, Cambridge: Polity.

Lopes, M. (1991) 'Text of fear in Puerto Rico', Discourse Analysis Conference, Manchester University.

Lopes, P. (1992) 'Innovation and diversity in the popular music industry, 1969–1990', *American Sociological Review*, 57: 56–71.

Lorente, R. (1994) 'MTV Latino pulsates from south beach', *Miami Herald*, 24 March: MBI.

Lull, J. (1995) *Media, Communication, Culture: A Global Approach*, New York: Columbia University Press.

—— and Miller, D. (1982) 'Media and interpersonal socialization to new wave music', paper presented to the annual convention of the International Communication Association, Boston, MA, May.

Lury, C. (1998) *Prosthetic Culture*, London: Routledge.

Mabey, R. (1969) *The Pop Process*, London: Hutchinson.

McClary, S. (1991) *Feminine Endings: Music, Gender and Sexuality*, Minneapolis, MN: University of Minnesota Press.

MacDougald, D. Jr (1941) 'The popular music industry', in P. F. Lazarsfeld and F. N. Stanton (eds) *Radio Research 1941*, New York: Duell, Sloan & Pearce.

McGowan, C. and Pessanha, R. (1998) *The Brazilian Sound: Samba, Bossa Nova and the Popular Music of Brazil*, Philadelphia, PA: Temple University Press.

McLeod, K. (2002) 'Between rock and a hard place. Gender and rock criticism', in S. Jones (ed.) *Pop Music and the Press*, Philadelphia, PA: Temple University Press.

McPhee, W. N. (1977) 'When culture becomes a business', in P. M. Hirsch, P. V. Miller and F. G. Kline (eds) *Strategies for Communication Research*, Beverly Hills, CA: Sage.

McRobbie, A. (1984) 'Dance and social fantasy', in A. McRobbie and M. Nava (eds) *Gender and Generation*, London: Macmillan.

—— (1991) *Feminism and Youth Culture: From Jackie to Just Seventeen*, London: Macmillan.

—— (1992) 'Post-Marxism and cultural studies', in L. Grossberg, C. Nelson and P. Treichler (eds) *Cultural Studies,* London: Routledge.

Maffesoli, M. (1996) *The Time of the Tribes: The Decline of Individualism in Mass Society*, London: Sage.

Mandela, N. (1990) Speech delivered in Detroit, MI, 29 June.

Manuel, P. (1993) *Cassette Culture – Popular Music and Technology in Northern India.* Chicago: University of Chicago Press.

—— (1995) 'Music as symbol, music as simulacrum: postmodern, pre-modern and modern aesthetics in subcultural popular music', *Popular Music*, 14(2): 227–39.

Martin, G. (ed.) *Making Music*, London: Muller.

Martin-Barbero, J. (1993a) 'Latin America: cultures in the communication media', *Journal of Communication*, 43: 18–30.

—— (1993b) *Communication, Culture and Hegemony: From the Media to Mediations*, London: Sage.

Martinez, R. (1994), 'The dance of neuvo L.A.', *Los Angeles Times Magazine*, 30 January.

Marx, K. and Engels, F. (1967) *The Communist Manifesto*, Harmondsworth: Penguin.

Meehan, E. (1984) 'Ratings and the institutional approach: a third answer to the commodity question', *Critical Studies in Mass Communication*, 1: 216–25.

Mercer, K. (1994) *Welcome to the Jungle: New Positions in Black Cultural Studies*, London: Routledge.

Merriam, A. (1964) *The Anthropology of Music*, Evanstown, IL.: Northwestern University Press.

Middleton, R. (1990) *Studying Popular Music*, Milton Keynes: Open University Press.

Middleton, D. and Edwards, D. (eds) (1990) *Collective Remembering*, London: Sage.

Mintel (1988a) *Mintel Special Report: Youth Lifestyles*.

—— (1988b) 'Attitudes to evenings out', *Mintel Leisure Intelligence* 4.

Mitchell, T. (1996) *Popular Music and Local Identity: Rock, Pop and Rap in Europe and Oceania*, London: Leicester University Press.

Moore, D. (1994) 'Latin rockers seek global roll', *Variety,* 28 March–3 April, 48: 64, 67.

Moore, S. (1988) 'Here's looking at you, kid', in L. Gamman and M. Marshment (eds) *The Female Gaze: Women as Viewers of Popular Culture*, London: The Women's Press.

Morgan, R. (1980) 'Musical time/musical space', *Critical Inquiry*, 7: 527–38.

Morley, D. and Robins, K. (1995) *Spaces of Identity: Global Media, Electronic Landscapes and Cultural Boundaries*, London: Routledge.

Morris, S. (1990) Interview, *Omni*, 12(9).

Muggleton, D. (1997) 'The post-subculturalist', in S. Redhead, D. Wynne and J. O'Connor (eds) *The Clubcultures Reader: Readings in Popular Cultural Studies*, Oxford: Blackwell.

Mulkay, M. (1988) *On Humor: Its Nature and its Place in Modern Society*, Basil Blackwell: New York.

Mulvey, L. (1989) 'Visual pleasure and narrative cinema', in *Visual and Other Pleasures*, Bloomington, IN: Indiana University Press.

Mungham, G. and Pearson, G. (1976) *Working Class Youth Cultures*, London: Routledge.

—— (1991) *Shots From The Hip*, London: Penguin.

Myers, D. (1987) '"Anonymity is part of the magic": individual manipulation of computer-mediated communication contexts', *Qualitative Sociology*, 10: 151–66.

Negus, K. (1992) *Producing Pop: Culture and Conflict in the Popular Music Industry*, London: Edward Arnold.

Obrecht, J. (1988) 'Pro's reply: Al Hendrikson: the way we were', *Guitar Player*, March.

Official Proceedings of the American Federation of Musicians (1929) July, 18.

O'Hagan, S. (1987) 'Yo bum, listen punk', *NME*, 18 April: 29.

Olson, M. (1998) 'Everybody loves our town: scenes, spatiality, migrancy', in T. Swiss, J. Sloop and A. Herman (eds) *Mapping the Beat: Popular Music and Contemporary Theory*, Oxford: Blackwell.

Overture [trade journal of Local 47 of the American Federation of Musicians] (1933), May.

—— (1938a) July.

—— (1938b) September.

—— (1942) January.

—— (1956).

Paiva, B. (1983) *The Program Director's Handbook*, Blue Ridge Summit, PA: Tab Books.

Pareles, Jon (1990) 'The midi menace: machine perfection is far from perfect', *New York Times*, 13 May: H25.

Parsons, T. (1964) *Essays in Sociological Theory*, New York: Free Press.

Partch, H. (1974) *Genesis of a Music* (2nd edn), New York: Da Capo.

Pauly, J. J. (1990) 'The politics of new journalism', in N. Sims (ed.) *Literary Journalism in the Twentieth Century*, Oxford: Oxford University Press.

Pena, M. (1985) *The Texas–Mexican Conjunto: History of a Working-Class Music*, Austin, TX: University of Texas Press.

Peterson, R. A. and Berger, D. G. (1971) 'Entrepreneurship in organizations: evidence from the popular music industry', *Administrative Science Quarterly*, 16: 97–107.

—— (1975) 'Cycles in symbol production: the case of popular music', *American Sociological Review*, 40: 158–73.

Peterson, R. and Kern, R. (1996) 'Changing highbrow taste: from snob to omnivore', *American Sociological Review*, 61: 900–7.

Plant, S. (1997) *Zeros and Ones: Digital Women and the New Technoculture*, London: Fourth Estate.

Polhemus, T. (1997) 'In the supermarket of style', in S. Redhead, D. Wynne and J. O'Connor (eds) *The Clubcultures Reader: Readings in Popular Cultural Studies*, Oxford: Blackwell.

Price, M. and Massey, G. (1990) *Melody Maker*, 8 December.

Pucket, J. (1995) 'Fine Prine: singing stories from everyday life', *The Courier Journal*, 27, May: 15.

Radley, A. (1990) 'Artefacts, memory and a sense of the past', in D. Middleton and D. Edwards (eds) *Collective Remembering*, London: Sage.

Raphael, A. (1995) *Never Mind the Bollocks: Women Rewrite Rock and Roll*, London: Virago.

Redding, N. (1996) *Are You Experienced? The Inside Story of the Jimi Hendrix Experience*, New York: Da Capo.

Redhead, S. (1993) 'The end of the end-of-the-century party', in S. Redhead (ed.) *Rave Off: Politics and Deviance in Contemporary Youth Culture*, Aldershot: Avebury.

——, Wynne, D. and O'Connor, J. (eds) (1997) *The Clubcultures Reader: Readings in Popular Cultural Studies*, Oxford: Blackwell.

Refior, E. (1955) *The American Federation of Musicians: Organization, Policies, and Practices*, Master's thesis, University of Chicago.

Regev, M. (1994) 'Producing artistic value. The case of rock music', *Sociological Quarterly*, 35(1): 85–102.

—— (1997) 'Rock aesthetics and musics of the world', *Theory, Culture and Society*, 14: 125–42.

Reitveld, H. (1994) 'Living the dream', in S. Redhead (ed.) *Rave Off*, Manchester: Manchester University Press.

Rheingold, H. (1997) 'Yo, netheads! Off with your masks!', *Yahoo Internet Life*, 26 June, www.zdnet.com/products/content/articles/1997/chat.netheads/.

Riley, D. (1988) *Am I That Name? Feminism and the Category of 'Women' in History*, Minneapolis, MN: University of Minnesota Press.

Robinson, D., Buck, E. and Cuthbert, M. (1991) *Music at the Margins: Popular Music and Global Cultural Diversity*, Newbury Park: Sage.

Rodriguez, R. (1993) 'Yo quiero mi MTV!', *Miami Herald*, 30 September: 1G.

Rojo, A. (1995) 'Participation in scholarly electronic forums', Ph.D. thesis, University of Toronto, www.oise.utoronto.ca/~arojo/.

Rosolato, G. (1972) 'Repetitions', *Musique en Jeu*, 9: 33–44.

Ross, A. (1992) 'New Age technoculture', in L. Grossberg, C. Nelson and P. Treichler (eds) *Cultural Studies*, London: Routledge.

Roth, M. (ed.) (1983) *The Amazing Decade: Women and Performance Art in America, 1970–1980*, Los Angeles, CA: Astro Artz.

Rothenbuhler, E. W. (1982) 'Radio and the popular music industry: a case study of programming decision making', unpublished Master's thesis, Department of Communication, Ohio State University.

—— (1985) 'Programming decision making in popular music radio', *Communication Research*, 12: 209–32.

Rowe, W. and Schelling, V. (1991) *Memory and Modernity: Popular Culture in Latin America*, London: Verso.

Rumsey, G. and Little, H. (1989) 'Women and pop: a series of lost encounters', in A. McRobbie (ed.) *Zoot Suits and Second Hand Dresses*, London: Macmillan.

Ryan, J. and Peterson, R. A. (1982) 'The product image: the fate of creativity in country music songwriting', in J. S. Ettema and D. C. Whitney (eds) *Individuals in Mass Media Organizations: Creativity and Constraint*, Beverly Hills, CA: Sage.

Said, E. (1985) *Orientalism*, Harmondsworth: Penguin.

Sales, G. (1984) *Jazz: America's Classical Music*, New York: Prentice-Hall.

Salewicz, C. and Boot, A. (2001) *Reggae Explosion: The Story of Jamaican Music*, London: Virgin Books.

Saralegui, M. (1994) 'MTV Latino attracts viewers in the U.S. and abroad', *Wireless International*, 14 March: 18.

Savage, J. (1988) 'The enemy within: sex, rock and identity', in S. Frith (ed.) *Facing the Music*, New York: Pantheon.

—— (1991) *England's Dreaming*, London: Faber & Faber.

Scannell, P. (1989) 'Public service broadcasting and modern public life', *Media, Culture and Society*, 11(2), April.

Scaramuzzo, G. (1986) 'The magic of Kassav', *Reggae and African Beat*, 5 (5/6): 46–51.

Schreiner, C. (1993) *Musica Brasileira: A History of Popular Music and the People of Brazil*, London: Marion Boyars Publishing.

Schuller, G. (1986) 'The future of form in jazz', in *Musings: The Musical Worlds of Gunther Schuller*, New York: Oxford University Press.

Schutz, A. (1970) in R. M. Zaner (ed.) *Reflections on the Problem of Relevance*, New Haven, CT: Yale University Press.

Scott, A. (2000) *The Cultural Economy of Cities: Essays on the Geography of Image-producing Industries*, London: Sage.

Sennett, R. (1990) *The Conscience of the Eye: The Design and Social Life of Cities*, London: Faber & Faber.

——— (1994) *Flesh and Stone: The Body and the City in Western Civilization*, New York: Norton.

Shank, B. (1994) *Dissonant Identities: The Rock 'n' Roll Scene in Austin, Texas*, London: Wesleyan University Press.

Sharma, S., Hutnyk, J. and Sharma, A. (eds) (1996) *Dis-Orienting Rhythms: The Politics of the New Asian Dance Music*, London: Zed Books.

Shepherd, J. (1991) 'Music and male hegemony', in *Music as Social Text*, Cambridge: Polity Press.

Shields, R. (1992a) 'Spaces for the subject of consumption', in R. Shields (ed.) *Lifestyle Shopping: The Subject of Consumption*, London: Routledge.

——— (1992b) 'The individual, consumption cultures and the fate of community', in R. Shields (ed.) *Lifestyle Shopping: The Subject of Consumption*, London: Routledge.

Silver, V. (1993) 'Tor MTV, a leap to Latin America', *The New York Times*, 27, September: C6(N), D6(L), col. 1.

Simon, B. S. (1997) 'Entering the pit: slam-dancing and modernity', *Journal of Popular Culture*, 31: 149–76.

Slobin, M. (1993) *Subcultural Sounds: Micromusics of the West*, London: Wesleyan University Press.

Small, C. (1980) *Music, Society, Education* (2nd edn), London: John Calder.

Smith, A. (1988) [former staff musician] Interview with James P. Kraft, Los Angeles, CA, 5 September and 21 November.

Stephens, M. (1998) 'Babylon's "natural mystic": the North American music industry, the legend of Bob Marley, and the incorporation of transnationalism', *Cultural Studies*, 12: 139–67.

Stokes, M. (1994) 'Introduction: ethnicity, identity and music', in M. Stokes (ed.) *Ethnicity, Identity and Music: The Musical Construction of Place*, Oxford: Berg.

Straw, W. (1991) 'Systems of articulation, logics of change: communities and scenes in popular music', *Cultural Studies*, 5(3): 368–88.

——— (1993) 'The booth, the floor and the wall: dance music and the fear of falling', *Public*, 8: 169–83.

Straw, W., Johnson, S., Sullivan, R. and Friedlander, P. (eds) (1995) *Popular Music: Style and Identity*, Montreal: The Centre for Research on Canadian Cultural Industries and Institutions/International Association for the Study of Popular Music.

Sturmer, C. (1993) 'MTV's Europe: an imaginary continent?', in T. Dowmunt (ed.), *Channels of Resistance: Global Television and Local Empowerment*, London: British Film Institute.

Sudjic, D. (1989) *Cult Heroes*, London and New York: Norton.

Sudnow, D. (1978) *Ways of the Hand: The Organisation of Improvised Conduct*, Cambridge, MA.: Harvard University Press.

Swiss, T., Sloop, J. and Herman, A. (eds) (1998) *Mapping the Beat: Popular Music and Contemporary Theory*, Oxford: Blackwell.

Takaki, R. (ed.) (1994) *From Different Shores: Perspectives on Race and Ethnicity in America*, Oxford: Oxford University Press.

Tate, G. (1992) 'The electric miles,' *Flyboy in the Buttermilk: Essays on Contemporary America*, New York: Simon & Schuster, pp. 73–4.

Taylor, T. (1995) 'When we think about music and politics: the case of Kevin Volans', *Perspectives of New Music*, 33: 504–36.

—— (1997) *Global Pop: World Music, World Markets*, Routledge: London.

TeGroen, J. (1989) Interview with James P. Kraft, Los Angeles, CA, 3 February.

—— and Fisher, P. [local 47 radio representative] (1988) Interview with James P. Kraft, Los Angeles, CA, 1 October.

Tennaille, F. (1987) 'Kassav', *Paroles et musique*, 70.

Tester, K. (ed.) (1994) *The Flâneur*, London: Routledge.

Théberge, P. (1989) 'The "sound" of music: technological rationalization and the production of popular music', *New Formations*, 8, 99–111.

Thede, M. (1967) *The Fiddle Book*, New York: Oak Publications.

Thompson, R. F. (1983) *Flash of the Spirit*, New York: Random House.

—— (1990) 'Kongo influences on African American artistic culture', in J.Holloway (ed.) *Africanisms in American Culture*, Bloomington, IN: Indiana University Press.

Thornton, S. (1990) 'Strategies for reconstructing the popular past', *Popular Music*, 9(1): 87–95.

—— (1994) 'Moral panic, the media and British rave culture', in A. Ross and T. Rose (eds) *Microphone Fiends*, New York: Routledge.

—— (1995) *Club Cultures: Music, Media and Subcultural Capital*, Cambridge: Polity Press.

Tokaji, A. (1985) 'Leftist political songs in Hungary before and after 1948', in D. Horn (ed.) *Popular Music Perspectives 2*, Exeter: International Association for the Study of Popular Music, pp. 307–17.

Tomlinson, J. (1991) *Cultural Imperialism: A Critical Introduction*, Baltimore, MD: Johns Hopkins University Press.

Toynbee, J. (1993) 'Policing Bohemia, pinning up the grunge: the music press and generic change in British pop and rock', *Popular Music*, 12(3): 289–300.

Truax, B. (1976) 'A communicational approach to computer sound programs', *Journal of Music Theory*, 20, 227–300.

Urry, J. (1996) 'How societies remember the past', in S. MacDonald and G. Fyfe (eds) *Theorizing Museums: Representing Identity and Diversity in a Changing World*, Sociological Review Monograph, Oxford: Blackwell.

Various Artists (2002) *Bollywood*, Greensleeves [LP], GRELD730.

Ward, A. (1993) 'Dancing in the dark', in H. Thomas (ed.) *Dance, Gender and Culture*, London: Macmillan.

Weber, M. (1958) *The Rational and Social Foundations of Music*, Carbondale, IL: Southern Illinois University Press.

Weinstein, D. (1999) 'Art versus commerce: deconstructing a (useful) romantic myth', in K. Kelly and E. McDonnell (eds) *Stars Don't Stand Still In The Sky: Music and Myth*, New York and London: Routledge.

Welburn, R. G. (1985) 'The early record review: jazz criticism's first-born child', *Annual Review of Jazz Studies*, 3: 120–9.

Welch, C. (1977) 'Zeppelin over America', *Melody Maker*, 25 June.

White, D. M. (1950) 'The gatekeeper: a case study in the selection of news', *Journalism Quarterly*, 27: 383–90.

Whitefield, M. (1995) 'As history marches forward, so does the reach of MTV', *Miami Herald,* 9 April: 1K–3K.

Wiebe, G. (1940) 'The effect of radio plugging on students' opinions of songs', *Journal of Applied Psychology*, 24: 721–7.

Williams, R. (1965) *The Long Revolution*, Harmondsworth: Pelican.

—— (1974) *Television: Technology and Cultural Form*, London: Fontana.

—— (1989) *Resources of Hope: Culture, Democracy, Socialism*, London: Verso.

Willis, P. (1978) *Profane Culture*, London: Routledge & Kegan Paul.

Wise, S. (1990) 'Sexing Elvis', in S. Frith and A. Goodwin (eds) *On Record: Rock, Pop and the Written Word*, New York: Routledge.

Wollen, P. (1992) *Raiding the Icebox: Reflections on Twentieth-Century Culture*, London: Verso.

Wyatt, R. O. and Badger, D. P. (1990) 'Effects of information and evaluation in film criticism', *Journalism Quarterly*, 67(2) Summer: 359–68.

Young, C. (1990) '"I'm not such an old hippie": Robert Plant stops being polite', *Musician*, June.

Zemp, H. (1979) 'Aspects of 'Are'are musical theory', *Ethnomusicology*, 23: 5–48.

Index

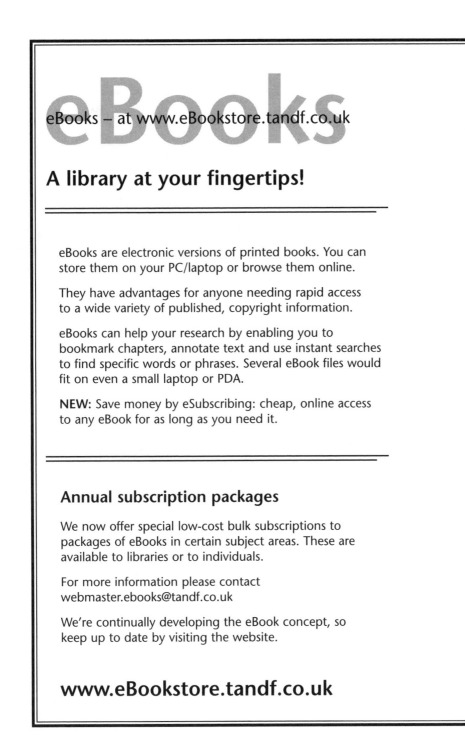